Jurisdiction and Arbitration Agreements in International Commercial Law

Arbitration and jurisdiction agreements are frequently used in transnational commercial contracts to reduce risk, gain efficacy and acquire certainty and predictability. Because of the similarities between these two types of procedural autonomy agreements, they are often treated in a similar way by courts and practitioners.

This book offers a comprehensive study of the prerequisites, effectiveness and enforcement of exclusive jurisdiction and arbitration agreements in international dispute resolution. It examines whether jurisdiction and arbitration clauses have identical effects in private international law and whether they have been or should be given the same treatment by most countries in the world. By comparing the treatment of these clauses in the US, China, the UK and the EU, Zheng Sophia Tang demonstrates how, in practice, exclusive jurisdiction and arbitration agreements are enforced. The book considers whether the Hague Convention on Choice of Court Agreements could be treated as a litigating counterpart to the New York Convention, and whether it could work successfully to facilitate judicial cooperation and party autonomy in international commerce.

This book breaks new ground in combining updated materials in EU, US and UK law with unique resources on Chinese law and practice. It will be valuable for academics and practitioners working in the field of private international law and international arbitration.

Dr Zheng Sophia Tang (LLB, LLM, PhD, Barrister, Accredited Mediator) is an Associate Professor in business law at the Centre for Business Law and Practice, University of Leeds. Her research interest lies in the field of private international law, arbitration and commercial corruption. She is the author of *Electronic Consumer Contracts in the Conflict of Laws* (Hart, 2009) and she has published extensively in internationally renowned, peer-reviewed journals.

Routledge Research in International Commercial Law

Available titles in this series include:

International Commercial and Marine Arbitration
Georgios I. Zekos

International Commercial Arbitration and the Arbitrator's Contract
Emilia Onyema

Jurisdiction and Arbitration Agreements in International Commercial Law
Zheng Sophia Tang

Jurisdiction and Arbitration Agreements in International Commercial Law

Zheng Sophia Tang

Routledge
Taylor & Francis Group
LONDON AND NEW YORK

First published 2014
by Routledge
2 Park Square, Milton Park, Abingdon, Oxon OX14 4RN

and by Routledge
711 Third Avenue, New York, NY 10017

Routledge is an imprint of the Taylor & Francis Group, an informa business

British Library Cataloguing in Publication Data
A catalogue record for this book is available from the British Library

Library of Congress Cataloging-in-Publication Data
Tang, Zheng Sophia, author.
Jurisdiction and arbitration agreements in international commercial law / Zheng Sophia Tang.
pages cm. – (Routledge research in international commercial law)
Includes bibliographical references and index.
1. Arbitration agreements, Commercial. 2. International commercial arbitration. 3. Jurisdiction. 4. Commercial law. I. Title.
K2400.T356 2014
343.08'7–dc23

2013033349

ISBN: 978-0-415-62554-8 (hbk)
ISBN: 978-0-203-71278-8 (ebk)

Typeset in Baskerville
by Wearset Ltd, Boldon, Tyne and Wear

MIX
Paper from responsible sources
FSC
www.fsc.org
FSC® C013604

Printed and bound by CPI Group (UK) Ltd, Croydon, CR0 4YY

Contents

Table of cases

English cases

EU cases

US cases

Chinese cases

French cases

German cases

Italian cases

Irish cases

Belgium case

Russian case

Luxembourg case

Brazil cases

Canadian cases

Singapore cases

Lithuanian cases

Swiss cases

Dutch cases

Awards

Table of statutes and legislative instruments

International conventions

EU legislation

UK

US

China statutes

China Supreme People's Court interpretation and other documents

Germany

France

Switzerland

Quebec

Brazil

Preface

Arbitration and jurisdiction agreements are frequently used in transnational commercial contracts. Sophisticated commercial parties adopt them to reduce risk, gain efficacy and acquire certainty and predictability. Both agreements have specific contractual requirements for their formation, incorporation and validity, have the prorogation effect to make the chosen forum competent and have the derogation power to deprive any otherwise competent fora of their jurisdiction. Both generate complex and interesting questions on the conflict of jurisdiction and interaction with anti-forum shopping measures, such as *lis pendens*, *forum non conveniens*, anti-suit injunction and anti-arbitration injunction. Because of the similarities between the two types of frequently used dispute resolution agreements, they are often treated in a similar way by courts and practitioners.

This book offers a comparative study on the prerequisites, effectiveness and enforcement of exclusive jurisdiction and arbitration agreements in international dispute resolution in order to determine whether the clauses have the identical effects in private international law and whether they have been or should be given the same treatment by most countries in the world. The book compares the treatment of jurisdiction and arbitration clauses in the US, China, the UK and the EU to demonstrate how, in practice, exclusive jurisdiction and arbitration agreements are enforced. In light of all this, the book considers whether the Hague Convention could be treated as a litigating counterpart of the New York Convention and whether it could work successfully to facilitate judicial cooperation and party autonomy in international commerce.

I gave a four-day training course on law relating to procedural autonomy in the EU-Macau Judicial Cooperation/Mutual Trust Programme in Macau during June 2011. This lecture inspired me to do further research on this issue and to compare detailed rules concerning validity, effectiveness and enforcement between jurisdiction and arbitration agreements. I would wish to express my gratitude and appreciation to Professor Paul Beaumont for his recommendation and Macao Law Reform and International Law Bureau for the invitation and organization.

I wish to thank my previous colleague, Dr Christa Roodt, for her stimulating discussions with me, and an anonymous reviewer for his/her positive and constructive comments. I want to thank Professor YongPing Xiao, who provided me with opportunities to do research and to use the resources at the Wuhan University in order to complete the writing on the Chinese law part.

I am grateful to my parents, Yang Cao and ZhuoLiang Tang, and my husband, Roy Rao. Their support and encouragement were important to me in completing this work.

Z.S. Tang
Leeds, 31 July 2013

1 Introduction

1 Introduction

Strategic manipulating of procedure is a potential risk in international commercial dispute resolution. Substantive and procedural advantages are relatively easy to gain in international compared with domestic transactions, caused by the conflict of different legal systems and substantive laws.[1] Effective dispute resolution is one of the key factors contributing to the success of international business practice. In order to achieve certainty and predictability, parties usually enter into dispute resolution agreements in their international civil and commercial relationship. Dispute resolution agreements record the parties' consent on the method, the forum and the special procedural conditions to resolve their commercial disputes. Various dispute resolution agreements exist, including choice of court/jurisdiction agreements, arbitration agreements, mediation agreements, class action waiver agreements, etc. The two most important and frequently used dispute resolution agreements are choice of court agreements and arbitration agreements, which are the focus of this book. For the purpose of this book, disputer resolution agreements/clauses, thus, refer only to jurisdiction and arbitration agreements.

The functioning of dispute resolution agreements is to direct the parties to the agreed forum, either a court or an arbitral tribunal, using the agreed method, adjudication or arbitration, to resolve their disputes.[2] Where the parties enter into jurisdiction or arbitration agreements, they expect greater certainty, procedural efficiency and lower litigation cost. They wish their dispute to be brought in the only forum or tribunal, as designated in their agreements, and no party can freely breach the promise.

If a dispute resolution agreement is the same as other contract terms, the expectation is realistic. However, dispute resolution agreements are

1 Fentiman, 2010: para 7.01.

2 A dispute resolution clause includes both choice of court agreements and arbitration agreements. For a general introduction of dispute resolution clause, see Taylor, 1993: 785; Lenhoff, 1960: 414; Pryles, 1976: 543.

different from normal contract terms in that they aim to grant jurisdictional competence to an authority, while derogating other competent authorities from their jurisdiction. While state sovereignty is involved, the agreement, though aiming to resolve private matters between private parties, cannot be classified as purely 'private'. The mixture of private rights and public power leads to the complexity of this issue. The recognition and enforcement of dispute resolution agreements, as a result, generate more perplexing problems than ordinary contract terms could. The forum, which has been designated by the parties, may not be able to accept the prorogated power because accepting such power might infringe the sovereignty of another state[3] or because exercising this power is impractical.[4] It is also possible that the subject matter concerns the interests of third parties, public policy or fundamental national interest, which is not privately disposable.[5] More difficulty may result from the derogation effect of dispute resolution clauses, as many countries traditionally object to the idea of having courts' authority ousted by the private agreement.[6] The attitude to dispute resolution agreements has been largely changed in the contemporary world.[7] However, the sceptical view of the 'ouster' effect has never been completely removed.[8] The effectiveness of dispute resolution clauses, especially jurisdiction clauses, is frequently questioned in international legal practice. The original purpose of commercial parties by adopting dispute resolution agreements in their contracts is not achievable if state attitude towards dispute resolution clauses is unclear or negative.

Regardless of practice in individual countries, the world clearly witnesses the trend to support party autonomy. This is demonstrated by the international effort to establish judicial cooperation or harmonized

3 Many matters subject to exclusive jurisdiction of a country fall into this category. For example, the dispute relates to the disposal of a land located in the territory of another country, validity of public registrar of another country, composition and dissolution of a company registered in another country, the validity and nullity of IP rights registered or deposited in another country.

4 For example, all relevant evidence of the dispute is located in another country, which renders proceedings extremely difficult, expensive and inconvenient. The traditional doctrine of *forum non conveniens* may be used to refuse jurisdiction granted by a valid jurisdiction clause. See *Eleftheria*, [1970] P 94; *Restatement (Second) Conflict of Laws* (1971), Ch 80.

5 See Ch 4 on arbitrability and the scope of jurisdiction agreements. Briggs, 2008: para 1.07.

6 English common law: Kahn-Freund, 1977: 843; *The Fehmarn* [1958] 1 WLR 159, 161; US history: *Mut. Reserve Fund Life Ins. v Cleveland Woolen Mills*, 82 F. 508 (6th Cir. 1897); Crystal and Giannoni-Crystal, 2012: 205; traditional Dutch vie: Kollewijn, 1961: 31.

7 Kahn-Freund, 1977: 843; Nygh, 1999: 15–28; Briggs, 2008.

8 This is demonstrated by the court reserving discretion to take jurisdiction where the parties have entered into a valid exclusive jurisdiction clause choosing another court. See *Eleftheria*, [1970] P 94; *Restatement (1st) Conflict of Laws* (1971), Ch 80.

jurisdiction rules on enforcement of procedural autonomy agreements.[9] It is reasonable to predict that the importance of dispute resolution agreements will continue to increase in the future. Countries will further relax national law on deciding the validity and enforceability of dispute resolution agreements, and more in-depth judicial cooperation will be established in the international context to improve efficiency of dispute resolution agreements and to prevent concurrent proceedings and irreconcilable judgments.

2 Jurisdiction and arbitration agreements: comparison

A sketchy observation may lead to a conclusion that jurisdiction and arbitration agreements are the same. They do share some characteristics. Both are based on the parties' genuine consent and need basic contractual requirements in order to be valid,[10] the effect of both stems from the principle of contract freedom,[11] both can provide procedural certainty and reduce cost,[12] both have the effect to grant jurisdiction to the chosen court/tribunal and both (except non-exclusive jurisdiction agreements) intend to exclude any otherwise competent non-chosen forum from taking jurisdiction. They are frequently equalized by courts, which apply the same principles to both jurisdiction and arbitration agreements.[13] In the USA, for example, the cornerstone case providing enforceability to jurisdiction agreements, *Bremen v Zapata off-Shore Company*,[14] has been frequently quoted in cases giving effects to international arbitration agreements, because 'an agreement to arbitrate before a specified tribunal is, in effect,

9 In the area of arbitration, the Convention on the Recognition and Enforcement of Foreign Arbitral Awards 1958 (New York Convention) requires a court to respect arbitration agreements, validity concluded, and to recognize and enforce arbitral awards given in the tribunal seated in a foreign state. The UNCITRAL also publishes the Model Law on International Commercial Arbitration and Arbitration Rules to provide further consistency in procedural rules. In the area of jurisdiction, the Council Regulation (EC) No 44/2001 of 22 December 2000 on jurisdiction and the recognition and enforcement of judgments in civil and commercial matters (Brussels I Regulation) provides uniform jurisdiction rules in deciding validity and enforceability of choice of court agreements, and facilitates recognition and enforcement of judgments made by the chosen court within EU. The Hague Choice of Court Convention 2005 is the international instrument in giving effectiveness to exclusive jurisdiction clauses among Contracting States in the world.

10 See Art II.3 of the New York Convention; Art 3(c), 5(1), 6(a) and 9(a) of the Hague Choice of Court Convention; Art 23 of the Brussels I Regulation.

11 Crystal and Giannoni-Crystal, 2012: 248.

12 Ibid., 248.

13 See discussion in Fawcett and Carruthers, 2008: 473–475. *Aggeliki Charis Compania Maritima SA v Pagnan SpA, The Angelic Grace* [1995] 1 Lloyd's Rep 87; *Welex AG v Rosa Maritime Ltd* [2003] 2 Lloyd's Rep 509.

14 407 US 1 (1972).

a specialized kind of forum-selection clause'.[15] In England, exclusive jurisdiction agreements and arbitration agreements have equivalent weight when courts exercise their discretion in granting anti-suit injunctions.[16] The principle of deciding whether to grant anti-suit injunctions in cases where there is an exclusive jurisdiction clause is summarized in *Donohue v Armco*,[17] which is followed by a few cases in which it was decided to grant injunctions in supporting arbitration agreements.[18]

The analogy raises a question: are jurisdiction and arbitration agreements completely identical in nature and, thus, require the same treatment? This is a misunderstanding. Jurisdiction and arbitration agreements share similarities in the perspective of contract law. However, they have fundamental diversity. Arbitration agreements submit disputes to arbitral tribunals, which are private bodies, acquiring their dispute resolution power from party autonomy. Parties could designate not only the seat of the tribunal, but also the composition of the tribunal, the law applicable to the arbitration agreement, the arbitration procedure and the substance/merit of the dispute.[19] They can also exclude the application of the domestic law of any countries and subject the merit of their disputes to flexible international commercial norms, such as the *lex mercatoria*.[20] Party autonomy is the foundation of arbitration. The flexibility in terms of merit and procedure exists in arbitration but not adjudication.[21] Although most countries allow the parties to choose courts to hear their disputes, the parties cannot intervene in the procedure and conflict of laws of the court. Party autonomy is a supplement rule in adjudication to improve certainty and procedural efficiency. It is, however, not the foundation of international adjudication.

Another difference between jurisdiction and arbitration agreements is that arbitration agreements provide an alternative dispute resolution method. It is the parties' agreement to resolve their disputes out of court, in a private tribunal. No matter how much a state wants to preserve its sovereignty, no country would demand the parties to resolve their disputes

15 *Scherk v Alberto-Culver, Co*, 417 US 506, 518. See also *Mitsubishi v Soler Chrysler-Plymouth*, 473 US 614, 631; Crystal and Giannoni-Crystal, 2012: 248.

16 See Fawcett and Carruthers, 2008: 474–475.

17 [2001] UKHL 64.

18 *Atlanska Plovidba v Consignaciones Asturianas SA (The Lapad)*, [2004] 2 CLC 886, para 28: 'An agreement to arbitrate has many similarities to an exclusive jurisdiction clause... This principle [of *Donohue*] applies equally to arbitration agreements'. See also *Noble Assurance Co v Gerling-Konzern General Insurance Co* [2007] 1 CLC 85, para 84–85; *Welex AG v Rosa Maritime Ltd* [2003] EWCA Civ 938, para 47–52. The principles applying to decline jurisdiction, however, differ between cases with exclusive jurisdiction agreements and with arbitration agreements. The former depends on discretion under *forum non conveniens*, while the latter is regulated by statute, i.e. the Arbitration Act 1996, s9.

19 Gertz, 1991: 163.

20 Lando, 1985: 747; Maniruzzaman, 1999: 657; Lowenfeld, 1990: 133; Elcin, 2012.

21 Briggs, 2008: para 1.09.

exclusively in courts. Out-of-court resolution of private differences is encouraged, or at least permitted, by most countries.[22] A court, as a result, would not have much discomfort, if the parties agree to submit their dispute to arbitration. Submitting disputes to the court of another sovereign state is different. The parties do not resolve their dispute out of court, but have made a private decision that another court is more competent, or more appropriate.

The difference between jurisdiction and arbitration agreements determines the fact that some countries provide the same contractual requirements in deciding their formation and validity, while providing more stringent restrictions to the enforcement of jurisdiction agreements.[23] In other countries, even the validity requirements differ between jurisdiction and arbitration agreements.[24] Nevertheless, the current development shows that more countries recognize the importance of efficient dispute resolution, the necessity to enforce freely entered agreements between the parties and the national interest to promote international comity. The enforcement of jurisdiction clauses has been gradually improved, first in domestic legislation and judicial practice, then in international legal framework. An optimistic view is that an increasing number of national courts will gradually accept party autonomy in international adjudication and abandon their traditional scepticism to the private choice of another court over the local one. Jurisdiction clauses may be enforced as effectively as arbitration clauses in international commerce in the future.

3 Terms and definitions

3.1 International

Arbitration and jurisdiction agreements may be entered into to deal with both domestic and international disputes. Although a country usually provides the same substantive law to decide the validity of dispute resolution agreements in both domestic and international contexts, domestic and international dispute resolution agreements are never treated in the same way. International dispute resolution agreements resolve disputes in a cross-border relationship, which usually involves the interests of more than one country. There are complicated conflict of law questions concerning

22 See Dundas, 2010: 343; Ahmed, 2012: 151; Wall, 2009: 78; Shipman, 2006: 181; Lord Phillips of Worth Matravers, 2008: 406.

23 For example, in the USA, the enforcement of jurisdiction clauses is more uncertain in state courts than arbitration agreements. See Haines, 2002: para 3 and para 19. In China, there is explicit legislation providing requirements to enforce arbitration agreements (Civil Procedure Law 2012, Art 271), while there is no such requirement to jurisdiction clauses.

24 An example is China, where more restrictive requirements are provided to jurisdiction agreements than arbitration agreements. See Chapter 2 below.

the applicable law to decide the validity of such clauses, and the forum that can determine the preliminary issues. Difference also exists as to the enforcement of dispute resolution agreements domestically and internationally. Domestic enforcement only requires a statutory provision of the domestic law, while effective international enforcement requires judicial cooperation between other countries and the balance of national interest, commercial efficiency and international comity. More perplex issues arise in international dispute resolution agreements.

The definition of 'international' differs among different instruments, depending on their specific purposes. In the UNCITRAL Model Law on International Commercial Arbitration, an arbitration is international if the parties have their place of business in different states at the time of contracting, if the place of arbitration, the place of performance of substantial obligations or the place most closely connected to the subject matter of the dispute is located out of the parties' place of business, or if the parties have agreed that the subject matter relates to more than one country.[25] In the New York Convention, on the other hand, 'international' only refers to the award, which seeks recognition and enforcement, being made in the territory other than the territory where recognition and enforcement is sought.[26] If the parties and all elements relating to the dispute are located in one country and the parties submit their dispute to the arbitral tribunal seated in another country, this agreement is not 'international' in the Model Law but the award is 'international' in the New York Convention if it seeks recognition and enforcement in the parties' place of business. The difference is caused by the different purpose of the instruments. The Model Law aims to reduce disparity between national arbitration law in enforcing arbitration agreements, while the New York Convention attempts to facilitate the global movement of arbitral awards between different countries. Different definitions for different purposes are recognized in the Hague Choice of Court Convention.[27] Article 1 of the Hague Convention provides that, for the purposes of jurisdiction,

> a case is international unless the parties are resident in the same Contracting State and the relationship of the parties and all other elements relevant to the dispute, regardless of the location of the chosen court, are connected only with that State.[28]

For the purpose of recognition and enforcement, 'a case is international where recognition or enforcement of a foreign judgment is sought'.[29]

25 Art 1(3).
26 Art I.1.
27 Art 1.
28 Art 1(2).
29 Art 1(3).

This book primarily focuses on enforcing dispute resolution agreements at the jurisdictional stage and defines 'international disputes' as disputes with all relevant elements, except the chosen forum or tribunal, located in different countries; in sections dealing with enforcement of judgments or awards made pursuant to a dispute resolution agreement, 'international' refers to the situation where recognition and enforcement are sought in a country other than the place where the judgments or awards are made.

3.2 Commerce

This book concerns dispute resolution agreements in international commerce. Commerce is given a wide definition, covering all business relationships, contractual or non-contractual. A non-exhaustive list of commercial relationships is provided in the UNCITRAL Model Law in International Commercial Arbitration, which includes:[30]

> any trade transaction for the supply or exchange of goods or services; distribution agreement; commercial representation or agency; factoring; leasing; construction of works; consulting; engineering; licensing; investment; financing; banking; insurance; exploitation agreement or concession; joint venture and other forms of industrial or business cooperation; carriage of goods or passengers by air, sea, rail or road.

Disputes arising out of these commercial activities may, or may not, be contractual in nature. If the parties have disputes on delictual liability, they may also submit their disputes to arbitration or to their chosen court for adjudication. Dispute resolution agreements can be entered into before or after disputes have arisen. If a dispute resolution agreement is entered into before the dispute has arisen and the concerned dispute is delictual, it is necessary to consider whether the dispute resolution clause is broad enough to cover delictual claims arising out of the parties' relationship.[31] Furthermore, not every country permits the use of jurisdiction

30 UNCITRAL Model Law 2006, footnote 2.

31 For jurisdiction agreements, see English case: *Provimi Ltd v Aventis Animal Nutrition SA* [2003] 2 All ER (Comm) 683 (QBD (Comm)); US case: *Marinechance Shipping, Ltd v Sebastian*, 143 F.3d 216 (5th Cir. 1998); Chinese cases: *Lai v ABN AMRO Bank*, Shanghai Municipal High People's Court (2010) No 49; *Watanabe v Culture & Art Press*, Shanghai Municipal No 1 Intermediate People's Court (2008) No 210; French case: *SIEPA v Micheline Lifestyle Ltd*, Cass. Civ 2nd, June 5, 2008. For arbitration agreements, see English cases: *Capital Trust Investments v Radio Design TJ* [2002] 1 All ER (Comm) 514; *Heyman v Darwins* [1942] AC 356; *Overseas Union Insurance v AA Mutual International Insurance* [1988] 2 Lloyd's Rep 63; *Fillite (Runcorn) v Aqua-Lift* (1989) 26 Con LR 66; US cases: *Mitsubishi Motors Co v Soler Chrysler-Plymouth, Inc.*, 473 US 614 (1985); *Re Kinoshita & Co.*, 287 F.2d 951 (2d Cir. 1961); *Prima Paint v Flood & Conklin Mfg*, 388 US 395, 421 (US NY 1967), at 406.

or arbitration agreements in resolving delictual disputes.[32] This broad definition also includes contracts with inequality of bargaining power, where the unsophisticated party may require special protection in terms of dispute resolution agreements.

3.3 Different types of jurisdiction agreements

Exclusive jurisdiction agreements

Unlike arbitration agreements, there is usually more than one type of jurisdiction agreement. The book will primarily focus on exclusive jurisdiction agreements. An exclusive jurisdiction agreement is a clause with the effect of both prorogation and derogation. It designates, for the purpose of deciding disputes which have arisen or may arise in connection with a particular legal relationship, the competent forum to the exclusion of any other courts.[33] An example of a typical exclusive jurisdiction clause is that: 'Any disputes arising out of the contract shall be decided exclusively by Chinese courts.' An exclusive jurisdiction clause attempts to have the same effect as an arbitration agreement with both prorogation and derogation power.

Non-exclusive jurisdiction agreements

Non-exclusive jurisdiction agreements have the effect of prorogation but not derogation. In other words, non-exclusive jurisdiction clauses grant jurisdiction to the chosen court but do not prevent the parties from bringing the dispute to other courts which are otherwise competent.[34] For example, a contractual clause states: 'Besides all the competent courts, any dispute arising out of the contract can also be brought to the court of Hong Kong.'

The exclusivity of a jurisdiction clause is crucial to its effect in the chosen court and to a non-chosen forum's decision to take or decline jurisdiction. Many jurisdiction clauses expressly state whether they are meant to be exclusive or non-exclusive. However, it is also common practice that a jurisdiction clause is drafted in neutral terms, which does not state its exclusivity. For example, a jurisdiction clause is drafted as follows: 'The parties agree to submit any disputes arising out of the transaction to the High Court of England.' There are different means to decide the exclusivity of

32 For example, Texas courts invalidated choice of court agreements in fraud or tort actions, *S.W. Intelecom v Hotel Networks*, 997 S.W.2d 322, 324 (Tex. Ct. App. 1999); Colorado District Court held choice of court agreements only cover contractual claims, *Xantrex Technology v Advanced Energy Industries*, Not Reported in F. Supp. 2d, 2008 WL 2185882, D.Colo., 2008. See Haines, 2002: para 8.

33 See the definition in the Hague Choice of Court Convention, Art 3(a).

34 Fawcett and Carruthers, 2008: 289.

such a jurisdiction clause. In the USA and Australia, a jurisdiction clause is presumed non-exclusive unless the parties clearly indicate otherwise;[35] in continental Europe, a jurisdiction clause is considered exclusive unless it explicitly states it is non-exclusive;[36] in other countries, there is no presumption and courts have to make a decision according to the 'true construction' of the clause, taking account of all the circumstances.[37]

Choice of more than one jurisdiction

There are also untypical jurisdiction agreements. Occasionally, a jurisdiction clause designates the competent courts of more than one country. For example, a contract provides: 'Disputes should be decided by the court of Hong Kong or China Mainland.' Different interpretations exist as to the exclusivity of such a jurisdiction clause. Under the law of some countries, such as China Mainland, a choice of court clause, either choosing more than one court in one country, or choosing the courts of more than one country, is invalid. In the Opinions on Some Issues Concerning the Application of the Civil Procedure Law of 1992, Article 24 provides that the parties could choose one of the related people's courts to hear a domestic dispute, but the choice of more than one court should be invalid.[38] The same view was repeated in subsequent judicial interpretations.[39]

Common practice, however, is not so restrictive. The choice of more than one jurisdiction is allowed in both the 2005 Hague Convention and the Brussels I Regulation. Article 3(b) of the 2005 Hague Convention provides that 'a choice of court agreement which designates *the courts of one Contracting State or one or more specific courts of one Contracting State* shall be deemed to be exclusive unless the parties have expressly provided otherwise' (emphasis added). Although the Convention does not prevent the parties from choosing the court of more than one country, a jurisdiction clause choosing more than one Contracting State shall be non-exclusive.[40] The Brussels I Regulation says the choice of the court of 'a Member State' shall be enforced. However, the ECJ has ruled that the choice of two Member States is valid and within the scope of the Regulation, and, more importantly, it can be exclusive in that it excludes all other non-chosen

35 Haines, 2002: para 9.

36 Brussels I Regulation, Art 23. See also Hague Choice of Court Convention, Art 3.

37 Such as English common law, Hong Kong, Japan and China. See Haines, 2002: para 9.

38 Discussed and adopted at the 528th meeting of the Judicial Committee of the Supreme People's Court, and promulgated by Judicial Interpretation No 22 [1992] of the Supreme People's Court on 14 July 1992.

39 Fa Han [1995] No 157.

40 If more than one court in one Contracting State is chosen, the jurisdiction clause can still be exclusive unless the parties provide otherwise.

states' jurisdiction.[41] This interpretation is appropriate because the parties may have chosen more than one country and allowed the claimant the option to select between the chosen courts to bring the action, while they want to derogate jurisdiction of all other competent courts.

Alternative choice of court agreements

The second type of unusual jurisdiction agreement permits the parties to choose alternative courts in different occasions. For example, the clause provides: 'The seller agrees to bring all the actions concerning disputes or differences arising out of the contract in the court of England; the buyer agrees to bring any actions in the court of Hong Kong.' In other cases, the parties could agree that 'any disputes should be brought to the court of jurisdiction where the defendant has his domicile'. This choice then provides alternative jurisdiction to each party and jurisdiction depends on which party brings the action.

Alternative choice of court clauses are different from clauses choosing more than one court. Although the latter is invalid under Chinese law, the former is valid and enforceable in Chinese courts. In alternative jurisdiction clauses, the claimant can only bring the action in one court. Although the other party can bring the same action in a different chosen court, it would not cause confusion as to which court is chosen by the parties in a single action.

The Chinese Supreme Court provided judicial guidance in 1994 that if the parties made an agreement that any action should be brought in the place of the claimant's domicile, this agreement was valid. If one party A brought the action in his domicile, while the other party B brought the same action in B's domicile, *lis pendens* rule should apply.[42] This interpretation was provided to determine the effect of a domestic choice of court agreement. It is uncertain whether the interpretation applies to an international choice of court agreement.

Asymmetric jurisdiction agreements

An asymmetric choice of court agreement is similar to an alternative choice of forum clause but it is clearly more favourable to one party than the other.[43] For example, the clause provides that: 'The lender may bring proceedings against the borrower in an English court, or in any other court having jurisdiction under its law, while the borrower may bring proceedings against the lender only in an English court.' This agreement is mostly used by banks in cross-border loan agreements.

41 Case 23/78 *Meeth v Glacetal Sarl* [1978] ECR 2133; Fawcett and Carruthers, 2008: 288.
42 Jing Han [1994] No 307.
43 Hartley, 2009: 164.

As alternative choice of court clauses, asymmetric choice of court clauses are different from clauses choosing more than one forum. Once a part brings the action, there is only one chosen forum available. As a common practice in the standard term contract of banks, an asymmetric jurisdiction clause is enforceable under the law of most countries. In a few Chinese cases, for example, the people's courts recognize the effect of asymmetric choice of court clauses, regardless of relevant bargaining power between the parties. In *The Sumitomo Bank v Xinhua Real Estate,*[44] disputes arose from a loan agreement between a bank (the lender) and a company (the borrower). The agreement included a jurisdiction clause providing:

> For the benefit of the lender, the Borrower irrevocably agrees that the courts of Hong Kong are to have non-exclusive jurisdiction to settle any disputes which may arise out of or in connection with this Agreement and that, accordingly, any legal action or proceedings arising out of or in connection with this Agreement ('Proceedings') may be brought in those courts and the Borrower irrevocably submits to the non-exclusive jurisdiction of those courts. Nothing in this Clause shall limit the right of the Lender to take Proceedings against the Borrower in any other court of competent jurisdiction nor shall the taking of Proceedings in one or more jurisdictions preclude the Lender from taking Proceedings in any other jurisdiction, whether concurrently or not.

This agreement was held valid and enforceable under the applicable law.[45] If this decision is said to be fair because parties shall be deemed to have equal bargaining power and have a fair bargain, asymmetric clauses are equally upheld in consumer contracts. In *Lai v ABN AMRO Bank,*[46] for example, a private investor entered into an investment agreement with a Dutch bank. Within this agreement, there was a choice of court clause to the effect that the investor could only sue the bank in Hong Kong to the exclusion of any other competent jurisdiction, while the bank could sue the investor in any competent fora. Both Shanghai Intermediate Court and Shanghai High Court upheld the choice of court agreement and declined jurisdiction in favour of Hong Kong courts.

In Europe, an asymmetric clause may be enforceable under the domestic law of Member States, and the Brussels I Regulation does not contain any rules that make an asymmetric clause invalid. In *Continental*

44 Supreme Court, (1999) Jing Zhong Zi No 194.

45 The court, however, used the governing law of the contract to interpret the jurisdiction clause, which was inconsistent with most courts' practice in China, where *lex fori* was applied.

46 Shanghai Municipality High Court, (2010) No 49.

Bank v Aeakos,[47] for example, the American bank and some borrowers entered into a loan agreement which provided that the borrowers could sue the bank exclusively in England while the bank could sue the borrowers in other competent jurisdictions. This agreement was upheld by the English courts under the Brussels Convention and domestic English law. The effect of an asymmetric jurisdiction clause, however, will be different in European Member States. A Member State may use a domestic law pursuant to its choice of law rules to invalidate such an agreement. For example, an asymmetric jurisdiction clause falling under Article 23 of the Brussels I Regulation was struck down by the French Supreme Court,[48] which applied French substantive law that invalidates a contract where one party has entire control over the event.[49] Similar decisions have also been reached by Bulgarian[50] and Russian courts.[51]

3.4 Arbitration agreements

Arbitration agreement is defined in the UNCITRAL Model Law as 'an agreement by the parties to submit to arbitration all or certain disputes which have arisen or which may arise between them in respect of a defined legal relationship, whether contractual or not'.[52] There may be two types of arbitration agreements, mandatory and non-mandatory. Non-mandatory arbitration agreements may allow the claimant the choice either to bring the dispute to the designated arbitral tribunal or to bring the dispute to the court. Arbitration agreements may also be classified into binding and non-binding agreements. The non-binding arbitration agreement means that the arbitral award may not bind the parties and the unsatisfied party has the option to bring the dispute to the court. Between them, there are also partial binding agreements, under which the arbitral award only binds one party but not the other.[53]

Non-mandatory, non-binding and partial binding arbitration agreements are very rare. Their nature has been questioned, as people doubt whether they are arbitration agreements at all. Arbitration is characterized by its mandatory, binding and final nature, which make arbitration popular due to business efficacy and certainty. Those usual types of

47 *Continental Bank NA v Aeakos Compania Naviera SA and Others*, [1994] ILPr 413.

48 *La société Banque privée Edmond de Rothschild Europe v Mme X, Cour de Cassation*, judgment of 26 September 2012.

49 Civil Code, articles 1170 and 1174.

50 2 September 2011 (Judgment No 71 in commercial case No 1193/2010).

51 *Sony v RTC*, Case No 1831/12, judgment dated 19 June 2012, reasons for the judgment published on 1 September 2012 (concerning one-way arbitration agreements).

52 Art 7.

53 Mostly in employment and consumer arbitration, see *Allen v Tenet Healthcare Corp.*, 370 F. Supp. 2d 682, 685 (M.D. Tenn. 2005); *Johnson v Long John Silver's Restaurants Inc.*, 320 F. Supp. 2d 656, 667 (M.D. Tenn, 2004). Haloush and Malkawi, 2008: 340.

arbitration agreements are usually used in special contracts, such as consumer contracts and employment contracts, to protect the weaker parties' rights to access to justice.[54] Besides, non-mandatory arbitration agreements are upheld in a few recent Chinese cases. For example, the Shanghai High People's Court ruled that the arbitration agreement read 'Arbitration, if any, in Hong Kong and English law to apply' is non-exclusive or non-mandatory, which only grants jurisdiction to the Hong Kong arbitral tribunal without depriving competent Chinese courts their jurisdiction.[55] This interpretation is criticized for being too arbitration unfriendly. There is also a question as to why the Chinese court does not interpret this clause pursuant to English law or Hong Kong law, under which the agreement shall be construed to submit disputes exclusively to arbitration.[56] These special arbitration agreements, anyway, are not covered by this book, which only considers rules relating to ordinary arbitration agreements in commercial contracts.

4 Objective of the book

Dispute resolution agreements are special contract terms. Their binding effects on the parties stem from the contractual nature, while their enforcement by courts stems from state sovereignty. Only after a country accepts that private parties have the power to agree on a competent forum and it is in the country's interest to recognize the full enforceability of this agreement, a dispute resolution clause could acquire the effectiveness that parties intend to have and could provide certainty and predictability to the parties. This book offers a systematic and comparative study on the prerequisites, effectiveness and enforcement of exclusive jurisdiction and arbitration agreements in international dispute resolution in order to determine whether the clauses have the identical effects in private international law. The book also investigates whether they are, or should be, given the same treatment by most countries in the world. The book compares the treatment of jurisdiction and arbitration clauses mainly in the US, China, the UK and the EU to demonstrate how, in practice, exclusive jurisdiction and arbitration agreements are enforced. Law and practice in other jurisdictions are also considered in due course. This book finally

54 See discussion in Padis, 2013: 665; Reich, 2009: 866; Grossberg, 2008: 673–674; Schmitz, 2004: 68–69; Ribstein and Kobayashi, 2002: 51.

55 Shanghai High People's Court, (2009) No 275. The same decision was also reached by the Fujian High People's Court in *Shanghai Youlixin International Freight Agency Co. Ltd v Xiamen Yaozhong Asia-Pacific Trading Co*, [2011] No 818.

56 Supreme People's Court, 'Interpretation of the Supreme People's Court concerning some issues on the application of the Arbitration Law of the People's Republic of China', Art 16 provides that in deciding the validity and effect of an arbitration agreement, the court shall apply the law chosen by the parties; in the absence of that, the law of the seat; in the absence of that, the Chinese law.

considers whether the Hague Convention could be treated as a litigating counterpart of the New York Convention and whether it could work equally successfully to facilitate judicial cooperation and party autonomy in international commerce.

5 Legal framework

5.1 English law

English law on jurisdiction agreements is complicated by the influence of EU legislation. England has two systems of law applying to jurisdiction agreements: the Council Regulation (EC) No 44/2001 of 22 December 2001 on jurisdiction and the recognition and enforcement of judgments in civil and commercial matters ('Brussels I')[57] applies to jurisdiction agreements concluded between the parties, one of which has its domicile within the EU and a court of an EU Member State is chosen in the agreement;[58] English common law applies to jurisdiction agreements out of the scope of the Brussels I Regulation.[59] The situation will change after 10 January 2015, when the Regulation (EU) No 1215/2012 of the European Parliament and the Council of 12 December 2012 on jurisdiction and the recognition and enforcement of judgments in civil and commercial matters (recast) ('Brussels I Recast')[60] will enter into force and replace the Brussels I Regulation in all Member States. Article 25(1) of the Brussels I Recast removes the domicile requirement to the application of this provision and applies to all jurisdiction clauses choosing one of the Member States. After this provision enters into force, English common law only applies in cases where the court of a third country is chosen and the English court decides whether to decline jurisdiction. English law is relevantly clearer in arbitration. The Arbitration Act 1996 provides uniform rules in arbitration, including domestic and international arbitration.

5.2 US law

The US has no federal statute on jurisdiction agreements, the effect of which is based on case law. The cornerstone case is *Bremen v Zapata Off-Shore*,[61] which established the common law test in deciding the enforceability of a jurisdiction clause. The effect of a jurisdiction clause is prima facie upheld, subject to the exception of public policy and unconscionability. This case has been followed in most Federal Courts. However, the

57 [2001] OJ L 44/1.
58 Art 23(1).
59 Art 4(1).
60 [2012] OJ L 351/1.
61 407 US 1 (1972).

enforcement of jurisdiction agreements in state courts is still uncertain. The enforcement of arbitration agreements, on the other hand, is set up in legislation, i.e. the Federal Arbitration Act 1925 clearly provides agreements to submit disputes to arbitration 'shall be valid, irrevocable, and enforceable, save upon such grounds as exist at law or in equity for the revocation of any contract'.[62]

5.3 Chinese law

Chinese law follows the civil law tradition. Laws exist in legislation and the Supreme Court judicial direction/interpretation. Case law only has referential value. Two statutes are particularly relevant: the Civil Procedure Law 2012 and the Arbitration Law 1994. The CPR Civil Procedure Law 1991 is the first legislation that recognizes the effect of choice of court agreements. Prior to that, the Civil Procedure Law (for Trial Implementation) 1982 said nothing about party autonomy, either in domestic or in international cases.[63] The 1991 Civil Procedure Law has been amended twice, in 2007[64] and 2012,[65] respectively. This Act provides provisions to decide the validity and enforcement of both jurisdiction and arbitration agreements. The effect of jurisdiction agreements has also been interpreted in a number of judicial directions published by the Supreme Court, including 'Opinion on Several Issues on the Application of the Civil Procedure Law of the People's Republic of China' ('1992 Opinion'),[66] and 'Summary of the Second National Conference on the Adjudication of Commercial and Maritime Cases with Foreign Elements' published in 2005 ('2005 Summary').[67]

The effect of an arbitration agreement is established in both the Civil Procedure Law 2012 and the Arbitration Act 1994.[68] Furthermore, the Supreme Court introduced a unique and controversial internal report-

62 Section 2.

63 For a general introduction to the Chinese civil procedure law and source of law, see Zhang, 2002: 59.

64 The Civil Procedure Law 1991 was amended in 2007 by the Decision of the Standing Committee of the National People's Congress on Amending the Civil Procedure Law of the People's Republic of China, adopted at the 30th Meeting of the Standing Committee of the Tenth NPC on 28 October 2007, and promulgated by the Order of the President No 75. It entered into effect from 1 April 2008. The translation of statutes in the article is available at the National People's Congress, the Database of Laws and Regulations, www.npc.gov.cn/englishnpc/Law/Integrated_index.html.

65 The Civil Procedure Law was further amended in 2012 by the Decision of the Standing Committee of the NPC, adopted at the 28th Meeting of the Standing Committee of the Eleventh NPC on 31 August 2012, entered into force from 1 January 2013.

66 [1992] No 22.

67 Supreme People's Court, [2005] No 6.

68 Adopted at the Ninth Meeting of the Standing Committee of the Eighth National People's Congress on 31 August 1994 and promulgated by Order No 31 of the President of the People's Republic of China on 31 August 1994.

and-review procedure to strengthen the effectiveness of arbitration agreements in its judicial direction 'Notice on Issues about the Handling of Cross-Border and Foreign Arbitration' ('1995 Notice').[69] Another important judicial interpretation on arbitration is the 'Interpretation of the Supreme People's Court Concerning some Issues on the Application of the Arbitration Law of the People's Republic of China' ('Interpretation 2006').[70] The Choice of Law on Foreign-Related Civil Relationships Act 2010 (Conflicts Act)[71] and its judicial interpretation, 'Interpretations of the Supreme People's Court on Several Issues Concerning Application of the Law of the People's Republic of China on Choice of Law for Foreign-Related Civil Relationships (I)',[72] also include choice of law rules relating to arbitration agreements.

5.4 International instruments

International harmonization of law is comparatively more advanced in arbitration than in jurisdiction agreements. The United Nation Convention on the Recognition and Enforcement of Foreign Arbitral Awards 1958 (New York Convention) has 144 signatory countries. It is remarked as the most successful international convention in the international commercial area.[73] Following the New York Convention, UNCITRAL published the Model Law on International Commercial Arbitration (amended 2006) and the Arbitration Rules (amended 2010), which aim to address difficulties caused by inadequacy and disparity of national arbitration law and to establish further harmonization and efficiency. Beside the important harmonization at the international level, there are also two regional arbitration conventions, which deserve some words. The first one is the European Convention on International Commercial Arbitration 1961, which entered into force in 1964. This Convention aims to improve international commercial practices involving European states;[74] 32 European countries are party, involving non-EU countries.[75] The second important regional arbitration convention is the Inter-American Convention on International

69 (1995) No 18.

70 The judicial interpretation was passed in the 1375th meeting of the Supreme People's Court Trial Committee on 26 December 2005 and entered into force from 8 September 2006, Fashi [2006] No 7. Some directions can also be found in the 'Notice of the Supreme People's Court of some issues on the enforcement of the Arbitration Law of the Peope's Republic of China' Fafa [1997] No 4.

71 Adopted at the 17th session of the Standing Committee of the 11th National People's Congress on October 28, 2010 and promulgated and entered into force on April 1, 2011.

72 [2012] No 24.

73 Strong, 2012: 127; Park and Yanos, 2006: 257; Westbrook, 2011: 640; Levi-Tawil, 2011: 613–614.

74 Born, 2009: 102.

75 United Nation Treaty Collection, http://treaties.un.org/pages/ViewDetails.aspx?src=TREATY&mtdsg_no=XXII-2&chapter=22&lang=en, last accessed on 16 April 2013.

Commercial Arbitration (the 'Panama Convention'),[76] with the US and 15 South American countries being party. Neither of these conventions conflict with the New York Convention, but they provide supplementary rules to help international arbitration practice.

In terms of jurisdiction, the international harmonization is less successful than arbitration, while regional harmonization is more influential. The European Union has harmonized jurisdiction rules and recognition and enforcement of foreign judgments among its Member States. The Brussels I Regulation, and its future successor, the Brussels I Recast, have been described above as part of enforcing law in England. At the international level, the Hague Conference on Private International Law adopted the Convention on Choice of Court Agreements in 2005, which intends to be the international instrument to facilitate the enforcement of jurisdiction agreements and enforcement of judgments given by the chosen country.

76 United Nations Panama Convention Establishing the Latin American Economic System (SELA), 17 October 1975, 1292 U.N.T.S. 21295.

2 Prerequisites

Contractual requirements

1 Introduction

Before a court considers the effectiveness and enforceability of a jurisdiction or arbitration agreement, the first condition that must be satisfied is that there is a valid conflicts clause between the parties. Existence and validity is the preliminary requirement of disputes resolution agreements.

The existence and validity of a dispute resolution agreement is closely related to the formation and validity of contracts or contract terms, but they are not the same. On the one hand, a dispute resolution clause is a contract term, the conclusion of which must follow the ordinary contractual concepts and principles, i.e. there must be a meeting of minds. On the other hand, a dispute resolution clause is a special contract term. The principle of severability usually separates them from underlying contracts and ordinary contract terms. The invalidity of the main contract or other contract terms could not automatically mean a conflicts clause in this contract is invalid. Different applicable law might be applied to decide the validity of a conflicts clause from the main contract. Even if the same applicable law applies, besides basic contractual principles, special rules are applied to determine the existence and validity of jurisdiction or arbitration clauses.

2 Existence and validity: the concepts

2.1 Classification between existence and validity

Existence and validity of conflicts clauses are two different concepts. The former refers to the conclusion of a conflicts clause and incorporation of this clause into a contract. The latter refers to the quality and authenticity of the parties' consent and other issues that may render a conflicts clause void or voidable.[1] In practice, however, it is sometimes hard to distinguish

1 *Albon v Naza Motor Trading SDN BHD* [2007] EWHC 665 (Ch), per Lightman J; *JSC BTA Bank v Mukhtar Ablyazov* 2011 EWHC 587 (Comm), para 34, per Clark J.

these two concepts. For example, one party may argue that there is an implied choice of forum agreement in their contract. It is unclear whether this is something relating to the existence of a conflicts clause, namely the dispute resolution agreement is concluded between the parties, or something relating to the validity of such a choice, namely the agreement, albeit unexpressed, demonstrates the authentic consents of the parties and meets specific formal requirements.

Some legislation does not clearly distinguish the existence and validity of a conflicts clause. In the EU, for example, Article 23(1) of the Brussels I Regulation (Art 25(1) of the Brussels I Recast) provides uniform requirements to determine the formal validity of a jurisdiction clause. Some of these requirements, however, relate to the existence of a jurisdiction clause. In *Segoura v Bonakdarian*,[2] for example, the dispute was whether the jurisdiction clause, which was not orally agreed on by the parties in their negotiation on the current transaction but existed in their previous transactions, could bind the parties in their current contractual obligations. The key consideration was whether the jurisdiction clause governing the parties' previous transactions was incorporated into the current agreement. It is a question in relation to the formation of the jurisdiction clause. The decision, however, was based on Article 23(1)(b) of the Brussels I Regulation, which provided formal validity requirements for jurisdiction clauses.[3]

In the US, before enforcing a jurisdiction clause, a court must be satisfied that the existence of the jurisdiction clause is reasonably communicated to the other party.[4] This is a requirement in relation to both the existence and validity of jurisdiction clauses. The expression 'reasonably communicate' concerns the formation of the agreement and the material validity relating to the quality of consent. First, a jurisdiction clause is not formed unless it is brought to the other party's attention. Second, if a jurisdiction clause is not made known to the other party, there is no authentic consent and the clause is not materially valid.

The UNCITRAL Model Law distinguishes between existence and validity of an arbitration agreement.[5] For example, Art 7(6) (option 1) states that an arbitration agreement is in writing if there is a reference in a

2 Case 25/76 [1976] ECR 1851.

3 See also Art 23(1)(c) Brussels I. See *Re Jurisdiction in the Case of a Sale Involving the Carriage of Goods* [2010] ILPr 29. There is also an opinion that, in the EU, the distinction is made between formal validity on the one hand and the formation and substantive validity on the other, which is mainly because the Rome I Regulation provides a distinct choice of law rules for them (Art 10 and Art 11). Fawcett and Carruthers, 2008: 286.

4 *Spataro v Kloster Cruise* 894 F.2d 44, 45–46 (2d Cir. 1990); *Hodes v SNC* 858 F.2d 905, 909–912 (3d Cir. 1988); *Denicola v Cunard Line*, 642 F.2d 5, 9 (1st Cir., 1981); *Effron v Sun Line*, 67 F.3d 7, 9 (C.A.2 (N.Y.), 1995).

5 UNCITRAL Model Law on International Commercial Arbitration 1985, with amendments as adopted in 2006.

contract to any document containing this arbitration clause, provided the reference makes this clause part of the contract. It shows that the court must decide first whether the reference has incorporated the arbitration clause into the contract. If it has not, the court should not use this article to grant the arbitration clause formal validity. However, regardless of the language suggesting a distinguished treatment to existence and validity of an arbitration clause, these issues are rarely treated separately in practice.

It seems that the distinction between existence and validity of a conflicts clause is frequently ignored in legislation process and in practice. It is true that even in theory the strict line between existence and validity of a conflicts clause is very often blurred and hard to draw. Especially in common law countries, strict dichotomy does not exist. It is unrealistic to require a court to always draw a clear line between existence and validity and apply different rules to determine each, which would induce extra burden, lead to unnecessary delay and increase litigation cost. On the other hand, it is necessary to recognize the fact that existence and validity of conflicts clauses are different issues in theory. If the argument is on the existence of a conflicts clause, the court should examine offer, acceptance and intention to create legal relationships.[6] Disputes on the existence of an agreement exist where no valid acceptance is expressed,[7] where a conflicts clause concluded in a previous contract or included in another document is incorporated into the current contract,[8] where a jurisdiction or arbitration clause is entered into impliedly[9] and where the latter behaviour of either party amounts to the repudiation.[10] If the dispute is on the validity of a clause, the focus should be the formal requirements set out by law and the quality of consent concerning such issues as fraud, mistake, undue influence, duress and misrepresentation.[11] It is accepted that in certain circumstances, where the issue falls on the borderline between existence and

6 English common law also requires consideration.

7 *Nordgemuse di Wihem Krogmann OHG v Gennaro Parrilli*, Giustizia civile 1996 I, 811–814; *Alfred Dunhill v Tivoli Group*, Giustizia civile 1996 I 2065–2070; *Duta Wajar Sdn v Pasukhas Constructions Sdn Bhd* [2012] 4 CLJ 844; Magnus and Mankowski, 2012: para 131.

8 *AEL v Socofi SA* [2009] EWHC 3223 (Comm); *AIG Europe SA v QBE International Insurance* [2001] All ER(D) 50; *7E Communications Ltd v Vertex Antennentechnik GmbH CA TLR* [2007] EWCA Civ 150; *TW Thomas v Portsea Steamship* [1912] AC 1; *Alfred McAlpine Construction Ltd v RMG Electrical* [1998] ADRLJ 33; *Extrudakerb (Maltby Engineering) Ltd v Whitemountain Quarries Ltd,* [1996] N.I. 567; *Roche Products Ltd v Freeman Process Systems Ltd,* (1996) 80 BLR 102; *TW Thomas & Co v Portsea Co Ltd* [1912] AC 1; *The Annefield* [1971] P. 168; *Skips AS Nordheim v Syrian Petroleum The Varenna* [1983] 2 Lloyd's Rep. 592; *Pine Ton Insurance v Unione Italiana Analo Saxon Reinsurance* [1987] 1 Lloyd's Rep. 476.

9 *Compagnie d'Armement Maritime SA v Compagnie Tunisienne de Navigation SA* [1971] AC 572; *Akai* [1996] 188 CLC 418; *Paul Smith Ltd v H&S International Holding Inc* [1991] 2 Lloyd's Rep 127; *Axa Re v Ace Global Markets Ltd* [2006] EWHC 216; *Interserve Industrial Services Ltd v ZRE Katowice SA* [2012] EWHC 3205 (TCC).

10 *Noble Power Investments Limited & Another v Nissei Stomach Tokyo Co Ltd,* CACV 398/2007; *Dubai Islamic Bank PJSC v PSI Energy Holding Co,* [2011] EWHC 1019 (Comm).

11 Haines, 2002: paras 12–19; Fawcett and Carruthers, 2008: 286–287.

validity, it is unnecessary to apply separate rules and the court could adopt a synthetic approach to consider the whole situation systematically. In other cases, where the dispute clearly concerns the formation of a contract term or the validity of this term, it is necessary to distinguish existence and validity of conflicts clauses and examine each respectively.

2.2 Classification between formal validity and substantive validity

Deciding validity of a conflicts clause is usually very complicated. Since there are different types of validity, i.e. formal validity and material validity, a court shall decide classification first. Formal validity concerns the external expression of an agreement, such as whether it is in writing, whether signatures are available, whether digital agreements are acceptable; while material validity includes all other issues, including the authenticity of the consent, the capacity of the parties, legality of the agreement and public policy. It is hard to draw a clear-cut line between formal and substantive validity, as the requirement as to form usually contains the consideration for the demonstration of consent.

Article 23 of the Brussels I Regulation, for example, provides very wide definition to formal validity, which concerns not only the external expression of the agreement and the consent, but also the quality of the consent. Agreements that are not presented in a way to catch another party's attention have been ruled as not being formally valid.[12] On the other hand, no substantive validity has been expressly provided in the Regulation. In common law countries, unless expressly provided by statutes, the courts do not examine formal and material validity of dispute resolution agreements separately. A court is usually ready to search the common consent without the requirement of rigid form.[13] In the US, for example, the only requirement for a dispute resolution clause to be valid is conscionableness.[14] It is accepted that strict requirement for separate treatments to form and substance of a dispute resolution agreement is not in accordance with commercial practice. However, although formal and material validity has been mixed in many cases in practice and cannot be clearly distinguished, for the purpose of analysis, the book still keeps the traditional dichotomy to separate validity into form and substance. A court usually uses the *lex fori* to decide the classification.

12 Case 24/76 *Colzani v RUWA* [1976] ECR 1831; *Marine Contractors v Shell Petroleum Development* [1984] 2 Lloyd's Rep 77; *7E Communications v Vertex Antennentechnik GmbH* [2007] EWCA Civ 140; Briggs, 2008: para 7.43; Yackee, 2004b: 1182.

13 *Roberts & Schaefer v Merit Contracting* 99 F.3d 248, 252–253 (7th Cir 1996); Yackee, 2004b: 1182; Tang, 2009: 135–139.

14 *M/S Bremen v Zapata Off-Shore* 407 US 1 (1972).

2.3 Applicable law to classification

Classification between existence, formal validity and substantive validity of a conflicts clause is a question of law and confronts choice of law issues. A court usually will use the *lex fori* to decide classification. After the classification, a court will continue to decide which substantive law applies to the preliminary issue in question.

3 Which law decides existence and validity?

There is a trend to harmonize preliminary requirements in jurisdiction and arbitration agreements in order to improve certainty in international commerce. In general, rules concerning formal validity of a conflicts clause are harmonized, at least partially, either at the regional or at the international level, while rules on formation and substantive validity are largely left untouched. It is because domestic laws of each country vary largely in substantive validity and substantive validity is, sometimes, relating to public interest. In the regional and international harmonization of conflict of laws, the harmonization on substantive validity of a conflicts clause incurs the greatest difficulty. A uniform substantive law cannot be accepted in the New York Convention, UNCITRAL Model Law, Brussels I Regulation and Hague Choice of Court Convention. The most recent harmonization in jurisdiction agreements only introduces harmonized choice of law rules to decide substantive validity.[15] Even if a court has used choice of law to answer this issue, the application of the governing law may be further restricted by the concern of public policy or mandatory rules of both the forum and a closely related third country.[16] Since there are different domestic laws deciding the preliminary issues of a conflicts clause, a court or tribunal will first decide which country's substantive law should apply to govern this issue.

3.1 Jurisdiction clauses

National courts adopt inconsistent choice of law in deciding the preliminary issues. Choice usually exists between the *lex fori*, the governing law to the main contract, or the law of the chosen court. When contractual parties enter into jurisdiction agreements, they aim to have a clear picture as to in which country they would sue or be sued. The diversity of approaches makes jurisdiction clauses easily evadable. In order to re-establish certainty and predictability, many countries enter into judicial

15 Regulation (EU) No 1215/2012 of the European Parliament and the Council of 12 December 2012 on jurisdiction and the recognition and enforcement of judgments in civil and commercial matters (recast), (Brussels I Recast), [2012] OJ L 351/1, Art 25(1); Hague Choice of Court Convention, Art 5(1) and 6(a).

16 E.g. Hague Choice of Court Convention, Art 6(b) and (c).

cooperation by harmonizing either substantive rules or choice of law rules. The two most important harmonization instruments are the European harmonization of jurisdiction rules in the Brussels I Regulation, which will be replaced by the Brussels I Recast from 10 January 2015,[17] and the Hague Convention on the Choice of Court Agreements of 2005.

EU approach

The current Brussels I Regulation harmonizes formal requirements in relation to jurisdiction clauses within the scope of the Regulation.[18] However, there is no uniform rule to decide the applicable law governing the existence of jurisdiction clauses or validity other than form. Although Article 10 of the Rome I Regulation has established uniform choice of law rules to decide the existence of consent to a contract or contract terms, Article 1(e) of the Rome I Regulation clearly excludes arbitration and choice of court agreements from its scope. This is because there has been harmonized Union law on jurisdiction clauses[19] and international treaties in arbitration,[20] and it is considered better to avoid overlapping and conflicts. Thus, Article 10 cannot be used to decide the existence and material validity of a jurisdiction or arbitration clause.[21]

Existence and material validity of a jurisdiction clause, thus, are left to be decided by the individual Member State. However, examining the formal requirements in Article 23(1) and the ECJ interpretation to this provision, it is not difficult to find that the meaning of the uniform formal requirement is very broad, which covers the issues relating to the existence and substantive validity of a jurisdiction clause.[22] The ECJ's construction in formal validity concerns more than simply the 'form', but also whether the form could in some ways demonstrate the parties' true intention. In the ECJ's interpretation, a court should look beyond 'writing' to figure out whether the jurisdiction clause is written in a way that the other party knows or ought to know the existence and meaning of this clause. The formal requirements require the clear demonstration of consent to, or

17 Brussels I Recast, Art 81.

18 Art 23(1) Brussels I.

19 The Brussels I Regulation, Art 23. See Guiliano-Lagarde Report, Art 1.5.

20 New York Convention of 1958. All Member States are parties.

21 However, many courts fail to make the distinction in practice and apply Article 10 equally to decide the existence and validity of dispute resolution clauses. *Welex AG v Rosa Maritime Ltd (The Epsilon Rosa) (No 2)* [2003] ILPr 18 (using Article 8 of the Rome Convention to decide the existence of an arbitration clause).

22 See Art 23(1) of Brussels I. Case 24/76 *Colzani v RUWA* [1976] ECR 1831; Case 25/76 *Galeries Segoura Sprl v Firma Rahim Bonakdarian* [1976] ECR 1851; Case 71/83 *'Tilly Russ' v Nova NV* [1984] ECR 2417; Case C-106/95 *Mainschiffahrts-Genossenschaft eG (MSG) v Les Gravieres Rhenanes Sarl* [1997] ECR I-911; Case C-159/97 *Transporti Castelletti Spedizione Internatzionali SpA v Hugo Trumpy SpA* [1999] ECR I-1597.

acceptance of, a jurisdiction clause, which concerns its formation of a jurisdiction clause and the quality of consent.[23]

As a result, there is an argument that the formal requirements in Article 23(1) are full and sufficient to ensure the genuine consent to a jurisdiction clause exists.[24] In other words, no choice of law rule is necessary to decide the existence and validity. This, however, is not true. Although some issues relating to the formation and material validity are covered by the broad wording of Article 23(1), many other issues are left out. The broad coverage of formal validity is not comprehensive to cover every issue concerning the authenticity of consent. It can only tackle situations where jurisdiction clauses are inserted in a contract in a way that prevents the other party from noticing its existence. It is incapable in dealing with cases where the jurisdiction clause is clearly expressed, the intention of the parties has been brought to it and the parties have demonstrated their consent clearly and unambiguously to the jurisdiction clause, but there exists coercion, duress or undue influence, which makes consent tainted.

In practice, most courts prefer to treat Article 23(1) separately from the existence and material validity of a jurisdiction clause. In *Coreck Maritime v Handelsveem*,[25] the ECJ held that each Member State could apply the conflict of law rules of the forum to decide material validity of a jurisdiction clause choosing a non-Member State. However, since no uniform choice of law exists within the EU Member States, the practice varies.[26] In Austria,[27] the Netherlands, Malta and Poland,[28] the failure of intent is subject to the *lex causae*; in Cyprus[29] and Greece,[30] issues beyond formal validity are decided according to the *lex fori*.[31]

In terms of the existence of a jurisdiction clause, Hamblen J said in *Polskie Ratownictwo Okretowe v Rallo Vito*[32] that Article 23 has two elements: (1) juris-

23 *Africa Express Line v Socofi SA* [2010] ILPr 15; Case 24/76 *Estasis Salotti di Colzani Aimo e Gianmario Colzani v RUWA Polstereimaschinen GmbH* [1976] ECR 1831, Case C106/95 *Mainschiffahrts Genossenschaft eG (MSG) v Les Gravieres Rhenanes Sarl* [1997] QB 731; Case C-387/98 *Coreck Maritime GmbH v Handelsveem BV* [2000] ECR I-9337; *Bols Distilleries BV (t/a Bols Royal Distilleries) v Superior Yacht Services Ltd* [2007] 1 WLR 12.

24 Case C-159/97 *Transporti Castelletti Spedizioni Internazionali SpA v Hugo Trumpy SpA* [1997] ECR I-1597, paras 49 and 51; *MSG v Les Gravieres Rhenanes Sarl*, para 15.

25 Case C-387/98, [2000] ECR I-9337.

26 Hess *et al.*, 2007: para 377.

27 OGH 7 Ob 320/00k, ZfRV 2001/71 = RdW2001/678; 7 Ob 38/01s, RdW 2001/676 = ÖRZ-EÜ 2001/70 =ZfRV 2001/63 = ecolex 2002, 420 = ELF 2001, 431; 5 Ob 130/02g; Parenti, 'Internationale Gerichtsstandsvereinbarungten: *Lex fori* oder *lex causae* Anknüpfung?', (2003) ZfRV 221. National Report Austria (Oberhammer/Domej), Study JLS/C4/2005/03.

28 25 October 2005, I CK 263/05.

29 C Michailidou, 'The application of Regulation 44/01/EC: National Report Cyprus', Study JLS/C4/2005/03.

30 National Report Greece, JLS/C4/2005/03.

31 Hess *et al.*, 2007: para 377.

32 [2009] ILPr 55.

diction agreements must exist and (2) the agreements must meet formal requirements in Article 23(1).[33] The claimant should show a good arguable case that there is a jurisdiction clause between the parties[34] and the court should decide 'if there was sufficient consensus between the parties as a question of fact, without recourse to any rules of national law'.[35] The defendant contested that the jurisdiction clause included in the standard form was not part of the contract subject to negotiation and acceptance. The court relied on the common commercial practice, the knowledge of the defendant, and the content of the contract to conclude that the standard terms were incorporated in the contract. The jurisdiction clause as part of the standard terms was equally incorporated in the contract even without being referred to specifically. Some types of commercial contracts regularly address standard terms, which were right within the knowledge of experienced commercial participants and their brokers. During negotiation, the existence of standard terms was brought to the attention of the other and some fundamental terms in the standard form were negotiated and agreed upon. *In Antonio Gramsci Shipping v Oleg Stepanovs*,[36] the English court held that the existence and interpretation of a jurisdiction clause is governed by the *lex fori*, while the formal validity and consensus are governed by the uniform EU law.[37] This approach, however, has been criticized as failing to see the inherent broad coverage of Article 23(1) of the Brussels I Regulation, the interpretation of which has covered all issues relating to the existence of consent.[38]

The situation will be clearer after the Brussels I Recast enters into force on 10 January 2015,[39] which provides uniform choice of law rules to decide the existence and material validity of a jurisdiction clause. The new Article 25(1) provides that the law of the chosen Member State should be applied to decide the substantive validity of a jurisdiction clause.[40] The Brussels I Recast also permits *renvoi* by allowing the application of the conflict of laws of the chosen Member State.[41]

Hague Convention on choice of court agreements

The Hague Convention also only harmonizes formal requirements for an exclusive jurisdiction agreement. However, it provides piecemeal require-

33 Ibid., para 35.

34 *Canada Trust Co v Stolzenberg (No 2)* [1998] ILPr 290; *Bols Distilleries BV (t/a Bols Royal Distilleries) v Superior Yacht Services Ltd* [2007] 1 WLR 12; *Kolmar Group v Visen Industries* [2010] ILPr 23.

35 *Polskie Ratownictwo Okretowe v Rallo Vito*, para 36. Collins *et al.*, 2006: paras 12–108.

36 [2011] EWHC 333 (Comm).

37 Ibid., para 31.

38 *Kolmar Group AG v Visen Industries Ltd* [2010] ILPr 23, para 25.

39 [2012] OJ L 351/1.

40 Art 25(1) and recital 20.

41 Brussels I Recast, recital 20.

ments for substantive validity. First, the substantive law of the chosen court can be used to decide the jurisdiction clause 'null and void' (Arts 5(1), 6(a), 9(a)); second, a non-chosen court can use its domestic law to decide if a party lacks capacity (Art 6(1)) or whether the agreement would lead to a manifest injustice or would be manifestly contrary to the public policy of this country (Art 6(b) and 6(c)).

During the negotiation of the Hague Choice of Law Convention, the applicable law to the substantive validity agreements confronted great controversy and debates. Applying the law of the chosen state can lead to certainty, i.e. wherever the dispute is brought, the same applicable law shall apply and the decision will be consistent. The weakness is that this approach may cause unfairness to the rejecting party, especially when this party enters into the contract under undue influence, fraud or duress. The other party may choose the competent court, bearing in mind that its domestic law would enforce contracts concluded under the above circumstances. Although the Convention eventually adopt the approach to apply the law, including choice of law, of the chosen state, exception is also given to the law of the non-chosen state, which is seized to decide the dispute. It is because a non-chosen court does not feel comfortable to enforce a jurisdiction clause which is valid under the law of the chosen country but nevertheless contradicts its overriding mandatory rules and public policy. Exception is thus given to capacity of a party and fundamental public policy of the non-chosen country. This exception could avoid moderate unfairness caused by the application of the law of the chosen court, and could provide the rejecting party with a certain level of protection.

Common law approach in England and the USA

The approach adopted in English and US common law is inconsistent and confusing. English and US common law usually directly applies the *lex fori* to decide the existence and validity of a jurisdiction clause.[42] Even if the parties have chosen the applicable law to govern the underlying contract, the courts would still apply the *lex fori* to a jurisdiction clause.[43] The application of *lex causae*, on the other hand, has not been completely

42 *Antonio Gramsci Shipping Corporation & Others v Oleg Stepanovs* [2011] EWHC 333 (Comm), per Burton J: 'English law (i.e. national law) governs the existence (i.e. scope and effect) and interpretation of a jurisdiction clause, and EU law governs formality and consensus'; *The Varenna* [1983] 2 Lloyd's Rep 592, 594; *The Emmanuel Colocotronis (No 2)* [1982] 1 Lloyd's Rep 286, 289; *Midgulf International Ltd v Groupe Chimiche Tunisien* [2010] 1 CLC 113; *Sotrade Denizcilik Sanayi Ve Ticaret A.S. v Amadou LO, Tiger Denrees Senegal, Axa Assurance Senegal, Axa France Assurance S.A. (The 'Duden')* [2008] EWHC 2762 (Comm), para 44.

43 Yackee, 2004a: 67; Symeonides *et al.*, 1998: 681. *Evolution Online Systems, Inc. v Koninklijke PTT Nederland N.V* 145 F.3d 505 (2d Cir. 1998); *Afram Carriers v Moeykens* 145 F.3d 298 (5th Cir. 1998); *Gen Elec Co v G Siempelkamp GmbH* 29 F.3d 1095 (6th Cir. 1994); *New Moon Shipping v MAN B & W Diesel AG* 121 F.3d 24 (2d Cir. 1997).

excluded in court practice,[44] and is advocated by some academic writers.[45] Although judicial practice generally uses the *lex fori* to decide validity of a jurisdiction clause, the American National Conference of Commissioners on Uniform State Laws drafted a Model Choice of Forum Act in 1968, which proposed to apply the law of the chosen court to decide validity of a jurisdiction clause.[46]

Chinese approach

In China, there is no legislative provision or judicial direction providing guidance in deciding existence of a jurisdiction clause. The practice shows great divergence. Most people's courts apply the *lex fori*,[47] while a few courts also apply the *lex causae*.[48]

The advantage of applying the *lex fori* is that Chinese courts are most familiar with Chinese law and could make decisions on the preliminary issue very quickly. However, some Chinese courts strictly apply the *lex fori* and apply Chinese domestic law even if the parties have chosen another country and that country's law to govern a jurisdiction clause. They classify jurisdiction clauses procedure which is exclusively governed by the Chinese law.[49] Since Chinese law has provided relatively more restrictive requirements for a jurisdiction clause to be valid—for example, a jurisdiction clause can only choose the court that has 'practical connections' to the dispute[50]—the application of Chinese law would provide possibility for forum shopping. The party, who wants to avoid a freely entered choice of court agreement choosing a neutral forum, might bring the action in China, where the clause would be invalid.

44 *Compagnie Tunisienne de Navigation S.A. v Compagnie d'Armement Maritime S.A.* [1971] AC 572; *Hoerter (Trading as C.F. Mumm) v Hanover Caoutchouc, Gutta Percha & Telegraph Works*, 10 T.L.R 103.

45 Kahn-Freund, 1977: 825.

46 Ibid., 830.

47 *Shandong Jufeng v Korea MGame* Supreme People's Court, (2009) No 4; Supreme People's Court, 'Annual Report of Intellectual Property Cases in the Supreme Court (2009)', [2010] No 173, case 44.

48 *The Sumitomo Bank Ltd v Xinhua Estate* Supreme People's Court, (1999) No 194.

49 *Shandong Jufeng v MGame*, Supreme People's Court, (2009) No 4; Guangdong Province High People's Court, 'Notice on Issues about Deciding the Five Intermediate People's Courts of Guangzhou Municipality on the Territorial Jurisdiction and Jurisdiction by Forum Level on Civil and Commercial Matters Relating to Hong Kong and Macau', [2002] No 191, Art 13; *China Point Finance Ltd v Zhuhai City Commercial Bank*, Guangdong Province High People's Court, (2004) No 263; *Zhongshan Shishen v Auli, Guangdong Province High People's Court*, (2004) No 239.

50 Chinese Civil Procedure Law (Amended) 2012, Art 34. See subsection 5.2 'Material validity' below.

3.2 Arbitration agreements

More diversity exists in deciding applicable law governing arbitration agreements and the decision may be different depending on whether a court or a tribunal is seized to decide this issue. If a party challenges the validity of an arbitration agreement in a court, some courts use domestic choice of law rules to decide the validity of an arbitration clause. In general, most countries permit the parties to choose the applicable law to govern an arbitration clause.[51] In the absence of choice, different approaches are adopted.

International harmonization

Both the New York Convention and the Model Law do not provide uniform rules on material validity of an arbitration clause, which is left to be decided by the national law designated by the conflict of laws. More difficulties arise because the New York Convention does not provide uniform choice of law rules to decide the material validity of an arbitration clause either. Article II(3) provides that a seized court should refer the dispute subject to an arbitration clause to arbitration 'unless it finds that the said agreement is null and void, inoperative or incapable of being performed'.[52] It does not clarify under which law the seized court could find the arbitration agreement null, void and inoperative. Some guidance may be found in Article V(a), which provides that a court may not enforce an award if the agreement 'is not valid under the law to which the parties have subjected it or, failing any indication thereon, under the law of the country where the award was made'. This provision suggests two laws may be used by the recognition court to refuse enforcing an arbitral award, namely the chosen law of the parties, and in the absence of choice the law of the seat of arbitration. Many have suggested that the same applicable law should be used by the seized court when asked to decide the validity of an arbitration clause.[53] Although the rules only apply at the stage of enforcement instead of referral, applying the same rule would help consistent decisions. For example, if the referral court applies the *lex fori* to find the arbitration agreement valid and refers the dispute to arbitration, while the enforcement court, by applying the law of the seat, finds the clause invalid, it will refuse to enforce the award. However, it is also argued that, during the negotiation of the New York Convention, the suggestion that the same conflict rules should be included in Article II(2) was refused because it was inappropriate to force a seized court to enforce an arbitration clause which was invalid under its national law, including conflict of

51 This approach is implied in Art V(1)(a) of the New York Convention and Art 34(2)(a) of the UNCITRAL Model Law. Greenberg, Kee and Weeramantry, 2011: 160.

52 The same provision is adopted in the UNCITRIAL Model Law, Art 8(1).

53 Tieder, 2003: 393; Moss, 1999: 291.

laws.[54] The only international instrument that provides clear guidance is the European Convention on International Arbitration of 1961, which provides that the existence or validity of an arbitration agreement should be decided by the law agreed by the parties, in the absence of which, under the law of the country where the award is to be made. If both countries cannot be determined, the conflict of laws of the seized court shall apply.[55]

English common law

In England, the court has applied different laws to decide the validity of an arbitration clause, such as the chosen law by the parties to govern the arbitration clause, the *lex causae*,[56] the law of the seat or the *lex fori*.[57] The current trend is that, where there is no choice of law clause choosing the governing law particularly to govern the arbitration clause, the law applicable should be the law of the country where the arbitration is to be seated.[58] The court gives reasons in *C v D*:[59]

> an agreement to arbitrate will normally have a closer and more real connection with the place where the parties have chosen to arbitrate than with the place of the law of the underlying contract in cases where the parties have deliberately chosen to arbitrate in one place disputes which have arisen under a contract governed by the law of another place.

This approach is consistent with the belief of most academic writers and arbitrators.[60] By choosing the place of arbitration, parties have impliedly given consent to be bound by the procedural law of the place applying to arbitration and other policy concerning arbitration agreements.[61] The question is whether the *lex arbitri* is still applicable if the parties have included a choice of law agreement in their contract. The choice of law clause may be interpreted narrowly as applying to the substance of the dispute only, or broadly as an intention to govern all non-procedural issues of arbitration. It is suggested that since the *lex arbitri* is based on the

54 Graffi, 2006: 697; Haight, 1958: 27–28.

55 Geneva, 21 April 1961, Art VI.2.

56 *BVI v Ferrell International Ltd* [2002] 1 All ER (Comm) 627; *Union of India v McDonnell Douglas* [1993] 2 Lloyd's Rep 48. Blackaby *et al.*, 2009: para 3.12. Applying the law of the seat to decide the validity of an arbitration clause is also adopted in the Scottish Arbitration Act 2010, s6.

57 *Black-Clawson v Papierwerke* [1975] AC 591; *C v D* [2007] EWHC 1541 (Comm); *XL Insurance v Owens Corning* [2000] 2 Lloyd's Rep 500; Blackaby *et al.*, 2009: paras 3.15–3.29.

58 *C v D* [2007] EWCA Civ 1282.

59 Ibid., para 22

60 Thrope, 1999: 20.

61 Ibid., 20.

presumption of 'implied consent', the possibility of 'implied consent' can be excluded by the express agreement that the true intention of the parties is to choose a different law. As a result, if the parties have chosen a different law, the chosen law should apply.

US law

Like jurisdiction clauses, the US courts usually directly apply the *lex fori* to decide the prerequisites of an arbitration agreement.[62] The US courts treat validity of arbitration agreements as a matter of procedure and continue to apply the Federal Arbitration Act (FAA) to decide the validity and interpretation of arbitration agreements, ignoring the parties' express choice of law.[63] Although directly applying the *lex fori* is straightforward and convenient to the court, this approach may be too rigid. First, it ignores the consent of the parties. The parties may have the intention to apply the chosen law to the interpretation and validity of an arbitration agreement. Second, it ignores the importance of the *lex arbitri*. Third, the judgment may be different between the court and tribunal due to the application of different applicable laws to the validity of arbitration agreements, and there may be concurrent proceedings due to the different decisions.

Chinese law

Compared to jurisdiction clauses, more mature and developed rules are established for arbitration agreements. Although the Arbitration Law 1994 is silent on this issue,[64] guidance has been provided by the 'Interpretation of the Supreme People's Court concerning Some Issues on Application of the Arbitration Law of the People's Republic of China' in 2006,[65] and updated in the PRC Conflicts Act and its Judicial Interpretation 2012. The parties could agree on the applicable law to decide the validity of an arbitration clause; in the absence of such a choice, the law of the place where the arbitration institution is located or the agreed place of arbitration should apply; if the parties do not agree on either the applicable law or the place of arbitration, the *lex fori*, i.e. Chinese law, should apply.[66] The law changes the tendency of some

62 *Chloe Z Fishing Co. v Odyssey Re (London) Ltd* 109 F. Supp. 2d 1236 (S.D. Cal. 2000); *Kamaya v American Property Consultants*, 959 P.2d 1140 (Wash. App. 1998); *Westbrook International v Westbrook Tech*, 17 F. Supp. 2d 681 (E.D.Mich. 1998); Yackee, 2004a: 74–76; Malloy, 2002: 51; Jiang, 1992: 188.

63 Ibid.; for criticism, see, in general, Thrope, 1999: 16.

64 PRC Arbitration Law 1994, Adopted at the Ninth Meeting of the Standing Committee of the Eighth National People's Congress on 31 August 1994 and promulgated by Order No 31 of the President of the People's Republic of China on 31 August 1994.

65 [2006] No 7, Article 16.

66 Art 18, PRC Conflicts Act 2010. 2012 Interpretations on the Conflicts Act, Fa Shi [2012] No 24, Art 14.

Chinese courts to directly apply Chinese law to all arbitration clauses regardless of the parties' intention or the international nature of the dispute. The choice of law rules for arbitration agreements are advanced and in line with international conventions. The Chinese practice clearly shows the influence of international conventions. Chinese practice has put jurisdiction and arbitration agreements on an unequal footing. Uncertainty, inconsistency and confusion continue to exist in jurisdiction clauses, while the applicable law to arbitration agreements has been clarified.

Other national approaches

Some countries adopt the principle in favour of arbitration and apply the law that could validate an arbitration clause. Alternative applicable laws are provided and the arbitration clause will be valid if it meets the requirement of any of them. An example is Swiss law. In Switzerland, an arbitration agreement will be valid if it conforms to any of the following: the law chosen by the parties, the law governing the subject matter of the disputes, or Swiss law.[67]

Other courts adopt a very flexible approach to seek the real intention between the parties. The French court, for example, has delivered decisions not to apply the governing law to decide the validity of an arbitration agreement, but to consider the fact of the case to decide whether the parties' common intention can be found.[68] French jurists and courts hold a strong view that arbitration agreements are a clause of party autonomy and independent from the main contract. The court does not need to refer to any national law to decide the validity of an arbitration agreement, but only needs to use discretion to check if there is common intention between the parties.[69] The need to protect parties' actual consent is more important than maintaining rigid formal and material validity rules.[70]

Arbitral tribunal

Where an arbitration tribunal is seized to decide the validity of an arbitration clause, a tribunal usually prefers to use the law of the seat to decide this issue;[71] others may use the same approach as the local court by relying

67 Art 178 of the Swiss Statute of Private International Law.

68 *Société d'études et représentations navales et industrielles (SOERNI) et autres v Société Air Sea Broker limited (ASB)*, 8 July 2009, Case no 08–16025; *Municipalité de Khoms El Mergeb v Société Dalico*, 20 December 1993, Case no 91–16828; *L'Entreprise Tunisienne d'Activités Pétrolières (ETAP) v Bomal Oil*, 9 November 1993, Case no 91–15194; *Société anonyme Française Entrepose GTM pour les Travaux Pétroliers Maritimes (ETPM) v Société anonyme Empresa Constructoria Financiera (ECOFISA)*, 4 December 1990, Case no 88–13336.

69 Graffi, 2006: 718–720.

70 Ibid., 721.

71 Redfern, 2004: 126; Born, 2009: 111.

on domestic choice of law to decide the applicable law to the validity of an arbitration agreement. However, a unique option that is only available to an arbitration tribunal is the application of non-state principles to decide the validity of an arbitration clause. This approach is particularly supported by French arbitral decisions, supported by courts.[72] It is argued that the validity of an arbitration clause is 'a matter of transnational law or arbitral practice, determined by the arbitrators themselves by reference to prior arbitral decisions, without reference to a domestic law'.[73] An arbitration clause thus will usually be valid as long as it is entered into in a way that is in accordance with ordinary commercial practice.

3.3 Capacity

Capacity is a special issue that can challenge the validity of a jurisdiction or an arbitration clause. However, it is different from the existence of, and other formal and substantive validity requirements in relation to, a dispute resolution agreement. It is necessary to use a separate section to deal with choice of law applying to capacity. Deciding capacity of the parties in a dispute resolution clause also involves the issue of choice of law. Since capacity of the parties is very different from the material validity relating to 'consent', different choice of law rules thus apply to govern them respectively. The Rome I Regulation provides partially harmonized rules to decide capacity of a natural person. If both parties have the same habitual residence and have capacity to conclude contracts, a party can invoke his incapacity pursuant to the law of another country only if the other party was aware of this incapacity at the time of contracting.[74] This provision, however, is not useful in deciding the capacity of the parties in a dispute resolution agreement because the Rome I Regulation has excluded an agreement on jurisdiction or arbitration from its scope of application.[75] Furthermore, in business contracts, capacity usually concerns whether the contractor could act on behalf of a company according to the substantive company law of a country,[76] instead of natural persons.

The Brussels I Regulation does not provide any provision on uniform rules in deciding parties' capacity in entering into a jurisdiction clause. The New York Convention does not provide relevant rules as to capacity at the stage of deciding jurisdiction of a court or tribunal but rules are provided at the stage of recognition of arbitral awards. Article V(1)(a) permits a court to refuse recognizing or enforcing an arbitral award if the parties are 'under

72 *Isover St Gobain v Dow Chemical France* (4131/1982) ICC I ICC Awards 146 at 465, affirmed 21 October 1983 [1984] Rev. Arb. 98 Cour d'Appel de Paris; *Hecht v Buismans* [1972] Rev. Arb. 67 Cour d'Appel de Paris. See Parish, 2010: 670.

73 Parish, 2010: 670.

74 Art 13.

75 Art 1(2)(e).

76 Schulz, 2002a: 6.

the law applicable to them' under some incapacity. However, this rule is modified in the UNCITRAL Model Law, which deletes the term 'under the law applicable to them' and comments that it is because the term in the New York Convention contains an 'incomplete and potentially misleading' choice of law rule.[77] It seems that a court seized to decide the capacity of the parties has the liberty to rely on its national law, including choice of law rules, under both the Brussels I Regulation and the New York Convention.

In the Hague Convention of 2005, a jurisdiction clause is invalid if either party lacks capacity in either the law of the chosen forum or the law of the seized forum, including the choice of laws in either country.[78] The chosen court will apply its own substantive law or choice of law to decide whether the jurisdiction clause is null because of the incapacity of a party; the seized non-chosen court could apply either the law of the chosen country or its own law to invalidate a jurisdiction clause.

4 Existence of conflicts agreements

4.1 Implied choice

Parties may enter into a conflicts clause impliedly. In practice, the parties may not specifically negotiate a conflicts clause, while by their conduct, their previous courses of dealing, their professional and commercial knowledge and other terms of the contract, the court could confidently conclude that the parties have made tacit choice.

An implied choice of jurisdiction or arbitration may not be recognized in all countries. For example, China requires all conflicts clauses to be concluded expressly. Article 34 of the Chinese Civil Procedure Law 2012 requires jurisdiction agreements in cross-border contracts to be entered into 'through written agreements'.[79] Article 16 of the Chinese Arbitration Law requires arbitration agreements to be included in contracts or formed by other written means.[80] No authorized interpretation, however, has been provided to jurisdiction agreements. However, under Chinese Contract Law, an acceptance can be made in light of trade practices.[81] Arguably, if a dispute resolution agreement is a contract term in the main contract and

77 Explanatory Note by the UNCITRAL secretariat on the 1985 Model Law on International Commercial Arbitration as amended in 2006, para 54.

78 Art 6(a) and (b). See Hartley/Dogauchi Report, para 150; Minutes No 8 of the Twentieth Session, Commission II, paras 50–59.

79 This is consistent with Art 242 and Art 25 of the Chinese Civil Procedure Law 2007. The 2012 amendment deleted the previous Art 242 and provides the uniform rules in Art 34 for jurisdiction agreements in both domestic and transnational disputes.

80 Adopted at the Ninth Meeting of the Standing Committee of the Eighth National People's Congress on 31 August 1994 and promulgated by Order No 31 of the President of the People's Republic of China on 31 August 1994, Art 16.

81 Arts 22, 26 PRC Contract Law 1999 (Adopted at the Second Session of the Ninth National People's Congress on 15 March 1999).

the main contract is entered into according to trade practice, the dispute resolution clause is valid. This suggestion, however, remains an academic argument, and most courts and tribunals require arbitration agreements to be formed expressly.

Common law countries traditionally accept contracts implied-in-fact. England, for example, accepts that both the choice of court and the arbitration clause can be entered into impliedly.[82] In the US, the Supreme Court said in *Baltimore & Ohio R Co v United States*[83] that an implied-in-fact contract is 'founded upon a meeting of minds, which, although not embodied in an express contract, is inferred, as a fact, from conduct of the parties showing, in the light of the surrounding circumstances, their tacit understanding'.[84] Trade usage and commercial custom are frequently used by US courts to validate arbitration agreements.[85] The courts hold that there is a valid arbitration clause even if it is not referred to and agreed upon by the opposing party if it is an industrial custom that an arbitration clause is likely to exist in certain contracts.[86] In the EU, the Brussels I Regulation provides that a jurisdiction clause exists if it is in a form according with common usage or practice in international trade or commerce.[87] Implied choice is also accepted in other civil law countries. Prior to the Brussels Convention coming into force, the French courts accepted that the choice of court can be inferred from parties' conduct.[88] The French courts also accept that the parties may demonstrate their intention to be governed by an arbitration agreement, either expressly or impliedly.[89] The German Supreme Court suggested that an arbitration agreement could be inferred in accordance with customary trade usage.[90]

However, it is necessary to note that contradict opinions exist, at least in the area of arbitration agreements. Some commentators believe an arbitration agreement should exist only with 'express, unequivocal

82 *Stella Shipping v Hudson Shipping Lines* [2010] EWHC 2985 (Comm) (arbitration clauses can be inferred from parties' conduct); *Habas Sinai Ve Tibbi Gazlar Isthisal Endustri AS v Sometal SAL* [2010] 1 All ER (Comm) 1143; *Sea Trade Maritime v Hellenic Mutual War Risks Association (The Athena)* [2006] 2 CLC 710; *Cable & Wireless v Muscat* 2005 WL 556663 (implied agreement to abandon an arbitration clause); *American Design Associates v Donald Insall* 2000 WL 33250594.

83 261 US 592 (1923).

84 Ibid.

85 Coakley, 2000: 148.

86 Ibid.

87 Art 23(1)(c) Brussels I.

88 *Société Jansen v Société Heurtey* Paris, 27 January 1955, Rev 1955 330. See Lenhoff, 1960: 426.

89 *Dallah Real Estate v Ministry of Religious Affairs of the Government of Pakistan* [2010] UKSC 46 (quoting the expert's opinion: 'is necessary to find out whether all the parties to the arbitration proceedings, including that person, had the common intention (whether express or implied) to be bound by the said agreement and, as a result, by the arbitration clause therein'.

90 Judgment of 12 March 1992. See Carbonneau and Janson, 1994: 220.

agreement'.[91] The concept of implied choice allows a court to impose contract terms even if it is not expressly entered into by the parties. A lot of courts infer the existence of implied arbitration agreements because 'arbitration may be the prevalent means of resolving dispute in an industry',[92] but very likely a meeting of minds might be lacking between the parties at the time of contracting. No doubt a lot of parties are subject to the implied arbitration agreements by surprise. Furthermore, it is questionable whether ordinary contractual principles are always applicable to arbitration agreements. An arbitration clause is severed from an ordinary contract and, more importantly, there is different public policy to govern an arbitration clause which affects a person's access to justice and ousts a court's jurisdiction.[93] It has been stated in a US case, *Marlene*:[94]

> by agreeing to arbitrate a party waives in large part many of his normal rights under the procedural and substantive law of the State, and it would be unfair to infer a significant waiver on the basis of anything less than a clear indication of intent.

However, even *Marlene* did not completely rule out the possibility of entering into an arbitration impliedly providing 'a clear indication of intent' can be proved by any means.

How could an implied choice be determined? The existence of such an agreement should be decided by considering all the facts of the case. In English law, the court uses the general contract principles to find out the existence of an implied contract. The general rule is that an implied choice must be inferred with certainty and should not be easily made unless it is necessary to do so and if the parties' conduct is more consistent with the intention to contract than with an intention not to contract.[95] In the US, some courts adopt the case-by-case approach, examining the 'degree of surprise or hardship' imposed on the opposing party by an arbitration agreement.[96] The opposing party must show both subjective and objective surprise. If an arbitration clause was unilaterally inserted in the confirmation letter, receipt or any document without negotiation or

91 *Marlene v Carnac*, 45 N.Y.2d 327, 334 (NY 1978); *Schubtex v Allen*, 49 N.Y.2d 1, 11 (per Gabrielli J).

92 *Schubtex*, 9 (per Gabrielli J).

93 *Matter of Weinroff*, 32 N.Y.2d 190, 198; *Woodcrest Fabrics v B&R Textile* 95 A.D.2d 656 (NYAD 1 Dept 1983), 663 (per Milonas J).

94 *Marlene v Carnac*.

95 *Cable & Wireless*, para 58; *The Aramis* [1989] 1 Lloyd's Rep 213; *Blackpool and Fylde Aero Club v Blackpool Borough Council* [1990] 1 WLR 1195.

96 *Bergquist v Sunroc Co* 444 F. Supp 1236 (E.D.Pa 1991), 1245; *Schulze v Tree Top; N&D Fashions v DHJ Injus* 548 F.2d 722, 726 (8th Cir 1976); *Dorton v Collins* 453 F.2d 1161 (6th Cir. 1972); *Dixie Aluminum v Mitsubishi International* 785 F. Supp. 157 (N.D.Ga 1992); *Stewart Sandwiches, Inc. v MSL Indus., Inc.*, 1990 WL 165630, 3 (N.D.Ill. Oct. 19, 1990); *Valmont Indus., Inc. v Mitsui & Co. (USA), Inc.*, 419 F. Supp. 1238 (D.Neb.1976).

sufficient notice, and the opposing party paid no attention to it, subjective surprise exists.[97] However, if the opposing party should have known a jurisdiction or an arbitration clause would be inserted according to the common practice between the parties, the previous courses of dealing and the industry custom, there will not be objective surprise.[98] Finally, the opposing party must prove hardship, namely enforcing the clause will cause substantial economic hardship, and mere inconvenience is not sufficient.[99]

Applicable law

There is no general practice to treat the parties' express choice of law agreement as the implied choice of jurisdiction. In traditional English law, the applicable English law is one ground that enables the court to exercise its discretion to serve a claim form on a defendant out of jurisdiction.[100] However, this is not because of the tacit choice, but because of the close connection and convenience of trial. The governing law is a connecting factor between the dispute and the court to justify the exorbitant jurisdiction. It is also a factor considered in *forum conveniens* for English courts to eventually take jurisdiction. The traditional practice does not suggest the choice of law is a factor that could be taken into consideration to decide the existence of implied jurisdiction.[101]

Common practices between the parties

The most common example is when the parties have long-term dealings or a commercial relationship between them and they had previously negotiated and agreed upon standard terms and conditions or a master contract. If the current contract does not expressly include or refer to a conflicts agreement, there is the possibility that both parties know or ought to have known their current transaction should be subject to the

97 *Avedon Engineering v Seatex* 112 F. Supp. ed 1090, 1095 (D.Colo., 2000).

98 Ibid., 1095–1096. *American v El Paso Pipe and Supply*, 978 F.2d 1185, 1191 (10th Cir. 1992); *Helen Whiting v Trojan Textile* 307 NY360 (1954); *N&D Fashions*, 722.

99 *American v El Paso Pipe and Supply* 978 F.2d 1185, 1191; *Avedon Engineering*, 1196–1197.

100 CPR, Practice Direction 6B, para 3.1(6)(c).

101 On the contrary, existence of a jurisdiction or arbitration clause has been considered as a strong factor in many English courts to demonstrate that the parties also wish the law of that country to apply. Recital 12 of the Brussels I Regulation.

same conflicts terms agreed in previous dealings.[102] Even if a previous master agreement was not in-print or orally agreed on,[103] if it is 'demonstrated clearly and precisely' that the parties have dealt on the basis that their disputes will be determined by certain forum or law, implied choice also exists.[104] That is because the course of dealing is such that it would be contrary to good faith for the other party to deny that there was a jurisdiction agreement which is essentially a species of estoppel. Furthermore, implied choice may also exist where the conclusion of a conflicts clause by certain means or conduct is a common understanding or common practice in a particular trade or commerce. To infer the existence of an implied jurisdiction in these situations is provided by the Brussels I Regulation.[105]

Article 23(1)(b) of the Brussels I Regulation provides that jurisdiction clauses are formally valid if they are consistent with the common practice between the parties. This usually occurs where there is a long-term relationship between the parties.[106] If the previous contracts between the parties have contained jurisdiction clauses choosing the same forum, or the parties have resolved their previous disputes in a particular forum, it is reasonable to conclude that there is common practice between the parties. If the current transaction does not include any negotiation on jurisdiction issues and there is no factor suggesting the parties want to act differently this time, the court could conclude that an implied choice of court agreement has been entered into by the parties. The ECJ, for example, provided in *Segoura v Bonakdarian*[107] that, although the jurisdiction clause, which was not agreed upon in oral agreement but later inserted in the invoice, was invalid, if the current transaction forms part of a continuing trading relationship between the parties and the dealings as a whole were governed by the same general conditions in the invoice, the clause should be binding. However, whether a common practice is established depends on the period of time of dealing. In an Austrian case, for example,

102 Case 221/84 *Berghoefer GmbH & Co KG v ASA SA* [1985] ECR 2699, para 18; AG opinion on *Berghoefer*, 2702; Case 71/93 *Tilly Russ v Haven & Vervoebedrijf Nova NV* [1984] ECR 2417, para 14; *Re Jurisdiction in the Case of a Sale Involving the Carriage of Goods (5 U 99/07)* (Oberlandesgericht (Stuttgart)) [2010] ILPr 29; *Fiandre v La Société Mothes* (French Cour de Cassation) [2001] ILPr 13; *Societa Trasporti Castelletti Spedizioni Internationali SpA v Hugo Trumpy SpA* (Corte di Cassazione) [1998] ILPr 216; *ISEA Industrie SpA v SA LU* (Cour d'Appel) [1997] ILPr 823. For US cases, see: *Insteel Wire v Dywidag* WL 2253198 (M.D.N.C. 2009); *Noble Drilling v M/V*, 2011 WL 1399243 (E.D.La, 2011)(NO CIV.A 10–2865); *Revlon v United Overseas* 1994 WL 9657 (S.D.N.Y 1994).

103 Case 25/76 *Galeries Segoura Sprl v Firma Rahim Bonakdarian* [1976] ECR 1851, para 11.

104 *Kolmar Group AG v Visen Industries Ltd* [2010] ILPr 23, para 29.

105 Art 23(1)(b) and (c) of the Brussels I Regulation.

106 It is provided by Austrian courts that if a party sent general terms to another at the start of their business relationship, it does not establish a common practice. OGH 7 Ob 336/97f.

107 Case 25/76, [1976] ECR 1851.

repeated delivery of bills and notes to the other party after conclusion of contracts during the 11-month relationship was not sufficient to establish common practice.[108] In a German case, *Re Jurisdiction in the Case of a Sale Involving the Carriage of Goods (5 U 99/07)*,[109] a French company and a German company had been in a business relationship for more than 10 years. In the recent transaction, the German company sued for non-payment of the purchase price for goods delivered by a carrier from Germany to France. The general conditions of the contract, which included a jurisdiction clause choosing German courts, were in German and printed on the reverse of the invoice. The court, however, found that there existed a valid jurisdiction clause, because it would be unreasonable for the party to argue that the general terms were not validly agreed on after 10 years' collaboration, where repeated conclusion of contracts and reference to the general terms existed between the parties. If both parties should have been aware of the existence of the jurisdiction clause, which is within the framework of their continuing business relationship, it is contrary to good faith to deny its existence.[110] Under the existing case law, jurisdiction clauses in standard terms in continuing relationship are usually construed as part of the parties' choice in their later transactions even if no express reference or acceptance exists; the common conduct of the parties in previous transactions which demonstrates common understanding can also show the existence of implied choice.[111]

The past conduct of dealing is also adopted in many courts to infer the existence of an arbitration clause.[112] In a US case, *Schutex v Allen Snyder*,[113] the court accepted that a prior course of dealing was relevant to decide if the parties had agreed to submit to arbitration. If a party argues that there is an oral agreement, the previous course of dealing can also be considered to decide whether the oral agreement on arbitration can be inferred.[114] In this case, however, the court found there were two prior dealings between the parties, an arbitration clause was inserted in the confirmation of an oral order sent to the buyer, no evidence to show the oral negotiation included arbitration agreements and there was no evidence to show the parties had ever used arbitration in prior dealings. The court refused to accept there was an implied choice. It shows that, although

108 OGH 7 Ob38/01s, RdW 2001/676 = RZ-EÜ 2001/70 = ZfRV 2001/63 = ecolex2002, 420.

109 [2010] ILPr 29.

110 Case 221/84 *Berghoefer GmbH & Co KG v ASA SA* [1985] ECR 2699, para 18; *Kolmar Group AG v Visen Industries Ltd* [2010] ILPr 23.

111 *Kolmar Group AG v Visen Industries Ltd* [2010] ILPr 23.

112 For the account of Lithuanian law, see *Svenska Petroleum v Lithuania* [2006] EWCA Civ 1529, para 23. English practice: *The Athena (No 2)* [2007] 1 Lloyd's Rep 280; *Habas Sinai v Sometal SAL*, [2010] EWHC 29 (Comm); US practice: *Nobel Drilling; WM Schloser v School Bd of Fairfax County* 980 F.2d 253 (C.A.4(Va) 1992); *Avedon Engineering v Seatex* 112 F. Supp. 2d 1090 (D.Colo, 2000).

113 49 N.Y.2d 1 (NY 1979).

114 Ibid., 5.

previous courses of dealing could demonstrate the existence of implied choice, evidence is required to prove that real consent exists between the parties.[115]

The *Schutex* approach, however, has been largely replaced by the modern approach to tackle the hardship and unfair surprise of a unilaterally inserted term. The previous course of dealing, again, is a relevant factor in the modern approach. If the parties have prior dealings with them and the opposing party should have known that a dispute resolution clause is likely and is usually included in invoices, receipts or confirmation documents, the party should not be surprised objectively by this clause. Without prompt objections, an implied acceptance of an arbitration clause exists.

Trade custom and usage

Industrial practice or trade custom or usage could help the court to infer implied jurisdiction or arbitration agreements. In *Mainschiffahrts-Genossenschaft eG (MSG) v Les Gravieres Rhenanes (LGR)*,[116] a German company, MSG, chartered a vessel to a French company, LGR, by oral agreement, without choice of court agreements. MSG sent a letter of confirmation containing a jurisdiction clause, as well as an invoice with the same term, which was paid by LGR. In deciding whether the jurisdiction clause is valid, the ECJ held that[117]

> under a contract concluded orally in international trade or commerce, an agreement conferring jurisdiction will be deemed to have been validly concluded under that provision by virtue of the fact that one party to the contract did not react to a commercial letter of confirmation sent to it by the other party to the contract or repeatedly paid invoices without objection where those documents contained a pre-printed reference to the courts having jurisdiction, provided that such conduct is consistent with a practice in force in the field of international trade or commerce in which the parties in question operate and the latter are aware or ought to have been aware of the practice in question.... A practice exists in a branch of international trade or commerce in particular where a particular course of conduct is generally followed by contracting parties operating in that branch when they conclude contracts of a particular type. The fact that the

115 *Jones Apparel v Petit* 75 A.D.2d 504 (NYAD 1980); *Woodcrest Fabrics; Just In-Material Designs v ITAD* 94 A.D.2d 103 (NYAD 1983); *Orkal Industries v Array Connector* 2011 WL 2138486 (NY Sup 2011); *Diskin v JP Stevens* 836 F.2d 47 (1st Cir. (Mass) 1987); *Schulze and Burch v Tree Top* 831 F.2d 709 (7th Cir. (Ill) 1987); *Conagra v William E Martin* 1994 WL 270304 (N.D Ill 1994); *Peterson v Beale* 1995 WL 479425 (S.D.N.Y. 1995); *J&C Dyeing v Drakon* 1994 WL 584669 (S.D.N.Y 1994); *Waldron v Goddess* 473 N.Y.S.2d 136 (NY 1984).

116 Case C-106/95, [1997] ECR 911.

117 Case C-106/95, [1997] ECR 911, para 25.

contracting parties were aware of that practice is made out in particular where they had previously had trade or commercial relations between themselves or with other parties operating in the branch of trade or commerce in question or where, in that branch, a particular course of conduct is generally and regularly followed when concluding a certain type of contract, with the result that it may be regarded as being a consolidated practice.

The decision is interpreted differently between Member States. For example, Austrian courts interpret it as meaning the existence of common usage is determined by *lex causae*,[118] while English courts believe common usage is given an independent definition.[119] Some Member States adopt a low standard to decide whether usages exist. For example, the Irish court gave effect to a jurisdiction clause written on the reverse side of an invoice without a reference on the face of it on the ground that this was common in international sale of hardware;[120] standard term insurance contracts were considered common usage by English courts.[121] A higher standard, however, is applied in more states, such as Germany, where a usage exists if it is the same practice recognized or practised in several countries,[122] and Italy, where a usage can only be found with well-established practice.[123]

In *O'Connor v Masterwood*,[124] the Irish Supreme Court decided that common usage includes the fact that businessmen are presumed to be aware of terms included in printed conditions. If they choose not to read them, they are still regarded as making consent and a jurisdiction clause is concluded.[125] This ground is accepted in the Brussels I Regulation.[126] A narrower interpretation was provided by Italian courts. In *Lloyd's Syndicate v Shifco*,[127] the Italian court ruled that the usage must not only exist in international commerce, but also relate to the specific sector. The usage thus is industry specific instead of applicable to international commerce in general. The presumed knowledge of the usage can be proved if the opposing party has either prior transactions with the same party or with other parties, or the particular course of conduct is generally and regularly

118 OGH 7 Ob38/01s.

119 'National Report England and Wales', Response to Report on the Application of Regulation Brussels I in the EU countries, Study JLS/C4/2005/03, 91–93.

120 *Clare Tavern's v Gill*, [2001] 1 IR 286.

121 *Standard Steamship Owners Protection & Indemnity Association (Bermuda) Ltd v GIE Vision Bail* [2004] EWHC 2919.

122 Oberlandesgericht Köln (12/21/2005–16 U 47/05).

123 *Corte di Cassazione*, 29.1.2002, n 1150. 'National Report Italy', Response to Study JLS/C4/2005/03, IT-15.

124 [2010] ILPr 18.

125 Ibid., para 19.

126 Art 23(1)(c).

127 (Italian Corte di Cassazione) [2009] ILPr 18.

followed to conclude this type of contract. The only reason that standard form contracts exist is because ordinary commercial practice is not sufficient. This mode to incorporate a dispute resolution agreement must also be regular practice within the specific industry and particular type of contracts.

Industry usage and customs are also frequently used to decide that an arbitration agreement exists, albeit not expressed.[128] However, the US court adopts restriction based on the test of unfair surprise and hardship.[129] Even if inserting an arbitration clause in standard terms unilaterally is a customary practice in certain industry, like textiles, the clause is not concluded if it causes an unreasonable surprise and harshness for performance.[130]

4.2 Incorporation

Jurisdiction and arbitration agreements can be incorporated in a contract by reference. In the Brussels I Regulation, a jurisdiction clause is formally valid if it is written on the reverse side of a contract, or is written in the general terms of the parties, and it is referred to by clear language in the contract.[131] Incorporation of an arbitration agreement by reference is clearly accepted in the UNCITRAL Model Law, Article 6(7) of which provides that: 'The reference in a contract to any document containing an arbitration clause constitutes an arbitration agreement in writing, provided that the reference is such as to make that clause part of the contract.'[132] Chinese law recognizes arbitration agreements incorporated from other contracts or documents.[133] However, it is unclear when arbitration agreements written in other documents are successfully incorporated in the current contract. More guidance has been provided by English courts. Although inconsistent decisions exist, English courts generally adopt different standards for incorporation of an arbitration clause in standard terms or in another contract between the same parties (single-contract case) and incorporation of such a term in a contract between different parties (two contracts case).[134] In the former, the general language of reference is sufficient to make the incorporation of arbitration

128 *Valmont Industries; Schubtex v Allen. Cf. Jones Apparel* ('vague, unspecific reference ... to the effect that "in the textile industry arbitration is the usual accepted method of resolving disputes" is not an acceptable substitute ... for finding a specific agreement to arbitrate').

129 *Bergquist v Sunroc Co; Schulze v Tree Top; N&D Fashions v DHJ Injus; Dorton v Collins; Dixie Aluminum v Mitsubishi International; Stewart Sandwiches, Inc. v MSL Indus., Inc; Valmont Indus., Inc. v Mitsui & Co. (USA).*

130 *Schulze v Tree Top*, 713.

131 *Estasis Salotti v RUWA; Credit Suisse Financial Products v Société Generale d'Enterprises.*

132 See also s6(2) of English Arbitration Act.

133 Supreme People's Court, 'Arbitration Law Interpretation 2006', Art 11.

134 Tweeddale and Tweeddale, 2010: 656.

agreements successful.[135] The same test is equally applied to jurisdiction clauses in Article 23(1) of the Brussels I Regulation (Art 25(1) of the Brussels I Recast). English courts have stated in a few cases that there is no need for specific reference to the jurisdiction clause to establish the real consent.[136] General reference to the standard terms should be enough and whether the other party has a copy of the standard terms is irrelevant.

In two-contract cases, however, it may not be obvious to one party that the proposed incorporation by another party refers not only to the substantive terms but also to the arbitration clause. The language used to incorporate the arbitration clause in the 'two-contract' case must specifically refer to the arbitration clause.[137] It is not clear whether the same approach is adopted for jurisdiction clauses under the Brussels I Regulation. However, in *AIG Europe v QBE International*,[138] the court refused to enforce a jurisdiction clause choosing French courts. The jurisdiction clause was concluded in the insurance contract and referred to by using general language, 'all terms as original', in the reinsurance contract. The court held that the word 'all' did not demonstrate clearly and precisely the consensus to include the jurisdiction clause in the original contract into the reinsurance contract. The court's reasoning is based on the strict interpretation of the consensus requirement in *Estasis Salotti*, and the rule of severability of a jurisdiction clause.[139] The reasoning, however, cannot survive the latter development in English law where the incorporation of jurisdiction clauses does not concern the rule of severability. A better justification for the *AIG* decision is that this is a two-contract case: the parties of the original insurance contract and those of the reinsurance contract are not identical. The decision may suggest that specific language is required to incorporate jurisdiction clauses in two-contract cases. However, it is necessary to admit that there are a lot of divergences in this issue and there is no consensus. Since the Brussels I Regulation should be given independent community meaning, the approach in other Member States is relevant for the consideration. In Italy, for example, specific reference to jurisdiction clauses is required even in a single-contract case.[140]

135 *Habas Sinai v Sometal*, [2010] Bus LR 880; *The Athena* [2007] 1 All ER (Comm) 183; *Modern Buildings (Wales) v Limmeer & Trinidad* [1975] 1 WLR 1281; *Tracomin v Sudan Oil Seed* [1983] 1 WLR 1026; *Excomm v Ahmed* [1985] 1 Lloyd's Rep 403; *Lexair v Edgar* (1993) 65 BLR 87; *Co-operative Wholesale v Saunders & Taylor* (1994) 39 Con LR 77.

136 *7E Communications v Vertex Antennentechnik* [2008] Bus LR 472; *Credit Suisse* [1997] CLC 168, 171–172. See also *Habas Sinai v Sometal SAL*, [2010] Bus LR 880, 898–899; *Coys of Kensington v Pugliese* [2011] EWHC 655 (QB).

137 *Sea Bridge Shipping v AC Orssleff's Eftf's A/S (The Delos)* [1999] 2 Lloyd's Rep 685; *The Athena*, ibid.; Cf. *Aughton*, 31 Con LR 60; *TW Thomas* [1912] AC 1; *Federal Bulker* [1989] 1 Lloyd's Rep 103; *Heyman v Darwins* [1942] AC 356; *Bremer Vulkan Schiffbau v South India Shipping* [1981] AC 909.

138 [2001] CLC 1259.

139 Para 26.

140 *Lloyd's Syndicate v Shifco-Somali High Seas* (Italian Corte di Cassazione) [2009] ILPr 18.

4.3 Variation of conflicts agreements

A conflicts clause, as a contract term, can be varied by the parties at anytime. The variation of a conflicts agreement is a new agreement, which equally requires demonstration of consent. The old conflicts agreement, after variation has been successfully made, will come to an end as soon as the new agreement is formed and enters into force.

As the formation of a conflicts clause, the variation of this clause can be done expressly or impliedly. Parties could enter into a new contract expressly including the new conflicts clause. Parties could also, by their conduct, vary the clause that they have previously entered into.

Intention of repudiation

A valid jurisdiction or arbitration clause can be repudiated at a later stage by the conduct of one party or both parties. If a jurisdiction/arbitration clause is repudiated by one party, he waived his benefit from the clause and cannot rely on it without the permission of the other party. In *Traube v Perelman*,[141] the parties entered into an arbitration agreement to submit all disputes to a specific arbitration tribunal. However, one party later argued that there were undetermined illegalities in the contract, which caused the chosen tribunal to refuse jurisdiction. This party has repudiated the arbitration clause and cannot rely on it to apply for an anti-suit injunction restraining the other party from bringing proceedings in courts.

The intention of repudiation must be communicated to the other party 'in clear and unequivocal terms'.[142] In *Downing v Al Tameer*,[143] the parties entered into an agreement with an arbitration clause. After one party denied that the contract was ever concluded, the other wrote to accept this was a repudiatory breach and claimed for damages in court. The Court of Appeal applied normal contractual principles and held that the statement of the party that no contract was concluded was a clear communication of repudiation and the commencing of court proceedings by the other party was an acceptance. The arbitration clause was thus repudiated. On the other hand, delay to bring arbitration proceedings[144] or the refusal to finance arbitration[145] does not clearly demonstrate the intention to repudiate.

141 2001 WL 1251816.

142 *The 'Kanchenjunga'* [1990] 1 Lloyd's Rep 391, 398; *The Mercanaut* [1980] 2 Lloyd's Rep 183; *The Golden Anne* [1984] 2 Lloyd's Rep 489.

143 *Downing v Al Tameer* [2002] CLC 1291.

144 *Andre et Cie SA v Marine Transocean Ltd (The Splendid Sun)* [1980] 1 Lloyd's Rep 333; *Paal Wilson & Co A/S v Partenreederei Hannah Blumenthal (The Hannah Blumenthal)* [1983] 1 AC 854; *Gulf Shipping Lines Ltd v Jadranska Slobodna Plovidba (The Matija Gubec)* [1981] 1 Lloyd's Rep 31; *Anna Maria*, [1980] 1 Lloyd's Rep 192.

145 *Paczy v Haendler & Natermann GmbH (No 2)* [1981] 1 Lloyd's Rep 302.

Suing in a non-chosen country in breach of an exclusive jurisdiction clause, or suing in a court instead of an arbitration tribunal, is normal in practice. Is the conduct of breaching the clause a valid expression of intention to repudiate? Some judges believe that commencing court proceedings for a dispute falling within an arbitration agreement is 'highly arguable' as being a repudiatory breach.[146] However, other cases hold that commencing court proceedings is not sufficient to bring an arbitration agreement to an end.[147] A very restrictive test is adopted in *Dubai Islamic Bank v PSI*,[148] where there was an exclusive jurisdiction clause in the contract in dispute choosing English courts. The bank later brought proceedings in Bahrain and the defendant brought the counter-claim. The question is whether the Bank's activity was repudiation and the counter-claim acceptance. The court said that the test for repudiatory breach is whether there is another explanation for the Bank's conduct. If there is, the court cannot infer an intention to repudiate. The reason for the bank to bring proceedings in Bahrain is that around $50 million of the bank's money was spent in Bahrain and the bank was advised that the only quick way of freezing assets in Bahrain is instituting proceedings. The court concluded that Bahraini proceedings did not 'clearly and unequivocally' point to an intention to no longer be bound by the jurisdiction clause.[149] Repudiation breach thus could not be inferred too lightly.

Acceptance

After one party has expressly stated, or has done a conduct which demonstrates, the intention to repudiate a conflicts clause, the other party could accept it by express communication or by conduct. The acceptance must also be communicated to the other party in a clear and unequivocal manner.[150] If after receiving the information of repudiation of an arbitration agreement, the other party commences legal proceedings as a response, this can be considered as acceptance, as stated by Potter LJ:[151]

> The question whether or not the issue in service of proceedings is an unequivocal acceptance of the repudiation will depend upon the previous communications of the parties and whether or not, on an objective construction of the state of play when the proceedings are commenced, the fact of the issue and service of the writ amounts to an unequivocal communication to the defendant that his earlier

146 *Delta Reclamation Limited v Premier Waste Management Limited* [2008] EWHC 2579 (QBD), para 35.
147 *Lloyd v Wright*, [1983] QB 1065.
148 [2011] EWHC 1019 (Comm), aff'd [2011] EWCA Civ 761.
149 Para 59.
150 *Downing v Al Tameer* [2002] CLC 1291, para 35.
151 Ibid.

> repudiatory conduct has been accepted, in the sense that it is clear that the issue of such proceedings (i) is a response to the defendant's refusal to recognise the existence of the arbitration agreement or any obligation thereunder and (ii) reflects a consequent decision on the claimant's part himself to abandon the remedy of arbitration in favour of court proceedings.

In terms of whether the counter-claim was an unequivocal acceptance presuming the proceedings were repudiation, the court in *Downing* said that the defendant by pleading counter-claim must demonstrate that further proceedings to be taken by the bank could not be brought in the chosen jurisdiction. Otherwise, simply entering a counter-claim is not enough to bring the jurisdiction clause to an end.[152]

5 Validity of dispute resolution agreements

5.1 Formal validity

Relaxation of written form

Requirements to formal validity vary largely from country to country. The written form is the most common and standard form of contracts. It can satisfy all the purposes as to the formal validity of a contract term, namely the evidence of the existence and content of the clause and the security and genuineness of such evidence. The black letter evidence cannot be easily revised without trace and forgery is relatively easy to identify. The literal meaning of 'in writing' is not difficult to understand. It means the parties write down or print the clause on paper. Almost all countries accept jurisdiction and arbitration agreements entered into in writing.

The international trend is the relaxation of requirements as to form. First, many countries have provided flexible interpretation as to what 'in writing' means. Given the development of modern technology and electronic communication, the meaning of 'in writing' has been extended to include all digital data stored in hardware devices, such as computers, mobiles, laptops, mailboxes and iPads®. For example, Chinese contract law extends the written form to cover any form capable of reproducing information contained in tangible forms.[153] Electronic data are qualified written forms, provided the information can be printed out.[154] The Supreme People's Court also provides that arbitration agreements made by 'written means' should include not only paper contracts and exchange of letters, but also electronic communication, such as telegraph, fax and

152 Paras 62–65.
153 PRC Contract Law, Art 11.
154 Art 11.

email.[155] The Hague Choice of Court Convention permits a jurisdiction clause to be concluded 'by any other means of communication which renders information accessible so as to be usable for subsequent reference'.[156] The UNCITRAL Model Law provides that 'in writing' includes written by electronic means, if the information is 'accessible so as to be useable for subsequent reference'.[157]

Second, the newest development shows that some countries and international harmonization of law do not require a dispute resolution clause to be concluded 'in writing'. Oral agreements 'evidenced in writing' are expressly accepted in, for example, the Brussels I Regulation,[158] the UNCITRAL Model Law on Arbitration,[159] and English Arbitration Act 1996.[160] The 2005 Hague Convention does not accept pure oral agreements, unless they are documented in writing and there is means to access the agreement for subsequent reference.[161] In China, Chinese Civil Procedure Law expressly requires the parties to choose the court 'through written agreement',[162] and the Chinese Arbitration Law states that arbitration agreements must be concluded by 'any written means',[163] which implies that dispute resolution agreements entered into orally are not valid;[164] neither are agreements concluded by conduct. It is not clear if a dispute resolution clause entered into orally and evidenced in writing is valid under Chinese law. The legislation does not clearly distinguish the concept of 'in writing' and 'evidenced in writing'. Nevertheless, in *Jufeng v MGame*,[165] the Supreme People's Court said that it accepts a jurisdiction agreement if certain written forms are there to confirm and ascertain this agreement. It implies that a jurisdiction agreement 'evidenced in writing' might be valid under Chinese law.

Third, further relaxation is witnessed where some conventions do not require any formal written evidence recording the dispute resolution

155 Interpretation to some issues in relation to the application of the Arbitration Law 2006, Art 1.

156 Art 3(c) of the Hague Convention 2005. Hartley and Dogauchi, 2007: para 112.

157 Art 7(4): Electronic communication means any communication that the parties make by means of data messages—information generated, sent, received or stored by electronic, magnetic, optical or similar means, including electronic data interchange, electronic mail, telegram, telex or telecopy.

158 Art 23(2).

159 Ibid.

160 s5(4).

161 Hartley and Dogauchi, 2007: para 114. The meaning of 'documented in writing' is the same as 'evidenced in writing', but the Hague Convention deliberately avoided using the term 'evidence' to avoid the impression of providing 'evidence' rules.

162 PRC Civil Procedure Law (Amended) of 2012, Art 34.

163 Supreme People's Court, 'Re the request for setting aside China International Economic and Trade Arbitration Commission [2008] No 44 Award', [2009] No 1.

164 *Quanshun v Jinsheng*, Chongqing Municipal No 1 Intermediate People's Court, 23 August 2001.

165 Supreme People's Court, (2009) No 4.

agreement but allow the agreement to be proved by trade custom, usages and previous dealings between the parties. For example, the Brussels I Regulation accepts jurisdiction agreements in a form pursuant to the common practice between the parties or in accordance with the common usage of international trade.[166] This very flexible formal requirement, nevertheless, has not been accepted in other jurisdictions.

Relaxation of formal requirements in arbitration

A typical example of the gradual relaxation of formal requirements is found in the United Nations in its harmonization of arbitration rules. In 1958, the New York Convention required an arbitration agreement to be 'in writing', 'signed by the parties' or 'contained in an exchange of letters or telegram'. This requirement is very restrictive and rigid.[167] It fails to take into account most common commercial practices where the parties agree terms orally without putting things in writing and the confirmation of terms is prepared by one party subsequently and sent to another; many arbitration agreements are contained in standard terms of a company, which is not directly included in the current written contract between the parties but only referred by written or non-written means; the letter or telegram restriction for the exchange of communications does not consider the development of modern technology, where many communications are done through electronic means. The UNICITRAL Model Law (Amended 2006) has provided a more flexible interpretation, which relaxes the 'in writing' requirement. Under the Model Law, 'in writing' includes: (1) agreements that are concluded in writing; (2) agreements entered into by any means and evidenced in writing[168] (this validates an arbitration agreement entered into orally or by conduct but recorded in written confirmation[169]); (3) agreements contained in an exchange of statements between the parties after disputes have arisen in which the existence of the agreement is alleged by one party and not denied by the other;[170] (4) a written arbitration agreement contained in another instrument;[171] and (5) written by electronic means, if the information is 'accessible so as to be useable for subsequent reference'.[172] The explanatory note also clarifies that the requirement of signature and the exchange of messages are not

166 Art 23(1). The same rule exists in the Brussels I Recast, Art 25(1).

167 For criticism, see Graffi, 2006: 691–692; Hill, 1998: 11; Cohen, 1997: 273.

168 Art 7(3).

169 Ibid.

170 Art 7(5).

171 Art 7(6).

172 Art 7(4): Electronic communication means any communication that the parties make by means of data messages—information generated, sent, received or stored by electronic, magnetic, optical or similar means, including electronic data interchange, electronic mail, telegram, telex or telecopy.

mandatory.[173] Many Contracting States of the New York Convention also provide more flexible interpretation to 'in writing'.[174] In England, for example, the Arbitration Act 1996 expressly requires an arbitration agreement to be 'in writing',[175] and provides constructions similar, but not identical, to that in the UNICITRAL Model Law. The term 'in writing' is construed to include three forms: (1) An agreement is made in writing,[176] including information being recorded by any means,[177] which implies that electronic communication is an accepted form for formation of arbitration agreements. The parties' signature is not mandatory.[178] (2) The agreement is made by exchange of communications in writing.[179] This means the agreement is contained in an exchange of statements between the parties in which the existence of the agreement is alleged by one party and not denied by the other.[180] (3) The agreement is evidenced in writing,[181] if the agreement not made in writing, but is recorded by the parties or their agents.[182] (4) If the parties, by other means, refer to written terms, the arbitration agreement meets the requirement of 'in writing'.[183]

Regardless of the trend to further relax the formal requirement of an arbitration clause and to adopt the more commercial sensational approach,[184] the written requirement for an arbitration agreement, however, remains in most countries. The common approach is to introduce more flexible interpretation to written forms, instead of abandoning the requirement of 'in writing' all together or permitting an arbitration agreement to be concluded by alternative means. Although most courts provide very flexible rules to the requirement of 'in writing', there must be, at least, written evidence demonstrating the existence of an arbitration clause. For example, in Netherlands, an arbitration agreement must be proved by documents 'in writing' if its existence is under challenge.[185] Although the court will not by its own motion invalidate the arbitration agreement not recorded in a written form if parties do not challenge the

173 Explanatory Note by the UNCITRAL secretariat on the 1985 Model Law on International Commercial Arbitration as amended in 2006, para 19.
174 Graffi, 2006: 692.
175 Art 5(1).
176 s5(2)(a).
177 s5(6).
178 s5(2)(a).
179 s5(2)(b).
180 s5(5).
181 s5(2)(c).
182 s5(4).
183 s5(3).
184 Kaplan, 1996: 27; Landau, 2002; Graffi, 2006: 693.
185 Art 1021(1) of the Dutch Code on Civil Procedure (amended). See Lazic, 2007: para 3.3.1.

existence of the arbitration agreement, a written form is compulsory once the agreement is challenged by one party.[186]

Finally, one issue that arises is whether the written requirement in the New York Convention must be met if the arbitral award is sought recognition and enforcement between Contracting States. If the New York Convention provides uniform rules for arbitration agreements falling within its scope, the restrictive formal condition must be met.[187] If an arbitration agreement only meets the more flexible standard of a national law but not the New York Convention, the court still recognizes its enforceability and refers the dispute to the chosen tribunal, but the award made cannot be enforced under the New York Convention.[188] A possible way out is that the court may construe that Article II(2) of the New York Convention provides the maximum standard for an arbitration agreement, which only prevents national courts from establishing more stringent rules to refuse to enforce an arbitration agreement or an arbitral award, but does not prevent any Contracting State from providing more arbitration-friendly rules to validate these clauses.[189] UNCITRAL also recommends that Article II(2) should be interpreted as providing a non-exhaustive circumstances where arbitration agreements may meet the requirement of being in writing.[190]

Signature

Must the written dispute resolution clause be signed by the parties before it can be valid? Signature is traditionally used to prove the identity of the signatories and their genuine consent. By signing their names on the document, the signatories expressly show that (a) they read, know and understand the terms of the contract, and (b) they express their consent to be bound by the terms. The practical functioning of signature is still important nowadays. However, many jurisdictions have abandoned the rigid requirement for the existence of signatures for a contract to be valid. If there are other means to establish parties' consent to an agreement, the agreement can continue to be binding. Signatures are not necessary in certain contracts where consent can be demonstrated by parties' conduct. For example, the offeree conducted the performance directly after

186 Cf. The French practice to look for common consent between the parties and to validate arbitration agreements may suggest an abandonment of written forms.

187 However, the national law of some countries may provide more restrictive formal requirement to an arbitration clause than that in the NYC. See e.g. the Italian case *Carapelli SpA v Ditta Otello Mantovani* [1981] ECC 183.

188 Graffi, 2006: 692; Pietro and Platte, 2001: 81.

189 Graffi, 2006: 692; Pietro and Platte, 2001: 81.

190 Recommendation Regarding the Interpretation of Article II, Paragraph 2, and Article VII, Paragraph 1, of the Convention on the Recognition and Enforcement of Foreign Arbitral Awards, Done in New York, 10 June 1958, Adopted by the UNCITRAL on 7 July 2006, at its Thirty-Ninth Session.

receiving the offer. In some cases, requiring signatures in every contract is impractical. For example, mass market contracts do not require the signature of every consumer, passenger or audience for making the purchase. Furthermore, in wrap contracts, the opening of a box by a party demonstrates the consent to the terms printed on the box. Requiring written signatures in every contract is no longer practical in the modern commercial world. However, although strict requirement of written signature is no longer necessary, there is much higher risk for a contract without signatures.

The Hague Convention 2005 abandons the requirement of signature for a written jurisdiction clause to be valid.[191] However, signature may be necessary for a jurisdiction clause concluded 'in writing' in the Brussels I Regulation. Although Article 23(1)(a) (and Art 25(1)(a) of Brussels I Recast) does not expressly require a written jurisdiction clause to be signed, it nevertheless provided, by the ECJ, that the written form must clearly and precisely demonstrate the consensus between the parties.[192] The ECJ held in *Galeries Segoura v FA Rahim Bonakdarian*[193] that the failure to object does not constitute acceptance of jurisdiction agreements, unless this is a common practice between the parties. In *Six Constructions v Paul Humbert*,[194] a jurisdiction clause was incorporated in the contract of employment and the employee performed its obligation without raising objection. The company argued it was sufficient evidence that the employee accepted the clause and there was no requirement of signature of the employee.[195] The French Supreme Court, based on the ECJ's decision, held that the lack of signature of the employee made the jurisdiction clause not compliant with the written requirement.[196] A more rigid approach is found in a decision of the Luxembourg Court of Appeal,[197] which held that a jurisdiction clause in the judgment convention could be considered as expressly and particularly accepted by a person if this particular clause was signed by this person. The signature of the contract as a whole was insufficient.[198] This approach, however, is not accepted by most latter cases because it is contrary to general trade practice and not commercially sensational. The only relaxation is that there is no need to

191 Hartley and Dogauchi, 2007: paras 110 and 112.

192 Case 24/76 *Estasis Salotti v RUWA* [1976] ECR 1831, 1841.

193 [1976] ECR 1851. See also *Société Microstof Textiles v Société Laine Freres* [1990] ILPr 364.

194 [1990] ILPr 22.

195 Ibid.

196 Such as German courts, see BGH NJW 2001, 1731; *Implants International v Stratec Medical* [1999] 2 All ER (Comm) 933; Magnus and Mankowski, 2012: 406–407. See also *Alpina Compagnia v Agenzia Marittima (the 'Ice Express')* (Italian tribunale), [1990] ILPr 263.

197 *Jurgen Weber v SA Eurocard Belgium-Luxembourg* (Luxembourg Court of Appeal) [1993] ILPr 55.

198 Para 11.

require special form of signature, a signature, thus, can be entered into by initials or stamps.[199]

The situation in arbitration is different. Before the New York Convention was established, English courts traditionally tried to find out the real intention of the parties and, as part of common law tradition, approve arbitration agreements without being signed if the parties' consent could be established by their conduct. In *Baker v Yorkshire Fire and Life Assurance*,[200] the court held the claimant submitted to arbitration included in the insurance policy even if he did not sign it, because the claimant relied on the policy to bring the action and could not disaffirm part of it while relying on another.[201] Although the New York Convention requires signature for an arbitration clause to be formally valid, signature of the parties is not mandatory in the domestic law of many countries.[202] In the US, the lack of signature was treated by the court as a possible lack of consent.[203] But once consent is proved, the lack of signature does not question the formal validity of the arbitration clause. The New York Convention also accepts a written arbitration agreement contained in an exchange of letters or telegrams.[204] In international commercial practice, where the parties exchange letters or telegrams, usually one or both parties would not sign. UNCITRAL Model Law further clarifies this issue by permitting any form of communication to be classified as 'in writing'. An arbitration agreement can also be contained in an exchange of statements of claim and defence in which the existence of an agreement is raised by one but not denied by the other.[205] The form of the original arbitration agreement is not important. There is also no need for signatures any more.[206]

Why is the signature generally required in Brussels I but not in the Hague Convention or in certain cases in the New York Convention? Does Brussels I provide more rigid formal requirements to a dispute resolution agreement on the cost of commercial efficacy? The reason is that Brussels

199 *Re Jurisdiction Agreement* (Case 2 Ob 280/05y) (Austrian Oberster Gerichtshof) [2008] ILPr 38.

200 [1892] 1 QB 144, 145.

201 Followed by *Hickman v Kent or Romney Marsh Sheepbreeders' Association* [1915] 1 Ch 881; *Morgan v William Harrison*, [1907] 2 Ch 137; *Anglo-Newfoundland Development v King*, [1920] 2 KB 214; *Bankers & Shippers Insurance v Liverpool Marine & General Insurance* (1925) 21 Ll. L. Rep 86; *Zambia Steel & Building Supplies v James Clark & Eaton*, [1986] 2 Lloyd's Rep 225.

202 English law: Arbitration Act, s5(2)(a). *Lafarge (Aggregates) v London Borough of Newham*, [2005] EWHC 1337 (Comm).

203 *Chastain v Robinson-Humphrey* 957 F.2d 851 (C.A.11(Ga), 1992); *Rollins v Foster* 991 F. Supp 1426 (M.D.Ala. 1998).

204 Art II(2).

205 Art 6(5).

206 Explanatory Note by the UNCITRAL secretariat on the 1985 Model Law on International Commercial Arbitration as amended in 2006, para 19.

I also establishes two alternative forms to validate a jurisdiction clause.[207] These alternative forms provide flexible conditions for a jurisdiction clause to be entered into, and all the situations where the party does not sign but demonstrates consent by other means fall into the alternatives. Brussels I also aims to protect the opposing parties from being subject to a jurisdiction clause by surprise. As a result, pure performance of a contract without negotiation on a jurisdiction clause unilaterally inserted into the contract by the other party will not be construed as consent in Article 23(1)(a) of the Brussels I Regulation (Art 25(1)(a) of the Brussels I Recast) unless this conduct is common in the parties' trading practice or in the international trade of custom.[208] The New York Convention does not provide alternative forms other than written ones, and the only means to provide flexibility in compliance with commercial practice is to provide flexible interpretation to the term 'in writing'.

However, is signature the only possible way to demonstrate parties' consent in a case where there is no trade usage or common practice between the parties? The answer should be negative. The exchange of letters between the parties or the record of negotiation could prove the consent, even though the final clause may not be signed. This form has been accepted in the New York Convention as being 'in writing' but its effect is in doubt in Brussels I if the parties do not have prior dealings or there is no such trade usage. It is thus suggested that, since the only requirement of 'in writing' is to show clear and precise consent, if parties' consent can be proved, there is no strict requirement that a signature is compulsory for Article 23(1)(a) of the Brussels I Regulation (Art 25(1)(a) of the Brussels I Recast) to be satisfied. This approach is also adopted in English decisions. In *Claxton Engineering v TXM Olaj-es Gazkutato Kit*,[209] the English court held an exclusive jurisdiction clause inserted by the offeree into the offeror's standard terms and conditions was validly 'in writing' even though there was no signature of both parties to certify the change, because the offeror's continued trading with the offeree amounted to acceptance.

Format

Another question that frequently arises is whether the 'manner' on which a dispute resolution clause is written down or expressed may invalidate this clause. The ECJ has ruled in a few cases that a jurisdiction clause does not satisfy the requirement of 'in writing' if it is not written in a way that can attract the other party's attention. For example, in *Estasis Salotti v*

207 Art 23(1)(b) and (c).
208 Art 23(1)(a) and (b).
209 [2011] ILPr 13.

RUWA,[210] a jurisdiction clause was held not to be in writing when it was printed on the reverse side of a contract without a reference to it on the front of the contract. Comparatively, in *Credit Suisse Financial Products v Société Generale d'Enterprises*,[211] a written contract referred to a master contract where an English jurisdiction clause was contained. The court held nevertheless that, since the offeree had signed the written contract with clear written reference on it, the offeree agreed to the incorporated terms of the main contract, including the jurisdiction clause.[212] Comparing the two case decisions, one could realize the difference. In *Salotti*, the jurisdiction clause was on the reverse side of the contract with no reference made on the face to it where the parties signed; in *Credit Suisse*, the contract showed the reference directing to the jurisdiction clause on its face where the parties signed. The court concerns whether the party that intends to insert the jurisdiction clause into the contract has made an effort to bring attention of the other party to the jurisdiction clause. In *Salotti*, it was very possible that the party who signed the contract did not turn it around to read the reverse side, while in *Credit Suisse*, the offeree should be able to read the reference in the contract which it signed. Whether or not the jurisdiction clause is expressly written in full in the contract is not crucial. It could be incorporated into the contract by referring to it, or to another contract that contains it. Where the standard terms are referred to expressly in the current contract, there is no need for a specific reference to the jurisdiction clause.[213]

This decision is also helpful in many contracts signed online. It is common practice that a website does not display full terms and conditions, including jurisdiction clauses, on the page where the party is required to click 'I agree' to show his consent. The website owner usually only provides a weblink referring to terms and conditions. The party who is required to 'sign' usually is required to tick a box showing 'I have read and agreed to the terms and conditions' to show he has read and fully understood those terms, including a jurisdiction clause. According to the above decisions, it is not crucial if the jurisdiction clause is not directly

210 Case 24/76. See also *Luz v Bertram* (Italian Corte di Cassazione) [1992] ILPr 537.

211 [1997] CLC 168 CA.

212 [1997] CLC 168 CA, 'a "guarantee" of real consent does exist where there is an express reference in the written contract itself by way of incorporation of other written terms which include a clause conferring jurisdiction. Indeed, given such an express reference, it seems to me self evident that the profferee of the written contract, by signing without reservation, has agreed in writing the incorporated terms (and thus the clause conferring jurisdiction) for the simple reason that the very words of the signed written contract itself are to that effect ... the consensus is incontrovertibly established by the express reference in the written contract itself.'

213 *7E Communications Ltd v Vertex Antennentechnik GmbH* [2007] 1 WLR 2175. For more discussion on formal validity in the Brussels I Regulation and the relevant case law, see Merrett, 2009: 551–553.

included in the page showing other contract terms, such as the description of goods and display of price, but included in a link directing to it.

The difficulty here is that such requirements may go too far and beyond the requirement as to form. It enters the field of substantive validity because it starts to consider not only the external expression of the consent, but also the inherent authenticity and quality of the consent. Because of this reason, many jurisdictions do not expand the formal validity to cover the circumstances when consent is made or the format of a written clause, and believe these should be left to the scrutiny of material validity. The additional requirement as to the format of writing is not adopted in the 2005 Hague Convention. The Hague Choice of Court Convention accepts agreements written in a foreign language; it does not require a jurisdiction clause to be written in a particular form and a clause in small and fine print or printed on the reverse side of the contract without a reference on the front would still be valid as to form.[214] If the authenticity of consent is in doubt, the court can refer to material validity requirements to invalidate it. It is questionable whether the ECJ requirements are still up to date. A particular reason for the ECJ to provide extended meaning to the requirement of 'in writing' is because of the lack of substantive requirements in the Brussels I Regulation. In a few cases, the ECJ decides that formal validity alone is sufficient to determine the substance of jurisdiction clauses.[215] Although this opinion is severely criticized by commentators, it is consistent with the ECJ's common approach to provide more valuable consideration to the written requirement and to require 'writing' to show substantive consent.

The New York Convention does not expressly require the format of writing to make an arbitration agreement formally valid. But the Contracting States may use their national law to invalidate an arbitration agreement on the ground that the format of writing taints the quality of consent. The German court has invalidated an arbitration clause in a consumer contract because it was one of those terms in small print extending over several pages and it was written in a way difficult even for an attentive and educated person to understand.[216] Japanese courts are also reluctant to allow an arbitration clause in small print to deprive a person of his access to courts.[217] In the US, a court might invalidate an arbitration clause concealed in excessively small print or on the reverse side of contracts, or one that uses unclear language, which may lead a court to find the

214 Hartley and Dogauchi, 2007: para 110.

215 C-214/89, *Powell Duffryn v Petereit*, ECR 1992, I-1745; C-106/95, *MSG Mainschiffahrtsgenossenschft v Le Gravières Rhenanes SARL*, ECR 1997 I-911.

216 *Richard Zellner v Phillip Alexander Securities* (Case 6 O 186/95) (Landgericht, Krefeld) [1997] ILPr 716. Hess *et al.*, 2007: para 376.

217 See discussion in *Oldendorff v Libera* [1996] CLC 482, 490.

procedural unconscionability.[218] However, the US courts enforced arbitration clauses printed on the reverse side of a contract with a reference to it on the front,[219] and clauses printed on the reverse side in bold form without a reference on the front.[220] Both are sufficient notices to the other party.

Oral agreements evidenced in writing

Pure oral agreements may be invalid in some countries. The most important reason is the impossibility to prove the existence and content of the agreement. Some jurisdictions, especially common law countries, do not require strict form of jurisdiction clauses. An oral agreement can be valid, as far as it can be proved in a certain way. If both parties accept that they have entered into a jurisdiction clause orally, there is no reason for a court to invalidate such an agreement simply because it is in an oral form.

However, if a country does not accept oral agreement per se, it may still accept the written evidence of an oral agreement. In some cases, the parties have entered into an oral agreement. Afterwards, one sends written confirmation containing this agreement to the other. If the other party does not object in any means, the written confirmation is acceptable written evidence of the agreement, which could make the agreement valid in form.[221] In *Berghoefer GmbH & Co v ASA SA*,[222] the parties entered into oral agreement, including jurisdiction clauses. One party sent the other written confirmation afterwards, which was not disputed by the recipient. The ECJ held that the jurisdiction clause was evidenced in writing and, thus, valid.[223] The UNCITRAL Model Law also provides that an arbitration agreement may be entered into orally and it is valid as far as the content is recorded.[224]

One important requirement for the 'evidence in writing' is that the subsequent written document must simply confirm what was already agreed upon orally, instead of inserting anything new in addition to what was discussed, or anything different from what was agreed upon. For example, in

218 *Velazquez v Brank Energe* 2011 WL 864857 (WDLa 2011) (validating arbitrating clauses in capital letters); *Stachurski v DirecTV* 642 F. Supp. 2d 758 (NDOhio 2009), 767–768 (validating arbitration clauses printed in bolded, capital letters); *In re Olympus Healthcare Group* 352 BR 603 (Bkrtcy.D.Del, 2006); *Harris v Green Tree Financial* 183 F.3d 173 (C.A.3(Pa), 1999), 182; *Rollins v Foster* 991 F. Supp. 1426.

219 *Troshak v Terminix* 1998 WL 401693 (E.D.Pa 1998).

220 *McCullough v Shearson Lehman Brothers* 1988 WL 23008, 3 (W.D.Pa, 1998). Cf *Harris v Green Tree* 183 F.3d 173 (C.A.3(Pa) 1999); *Doctor's Assocites v Casarotto* 517 US 681 (1996).

221 Hague Convention, official documents.

222 Case 221/84, [1985] ECR 2699.

223 For more discussion, see Merrett, 2009: 559–560.

224 Explanatory Note by the UNCITRAL secretariat on the 1985 Model Law on International Commercial Arbitration as amended in 2006, para 19.

Segoura v Bonakdarian,[225] the parties entered into an oral contract for the sale of goods, but they did not discuss jurisdiction issues during negotiation. When the seller performed his obligation, he delivered a document/receipt stating the sale was subject to terms and conditions printed on the reverse side of the document, which included a jurisdiction clause. The buyer did not raise objection. The ECJ, however, believed that in this case there was no valid jurisdiction agreement. The jurisdiction clause contained in the terms and conditions was not agreed orally. The latter document provided a new term which was consented by the other party, instead of only confirming the agreement that was entered into by the parties, which does not require the re-expression of consent.

5.2 Material validity

Lack of genuine consent

Parties should enter into agreements with authentic consent. Consent that is tainted by misrepresentation, mistake, fraud, duress or undue influence will make jurisdiction or arbitration clauses invalid. However, if the claim is that duress or undue influence makes the main contract void, it will not necessarily make jurisdiction or arbitration agreements void under the doctrine of severability.[226] In English common law, the court will consider each case to decide whether the nature of duress or fraud could directly invalidate the dispute resolution agreement.[227] The same decision is held in US courts. Although fraud or duress is sufficient to render a dispute resolution clause unenforceable,[228] general claims that fraud or duress exists in conclusion of the underlying contract cannot invalidate the dispute resolution clause.[229] The opposing party must prove the dispute resolution

225 Case 25/76.

226 *AstraZeneca v Albemarle International* [2010] 1 CLC 715; *El Nasharty v J Sainsbury* [2007] EWHC 2618 (Comm); *Harbour Assurance v Kansa General International* [1993] QB 701; *Westacre v Jugoimport-SDPR Holding*, [1998] CLC 409. See Ch 3 below.

227 *Westacre v Jugoimport-SDPR Holding*; *Israel Discount Bank of New York v Hadjipateras*, [1984] 1 WLR 137.

228 *Nagrampa v Mailcoups*, 469 F.3d 1257 (C.A.9 (Cal) 2006); *Walker v Ryan's Family Steak Houses*, 400 F.3d 370 (C.A.6 (Tenn) 2005); *Cooper v MRM Investment* 367 F.3d 493 (C.A.6 (Tenn) 2004); *Great Earth Companies v Simons* 288 F.3d 878 (C.A.6 (Mich) 2002); *Perry v Thomas* 482 US 483 (1987); *Doctor's Associations v Casarotto* 517 US 681 (1996); *Mitsubishi Motors v Soler Chrysler-Plymouth* 723 F.2d 155 (1st Cir. 1983); *KKM v Gloria Jean's Gourmet Coffees Franchising* 184 F.3d 42 (C.A.1(R.I.) 1999).

229 *Preferred Capital v Associations of Urology*, 453 F.3d 718, 722 (6th Cir. 2006) *Wong v Party Gaming Ltd* 589 F.3d 821 (C.A.6 (Ohio), 2009); *Buckeye Check Cashing v Cardegna*, 824 So.2d 228, 230 (Fla.Dist.Ct.App. 2002); *Southland v Keating*, 465 US 1 (1984); *Afram Carriers v Moeykens* 145 F.3d 298 (C.A.5 (Tex) 1998).

agreement itself is included as the result of fraud or duress.[230] This could be the case where the dispute resolution is unilaterally imposed, or is unilaterally inserted by one party after the main contract is concluded.[231]

Connection between the chosen court and the dispute/defendant

The neutral nature of arbitration makes it common practice to select an arbitral tribunal seated in a country with no connections to the dispute. This restriction only applies to jurisdiction agreements but not arbitration agreements. Most countries permit the parties to choose a neutral court to decide their disputes,[232] but some countries provide extra requirements as to which courts can be chosen.[233] For example, China Mainland requires 'practical connections' between the chosen court and the dispute,[234] which include the place where the defendant has his domicile, where the contract is performed, where the contract is concluded, where the plaintiff has his domicile or where the object of the action is located.[235]

Restricting the scope of courts that can be chosen may serve the purpose of preventing parties from abusing the process and protecting the parties from being deprived of their legal rights. However, the restriction is no longer necessary. First, the nature of party autonomy is to give the parties the right to decide their disputes. The law usually adopts a hands-off approach to the choice, with the exception of certain sensitive and fundamental issues and safeguarding of mandatory rules and public policy. It is common practice for the parties to take their disputes to a neutral forum where none of the parties may receive any advantage or prejudice. Second, most countries have adopted exclusive jurisdiction to prohibit choice of jurisdiction in actions where subject matters of which concern the fundamental national interest or are under absolute and effective state control, where jurisdiction should be taken exclusively for the purpose of administration and enforcement. For all other issues, there is no strong state interest involved and it is permissible for the parties to decide on their own courts. Third, there are already formal requirements and substantive contract law that supervise the background and circumstances under which jurisdiction clauses are entered into. Additional

230 *Great Earth v Simons*, 288 F.3d 878, 884, 890 (6th Cir. 2002); *Associations of Urology; Binder v Medicine Shoppe* 2010 WL 2854308 (E.D.Mich. 2010); *Fazio v Lehman Brothers* 340 F.3d 386 (6th Cir. (Ohio) 2003); *Inland Bulk Transfer v Cummins Engine* 332 F.3d 1007 (6th Cir. (Ohio) 2003); *Greenview Hospital v Wooten* 2010 WL 2835742, 5 (W.D.Ky. 2010); *Albert M. Higley v N/S Co* 2004 WL 5550700 (N.D.Ohio, 2004).

231 *Nagrampa v MailCoups*. For the EU approach under Article 23 of the Brussels I Regulation, see Merrett, 2009: 557–560.

232 Haines, 2002: para 2.

233 Ibid., paras 2–4.

234 Chinese Civil Procedure Law (Amended) 2012, Art 34.

235 Ibid., Art 34.

restrictions as to which court can be chosen in order to protect the parties from being abused in process are redundant. The most recent international development in choice of court agreements, the 2005 Hague Convention and the Brussels I Regulation and the Brussels I Recast, do not require the chosen court to have any connections to the dispute.

Public interest

Dispute resolution clauses are substantively invalid if they are contrary to the public interest. The definition of public interest is, again, uncertain. It may be classified into different categories. First, there is public interest to prevent a party from abusing its bargaining power in contracts with the inequality of bargaining power. This will render dispute resolution clauses invalid in certain contracts, such as consumer contracts,[236] insurance contracts,[237] employment contracts,[238] agency contracts[239] and franchise contracts.[240] Second, there is public interest to ensure the parties will not escape overriding mandatory rules or public policy of the state which is affected by the parties' contractual activities. If the parties choose a foreign country to hear the dispute in order to evade the overriding mandatory rules of the state of performance, the state of performance has sufficient reasons to invalidate the jurisdiction clause even if it is concluded with the authentic consent of both parties.[241] Third, there is policy not to permit party autonomy in areas concerning important public interest, the functioning of public authority or administrative agencies, and the interest of third parties. Law does not allow parties to choose the competent forum in every matter. Some subject matters have been considered essential in terms of a country's sovereignty, public interest and policy. A country claims exclusive jurisdiction over it and precludes party autonomy from playing. For example, the parties cannot choose the competent court in deciding the transaction of immoveable property.[242] There are other issues, where the parties could make agreement on the competent court, but they cannot submit the subject matter to arbitration. This is relating to arbitrability. It is recognized that not every subject matter is arbitrable. Arbitrability is a matter of domestic law. National law could make reservation as to which subject matter should be heard exclusively in court. Although most commercial matters are arbitrable, exceptions exist in

236 Section 4 of the Brussels I Regulation.
237 Section 3 of the Brussels I Regulation.
238 Section 5 of the Brussels I Regulation.
239 Case C-381/98 *Ingmar GB Ltd v Eaton Leonard Technologies Inc.* 2000 ECR I-9305.
240 Zimmerman, 1998: 759; *Kubis & Perszyk Assocsiation v Sun Microsystems*, 680 A.2d 618 (N.J. 1996); Haines, 2002: para 21.
241 Haines, 2002: para 21; *Ingmar GB Ltd v Eaton.*
242 Hartley and Dogauchi, 2007: para 67. For more on the exclusive jurisdiction, see Ch 4.

antitrust matters,[243] crimes, capacity of the parties, family law issue and contracts including the weaker party.[244] Fourth, enforcing agreements entered into under duress or fraud can also be held against public policy.[245] Finally, public policy may also come into play if the enforcement of jurisdiction or arbitration clauses will cause, directly or indirectly, the loss of statutory interest or access to justice of a party. For example, dispute resolution agreements which may prevent a consumer from participating in class action held in another state had been held against public policy of California.[246]

US courts frequently use public policy to invalidate jurisdiction or arbitration agreements. Dispute resolution clauses are invalidated if they are 'unconscionable'.[247] As the common law tradition, the concept of 'conscionableness' is uncertain. It may cover the situation where a dispute resolution clause designates an unfriendly/hostile jurisdiction,[248] a clause provides biased conditions between the parties and one party is obviously in a disadvantageous situation compared to another[249] or the process of conclusion of the clause is unfair.[250] All factors, including the presentation of a clause, the circumstances to conclude the clauses and the consequence of applying the clause, are all relevant. A dispute resolution clause is invalid if it is obtained by fraud or overreaching, or the enforcement is unreasonable or unjust.[251]

However, commercial soundness is a very important principle adopted by US courts to decide the validity of a forum selection clause. US courts have, in many cases, upheld dispute resolution clauses contained in

243 It was not arbitrable in old US law. See *Mitsubishi Motors v Soler Chrysler-Plymouth*, 473 US 614 (1985).

244 Private tenancy agreements are not arbitrable in Germany. See s1030(2) Zivilprozessordnung.

245 *Kaufman v Gerson* [1904] 1 KB 591; *Royal Boskalis Westminster NV v Mountain* [1999] QB 674 (CA).

246 *Doel v AOL LLC*, 2009 WL 103657 (9th Cir. Jan. 16, 2009).

247 Haines, 2002: paras 17–19.

248 In *Continental Grain Export v Ministry of War Etka*, 603 F. Supp. 724 (1984), the choice of Iranian courts was held unreasonable; *Scott v Tutor Time Child Care Systems, Inc.* 33 S.W.3d. 679 (Mo, 2000); *Investors Guaranty Fund, Ltd v Compass Bank*, 779 So.2d 185 (Ala. Sup. Crt. 2000).

249 *Bolter v Superior Court*, 87 Cal.App. 4th 900, 908 (2001); *Nagrampa v MailCoups, Inc.* 469 F.3d 1257 (C.A.9 (Cal.),2006); *Leasefirst v Hartford Rexall Drugs, Inc.*, 168 Wis.2d 83, 483 N.W.2d 585 (Wis.Ct.App.1992); *First Federal Financial Service, Inc. v Derrington's Chevron, Inc.*, 230 Wis.2d 553, 602 N.W.2d 144 (Wis.Ct.App.1999); *Feldman*, 513 F. Supp. 2d, 242–243; *Carnival Cruise Lines, Inc. v Shute*, 499 US 585 (1991), 593; *Swain v Auto Services, Inc.*, 128 S.W.3d 103, 108–109 (Mo.Ct.App.2003).

250 *Cottonwood Financial, Ltd v Estes*, 339 Wis.2d 472, 810 N.W.2d 852, 856 (Wis.Ct.App.2012); *Tricome v Ebay Inc.*, No 09–2492, 2009 WL 3365873, at 2 (E.D.Pa. Oct.19, 2009); *Alexander v Anthony Int'l., L.P.*, 341 F.3d 256, 265 (3d Cir.2003); *Grant v Phila. Eagles*, LLC, No 09–1222, 2009 WL 1845231, 6. (E.D.Pa. June 24, 2009).

251 *Bremen v Zapata Off-Shore*, 15.

standard form contracts with or without the signature of the other party. In such contracts, the courts examine the size and the format of the warning notice, whether it could direct the reader's attention to its terms and conditions,[252] and the language used in the clause—whether it is drafted in a clear and unambiguous manner.[253] As far as the clause is demonstrated clearly and made available to the other party, it is valid, and whether the reader in fact takes the chance to read it is not a serious concern.[254] Furthermore, even if a clause chooses a foreign country to decide a dispute between two parties with the same habitual residence, and the other party is a weaker one, such as passengers, as far as the chosen forum has connections to the contract, the clause should be valid.[255]

6 Interpretation and scope of dispute resolution agreements

6.1 Introduction

Sometimes, there is no dispute over the existence and validity of a dispute resolution agreement, but the disagreement is over whether the disputed matter is subject to the dispute resolution agreement, which requires the forum to consider the construction and scope of an agreement. A classic challenge on the scope of a dispute resolution agreement is whether it covers non-contractual claims. In international commercial practice, a dispute resolution agreement is usually concluded before a dispute has arisen and concluded as part of commercial contract. The wording usually says any dispute 'arising out of', 'in connection with' or 'in relation to' the contract should be submitted to the chosen forum. While disputes occur on tort or other non-contractual claims, one party that wants to escape the dispute resolution agreement always argues that the dispute in question does not fall within the scope of the agreement.

It is necessary to know that not all countries permit the parties to choose a competent forum to decide non-contractual disputes. In arbitration, the New York Convention accepts that parties could submit all disputes, 'contractual or not', to arbitration.[256] Contracting States thus have treaty obligations to permit the parties to enter into an arbitration agreement to resolve their non-contractual dispute. English courts accept an arbitration clause could cover tort claims if there was a sufficient close

252 *Effron v Sun Line*, 9.
253 Ibid., 9.
254 Ibid., 9.
255 Ibid., 9; *Hollander v K-Lines Hellenic Cruises*, 670 F. Supp. 563, 566 (S.D.N.Y. 1987); *Damigos v Flanders Companiea Naviera*, 716 F. Supp. 104, 107 (S.D.N.Y. 1989).
256 Art II.1.

connection between the tort and the contract.[257] The construction of an arbitration agreement only concerns whether it covers all, or some, of the disputed matter. In *JSC BTA Bank v Ablyazov*,[258] for example, the arbitration agreement reads: 'Any disputes, differences or claims arising from this contract (agreement) or in connection therewith, including the ones relating to its performance, breach, termination or invalidity.' The claimant bank sued the defendant for intentional fraud and wrongdoing, and claimed that the agreement did not cover non-contractual obligations. The parties agreed that Kazakh law governed the agreement. Kazakh law requires an arbitration agreement to be interpreted according to its literal meaning.[259] The English court considered the literal interpretation of 'arising from' and 'in connection therewith' should include a tort claim relating to the contract.[260] The claimant's claim is dismissed.

In jurisdiction agreements, the common practice in the world is that parties are permitted to choose competent courts in almost all civil and commercial matters except those subject to exclusive jurisdiction. For example, choice of court is allowed in both contractual and tort actions in the Brussels I Regulation.[261] The Hague Convention 2005 does not exclude the choice of court in tort from its scope.[262] However, some countries restrict the scope of jurisdiction clauses and permit only choice of court for contractual relationships. For example, Article 34 of the Chinese Civil Procedure Law 2012 permits the parties to choose the competent court for 'a dispute over a contract concluded with foreign element or over property rights and interests involving foreign element'. A strict literal reading may suggest that parties are not allowed to choose the competent forum for non-contractual, non-property obligations, such as tort. However, Chinese courts in practice prefer more flexible interpretations and would apply jurisdiction clauses to at least contract-related tort claims.[263]

6.2 Construction of dispute resolution agreements

If a country permits the parties to choose a forum in any cross-border relationship not subject to exclusive state control or restriction, the parties are

257 *Empresa Exportadora De Azucar (CUBAZUCAR) v Industria Azucarera Nacional SA (IANSA)* [1983] 2 Lloyd's Rep 171; *Aggeliki Charis Compania Maritima SA v Pagnan SpA (The Angelic Grace)* [1995] 1 Lloyd's Rep 87.

258 [2011] EWHC 587 (Comm).

259 Para 64.

260 Ibid.

261 Art 23(1) of the Brussels I Regulation.

262 Hartley and Dogouchi, 2007: 16 and para 39.

263 See *Lai v ABN AMRO Bank*, Shanghai Municipality High Court, (2010) No 49; *Watanabe v Culture & Art Press*, Shanghai Municipality No 1 Intermediate Court, (2008) Hu Yi Zhong Min Wu (Zhi) Chu No 210. Discussed below.

free to draft dispute resolution clauses to govern particular relationships or to cover all disputes arising between them. The scope of a conflicts clause is usually decided by considering the language used and all the circumstances of contracting. For example, if a jurisdiction clause provides that: 'All contractual disputes arising between the parties shall be heard by the court of Hong Kong', it shows that the jurisdiction clause does not apply to non-contractual obligations. If, on the other hand, the parties enter into jurisdiction agreements after the tort activity has been done to address the dispute arising out of the tort action, the jurisdiction clause clearly governs the dispute in question. Questions may arise if the parties use ambiguous language by saying, for example, 'The parties agree to submit disputes to English courts'. It then depends on the court to interpret whether the parties submit only their contractual disputes to English courts, or the parties intend to submit all contract-related, non-contractual disputes to English courts.

In England, construction of a conflicts clause 'should start from the assumption that the parties, as rational businessmen, are likely to have intended any dispute arising out of the relationship into which they have entered or purported to enter' to be governed by the conflicts clause unless the language clearly suggests to the contrary.[264] It is stated by Lord Hope that[265]

> The proposition that any jurisdiction or arbitration clause in an international commercial contract should be liberally construed promotes legal certainty. It serves to underline the golden rule that if the parties wish to have issues as to the validity of their contract decided by one tribunal and issues as to its meaning decided by another, they must say so expressly. Otherwise they will be taken to have agreed on a single tribunal for the resolution of all such disputes.

It is clear that the presumption will be made that a conflicts clause will be broad enough to cover all the disputes arising out of the agreement, unless the language clearly states otherwise. Furthermore, some clauses are drafted in a particularly broader manner that they should cover disputes arising 'in relation to the contract', which could extend the coverage to closely related matters or other related contracts.[266] However, English courts also held that this presumption is rebuttable. If the applicable law requires the dispute resolution clause to be construed according to its literal meaning, the court cannot apply the 'rational businessman'

264 *Fiona Trust and Holding v Privalov* [2007] UKHL 40, para 13, per Lord Hoffmann.

265 *Fiona Trust and Holding v Privalov*, para 26.

266 *Cinnamon European Structured Credit Master Fund v Banco Commercial Portugues SA* [2010] ILPr 11.

presumption but have to consider the actual words used and the literal meanings of the dispute resolution agreement.[267]

In the US, courts consider the 'factual allegations' rather than 'the causes of action asserted' to decide whether jurisdiction clauses cover the action.[268] In *Terra v Mississippi Chem*,[269] proceedings may arise out of a contract if: (1) they 'ultimately depend on the existence of a contractual relationship between the parties'; (2) 'resolution of the claims relates to interpretation of the contract'; or (3) 'contract-related tort claims involve the same operative facts as a parallel claim for breach of contract'.[270] In *Cfirstclass v Silverjet*,[271] the buyer claimed against the successor of a seller for tortious interference with an advantageous business relationship, tortious interference with contract and unjust enrichment. All the claims were fundamentally based on terms of sales agreements between the seller and the buyer and should be subject to the jurisdiction clauses in the sales agreement. In *Attachmate v Public Health Trust*,[272] for example, a manufacturer of software sued the purchaser for infringement of copyright and breach of the licence agreement. The purchaser purchased the software by issuance of purchaser orders which contained a clause agreeing that any litigation regarding the performance of the contract shall be submitted to Florida. The purchaser then was provided with copies of the end user licence agreement. The question is whether the jurisdiction clause in the purchaser order can be used to govern the claim on infringement of copyright. The action does not involve interpretation of the term in, or the performance of, the purchase order, instead it is based solely on the license agreement, which is a separate contract. The court believed that the two contracts concerned different matters and were independent of each other. The jurisdiction clause thus did not cover the claim in action.

Delictual claims frequently arise out of contracts. In England, for example, if an employee is injured during the course of his employment, an audience is injured in a premise, a passenger is injured during carriage or a consumer is injured by the defect of a product, the victim could sue the other party for breach of common law duty of care and statutory duty, and/or for the breach of contractual obligations. Non-contractual obligations also arise during the negotiation or the conclusion of a contract,

267 *JSC BTA Bank v Ablyazov*, para 64.

268 *Phillips v Audio Active* 494 F.3d 378, 388 (C.A.2 (NY) 2007); *Roby v Co of Lloyd's 996 F.2d 1353*, 1360–1361 (2d Cir. 1993); *Worldwide Network v DynCorp International* 496 F. Supp. 2d 59, 63 (D.D.C.2007); *Cheney v IPD Analytics* 583 F. Supp. 2d 108, 122 (D.D.C., 2008).

269 119 F.3d 688, 693–694 (8th Cir. 1997).

270 Ibid., 694, as cited in *Cheney v IPD Analytics*, 122; *Coastal Steel Corp. v Tilghman Wheelabrator Ltd*, 709 F.2d 190, 203 (3d Cir.1983); *Manetti-Farrow, Inc. v Gucci America, Inc.*, 858 F.2d 509, 514 (9th Cir.1988); *Lambert v Kysar*, 983 F.2d 1110, 1121–1122 (1st Cir. 1993)); *Worldwide Network Servs.*, 496 F. Supp. 2d at 62; *Gullion v JLG Serviceplus, Inc., Civil Action* No H-06-1015, 2007 WL 294174, 5 (S.D.Tex. Jan. 29, 2007).

271 560 F. Supp. 2d 324 (S.D.N.Y 2008).

272 *Attachmate Co v Public Health Trust* 686 F. Supp. 2d 1140, 1150 (W.D. Wash., 2010).

such as fraud or misrepresentation, which causes the conclusion of a contract, *negotia gestro* and *contra in comprehendo*. The third situation is where the parties have entered into a contract to build up a long-term commercial relationship and, during the relationship, one party commits business-related tort, such as infringement of the other parties' property rights.

In practice, some plaintiffs may try to avoid a valid conflict clause by relying on non-contractual claims. Some US judges adopted a narrow interpretation to a jurisdiction clause. If a clause does not clearly state that it will apply to 'any' claims between the parties, or specify it applies to non-contractual obligations, the courts refuse to apply jurisdiction clauses to non-contractual claims.[273] However, most courts prefer to provide jurisdiction clauses a broad meaning. Unless the parties provide otherwise, a jurisdiction clause shall be applied to non-contractual obligations arising out of or in relation to the contract which contains the jurisdiction clause. The same approach is adopted in China in order to prevent the party from manipulating the claim in order to avoid the dispute resolution clause. In *Lai v ABN AMRO Bank*,[274] for example, the claimant wanted to avoid the jurisdiction clause in the investment agreement by formulating his claim on fraud. The claimant argued that the jurisdiction clause only applied to contractual obligations. The court decided that the scope of a jurisdiction clause is broad enough to cover not only contractual claims, but also other claims arising out of or in relation to the contract where the jurisdiction clause is included. In another case, *Watanabe v Culture & Art Press*,[275] a Japanese writer and a Chinese press concluded a publication contract, choosing Japan as the exclusive forum. Watanabe sued the Chinese publisher in China for infringement of his copyright, and claimed that the jurisdiction clause was invalid because the dispute was not one based on the publication contract. The court decided that, if the contractual parties have expressly agreed on the competent court to decide disputes, they should not freely choose or change the basis of the claim to escape their agreement. The Supreme People's Court also expressly provides in the Arbitration Law Judicial Interpretation (2006 Interpretation) that, if the parties state that 'contractual disputes' (*he tong zheng yi*) are subject to arbitration, any disputes arising out of contracts should be submitted to arbitration.[276]

7 Harmonization and cooperation

It is ideal that, after the parties enter into a dispute resolution agreement, they will voluntarily perform their promise. However, in practice, disputes

273 See e.g. *Morgan Trailer Mfg. Co. v Hydraroll, Ltd*, 759 A.2d 926, 931 (2000); *Jacobson v Mail-boxes, Etc. USA, Inc.*, 419 Mass. 572 (1995). Haines, 2002: para 8.

274 *Lai v ABN AMRO Bank*, Shanghai Municipality High Court, (2010) No 49.

275 *Watanabe v Culture & Art Press*, Shanghai Municipality No 1 Intermediate Court, (2008) Hu Yi Zhong Min Wu (Zhi) Chu No 210.

276 Art 2.

concerning the existence and validity of dispute resolution agreements arise frequently. Different national law in this issue causes uncertainty, while jurisdiction or arbitration agreements are held valid in one country, but not in another. This level of disparity can lead to the ineffectiveness of dispute resolution agreements. International harmonization, as a result, is necessary and helpful.

The current legal framework shows that harmonization in formal validity of a dispute resolution agreement is much easier than harmonization of substantive validity. Domestic contract law of most countries represents great similarity in the formal requirements of a contract. The contract freedom principle and idea to reduce business costs and to improve efficiency call for the relaxation of the requirements for formation and formal validity, especially as the result of the development of telecommunications technology. Against this background, harmonization of formal validity of dispute resolution agreements is fairly successful at both the international and the regional level and in both jurisdiction and arbitration agreements.

Harmonization of substantive validity, on the other hand, is more difficult. Domestic law varies largely in its content on material validity. Furthermore, some issues relating to substantive validity connect closely with a country's policy, public interest and concept of justice and fairness. Substantive validity covers a large number of issues, including the subject and scope of a dispute resolution agreement, the requirement of genuine consent and fair deal, including duress and coercion, capacity of a party, protection of the weaker parties, the effect and influence of dispute resolution agreements and the involvement of third parties. It is difficult, if not impossible, to harmonize these issues, even at the regional level. Harmonization can only be achieved in uniform choice of law rules. However, exceptions should be given to public policy of a country. In arbitration, the general concept is not to harmonize either substantive law or choice of law in arbitration agreements. The same level of certainty does not exist in arbitration, but it does not seriously hamper the effectiveness of arbitration agreements in international commerce. It is because most national courts understand the importance of party autonomy in international arbitration and bear in mind the general policy to validate and enforce arbitration agreements in the absence of fundamental public policy infringement.

A question arising during the comparative study is whether the preliminary requirements are identical for jurisdiction and arbitration agreements, and whether it is necessary and practical to provide the same set of rules to decide existence and validity for the two different types of dispute resolution agreements. The practice in common law countries clearly shows a level of similarity and the court, when being asked to decide validity of jurisdiction agreements, frequently refers to previous judgments in arbitration agreements, and vice versa. In China, however, the legislative provisions differ widely between jurisdiction and arbitration agreements. It is because the rules applying to arbitration agreements have mirrored relevant provisions in the New York Convention, and the law-markers fail to consider the relevance and connection between the two dispute resolution agreements when drafting provisions on jurisdiction agreements.

Arguably, the contractual characteristic of both agreements makes it possible to impose the same rules for formation and validity. Applying the same rules to them could provide certainty and efficiency to the parties. In practice, however, more flexibility may be given to validate arbitration agreements than jurisdiction agreements. Especially when an arbitral tribunal is seized to decide the validity of an arbitration agreement, the tribunal may not apply the law of any particular country but instead find out the genuine intention of the parties at the time of contracting. Even if a court is seized to decide this issue, a court may nevertheless preserve more judicial discretion to validate arbitration agreements.[277] Further difference exists in substantive validity, where public policy may be used more frequently to invalidate judicial agreements than arbitration agreements. The subjective matter scope also differs between jurisdiction and arbitration agreements. While some countries prevent the parties from submitting issues relating to state sovereignty or public interest to the other country's jurisdiction, some of these issues are nevertheless arbitrable. This is why the same validity requirements for jurisdiction and arbitration agreements are rarely found in civil law jurisdictions. The common law jurisdictions provide the same test for both agreements and leave discretion to the court to make decisions on a case-by-case basis. It is thus submitted that jurisdiction and arbitration agreements are similar, but not identical, in the perspective of contractual law. The same rules on prerequisites, thus, are inappropriate for jurisdiction and arbitration agreements.

277 Such as French courts, see e.g. *SOERNI v ASB*; *Municipalité de Khoms El Mergeb v Société Dalico*; *ETAP v Bomal Oil*; *ETPM v ECOFISA*.

3 Prerequisites

Which forum decides?

1 Introduction

If a party challenges the existence and validity of a dispute resolution clause, which courts or tribunals have jurisdiction to decide the preliminary issue and jurisdiction of either themselves or others? The challenge to the preliminary issue of a dispute resolution clause may arise in two circumstances. First, the claimant may argue that the main contract has never been concluded or the main contract is invalid. Since a dispute resolution clause is part of the contract, this argument also questions the existence and validity of the dispute resolution clause. The doctrine of separability usually applies to deal with this situation, under which the dispute resolution agreement is deemed independent from the main contract and the non-existence or invalidity of the main contract cannot necessarily invalidate the dispute resolution agreement. Second, a claimant may directly challenge the existence or validity of a dispute resolution agreement. The question is whether the chosen forum is competent to rule on its own jurisdiction when the dispute resolution agreement that confers power to this forum is under challenge. The doctrine of *kompetenz-kompetenz* applies to grant the chosen forum the competence to examine its own jurisdiction. The doctrines of separability and *kompetenz-kompetenz* work together to promote the effectiveness of dispute resolution agreements and party autonomy.[1] This chapter examines the theory and the practice of the doctrine of separability and *kompetenz-kompetenz* in cross-border dispute resolution.

2 The doctrine of separability

2.1 Introduction

In practice, the existence and validity of the main contract is frequently under dispute. The claimant could commence the action arguing that the

1 Coe, 2009: 1378. These two doctrines are related but are different and work in different situations. See Rosen 1994: 602.

alleged contract is terminated, repudiated, invalid or not concluded. The court or tribunal thus is required to decide the alleged non-existence or invalidity of the main contract. Before a court or tribunal could decide the substance of a dispute, it must be satisfied that, first of all, it has jurisdiction. If the claimant sues in the chosen court challenging the validity and existence of the main contract, the defendant may argue that when the claimant raises this claim the claimant must believe the jurisdiction clause, as part of the contract, does not exist or is invalid. The claimant is thus estoppeled from relying on the jurisdiction clause in bringing the action in the chosen court. Furthermore, the chosen court cannot assert jurisdiction while the existence and validity of the jurisdiction clause is in question. The same difficulty arises in arbitration agreements.

If a party is barred from bringing proceedings in a chosen forum whenever he starts to question the validity and existence of a contract, it makes exclusive jurisdiction clauses or arbitration agreements practically useless. It may also violate the intention of the parties, who, when entering into the agreement, consented to submit literally 'all' disputes to the chosen forum. The party who wants to breach the dispute resolution clause that is freely entered into can do it simply by adding an additional claim questioning the validity of the main contract and bringing the case to another country. In order to protect party autonomy and to hold parties to their agreement, the common practice in deciding jurisdiction on the existence and validity of a main contract is the doctrine of separability. It means that jurisdiction and arbitration clauses are treated severable and independent from the main contract. The non-existence or invalidity of the main contract does not affect the parties' right to bring the action to the chosen court.[2]

2.2 The doctrine of separability in English law

The doctrine of separability has been accepted widely in the world but not without scepticism. In England, some early authorities believed that arbitrators could not decide the validity of a contract because a challenge on the validity of the underlying contract simultaneously challenges the validity of an arbitration agreement.[3] Limited separability was adopted in some early authorities, distinguishing arguments between the initio invalidity or inexistence of a contract, and the latter repudiation or frustration of a

2 *UR Power v Kuok Ails* [2009] 1 Lloyd's Rep 495, 503; *Novasen S.A. v Alimenta S.A.* 2011 EWHC 49 [Comm]; *Scherk v Alberto-Culver Co* 417 US 506 (1974); *Mackender v Feldia AG* [1967] 2 QB 590; *Deutsche Bank AG v Asia Pacific Broadband Wireless Communications* [2008] EWCA (Civ) 1091, para 24; *Mackender v Feldia* [1967] 2 QB 590; *Fiona Trust v Privalov* [2008] 1 Lloyd's Rep 254; *Ryanair v Bravofly* [2009] ILPr 41.

3 *Johannesburg Municipal v D Stewart* 1909 SC(HL) 53; *Jureidini v National British and Irish Millers Insurance* [1915] AC 499; *Hirji Mulji v Cheong Yue Steamship* [1926] AC 497. *Halsbury's Laws of England*, (4th ed., 1991), para 612.

contract.[4] If a contract ceases to exist or is rendered unenforceable at a later stage, the dispute resolution clause in the contract continues to have effect;[5] if the contract is *void ab initio*, so is the dispute resolution agreement.[6] The logic of the orthodox view is 'nothing can come from nothing'.[7] However, the justification is later criticized as failing to construe the meaning and coverage of an arbitration agreement.[8] Even if the parties have intention to have 'everything' arising out of their relationship submitted to arbitration, including the alleged initio invalidity or non-existence of a main contract, their intention cannot survive if the contract is *void ab initio*.[9]

English courts gradually adopt the doctrine of separability in full, by regarding a dispute resolution agreement 'a self-contained contract collateral to the containing contract'.[10] However, at the early stage, a 'construed intention' approach is adopted, under which the effect of a dispute resolution clause largely depends on the language used. For example, it is construed by some judges that an arbitration clause covering all disputes 'arising under' the contract does not show the parties have the intention to submit the *void ab initio* contract to arbitration, but a clause expressly covering disputes 'arising out of' the agreement does.[11] The House of Lords later said in *Fiona Trust v Privalov* that the language used to draft a dispute resolution clause was not decisive[12] because the different word made no difference in commercial practice.[13] While an underwriter drafts a standard term contract including an arbitration or jurisdiction clause, the underwriter will not consider the slightest difference between 'under' and 'out of'.[14] Based on this reason, a 'presumed intention' approach is established. It is presumed that, by inserting a dispute resolution clause, the parties have the intention to have all disputes in relation to their contract decided by the chosen forum irrespective of the invalidity of the main contract,[15] unless the parties explicitly state otherwise.[16]

4 *Heyman v Darwins* [1942] AC 356; *Harbour Assurance v Kansa General International Insurance* [1993] QB 701
5 *Heyman v Darwins.*
6 Ibid.
7 *Harbour Assurance v Kansa General*, 710.
8 Ibid., 711.
9 Ibid., 711.
10 Ibid., 711.
11 *Heyman v Darwins; Overseas Union Insurance v AA Mutual International Insurance* [1988] 2 Lloyd's Rep 63; *Fillite (Runcorn) v Aqua-Lift* (1989) 26 Con LR 66, 76; *MacKender v Feldia AG* [1967] 2 QB 590. *Cf Union of India v EB Aaby's Rederi A/S* [1975] AC 797.
12 [2007] 4 All ER 951, para 12.
13 Ibid.
14 Ibid.
15 Ibid., para 13. See the reference to German law, Decision of 27 February 1970 of the Federal Supreme Court of the Federal Republic of Germany (Bundesgerichtshof) (1970) 6 *Arbitration International* 79, 85.
16 *Vee Networks v Econet Wireless* [2005] 1 All ER (Comm) 303.

The 'presumed intention' approach saves the court effort in considering the specific language used by a dispute resolution agreement to decide whether the parties have intention to submit disputes on the very existence and initio validity of a contract to their chosen forum. The technical analysis of the language used is not realistic and may depart from the actual intention of the parties. This approach is certain, efficient and easy to apply; it is consistent with the commercial practice and reality. This approach is consistent with section 7 of the Arbitration Act 1996, which provides:[17]

> Unless otherwise agreed by the parties, an arbitration agreement which forms or was intended to form part of another agreement (whether or not in writing) shall not be regarded as invalid, non-existent or ineffective because that other agreement is invalid, or did not come into existence or has become ineffective, and it shall for that purpose be treated as a distinct agreement.

The English courts justify the doctrine of separability primarily on the grounds of party autonomy and commercial practicability. However, although the commercial parties, by entering a dispute resolution clause, have intention to submit their contractual disputes to the chosen forum, which will not be affected by the later frustration and repudiation, it is questionable whether such intention exists where the contract is not formed from the very beginning. Furthermore, a contract may be rendered *void ab initio* by different reasons, some of which concern the substance of the contract, such as the illegality of the transaction, and some of which concern the existence and quality of consent. Within the latter, difference exists between consent to the main contract terms and consent to the contract as a whole. If a contract is unenforceable, because a party is adduced into the contract by fraud, duress or undue influence relating to terms of price, delivery, quality and quantity of goods, it does not affect the intention of the parties to conclude the dispute resolution clause; if a party has no intention to enter into the contract at all but is forced to sign the agreement under duress, the duress also taints the intention to enter into the dispute resolution clause. The doctrine of separability could provide practical convenience for a court to decide a dispute, but separating a dispute resolution clause from the main contract is not always a realistic option.

17 Although there is no domestic legislation confirming the same approach is applicable to jurisdiction agreements, the English courts rule that the same treatment should be used for the choice of jurisdiction. *Deutsche Bank v Asia Pacific Broadband Wireless*, [2009] ILPr 36.

2.3 Doctrine of separability in the European law

The doctrine of separability has been accepted in the EU. The ECJ affirmed the doctrine of separability in *Benincasa v Dentalkit*.[18] Mr Benincasa and a company entered into a franchising contract, which contained an exclusive choice of court agreement choosing Italian courts. Benincasa later brought proceedings in Germany seeking to declare the franchising contract void under German law. He claimed that the choice of court clause could derogate German courts of jurisdiction because the action was to declare the main contract void, including the jurisdiction clause as a contract term. The German court referred the question to the ECJ for the clarification as to whether the court of a Member State designated in an exclusive jurisdiction clause under the Brussels Convention (precedent of the Brussels I Regulation) had exclusive jurisdiction when the action was for a declaration of the invalidity of the main contract.[19] The ECJ answered the question by applying the principle of separability. The ECJ drew a distinction between a jurisdiction clause and other substantive contractual provisions.[20] The former served a procedural purpose and was governed exclusively by the uniform jurisdiction rules of the Brussels Convention, while the latter was governed by the lex causae.[21] The invalidity of the underlying contract may not mean the invalidity of a jurisdiction clause given the different applicable law. Furthermore, the aim of legal certainty requires the seized court to decide its jurisdiction without having to consider the substance of the case.[22] This requires the court not to consider the validity of the contract before deciding whether or not to take jurisdiction. This purpose, however, would be jeopardized if one party simply claimed the contract was void and was permitted to sue in a non-chosen forum.[23] The doctrine of separability is further ascertained in the Brussels I Recast; Article 25(5) expressly provides that:

> an agreement conferring jurisdiction which forms part of a contract shall be treated as an agreement independent of the other terms of the contract. The validity of the agreement conferring jurisdiction cannot be contested solely on the ground that the contract is not valid.

18 Case C-269/95, *Benincasa v Dentalkit* [1997] ECR I-3767.
19 Ibid.
20 Para 24.
21 Para 25.
22 Para 27.
23 Para 29. Prorogation jurisdiction 'sets out to designate, clearly and precisely, a court in a Contracting State which is to have exclusive jurisdiction in accordance with the consensus formed between the parties, which is to be expressed in accordance with the strict requirements as to form laid down therein. The legal certainty which that provision seeks to secure could easily be jeopardised if one party to the contract could frustrate that rule of the Convention simply by claiming that the whole of the contract was void on grounds derived from the applicable substantive law.' For comments, see Purdie, 2008: 1489; Harris, 1998: 279.

2.4 Doctrine of separability in the USA

Most modern US cases adopt the doctrine of separability to all types of dispute resolution agreements unless the clauses express to the contrary.[24] The doctrine of separability in the US is first accepted in arbitration agreements. US courts traditionally treated an arbitration agreement severable from the main contract in order to, ironically, invalidate the arbitration agreement but enforce the terms of the main contract.[25] After the Federal Arbitration Act entered into force,[26] many courts used the doctrine of separability to enforce an arbitration agreement in an alleged invalid contract based on the federal policy to promote arbitration.[27] The doctrine of separability is later extended to jurisdiction clauses by the liberal and flexible interpretation of the judgment in *Bremen v Zapata*.[28] The *Bremen* case states that a choice of forum clause is effective if it is freely negotiated and unaffected by fraud.[29] This decision is interpreted by some courts to mean that a dispute resolution clause is unenforceable only if the clause itself, instead of the main contract, is the product of fraud or coercion.[30]

However, the US courts do not unanimously adopt the doctrine of separability to all jurisdiction clauses. Some courts use a 'consent test' by enquiring 'whether the parties assented to all the promises as a single whole, so that there would have been no bargain whatever, if any promise or set of promises were struck out'.[31] Others consider the whole circumstances of the case to decide if the parties have real intention to submit the claim challenging the main contract to the chosen forum. In *eBay v*

24 *Robert Lawrence v Devonshire Fabrics* 271 F.2d 402 (CA2 1959); *Watkins v Hudson Coal* 151 F.2d 311 (3 Cir 1945); *Petition of Prouvost Lefebvre* 102 F. Supp 757 (1952); *Kulukundis Shipping v Amtorg Trading* 126 F.2d 987 (2 Cir 1942); *Almacenes Fernandez v Golodetz*, 148 F.2d 625; *In re Pahlberg Petition*, 131 F.2d 968 (2 Cir 1942); *Arnold v Goldstar Financial Systems*, 2002 WL 1941546 (N.D.Ill 2002); *Haynsworth v Corporation*, 121 F.3d 956, 964 (C.A.5 (Tex) 1997); *Robert Lawrence v Devonshire Fabrics*, 410; *Intecall Telecommunication v Instant Impact*, 376 F. Supp. 2d 155, 160 (D.Puerto Rico, 2005); *Curran v Radiaguard Intern*, 2009 WWL 276793 (D.Puerto Rico, 2009); *Mitsui & Co (USA) v Mira*, 111 F.3d 33 (C.A.5 (La) 1997). Force 2011: 413.

25 *Hamilton v Hoe Insurance* 137 US 370 (1890); *US Asphalt Refining v Trinidad Lake Petroleum*, 222 F 1006 (1915).

26 It was established in 1925. *Robert Lawrence*; *Watkins v Hudson Coal*; *Petition of Prouvost Lefebvre*; *Kulukundis Shipping*; *Almacenes Fernandez v Golodetz*; *In re Pahlberg Petition*; *Arnold v Goldstar Financial Systems*; *Haynsworth v Corporation*.

27 *Robert Lawrence*; Cf. *Prima Paint v Flood & Conklin Mfg*, 388 US 395, 421 (US NY 1967).

28 *Bremen v Zapata*, 407 US 1 (1972). *Intecall Telecommunication*; *Curran v Radiaguard Intern*; *Mitsui & Co (USA) v Mira*.

29 407 US 1, 13.

30 *Scherk v Alberto*, 417 US 506, 519 (1974).

31 *US v Bethlehem Steel* 315 US 289, 298 (1942); *Lichter v US*, 68 S.Ct 1294, 1302 (US.Cal. 1948); *Hellenic Linces v Louis Dreyfus* 372 F.2d 753, 756 (2nd Cir. (NY) 1967); *Weaver v American Oil* 276 NE2d 144, 147 (Ind. 1971); *Muschany v US*, 65 S.Ct 442, 447 (1945); *Whitin Machine v US*, 175 F.2d 504, 507 (1st Cir. (Mass) 1949); *First Nat Bank v Pepper*, 454 F.2d 626, 636 (2nd Cir. (NY) 1972).

Digital Point Solutions,[32] the court refused to apply the doctrine of separability when the dispute was on whether the defendant was a party to the contract. The court distinguished the challenge to the very existence of a contract from the challenge to the invalidity of a contract. If a contract was invalid due to fraud, it did not invalidate the parties' intention to have all disputes between them submitted to the chosen forum; if a contract did not exist at all, there was no such intention between the parties.

2.5 Doctrine of separability in Chinese law

PRC Arbitration Law 1994 explicitly adopts the doctrine of separability for the arbitration agreement. It states that the arbitration agreement is independent from the main contract. The termination or invalidity of the main contract does not affect the validity of an arbitration agreement.[33] The position has been restated in the Supreme People's Court in its Interpretation Concerning Some Issues on Application of the Arbitration Law of PRC.[34]

Chinese law, however, does not contain any provisions granting the doctrine of separability to choice of court agreements. Neither is there any judicial direction provided by the Supreme People's Court. However, such a position can be implied in some courts' practice. First of all, most Chinese courts apply the *lex fori* to decide the validity of a jurisdiction clause, instead of the *lex causae*.[35] It shows these courts have treated jurisdiction clauses separately from other contract terms. By applying different applicable law, the validity of the jurisdiction clause may not follow the validity of the main contract. Second, some Chinese courts have classified jurisdiction clauses' procedural issues.[36] This position may not be theoretically sound, but it clearly distinguishes the jurisdiction clause from the

32 2009 WL 2523733 (N.D.Cal 2009).

33 Art 19(1).

34 [2006] No 7, Art 10.

35 *Shandong Jufeng v Korea Mgame*, Supreme People's Court, (2009) No 4; Supreme People's Court, 'Annual Report of Intellectual Property Cases in the Supreme Court (2009)', [2010] No 173, case 44. Cf. *The Sumitomo Bank Ltd v Xinhua Estate*, Supreme Court, (1999) No 194.

36 *Shandong Jufeng v Mgame*; Supreme People's Court, 'Answers to economic disputes relating to Hong Kong or Macau', [1987] No 28, Art 3(1) and (2); Guangdong Province High People's Court, 'Notice on Issues about Deciding the Five Intermediate Courts of Guangzhou Municipality on the Territorial Jurisdiction and Jurisdiction by Forum Level on Civil and Commercial Matters Relating to Hong Kong and Macau', [2002] No 191, Art 13; *China Point Finance Ltd v Zhuhai City Commercial Bank*, Guangdong Province High People's Court, (2004) No 263; *Zhongshan Shishen v Auli*, Guangdong Province High People's Court, (2004) No 239.

underlying contract.[37] Since the doctrine of separability has not been firmly established in law, in practice, some courts might fail to treat a jurisdiction clause as a separate agreement from the main contract.

2.6 Conclusion

The doctrine of separability is justified on the grounds of respecting the parties' intention,[38] protecting legal certainty,[39] promoting international comity[40] and facilitating the effectiveness of the dispute resolution clause.[41] No matter which reason is adopted, the doctrine of separability eventually shows the importance of practicability and pragmatism in cross-border dispute resolution. It can simplify litigation procedure, reduce cost and time in arguing jurisdiction, and provide certainty and predictability. However, it has to be admitted that this approach is sound in practice but not in theory. The doctrine of separability is based on a 'presumption' that a dispute resolution clause is independent from the main contract. Nevertheless, a dispute resolution clause is, as a matter of fact, integrated part of the underlying contract. It is concluded during the same procedure and in the same backgrounds with the main contract. If one party did not give authentic consent to the main contract, nor did he to the jurisdiction clause; if one party is incapable of expressing consent at the time of contracting, he cannot consent the jurisdiction clause either; where the total context for the conclusion of the contract is so unconscionable that it makes the contract invalid, so is the jurisdiction clause as a contract term. Although some countries provide extra validity requirements to a dispute resolution clause,[42] these additional requirements only make such a clause more easily invalidated than the main contract.

3 The doctrine of *kompetenz-kompetenz*

In a contract with a dispute resolution agreement, the doctrine of *kompetenz-kompetenz* specifically means the chosen forum should have the

37 Jurisdiction agreements relate to procedure but they are different from pure procedure. They are agreements concluded by parties. Although there are additional rules concerning their enforceability, the existence and validity of jurisdiction clauses are subject to contract principles.

38 *Fiona Trust v Privalov*. Rosen, 1994: 607.

39 *Benincasa*.

40 *Mitsubishi Motors v Soler Chrysler-Plymouth*.

41 *Mitsubishi Motors v Soler Chrysler-Plymouth*. Rosen, 1994: 607.

42 For example, in China, jurisdiction clauses must be in writing, while a contract can be concluded orally.

competence to decide its own jurisdiction.[43] There is a logic circle in the application of the doctrine of *kompetenz-kompetenz*.[44] Where the existence and validity of party autonomy is under challenge, the doctrine of *kompetenz-kompetenz* requires the chosen forum to presume, first of all, the valid consent exists, and to take jurisdiction based upon the presumption. If the chosen forum, after taking jurisdiction, finds the dispute resolution agreement invalid, it will decline jurisdiction in hearing the substance of the dispute. However, the decision cannot affect the fact that jurisdiction has already been taken to decide the validity of the dispute resolution clause. The resisting party has been prejudiced by being forced to attend the proceedings in a forum not agreed upon by him. Nevertheless, the doctrine of *kompetenz-kompetenz* is fundamental and inherent to civil procedure of every country. Without this doctrine, a court can never decide jurisdiction and assert a dispute.[45] No country will prevent its court from deciding its own competence under a dispute resolution clause.

The doctrine of *kompetenz-kompetenz*, however, cannot preclude conflicts of jurisdiction, parallel proceedings and irreconcilable decisions. Countries also permit their courts, if competent otherwise, to decide the preliminary issue of the dispute resolution agreement. A broad application of *kompetenz-kompetenz*, or negative *kompetenz-kompetenz*, requiring the dispute on the preliminary issue of a dispute resolution agreement to be decided exclusively by the chosen forum, may prevent the conflict of jurisdiction.[46] Pursuant to the negative *kompetenz-kompetenz* a non-chosen forum that is competent otherwise should always refer the dispute on the existence, validity and scope of the dispute resolution agreement to the chosen forum. However, the negative *kompetenz-komptenz* is barely adopted by any countries.[47]

Examining the application of the doctrine of *kompetenz-kompetenz* in dispute resolution clauses requires one to consider four issues: first, is the chosen forum competent to decide its own jurisdiction where the existence, validity and scope of the dispute resolution clause are under challenge? Second, if the chosen forum is competent to rule on its own jurisdiction, does it preclude other fora from taking jurisdiction to decide the same issue at the adjudication stage? Third, if both the chosen forum and the seized forum take jurisdiction to decide the preliminary questions

43 Rosen, 1994: 608. Two reasons are provided to support the doctrine: (1) there is a rebuttable presumption that the parties have intention to grant the chosen forum jurisdiction to decide arguments on the dispute resolution clause; (2) the doctrine is inherent in all judicial organs to permit them to function well. There is no reason to deprive this power in cases with dispute resolution agreements.

44 Schlosser, 1992: 203.

45 Fraterman, 2011: 913–914.

46 Inoue, 2006: 178; McLachlan, 2008: 233–234; Walt, 1999: 375–376.

47 Even where there is judicial cooperation, such as the Brussels I Regulation and the Hague Convention on Choice of Court Agreements, the negative *kompetenz-kompetenz* is not accepted.

at the adjudication stage, which forum has priority? Fourth, if a non-chosen forum does not take jurisdiction to decide the preliminary issue at the adjudication stage, does it have the power to review this issue at the recognition and enforcement stage?

3.1 Kompetenz-kompetenz *in jurisdiction agreements*

Competence of the chosen court

Every country accepting the prorogation power of a jurisdiction agreement does not prevent the chosen court from taking jurisdiction to decide its own jurisdiction. Based on party autonomy, there is a rebuttable presumption that the parties would wish all disputes, including the dispute on the existence of the valid jurisdiction clause, to be heard by the chosen court. This presumption is adopted for the purpose of commercial convenience. The claimant may submit a few claims in relation to one contract and the parties would not have the intention to split the procedure by submitting different issues to different courts.

Competence of the non-chosen forum

Most countries do not provide the chosen forum exclusive jurisdiction to decide the existence and validity of a jurisdiction clause. Even though the jurisdiction clause is exclusive in nature, a non-chosen forum, if competent under other jurisdiction grounds, is still entitled to decide the preliminary issues. When a non-chosen court is seized by the claimant to hear a case with a foreign jurisdiction clause, this court will usually not directly refer the parties to the chosen court, but decide, first of all, whether the jurisdiction clause is valid.[48] The doctrine of *kompetenz-kompetenz* also

48 English cases: *Mackender v Feldia AG.* [1967] 2 QB 590 (English courts decided the validity of a Belgium jurisdiction clause); *Dubai Electricity v Islamic Republic of Iran Shipping Lines (The Iran Vojdan)* [1984] 2 Lloyd's Rep 380 (deciding whether a German jurisdiction clause is valid under German law); *Trendtex Trading v Credit Suisse* [1980] QB 628 (English court decided whether to stay jurisdiction in favour of an exclusive Geneva jurisdiction clause and whether the clause was valid). Chinese cases: *Shandong Jufeng v Korea Mgame*, the Supreme Court, (2009) No 4 (Chinese court decided whether a Singapore jurisdiction clause was valid under Chinese law [*lex fori*]); *Lai v Abn Amro Bank*, Shanghai Municipality High Court, (2010) No 49 (Shanghai court decided whether an exclusive jurisdiction clause choosing Hong Kong court was valid). US cases: *Bremen v Zapata*, 407 US 1 (1972); *Wong v PartyGaming* 589 F.3d 821 (C.A.6 (Ohio), 2009) (Court of Appeals Sixth Circuit [Ohio] decided whether the clause choosing Gibraltar was valid); *Krendel v KerznerIntern Hotels*, 579 F.3d 1279 (C.A.11(Fla) 2009) (Florida courts considered whether a jurisdiction clause choosing the court of Bahamas was reasonably communicated to the consumers); *Braspetro Oil v Modec (USA)* 240 Fed.Appx 612 (C.A.5 (Tex) 2007) (Texas court decided whether the Brazil jurisdiction clause was invalid under US law); *Abbott Laboratories v Takeda Pharmaceutical* 476 F.3d 421 (C.A.7 (Ill) 2007) (Illinois court decided the validity of a jurisdiction clause choosing Japanese courts).

provides the non-chosen forum the competence to decide its own jurisdiction. Without judicial cooperation, there is no reason to expect a non-chosen court to give up its judicial capacity and to rely on the decision of the chosen court.

Although judicial cooperation creates a context where the negative *kompetenz-kompetenz* is possible to be adopted between the Contracting States, it is not adopted in either the EU or the Hague Convention. Under the Hague Convention on Choice of Court Agreements 2005, both the chosen court and the non-chosen court have the competence to decide the validity of a jurisdiction clause. Article 5(1) provides that:

> The court or courts of a Contracting State designated in an exclusive choice of court agreement shall have jurisdiction to decide a dispute to which the agreement applies, unless the agreement is null and void under the law of that State.

It means the chosen court could use its own domestic law, including choice of law, to decide whether a jurisdiction clause is valid as to substance. Article 6 further provides that a non-chosen court shall stay or dismiss proceedings in favour of the chosen court unless the jurisdiction agreement is invalid under the law of the chosen court,[49] a party is incapable to conclude a jurisdiction clause under the law of the seized court,[50] the enforcement of the jurisdiction clause leads to a manifest injustice or would be manifestly contrary to its public policy,[51] or the agreement cannot be enforced for unexpected reasons.[52] It suggests that a non-chosen court, if seized by the claimant, also has the power to decide whether the foreign jurisdiction clause is valid or unenforceable. During the negotiation of the Hague Convention, the delegates felt that the practice to permit any seized court to decide the preliminary questions of a jurisdiction clause should be changed only if different decisions would be given by different courts seized, which jeopardizes consistency and predictability.[53] Since the Convention provides uniform rules on formal validity and partially harmonizes choice of law rules to decide the substantive validity,[54] the level of harmonization can largely reduce the inconsistent results. There is no need to introduce negative *kompetenz-kompetenz* to the Convention, which may be too radical and may prevent many countries from signing or ratifying the Hague Convention.

In the EU, the current Brussels I Regulation does not clarify which court is competent to hear the dispute on the preliminary questions of an

49 Art 6(a).
50 Art 6(b).
51 Art 6(c).
52 Art 6(d).
53 Schulz, 2002b: 11.
54 Arts 5 and 6 of the Hague Convention.

exclusive jurisdiction clause either. Under the civil law tradition, a court that has jurisdiction granted by law should not decline exercising it without the legislative support. Pursuant to the civil law tradition, if a Member State has jurisdiction under any grounds of the Brussels I Regulation and the Regulation does not include a provision to permit the competent forum to stay or decline jurisdiction, it cannot decline jurisdiction by using its discretion. The presence of an exclusive jurisdiction clause does not prevent a non-chosen Member State from taking jurisdiction to decide the existence and validity of this clause, given this Member State is competent under other jurisdictional grounds of the Brussels I Regulation. In *Gasser v MISAT*,[55] an Austrian company and an Italian company entered into a contract allegedly containing an exclusive jurisdiction clause choosing the Austrian courts. After disputes arose, the Italian company questioned the existence and validity of this jurisdiction clause and brought an action in Italy. The Austrian company subsequently sued in Austria based on the jurisdiction clause. The ECJ recognizes that the Italian court, though not chosen in the agreement, has jurisdiction to decide the preliminary issue of the jurisdiction clause.[56] It is true that under the current law the EU has only accepted *kompetenz-kompetenz* in a narrow sense. Any court, including the chosen court and an otherwise competent court, can take jurisdiction to decide the existence and validity of an exclusive jurisdiction clause.

Broad *kompetenz-kompetenz*, or negative *kompetenz-kompeetenz*, however, is adopted in the Brussels I Regulation to decide the preliminary issues of a jurisdiction clause entered into between the parties domiciled in non-EU countries choosing one of the Member States as the competent court. Article 23(3) of the Brussels I Regulation provides that, in such circumstances, 'the courts of other Member States shall have no jurisdiction over their disputes unless the court or courts chosen have declined jurisdiction'. This type of jurisdiction clause falls outside the uniform jurisdiction rules of the Brussels I Regulation, which only applies to jurisdiction clauses concluded by at least one EU domiciliary and one of the Member States is chosen. The possible explanation for the different treatments to jurisdiction clauses within and outside the scope of the Brussels I Regulation is that, where a jurisdiction clause is outside of the regulation of Brussels I, each Member State uses its domestic rule to decide the exclusivity, validity and existence of the jurisdiction clause.[57] Inconsistent judgments are likely to be given by different Member States. If a jurisdiction clause is within the scope of Brussels I, there are uniform rules to decide its formal validity,

55 Case C-116/02 *Gasser v MISAT* [2003] ECR 14693.

56 The most important decision of the *Gasser* case is not the competence to decide the preliminary question of a jurisdiction clause, but the priority between different courts when seized to make decision.

57 Art 4(1).

exclusivity and enforceability. Although discrepancy still exists in issues such as material validity, uniform decisions are expected to be achievable in most cases.[58] The negative *kompetenz-kompetenz* adopted in Article 23(3) is so strong that it excludes all non-chosen Member States the competence to decide the preliminary issue of a jurisdiction clause even if the jurisdiction clause is non-exclusive in nature. Applying the negative *kompetenz-kompetenz* rule to non-exclusive jurisdiction clauses is controversial, which can hardly be justified in terms of commercial certainty and party autonomy. Furthermore, Article 23(3) cannot completely prevent parallel proceedings from arising. Since the Brussels I Regulation cannot bind any third countries, a non-chosen third country still can take jurisdiction under its domestic law to examine the chosen Member State's jurisdiction.

The negative *kompetenz-kompetenz* doctrine is not adopted in the Brussels I Recast either. Although Article 29(2) provides that, if the court chosen in an exclusive jurisdiction clause is seized, other courts shall stay jurisdiction until the chosen court makes decision on its competence. It means that if the chosen court is not seized to decide the validity of a jurisdiction clause, courts of other Member States are competent to decide this issue. Non-chosen courts only have the obligation to stay jurisdiction in cases, where both the non-chosen and the chosen courts are seized, in order to avoid parallel proceedings in deciding the preliminary issue.

Conflict of jurisdiction between the chosen and non-chosen forum

Since the negative *kompetenz-kompetenz* in jurisdiction clauses is not adopted, where the parties have disagreement on the preliminary issues of a jurisdiction clause, there may be parallel proceedings. Suppose a US company and a UK company agreed that all disputes arising out of their contract should be heard exclusively by the English courts. The UK company brought the action in England according to the jurisdiction clause, while the US company commenced proceedings in the US, challenging the existence and validity of the jurisdiction clause. Both countries have jurisdiction to decide the preliminary issue and both may proceed to give judgments.

Many countries have adopted some instruments to prevent concurrent proceedings. In common law countries, a court can use *forum non conveniens* to stay jurisdiction in favour of a foreign court if the court is satisfied that the foreign court will be a more appropriate forum and it is in the

58 Especially when the interpretation to the formal validity is very broad, which covers issues beyond a written form and examines the authentic consent of the parties. See e.g. Case 24/76 *Estasis Salotti v RUWA* [1976] ECR 1831; *Galeries Segoura v FA Rahim Bonakdarian*[1976] ECR 1851; *Credit Suisse Financial Products v Société Generale d'Enterprises* [1997] CLC 168 CA; *7E Communications Ltd v Vertex Antennentechnik GmbH* [2007] 1 WLR 2175; Case 221/84, *Berghoefer GmbH & Co v ASA SA* [1985] ECR 2699.

interest of justice to do so;[59] a court can also issue an anti-suit injunction restraining a party from continuing or commencing proceedings in another country if the foreign proceedings are vexatious or oppressive.[60] It is relatively easy to satisfy an English court that it should exercise its discretion to stay jurisdiction if there is a valid exclusive jurisdiction clause choosing a foreign country, or to issue an anti-suit injunction if the English court is granted exclusive jurisdiction by the agreement.[61] However, the presence of a jurisdiction clause cannot automatically generate *forum non conveniens* or anti-suit injunctions. Before a court can make such decisions, it should satisfy that such a jurisdiction clause does exist and is valid. *Forum non conveniens* and anti-suit injunctions can only tackle parallel proceedings in deciding the substance of a dispute, but cannot prevent concurrent proceedings from deciding the existence and validity of a jurisdiction clause.

The conflict of jurisdiction in deciding the preliminary issue of a jurisdiction clause cannot be prevented by the unilateral approach such as *forum non conveniens* and anti-suit injunctions, which do not establish priority between different competent courts. The order of priority is usually provided between the countries with judicial cooperation. In the EU, judicial cooperation and mutual trust are established between the Member States, and the order of priority in deciding the existence and validity of a jurisdiction clause is created by the doctrine of *lis pendens. Lis pendens*

59 See Fawcett and Carruthers, 2008: 426–455; *Spiliada Maritime v Cansulex*, [1987] AC 460; *Connelly v RTZ* [1998] AC 854; *Lubbe v Cape* [2001] 1 WLR 1545; *Cherney v Deripaska* [2010] 2 All ER (Comm) 456; *Novus Aviation v Onur Air Tasimacilik* [2009] 1 Lloyd's Rep 576; *Chadha v Dow Jones* [1999] ILPr 829; *Askin v Absa Bank* [1999] ILPr 471; *Vao Exportkhleb v Navigation Maritime Bulgare (No 2)* [1994] 2 Lloyd's Rep 41; *Hamed el Chiaty v Thomas Cook* [1994] 1 Lloyd's Rep 382; *Re Harrods (Buenos Aires)* [1991] 4 All ER 335; *Irish Shipping v Commercial Union Assurance* [1990] 2 WLR 117; *Holmes v Holmes* [1989] 3 WLR 302.

60 *Airbus Industries v Patel* [1999] 1 AC 119; *Continental Bank v Aeakos Compania Naviere* [1994] 2 All ER 540; *General Star International Indemnity v Stirling Cooke Brown Reinsurance Brokers* [2003] ILPr 19; *Lubb v Cape* [2000] 1 WLR 1545; *Donohue v Armco* [2002] 1 All ER 749; *Kuwait Oil Tanker v Qabazard* [2004] 1 AC 300; *Sabah Shipyard v Pakistan* [2003] 2 Lloyd's Rep 571; *Royal Bank of Canada v Cooperative Centrale Raiffeisen-Boerenleenbank BA* [2004] 2 All ER (Comm) 847; *Jameel v Dow Jones* [2005] QB 946; *OT Africa Line v Magic Sportswear* [2006] 1 All ER (Comm) 32; *Seismic Shipping v Total E&P* [2005] 2 All ER (Comm) 515; *Grovit v De Nederlandsche Bank* [2008] 1 All ER (Comm) 106; *Kolden Holdings v Rodette Commerce* [2008] 3 All ER 612; *Glaxo Group v Genentech* [2008] Bus LR 888; *Masri v Consolidated Contractors International Co* [2009] QB 503; *Elektrim v Vivendi Holdings* [2009] 2 All ER (Comm) 213; *Deutsche Bank v Highland Crusader Offshore Partners* [2010] 1 WLR 1023.

61 *Koonmen v Bender* [2007] WTLR 293; *Breams Trustees v Upstream Downstream Simulation Services* [2004] EWHC 211 (Ch); *Limit v PDV Insurance* [2005] 2 All ER (Comm) 347; *Dornoch v Mauritius Union Assurance* [2006] 2 All ER (Comm) 385; *HIT Entertainment v Gaffney International Licensing* [2007] EWHC 1282 (Ch); *Donohue v Armco; Sabah Shipyard v Pakistan; American International Specialty v Abbott Laboratories* [2003] 1 Lloyd's Rep 267; *Welex v Rosa Maritime ((No 2)* [2003] 2 CLC 207; *Royal Bank of Canada; OT Africa Line; Advent Capital v GN Ellinas* [2005] 1 CLC 1058; *Samengo-Turner v J&H Marsh & McLennan* [2007] 2 All ER (Comm) 813.

establishes the order of priority between the competent courts depending on the chronological order in which the court is seized to hear the dispute.[62] The second seized court must, by its own motion, stay jurisdiction in favour of the court first seized in deciding the same cause of action between the same parties. In the *Gasser* case,[63] the non-chosen Italian court was seized first to make a negative declaration of the existence of a valid Austrian exclusive jurisdiction clause. The Austrian court, which was chosen by the parties but seized second in time, must stay jurisdiction and wait for the Italian court to make decision.[64] It means that, under the current Brussels I Regulation, the non-chosen court not only has the competence to decide the preliminary issue of a jurisdiction clause, but also may take priority over the chosen court if the non-chosen court is seized earlier to make decision.[65]

The Hague Convention, on the other hand, completely leaves the priority issue undetermined. No court is obliged to give priority to another when it is seized to decide the preliminary issue of the same jurisdiction clause. This could sometimes lead to inconsistent decisions.[66] The Hague Convention deals with the inconsistency at the recognition stage, by making the chosen forum's decision decisive. In other words, if the non-chosen court decides the jurisdiction clause invalid, while the chosen court holds it valid, the recognition court should enforce the chosen court's decision.[67] As a result, when a non-chosen court is seized to answer the preliminary question while the same issue is pending in the chosen court, the non-chosen court, by considering the possible effect of recognition and enforcement of judgment, and the efficient management of cost and administration of judicial resources, might voluntarily stay jurisdiction.

Recognition and enforcement of judgments, however, cannot offer a perfect solution. First, staying jurisdiction depends on the motive of a non-chosen court and is not compulsory. If a non-chosen court continues jurisdiction, nothing could prevent it from doing so. The judgment cannot be recognized in the recognition country, but the procedure itself leads to burden, inconvenience and cost to the resisting party. Second, there is a possibility that the non-chosen country will be the requested country to recognize and enforce the judgment. The Hague Convention requires the

62 Art 27(1) of the Brussels I Regulation.

63 Case C-116/02 *Gasser v MISAT* [2003] ECR 14693.

64 Ibid.

65 For criticisms, see Fentiman, 2006; Hartley, 2005; Mance, 2004; Hartley, 2009: 255; Simons, 2003; Sifakis, 2006: 307–312; Hueske, 2009: 433; Clarke, 2007: 105, 124; Kulpers, 2009: 1510–1516.

66 For example, the jurisdiction clause is valid under the law of the chosen country, but it is invalid because one of the parties has no capacity to conclude this agreement under the law of a seized non-chosen country.

67 Arts 8(1) and 9(a).

requested court to recognize the chosen court's decision if the chosen court has determined the agreement valid,[68] but recognition can be denied if a party lacks capacity under the law of the requested country to conclude the jurisdiction clause,[69] or recognition would be manifestly incompatible with the public policy of this country.[70] This provides ground for the non-chosen court to continue jurisdiction. Furthermore, the recognition country may be a non-Contracting State of the Hague Convention.

Review at the recognition stage

In the Brussels I Regulation, a court, either chosen or non-chosen, should have no competence to review the basis of jurisdiction at the recognition stage.[71] That means, if a party has sued in a non-chosen Member State challenging the validity of a jurisdiction clause falling in Article 23(1) of the Brussels I Regulation, and the seized Member State makes decision denying the validity of such a clause, this decision is automatically enforceable in other Member States. If the recognition court is the chosen court, and if the chosen court may reach a different decision on the validity of the jurisdiction clause, the chosen court has no power to challenge the decision of the non-chosen court at the recognition stage. Based on the strict application of *lis pendens* rule in the *Gasser* case, within the context of the EU, a non-chosen Member State, if seized first, could provide decision on the validity of a jurisdiction clause choosing another Member State, and the chosen Member State, while being seized second, must stay jurisdiction. Once the first seized court makes decision to take jurisdiction by holding the jurisdiction clause invalid, the chosen court must dismiss the case even though it might decide otherwise. After the first seized court gives judgment, the judgment will be recognized and enforced in the chosen Member State.

The power of review, however, partially exists in the Hague Convention. Article 8(1) of the Hague Convention provides:

> A judgment given by a court of a Contracting State designated in an exclusive choice of court agreement shall be recognized and enforced in other Contracting States … Recognition or enforcement may be refused only on the grounds specified in this Convention.

The grounds to refuse recognizing the judgment given by the chosen state are provided in Article 9, one of which is that 'the agreement was null and void under the law of the State of the chosen court, unless the chosen

68 Arts 8(1) and 9(a).
69 Art 9(b). Hartley and Dogauchi, 2007: para 183–184.
70 Art 9(e).
71 Arts 32 and 33 of the Brussels I Regulation.

court has determined that the agreement is valid'. It means that if the chosen Contracting State decides that the jurisdiction clause is valid and gives the judgment to the substance of the case, a requested Contracting State must enforce the judgment.[72] The chosen state's decision upholding the validity is unreviewable at the recognition stage. However, if the chosen court directly takes jurisdiction to decide the substance of the dispute without examining the validity of the jurisdiction clause, a requested court is allowed to review this issue by applying the law of the chosen country at the recognition stage. Furthermore, whether or not the chosen court has made the decision on the validity of the jurisdiction clause does not prevent the requested Contracting State from reviewing the capacity of the parties in concluding this agreement under the law of the requested state.[73]

The Hague Convention does not provide any rule in recognizing and enforcing the judgment delivered by a non-chosen Contracting State. If a non-chosen Contracting State decided that a jurisdiction clause is invalid because a party is incapable of concluding such an agreement under its domestic law and gave the judgment on the substance of the case, the requested Contracting State is not required to recognize the judgment. Recognition and enforcement of the judgment fall outside of the scope of the Hague Convention and the requested state should rely on its domestic law to decide whether it should review the validity of the jurisdiction clause and whether to enforce the judgment of the non-chosen state.

3.2 **Kompetenz-kompetenz** *in arbitration agreements*

The application of *kompetenz-kompetenz* is more complicated in arbitration. An arbitration clause designates a private tribunal to the exclusion of the competence of a court. In the old days, it was contrary to public policy to permit the parties to grant a private organ the power superseding a court. In both the US and the UK, arbitration clauses were treated unfavourably.[74] Arbitration is now accepted as one of the most popular alternative dispute resolution methods in transnational commerce, and it is established in both international instruments and domestic law that a court shall stay jurisdiction or refer the parties to arbitration if a valid arbitration agreement exists.[75] However, the power of an arbitrator to decide its own jurisdiction is nevertheless more restrictive than that of a court. A court has inherent power generated from state sovereignty to examine its jurisdiction. An arbitral tribunal has all its competence stemmed from party

72 Art 9(a).
73 Art 9(b).
74 Rosen, 1994: 617 and 628; Korn, 1991: 74; *Dean Witter Reynold v Byrd*, 470 US 213, 219–221 (1985).
75 Art II.3 of the New York Convention; Art 8(1) of the UNCITRAL Model Law.

autonomy and the effect of party autonomy usually needs to be verified by authorities, namely the court.[76] The doctrine of *kompetenz-kompetenz* in arbitration permits a tribunal to rule on its own competence,[77] but a supervisory court has inherent power to supervise and review the tribunal's decision.

Competence of arbitral tribunals and supervisory courts

Although the New York Convention does not expressly provide that an arbitral tribunal has the competence to decide its jurisdiction, the doctrine of *kompetenz-kompetenz* is expressly accepted in both the UNCITRAL Model Law[78] and the UNCITRAL Rule of Arbitration;[79] both provide that '(t)he arbitral tribunal may rule on its own jurisdiction, including any objections with respect to the existence or validity of the arbitration agreement'.

The arbitral tribunal's competence, however, is limited by the review power of the supervisory court. That means an arbitral tribunal's ruling on its jurisdiction may not be final.[80] In English law, the Arbitration Act 1996 provides that, unless the parties agree otherwise, an arbitral tribunal may rule on its own jurisdiction as to the validity and the scope of the arbitration agreement.[81] However, a person who does not take any steps in the arbitral proceedings can require the court to review the jurisdiction of the arbitral tribunal and apply for a negative declaration or an injunction preventing the other party from commencing or continuing arbitration.[82] Where arbitration is already in progress and both parties have taken part in the proceedings, the court has the power to review the arbitral tribunal's jurisdiction upon the application by both parties,[83] or with the permission of the arbitral tribunal, if the court is satisfied that taking jurisdiction is likely to save adjudication cost, the application is made promptly and there are good reasons to decide the issue by the court.[84] Furthermore, in *Excalibur Ventures v Texas Keystone*,[85] Globster J said that s30 of the Arbitration Act 1996 only permits but does not require an

76 For example, the USA refused to accept the doctrine of *kompetenz-kompetenz* in relation to arbitration for a long time. See Wyss, 1997; *Interocean v National Shipping and Trading* 462 F.2d 673, 676 (2d Cir. 1972); *Pollux Marine Agencies v Louis Dreyfus* 455 F. Supp. 211, 216–217 (S.D.N.Y. 1978).

77 *China Minmetals Materials Import and Export v Chi Mei*, 334 F.3d 274, 288, 9C.A.3 (N.J.) 2003.

78 Arts 16(2) and (3). Explanatory Note, para 26.

79 UNCITRAL Arbitration Rules (revised in 2010), Art 23.

80 Rosen, 1994: 635. *Harbour Assurance v Kansa General International*; Shine, 2008: 202.

81 s30(1). Departmental Advisory Committee Report on the Arbitration Bill 1996, para 137–139, cited in *Azov Shipping v Baltic Shipping (No 3)* [1999] CLC 1425.

82 72(1).

83 s32(2)(a).

84 s32(2)(b).

85 2011 EWHC 1624 (Comm). For more comments, see Holland, 2012: 81.

arbitral tribunal to decide its own jurisdiction.[86] The Act also 'does not require a party who maintains that there is no arbitration agreement to have the question decided by an arbitral tribunal'.[87]

In China, the challenge to the validity of an arbitration clause can be brought either to the chosen tribunal or to the people's court.[88] If the same challenge has been brought to both fora, priority should be given to the court.[89] Although China accepts the doctrine of *kompetenz-kompetenz* in arbitration agreements, the competence of an arbitral tribunal is superseded by that of a court.[90] However, if the arbitral tribunal has ruled on the validity of an arbitration agreement, the parties should not bring the same preliminary issue to the courts.[91] French law, however, provides more comprehensive authority to an arbitration tribunal.[92] Although judicial review is also available, a review on arbitrability can only be conducted after the arbitral procedure is completed, or before the commencement of such a procedure if the clause is obviously invalid.[93] The French courts frequently refuse jurisdiction in deciding the validity of a French arbitration agreement and refer the parties back to the arbitral tribunal.[94]

It is fair to say that the practice in different countries shares the similar component: restricted *kompetenz-kompetenz* is provided to arbitral tribunals. Although every tribunal is competent to decide the preliminary issue of an arbitration agreement, it is subject to judicial control.[95] Practice varies on the level of control permissible. However, there is no one regime that has adopted negative *kompetenz-kompetenz* to exclude the supervisory court's review power in arbitration.

Competence of a non-supervisory court to review a foreign tribunal's jurisdiction

A supervisory court usually has inherent power to review the jurisdiction of a tribunal seated in this country. The power of a non-supervisory court

86 Para 64.
87 Para 64.
88 Art 20 of the Arbitration Law of China.
89 Ibid.
90 Wang, 2009: 321; Zhao, 2006: 439.
91 Supreme People's Court, 'Interpretation of the Supreme People's Court concerning some issues on the application of the arbitration law of the People's Republic of China', 2006, Art 13.
92 Rosen, 1994: 638.
93 *China Minmetals Materials Import and Export*, 288; Rosen, 1994: 643–647; French Civil Procedure Code, Arts 1458 and 1466.
94 Rosen, 1994: 642–643; *Société Impex v Société PAZ*, 18 May 1971, Cass. Civ. 1re, 1971 Bull. Civ. I, No 161, at 134.
95 *China Minmetals Materials Import and Export*, 288; *Telenor Mobile Communications v Storm LLC*, 524 F. Supp. 2d 332, 351 (S.D.N.Y. 2007); UNCITRAL Model Law, Art 16; Walt 1999: 378.

to decide the primary issue of an arbitration agreement choosing foreign arbitration is more controversial. Neither the New York Convention nor the Model Law precludes the power of a foreign court from reviewing the competence of an arbitral tribunal. The review may exist where the parties have entered into an agreement choosing the arbitral tribunal seated in another country, but one party later submitted the dispute to a non-supervisory court that may otherwise have jurisdiction to hear the substance of the dispute, alleging the arbitration agreement invalid.

In England, the review power granted in s30 and s72 of the Arbitration Act 1996 does not apply when the English courts are non-supervisory courts.[96] An English court may take jurisdiction to decide the validity of an arbitration agreement choosing a foreign tribunal according to its jurisdiction rules.[97] In practice, the English court may nevertheless decide to stay jurisdiction under the doctrine of *forum non conveniens* because it is more appropriate for the supervisory court to review the competence of an arbitral tribunal.[98] In most cases, if the claimant applies for an English court to examine the validity of a foreign arbitration clause, the English court will be reluctant to do so based on the ground of *forum non conveniens*. The English courts, however, are more ready to take jurisdiction to examine a foreign tribunal's jurisdiction if the applicant argues that the arbitration agreement is not concluded at all between the parties. The English court in such cases will consider it inappropriate and unfair to send the applicant to a jurisdiction which it has never given consent to subject itself to. In *Albon v Naza Motor Trading*,[99] the English court took jurisdiction to decide the competence of a Malaysian tribunal because the claimant proved an arguable case that his signature to the arbitration agreement was forged; in *Excalibur Ventures v Texas Keystone*,[100] the English court took jurisdiction to decide whether the claimants were parties of the New York arbitration agreement; in *Claxton Engineering v TXM*,[101] the English court took jurisdiction where the applicant challenged the very existence of the arbitration agreement between the parties.

96 s2(1) and 2(2) of the AA 1996.

97 *Dallah Real Estate & Tourism Holding Co v Pakistan* [2010] UKSC 46, [2011] 1 AC 763; *Al-Naimi (t/a Buildmaster Construction Services) v Islamic Press Agency Inc* [2000] 1 Lloyd's Rep. 522; *AES Ust-Kamenogorsk Hydropower Plant LLP v Ust-Kamenogorsk Hydropower Plant JSC* [2011] EWCA Civ 647, (2011) 108(25) L.S.G. 18; *Glencore International AG v Metro Trading International Inc. (No 3)* [2002] EWCA Civ 528; *Albon (t/a NA Carriage Co) v Naza Motor Trading Sdn Bhd* [2008] 1 All ER (Comm) 351; *Elektrim SA v Vivendi Universal SA* [2007] 2 Lloyd's Rep. 8. See CPR, PD 6B. See also R Merkin, *Arbitration Law* (looseleaf) (Informa, 2011 update), para 9.35.

98 *Weissfisch*, [2006] 1 CLC 424.

99 [2007] 2 CLC 782.

100 [2011] EWHC 1624 (Comm).

101 [2011] 2 All ER (Comm) 128.

Conflict of jurisdiction between a non-supervisory court and a tribunal

An arbitral tribunal does not need to wait for the court, either supervisory or not, to make decision before taking jurisdiction. If a supervisory court has given judgment on the validity of an arbitration agreement, the tribunal usually is expected to follow the court's decision. Otherwise, the arbitral award may be set aside by the supervisory court.[102] On the other hand, a non-supervisory court's judgment does not need to be followed by the arbitral tribunal at all. Parallel proceedings and inconsistent decisions may occur if a non-supervisory court and an arbitral tribunal decide differently on the existence and validity of an arbitration agreement.

Because of the existence of the risk of irreconcilable judgments, an arbitral tribunal and a court can use interim measures to prevent the proceedings from continuing in another forum. Some countries adopt the instrument of anti-arbitration injunctions to restrain a party from suing in an arbitration tribunal.[103] In England, the court has power to grant an anti-arbitration injunction against a tribunal seated in another country under the Senior Courts Act,[104] though in exceptional circumstances.[105] The English courts must be satisfied that the foreign arbitration proceedings are vexatious or oppressive and that continuing the arbitration proceedings would infringe the applicant's equitable rights. In practice, an English court usually will not grant an anti-arbitration injunction to restrain foreign arbitration because doing so would infringe the doctrine of *kompetenz-kompetenz*,[106] and the natural forum to decide the competence of a foreign arbitral tribunal usually should be the supervisory court.[107] An anti-arbitration injunction will be granted if there is probability that the

102 E.g. s67, AA 1996.

103 Brazil: *Campanhia Paranaense de Engergia-COPEL v UEG Araucaria Ltda*, Case No 24.334/2003, 3rd State Court of Curitiba, PR (Brazilian court issues an injunction preventing ICC proceedings based on the finding that the arbitration agreement was null and void). US cases: *In re Neutral Posture*, 135 S.W.3d 725 (Tex.App-Houston [1 Dist] 2003); *Certain Underwriters at Lloyd's v Bristol-Myers Squibb Co.* 51 F. Supp. 2d 756 (E.D.Tex 1999). English cases: *Claxton Engineering Services v TXM Olaj-Es Gazkutato Ktf*, [2011] EWHC 345; *Kazakhstan v Istil Group Inc* [2007] EWHC 2729 (Comm); *Excalibur Ventures LLC v Texas Keystone Inc* 2011 EWHC 1624 (Comm); *Albon (t/a NA Carriage Co) v Naza Motor Trading Sdn Bhd* [2007] EWCA Civ 1124; *Elektrim SA v Vivendi Universal SA* [2007] 1 CLC 227; *Intermet FZCO v Ansol Ltd* [2007] EWHC 226 (Comm).

104 s37. *Excalibur Ventures LLC v Texas Keystone Inc*, para 54–60.

105 *Black Clawson International Ltd v Papierwerke Waldhof-Aschaffenberg AG* [1981] 2 Lloyd's Rep. 446, 458; *Cetelem SA v Roust Holdings Ltd* [2005] 2 Lloyd's Rep 494, para 74 (per Clarke LJ); *Weissfisch v Julius* [2006] 1 Lloyd's Rep 716, para 33, per Lord Phillips CJ; *Elektrim SA v Vivendi Universal (No 2)* [2007] 2 Lloyd's Rep 8, para 51; *Albon v Naza Motor Trading Sdn Bhd (No 4)* [2007] 2 Lloyd's Rep 420; aff'd [2008] 1 Lloyd's Rep 1 ; *Claxton Engineering Services v TXM* [2011] EWHC 345; *Excalibur Ventures v Texas Keystone*, [2001] EWHC 1624 (Comm).

106 *Weissfisch v Julius* [2006] 1 CLC 424.

107 Ibid. See also *supra* subsection B.

arbitration agreement has never been concluded between the parties.[108] Such an injunction is issued where there is an arguable case that the applicant's signature was forged,[109] where the applicant is a third party to the arbitration agreement[110] and where the parties did not enter the arbitration agreement at all or replaced the arbitration clause with a jurisdiction clause in their latter agreement.[111]

An arbitral tribunal, at the same time, also has the power to issue an anti-suit injunction preventing the parties from bringing the issue to a foreign court. Such a power is accepted by the UNCITRAL Model Law.[112] The English Arbitration Act 1996 permits arbitrators to issue interim measures, including anti-suit injunctions.[113] The US courts also accept such power of arbitral tribunals.[114] However, the power of an arbitrator to issue an injunction against court proceedings is very restrictive. In Quebec, for example, arbitral tribunals do not have the autonomy to adjunct court jurisdiction and, if such an injunction is granted, it can only have legal effects after being recognized and enforced by courts.[115] In *Service Bérubé ltée c. General Motors du Canada ltée*,[116] the Quebec Court of Appeal accepted that injunctions can be granted by arbitral tribunals in limited circumstances and only when the parties had shown intention to be bound by arbitration. It clearly excludes the possibility for a tribunal to grant injunction against the court proceedings where the parties' intention to submit to arbitration is in challenge.

If both the non-supervisory court and the arbitral tribunal have issued injunctions to restrain each other's proceedings, neither fora believe the other has jurisdiction and will enforce the other's injunction. In *Claxton Engineering v TXM*[117] an anti-arbitration injunction was issued by the English court against the Hungarian arbitration proceedings, while an anti-suit injunction was issued by the Hungarian tribunal against the English court action. The non-supervisory court and the tribunal do not need to enforce each other's injunctions. The injunctions may be rendered useless in practice. The chance for the issuing court or tribunal to

108 Collins *et al.*, 2010: para 16–0–88; *Dallah Real Estate and Tourism v Ministry of Religious Affairs of the Government of Pakistan* [2010] UKSC 46; *Excalibur Ventures v Texas Keystone*, para 56–57.
109 *Albon v Naza Motor Trading* [2007] 2 CLC 782.
110 *Excalibur Ventures v Texas Keystone*.
111 *Claxton Engineering v TXM*.
112 Art 17: Unless otherwise agreed by the parties, the arbitral tribunal may, at the request of a party, order any party to take such interim measure of protection as the arbitral tribunal may consider necessary in respect of the subject matter of the dispute. The arbitral tribunal may require any party to provide appropriate security with such measure.
113 Arts 38 and 39 of the English AA 1996. *CMA v Hyundai* [2009] 1 Lloyd's Rep 213.
114 *Merrill Lynch v DeCaro*, 577 F. Supp. 616 (W.D.Mo 1983); Levy, 2005: 122.
115 *Canadian Royalties Inc v Nearctic Nickel Mines Inc* [2010] QCCS 4600.
116 [2011] J 2781.
117 [2011] ILPr 13.

enforce its injunctive order depends on: (1) whether the enjoined party has assets in its country, which it can freeze to enforce a penalty; (2) whether the final decision can be enforced. As to the arbitral tribunal, its awards will be enforced in the court of all Contracting States of the New York Convention, unless the enforcement court finds the arbitration agreement invalid. If the award is expected to be enforced by the non-supervisory court, the arbitral tribunal might have to seriously consider the effect of the anti-arbitration injunction. In other cases, an arbitral award has more chance of being enforced than a court judgment because there is not yet an international treaty in force which facilitates the recognition and enforcement of court judgments.[118]

Conflicts of jurisdiction between the supervisory and non-supervisory courts

Conflicts may also arise if both the supervisory and the non-supervisory courts take jurisdiction to decide the arbitral tribunal's jurisdiction. As stated above, the power to supervise arbitral jurisdiction is more appropriately exercised by the supervisory court.[119] However, nothing can prevent a non-supervisory court from examining the preliminary issue upon the claimant's application pursuant to its domestic law. The competence of an arbitral tribunal may cause conflict not only between a tribunal and a court, but also between the courts in different countries.

England believes that a supervisory court usually should be the natural forum to decide the competence of an arbitral tribunal.[120] If the English court is the supervisory court, it has the inherent power to restrain a foreign court from taking jurisdiction to decide the competence of an arbitration tribunal seated in England.[121] The Arbitration Act 1996[122] provides that an English court has the power to make orders in support of arbitral proceedings, including granting an interim injunction.[123] CPR 62.5 permits the English courts to serve a claim form out of jurisdiction for the injunction order (s44 order).[124]

From the perspective of international comity, every country has the competence to decide its own jurisdiction free from the intervention or guidance from other countries. An anti-suit injunction cannot be issued

118 The Hague Convention on Choice of Court Agreements 2005 has not entered into force yet. In the EU, although judicial cooperation is established between the Member States to enforce each other's judgments, the New York Convention will take priority. The Brussels I Regulation only has effects within the territory of the EU.

119 *Claxton Engineering Services v TXM Olaj-Es Gazkutato Ktf*, para 44.

120 *Weissfisch*.

121 *Midgulf International Ltd v Groupe Chimiche Tunisien* [2010] 2 Lloyd's Rep. 543.

122 s44(2)(e).

123 s44(1), s11(2)(e).

124 R62.5(1)(b).

lightly. Usually, an injunction can be granted to enforce contractual obligations. If an English court finds there is a valid English arbitration clause and a party brings the dispute subject to arbitration to a foreign court in breach of agreement, an injunction is usually granted based on the breach of contract.[125] However, if the resisting party does not directly bring the substantive claim to a foreign court, but applies for a declaration on whether the alleged arbitration agreement was concluded or valid in a foreign court, the party does not breach its contractual obligation. The court has to consider the purpose in commencing the foreign court action and whether the foreign action is vexatious or oppressive. In *Midgulf International Ltd v Groupe Chimiche Tunisien*,[126] the defendant disputed the existence of a London arbitration agreement and pursued the Tunisian court for a declaratory relief after the London arbitration was commenced. The claimant applied for an anti-arbitration injunction from the English court. The English court asserted jurisdiction to decide the competence of the London tribunal. After holding a valid arbitration agreement existed, the English court restrained the defendant from asking the Tunisian court for the declaratory relief, holding that the sole purpose of the Tunisian proceedings was to undermine the English arbitration.

What if the supervisory court and the non-supervisory court make different decisions on the preliminary issue? The worst situation could occur where the non-supervisory court finds the arbitration agreement invalid, while the supervisory court rules differently. Because there is not yet harmonized choice of law rules provided by any international instruments, different judgments likely exist. The supervisory court might issue an anti-suit injunction against further proceedings in the non-supervisory court, while the non-supervisory court may grant an anti-arbitration injunction to prevent the party from continuing foreign arbitration.[127] The conflict of injunctions thus occurs, which generates difficult questions in terms of international comity, certainty and predictability, and the ends of justice.

Review at the enforcement stage

An arbitral tribunal's decision on its jurisdiction is frequently challenged at the enforcement stage. The New York Convention permits the courts of a Contracting State to refuse recognizing or enforcing an arbitral award if a party has no capacity to enter into the agreement, the arbitration agreement is invalid either under the law chosen by the parties to govern this agreement or, in the absence of choice, under the law of the country where the award was made,[128] the award deals with issues outside the scope

125 *XL Insurance v Owens Corning*, [2001] CLC 914.
126 [2010] 2 Lloyd's Rep. 543.
127 *Telenor Mobile Communications v Storm* 584 F.3d 396 (C.A.2(NY) 2009).
128 Art V(1)(a).

of the arbitration agreement[129] or the subject matter is not arbitrable.[130] It is clear that the courts of a Contracting State have the power to comprehensively review the preliminary issue before enforcing the award.

3.3 **Kompetenz-kompetenz** *in dispute resolution clauses*

Although the doctrine of *kompetenz-kompetenz* grants the chosen forum jurisdiction to determine its own jurisdiction, the doctrine has quite a few limitations. Although international cooperation exists in both jurisdiction and arbitration, none of the instruments have adopted a negative *kompetenz-kompetenz* rule to exclude all non-chosen fora their jurisdiction to examine the existence and validity of a dispute resolution clause. This is an unfortunate situation. If the chosen forum's competence to rule on its own jurisdiction is not exclusive, conflicts of jurisdiction in deciding the existence and validity of a dispute resolution clause would likely occur.

The negative *kompetenz-kompetenz* doctrine can be established within a regime with sufficient judicial cooperation. Cooperation requires Contracting States to have mutual respect to each other's jurisdictional competence and to trust each other to decide its own jurisdiction. Against this background, it is possible to set up the rule requiring only the chosen forum to take jurisdiction to decide the preliminary issues of the dispute resolution clause, and to demand all other courts suspend proceedings until the chosen forum makes decision.[131]

Compared to exclusive jurisdiction clauses, more difficulties and controversies exist in arbitration. Parallel proceedings may exist between an arbitral tribunal and its supervisory court, between an arbitral tribunal and a non-supervisory court, and between the supervisory court and the non-supervisory court. The negative *kompetenz-kompetenz* doctrine certainly cannot be accepted to exclude the supervisory court's jurisdiction from reviewing the competence of an arbitral tribunal. Instead, an alternative form of *kompetenz-kompetenz* doctrine may be accepted to grant the chosen tribunal jurisdiction to decide its own competence, and only the supervisory court the jurisdiction of supervision. All non-supervisory courts should decline jurisdiction in deciding the preliminary issues of an arbitration agreement. This approach is more consistent with the doctrine of arbitral autonomy and compatible with international arbitration practice.

129 Art V(1)(c).

130 Art V(2)(a).

131 This proposal has been accepted in European Commission, *Proposal for a Regulation of the European Parliament and of the Council on jurisdiction and the recognition and enforcement of judgments in civil and commercial matters (Recast)*, December 2010, COM(2010) 748 final, Article 32 of which provides that 'where an agreement ... confers exclusive jurisdiction to a court or the courts of a Member State, the courts of other Member States shall have no jurisdiction over the dispute until such time as the court or courts designated in the agreement decline their jurisdiction'.

4 Conclusion

Dispute resolution clauses could provide certainty and predictability, reduce dispute resolution cost, simplify the process to decide jurisdiction and reduce parallel proceedings and conflicts of jurisdiction. However, all these benefits are compromised if the existence and validity of the dispute resolution clause is subject to dispute. When the dispute is whether the chosen forum is indeed 'chosen' by the parties, it is questionable whether the chosen forum or an otherwise competent non-chosen forum has the competence to decide this issue.

The current practice worldwide demonstrates the triumph of pragmatism over theoretical soundness. The establishment and adoption of both the doctrine of separability and the doctrine of *kompetenz-kompetenz* shows the trend. Both doctrines have the advantage of producing practical convenience and both are justified by the presumption that the parties should have agreed to submit the dispute, including the dispute relating to the chosen forum's competence, to the chosen forum. The two doctrines help to simplify the complicated issue, but neither could escape the logic dilemma by permitting a forum, the jurisdiction of which stems from party autonomy, to examine the existence and validity of the autonomy. Regardless of the logic circle, there is, by far, no better approach to decide jurisdiction in the existence of choice of jurisdiction. If the chosen forum has no jurisdiction to decide its own jurisdiction, it fundamentally undermines the doctrine of party autonomy. If only a competent non-chosen forum can decide the competence of the chosen forum, the chosen forum has to enforce a non-chosen forum's decision and cannot decide the issue by itself. This result is impractical and unrealistic. As a result, the doctrines of separability and *kompetenz-kompetenz* should continue to be used in deciding jurisdiction of the chosen forum.

From the practical perspective, applying the doctrine of separability does not generate many difficulties. However, the current application of the doctrine of *kompetenz-kompetenz* proves insufficient to prevent parallel proceedings and irreconcilable judgments. It has been suggested that, in a regime where international cooperation is established, negative *kompetenz-kompetenz* can be adopted to provide an order of priority between different competent fora. An alternative negative *kompetenz-kompetenz* doctrine should be adopted in arbitration to grant only the arbitral tribunal the power to decide its jurisdiction and only the supervisory court the power to review, while depriving any non-supervisory courts the power to examine the competence of a foreign arbitration.

4 Subject matter scope

1 Introduction

Not all disputes can be submitted to the chosen court or arbitral tribunal. Procedural autonomy in deciding the method and forum of dispute resolution is limited by the subject matter. Whether a subject matter can be submitted to arbitration is called 'arbitrability'. Arbitration is widely known as having 'a private proceeding with public consequences';[1] some matters are reserved exclusively by courts, in order to protect public interest.[2] Arbitrability is determined exclusively by state law and there is no international uniform standard.

Comparatively, the scope of jurisdiction agreements is much broader. Although the parties, by using private agreements, decide the forum to dispose their disputes, the disputes are determined by court authorities, with state power behind the proceedings and judgments. Most disputes, as a result, can be subject to jurisdiction agreements, except those where state interest is involved and foreign disposal is inappropriate in relation to state sovereignty.

2 Arbitrability

Some states adopt the concept of public policy to ring-fence arbitrable matters,[3] while others do not blindly exclude all public policy related disputes from arbitration.[4] It is suggested that developing countries may have more political interest to reserve public-related disputes for the courts, worrying liberal rules and private disposal of disputes may render the national interest to unfair advantages of parties stronger in economic power.[5] Regardless of the divergence in domestic law, public policy is one

1 Blackaby *et al.*, 2009: para 2.113; Mante, 2012: 34.

2 Blackaby *et al.*, 2009: para 2.111 ff.

3 Mante, 2012: 34; Greenberg *et al.*, 2011: 188–189.

4 Mante, 2012: 34; Brekoulakis, 2009: 20; *Premium Nafta Products Ltd v Fili Shipping company Limited* [2007] UKHL 40.

5 Mante, 2012: 34–35.

criterion in determining whether a subject matter is arbitrable. The difficulty is that the concept of public policy is also ambiguous.

Another criterion is whether the subject matter is freely disposable by its owner or whether it has an economic value.[6] Under German law, any claim involving an economic interest is arbitrable. 'Claims not involving an economic interest shall have legal effects to the extent that the parties are entitled to conclude a settlement on the dispute in question.'[7] Swiss law also provides that 'any dispute involving property can be the subject matter of arbitration'.[8] If the claim is characterized as 'economic' the dispute involves property.[9] English law has not drawn a clear line to distinguish arbitrable and non-arbitrable matters.[10] The court should consider arbitrability on a case-by-case basis. However, in general, matters may not be arbitrable if they concern public interest or affect the interests of third parties.[11]

Although national law on arbitrability differs in different jurisdictions, some disputes are commonly excluded from arbitration, including civil status of persons (citizenship), validity of marriage, child custody and criminal liability.[12]

Arbitrability may be decided at different stages of the procedure and by different authorities. In most cases, arbitrability is determined by arbitral tribunals; it can also be determined by courts, when the opposing party challenges it in courts; it may be decided by the enforcement court at the recognition and enforcement stage.[13]

2.1 Choice of law

Arbitrability is a question of law and is determined by the applicable law. Practice differs from different jurisdictions and depends on whether arbitrability is decided by courts or tribunals. Options usually are made between the chosen law by the parties, the governing law of the contract, the law of the seat, the *lex fori* (if a court is seized to hear the disputes) and the law of the enforcement courts.[14]

6 De Werra, 2012: 301.
7 German Code of Civil Procedure of 1998 (CCP), s1030.
8 Swiss Federal Act on International Private Law of 1987, Art 177.1.
9 Levy, 2002: 77.
10 Mustill and Boyd, 1989: 149.
11 Born, 2009: 768; cited in *Fulham Football Club (1987) v Richards*, [2011] EWCA Civ 855, para 39.
12 Singaporean Law, *Aloe Vera of America v Asianic Food* [2006] 3 SLR 174, 205; Chinese Arbitration Law 1994, Art 3(1).
13 Hanotiau, 1998: 756.
14 Moses, 2012: 72.

Arbitrability decided by courts

The issue of arbitrability may be raised in courts at different stages of arbitration. The party may directly apply to the supervisory court challenging the enforceability of an arbitration agreement before the commencement of arbitration proceedings; it may apply to the supervisory court to set aside the arbitral awards after the arbitration proceedings commence on the ground of non-arbitrability; it may challenge recognition and enforcement of arbitral awards in the enforcement courts at the enforcement stage.

A court usually intends to apply the *lex fori* to decide arbitrability of a dispute. It is because arbitrability concerns public interest and the national provisions determining arbitrability are usually classified as mandatory rules. The New York Convention clearly provides that, at the stage of recognition and enforcement of arbitral awards, the enforcement court will consider the *lex fori*. If the subject matter is not arbitrable at the *lex fori*, recognition and enforcement will be refused.[15] Although without express support from international legal instruments, the supervisory court usually will apply the *lex fori*, i.e. the law of the seat, to decide arbitrability.

Nothing can prevent a court from applying the *lex fori* to an issue concerning public interest. However, it is questionable whether applying the *lex fori* in all cases irrespective of the parties' intentions and the connections with the dispute is reasonable. It is hard to argue that arbitrability concerns matters that are 'crucial' to safeguard a country's fundamental social order. In other words, national provisions on arbitrability are not classified as 'overriding mandatory rules' which should override the otherwise governing law.[16] Where disputes have no connections with the enforcement forum or the place of the seat, it is doubtful whether the court should use the *lex fori* to invalidate an arbitration agreement.

Arbitrability decided by arbitral tribunals

It is even harder to ascertain the applicable law by an arbitral tribunal. In some tribunals, the law applicable to arbitrability will be the law governing arbitration agreements.[17] If the parties have expressly chosen the national law to govern the arbitration agreement, the chosen law shall apply.[18] In most cases, the parties may only choose the law governing the substance of the contract without designating the law governing the arbitration agreement. Most countries will apply the chosen law to decide the validity of an

15 New York Convention, Art V(2)(a).

16 See Art 9(1) of the Rome I Regulation on the definition of overriding mandatory rules. Fawcett and Carruthers, 2008: 728–741; Clarkson and Hill, 2011: 230–236.

17 Arts II(1) and V(1)(a) of the New York Convention.

18 Hanotiau, 1998: 764.

agreement.[19] Without any express choice, arbitrators have the wide power to determine the applicable law and may even decide that non-state law/ *lex mercatoria* applies.

Subject of arbitrability to party autonomy is not free from doubt. The parties may choose the law of a country that would validate such a choice in order to avoid the mandatory rules of a country which has close connections to the transactions or the arbitration proceedings. Furthermore, such a choice may be ignored by a supervisory court or an enforcement court. A dispute that is held arbitrable by the tribunal may be considered non-arbitrable by a court.[20] Regardless of the above concerns, this approach is frequently adopted in arbitration practice. Arbitrators are not judges in courts. They usually do not consider themselves servants of national law or that they should enforce any national mandatory rules in particular. Their power is originated from the parties' agreement. As a result, they apply the parties' choice of law to decide arbitrability in practice and do not consider the doctrine of mandatory rules or public policy.

Although arbitrators are likely to apply the chosen law, the law of the seat usually will also be relevant. Parties may have the intention to validate their arbitration agreements and deliberately choose the law of a country that recognizes the arbitrability of the subject matter, as against the seat of arbitration. However, if the subject matter is not capable of settlement by arbitration under the law of the seat, the award may be vacated by the supervisory court.[21] If the supervisory court is seized to decide arbitrability, it is likely that the court will apply the law of the seat to invalidate arbitration agreements. A tribunal usually should also consider the consequence and apply the law of the seat. Applying the law of the seat, however, is criticized by some commentators as the 'seat' usually is chosen for the convenience of the parties, instead of any real connections between the country and the dispute.[22]

Although arbitral tribunals are not obliged to consider the law of the enforcement jurisdiction, from a pragmatic perspective, arbitral tribunals would consider the risk of refusal to recognize and enforce arbitral awards. The law of the enforcement court thus will have practical effect which obliges arbitrators to take it into consideration. However, the law of the enforcement court may not be relevant if the parties agree to voluntarily enforce the awards or if the awards can be enforced in more than one jurisdiction.[23] Furthermore, a tribunal can only consider the law of the enforcement court after it can reasonably predict which party is likely to win and which country is likely to be the place of enforcement. If both

19 Ibid., 764.
20 Lehmann, 2004: 758–759.
21 Moses, 2012: 72–73; UNCITRAL Model Law of Arbitration, Art 34(2)(b)(i).
22 Lehmann, 2004: 758.
23 Moses, 2012: 73.

parties have assets located in more than one country, it is unpractical to take this issue into consideration.

2.2 Controversial matters

Bribery and corruption

Corruption is defined in a broad term. It includes not only the abuse of power by government officials but also other private misuse of power or position for illegitimate gain or benefits.[24] The corruption of government officials by abusing their authorities or by receiving bribes are usually punishable as criminal offences, which will be excluded from the scope of arbitration. Disputes, however, concerning the enforceability or performance of a contract allegedly being procured by corruption or allegedly facilitating the payment of bribes, could be brought to arbitration.[25]

Bribery was not arbitrable at an early stage[26] because the activity is against international public policy which forfeits the parties their rights to seek remedies and justice in arbitration.[27] Regardless of the early position held by international organizations,[28] matters concerning commercial bribery or corruption are arbitrable in modern times.[29] The early development of the modern approach is due to the confusion of the issue of arbitrability in corruption with separability.[30] Many tribunals or courts decided that arbitrators have the power to rule whether a contract is tainted by corruption upon the allegation, because the illegality of the underlying contract would not affect the validity of an arbitration agreement.[31] In England, the ICC award made in Switzerland was enforced though the tribunal ruled on the allegation of bribery.[32] The court bases the decision on three grounds: first, the parties entered into arbitration agreements and the intention should be respected; second, the doctrine of *kompetenz-kompetenz* grants jurisdiction to the arbitral tribunal; and third, the doctrine of separability decides that the illegality of the underlying contract

24 Transparency International UK (TI UK), 'Corruption in the UK: Overview and Policy Recommendations', 1.
25 Youssef, 2009: 54.
26 ICC Award No 1110 of 1963.
27 Wetter, 1994: 277, cited in Redfern, 2004: 143.
28 Blackaby *et al.*, 2009: para 2.134.
29 Hwang and Lim, 2011: paras 92–93; *National Power v Westinghouse*, Tribunal Federal, Lere Cour Civile, Recours de Droit Public du Sept 2, 1993, (1994) 12 ASA Bull 244; McDougall, 2005: 1041; *Westacre Investments Inc. v Jugoimport-SPDR Holding Co. Ltd*, [1998] 2 Lloyd's Rep. 111 (QB).
30 Youssef, 2009: 54; Redfern, 2004: 143.
31 Muller, 2004: 178–3.6, 178–3.6; Art 16.1, UNCITRAL Model Law 2006; Art 23.1, UNCITRAL Arbitration Rules 2010; Art 23.1, LCIA Arbitration Rules.
32 *Westacre Investments v Jugoimport SPDR Holding Co*, [1999] QB 740; Zadkovich, 2011: 106.

will not affect the validity of the arbitration agreement.[33] This, however, is not the same as arbitrability. Arbitrability concerns whether arbitrators have power to adjudicate the existence of corruption or bribery, or whether corruption should be reserved by judicial authorities.

Nonetheless, some countries still exclude corruption claims from arbitration. In Pakistan, for example, the Supreme Court decided in *Hubco v Wapad*[34] *that prima facie* corruption cases were inarbitrable. This decision was primarily based on public policy. The Supreme Court of Pakistan stated that public policy required issues relating to corruption to be decided by the court.[35] This view remains in the minority. However, although corruption is genuinely held arbitrable, arbitrators' power is simply limited to civil remedies, and arbitrators do not have authority to impose criminal sanctions against corruption.[36]

Insolvency

Although the insolvency law of every country differs, the common practice is that insolvency per se is inarbitrable.[37] It is justified by two reasons. First, 'pure' insolvency proceedings do not concern commercial disputes but execution of debts.[38] Pure bankruptcy proceedings are described by Lord Hoffmann as proceedings not to determine the existence of rights but 'to provide a mechanism of collective execution against the property of the debtor by creditors whose rights are admitted or established'.[39] Second, insolvency proceedings affect not only private interests between immediate contractual parties but the public at large, which should be reserved for jurisdiction of courts.[40] However, disputes that are not 'pure' insolvency matters, but in relation to insolvency proceedings, such as the existence of debt, restitution claims and post-insolvency sales, are generally arbitrable.[41] In the USA, disputes between the estate representatives of

33 *Westacre Investments v Jugoimport SPDR Holding Co*, [1999] QB 740; Zadkovich, 2011: 106.
34 *Hub Power Co Ltd (HUBCO) v Pakistan WAPDA and Federation of Pakistan* (2000) 15(7) Mealeey's International Arbitration Report, Section A.1, A-15 and 16.
35 Ibid.; Nicholls *et al.*, 2011: 330.
36 Zadkovich, 2011: 106.
37 Blackaby *et al.*, 2009: para 2.128; Mantilla-Serrano, 1995: 69; Lazic, 1999: s4. Singapore cases: *Re Sanpete Builders (S) Pte. Ltd*, High Court, Singapore, [1989] SLR 164; *Petroprod Ltd (in official liquidation in the Cayman Islands and in compulsory liquidation in Singapore) v Larsen Oil and Gas Pte Ltd* [2010] SGHC 186; Lithuanian cases: *BUAB Briauna v BITC Mobel AB* (2–178/2009); *Belaja Rus v Westintorg Corp* (3K-3–562/2008); *UAB Rimi Lietuva v UAB Vegida* (3K-3–142); *AMIR-S v BUAB Ekoela* (2T-44/2009).
38 Lew *et al.*, 2003: 206.
39 *Cambridge Gas Transportation v Official Committee of Unsecured Creditors of Navigator Holdings* [2007] 1 AC 508, para 14.
40 Mistelis, 2006: 367.
41 Poudret and Besson, 2007: 307.

affiliated companies are arbitrable, but court approval is required where bankruptcy proceedings are pending.[42]

Others may argue that insolvency of a company may make an arbitration agreement invalid as the original contractual party subject to the agreement loses its legal personality.[43] This, however, is overruled by most courts in practice.[44] Where a company is bankrupt, its rights and obligations under arbitration agreements may be transferred to its estate.[45] When the insolvency proceedings start in courts, arbitration proceedings will not be terminated automatically.[46] The (potential) bankruptcy of one party does not affect the enforceability of an arbitration agreement.[47] This practice is adopted in the USA,[48] Germany, France,[49] Switzerland and Spain.[50]

Competition and antitrust

Competition concerns public interest and state regulation of economic order. Competition claims are traditionally non-arbitrable based on the grounds of public policy.[51] Some competition disputes, especially antitrust disputes, involve companies with dominant power and may deprive the weaker party's right by forcing the adhesive party into a dispute resolution method out of court.[52] The complexity of antitrust disputes also overweighs the arbitral procedure.[53] The restriction, however, is relaxed in the modern commercial world.[54] The US Supreme Court decided in *Mitsubishi* that competition/antitrust disputes are arbitrable,[55] subject to

42 Gropper, 2012: 229; *Zimmerman v Continental Airlines*, 12 F.2d 55 (3rd Cir. 1983), *cert. denied*, 464 US 1038, 104 S.Ct. 699, 79 L.Ed.2d 165 (1984); *Hays and Co. v Merrill Lynch, Pierce, Fenner and Smith, Inc*, 885 F.2d 1149 (3rd Cir. 1989). Lazic, 1999.

43 Poudret and Besson, 2007: 306.

44 Swiss cases: 16 October 2012 (Case reference cases: 4A_50/2012); *Vivendi SA and others v Deutsche Telekom AG and others*, 4A_428/2008; Dutch cases: Rb. Amsterdam, 24 November 1906, W 8561; Rb. Amsterdam, 13 June 1979, NJ 1980, 254; Rb. Zwolle, 16 October 1987, upheld by Hof Arnhem, 3 March 1987; French cases: *Société Soules v Société Henry-Maitre Texier*, Cass. com. 4 February 1986, (1988) Rev. Arb. 718; *Société Technique d'avant-garde (T.A.G.) v Société Entertainment Media France Corp. (B.M.P.C.) et autres*, Cass. com., 12 February 1985, (1985) Rev. Arb. 275. See Lazic, 1999: s3.1.

45 Poudret and Besson, 2007: 306; Lazic, 1999: s3.1.

46 Poudret and Besson, 2007: 306; and cases in footnote 44.

47 Gropper, 2012: 237; Lazic, 1999: s3.1; cases in footnote 44.

48 Gropper, 2012: 237; *US Lines, Inc. v Am. S.S. Owners Mut. Prot. (In re US Lines, Inc.)*, 197 F.3d 631, 641 (2d Cir. 1999); *MBNA American Bank v Hill*, 436 F.3d 104 (2d Cir. 2006).

49 Gropper, 2012: 237–239.

50 Blackaby *et al.*, 2009: para 2.131.

51 *American Safety Equipment v J.P. Maguire & Co.*, 391 F.2d 821 (2d Cir. 1968).

52 Soltysinski, 1986: 349.

53 Ibid., 349.

54 For more discussion, see Landi, 2005.

55 *Mitsubishi Motors Co v Soler Chrysler-Plymouth*, 473 US 614 (1985).

the condition that arbitrators are bound to apply national competition law as a court does.[56] In the EU, there is no case specifically dealing with arbitrability of competition disputes. However, many commentators believe the ECJ decision in *Eco Swiss China Time Ltd v Benetton International NV*[57] infers EU competition law is arbitrable.[58]

Supporters of arbitrability of antitrust disputes argue that this approach improves party autonomy and prevents a party from avoiding arbitration by maliciously bringing antitrust elements into their disputes.[59] Opponents basically base their objections on public policy grounds and on the limit of arbitral tribunals to impose sanctions, though damages are available. It is also likely that awards concerning competition/antitrust are difficult to enforce in another country, which holds a strong stand in public policy.

Intellectual property disputes

Intellectual property (IP) disputes involve different types of claims. In general, rights between private parties—for instance, patent owners license others to use the patent, or copyright owners assign copyright to publishers—are freely disposable by the right owners. Disputes arising out of these activities can be arbitrated as all other private civil and commercial activities.[60] On the other hand, claims on validity and nullity of IP rights may not be completely private. In some countries, IP disputes concerning purely the power of state authorities, such as deposition and registration of patents, trademarks, designs, etc., are not arbitrable.[61] It is also believed by some countries that the 'adjudication of industrial property monopolies is a matter of public interest and should belong to the exclusive jurisdiction of courts or special administrative agencies'.[62] Other countries, however, take a more flexible approach allowing arbitrators to rule on the validity of IP rights.[63] In the USA, for example, section 294 of the US Code 1983 provides that disputes relating to patent validity or infringement can be submit to arbitration, and the arbitral awards only bind the current parties and have no effect on any third parties.[64]

Problems may arise if the parties submit disputes on the licence of trademarks or patents between private parties to arbitration, but the ruling depends on the determination of the validity of the IP right. In judicial

56 Ibid.
57 Case C-126/97, [1999] ECR I-3055.
58 Landi, 2005: 322.
59 Soltysinski, 1986: 349.
60 Blackaby *et al.*, 2009: para 2.118; De Werra, 2012: 301; Moses, 2012: 32.
61 Blackaby *et al.*, 2009: para 2.118; Soltysinski, 1986: 348.
62 Soltysinski, 1986: 348.
63 Such as the USA, Canada and Switzerland. See De Werra, 2012: 303; Soltysinski, 1986: 348.
64 Soltysinski, 1986: 348.

practice, if the defendant argues the IP rights in dispute are void, as a defence to the alleged breach of contract or infringement, it becomes an 'Italian Torpedo'. The court proceedings on the substantive dispute will be stayed until the court that has exclusive jurisdiction to decide the validity of IP rights decide this issue first.[65] This, however, is not the case in arbitration. Arbitrators can make decision on validity as a prerequisite to decide the substantive dispute between the parties. As far as the decision on validity does not have an effect *erga omnes*, this should not be a problem.[66]

Contracts with the inequality of bargaining power

There is no common practice to make contracts with the inequality of bargaining power non-arbitrable. In Italy, employment disputes are arbitrable.[67] In the USA, employment and consumer disputes are arbitrable in principle, subject to fairness and conscionability.[68] The fairness and conscionability test, however, in theory challenges the material validity of the arbitration agreements instead of the arbitrability of these claims. On the other hand, in Brazil, the Employment Appeal Tribunal stated in *Righetti v Organizacao das Nacoe Unidas (ONU)*[69] that employment disputes are arbitrable and the view that labour rights are indispensable is outdated. The Superior Labour Tribunal, however, held that labour disputes generally are non-disposable and should not be subject to arbitration. The arbitration agreement was upheld in this case on exceptional factual grounds.[70] Under the EU Unfair Terms in Consumer Contracts Directive, compulsory arbitration agreements deprive consumers' access to justice and are unenforceable against consumers.[71] Such agreements are nevertheless enforceable against businesses and non-compulsory arbitration agreements are still valid.[72] It is hard to argue that consumer disputes are completely non-arbitrable.

2.3 Conclusion

Although it is commonly understood that disputes concerning public interest are not arbitrable, the general trend is that the threshold for

65 *Knorr-Bremse Systems v Haldex Brake Products GmbH* [2008] ILPr 26; Fawcett and Torremans, 2011: 386.

66 De Werra, 2012: 303.

67 Sasson, 2007: 2.

68 Finizio, 2004: 89. E.g. *United Steelworkers of America v American Manufacturing Co*, 363 US 564 (1960) (labour disputes are arbitrable); *United Steelworkers of America v Warrior & Gulf Navigation Co.* 363 US 574 (1960); *Green Tree Financial Corp.-Alabama v Randolph*, 531 US 79 (2000); Berger, 2004: 753.

69 Unreported case. See comments in de Oliveira, 2012: N25.

70 *Righetti v Organizacao das Nacoe Unidas (ONU)*, ibid.; de Oliveira, 2012: N25.

71 Council directive 93/13/EEC of 5 April 1993 on unfair terms in consumer contracts, [1993] OJ L 95/29, Annex 1(q).

72 Hill, 2008: 215; Tang, 2009: 157.

arbitrability is gradually lowered. Most countries now allow matters that are non-arbitrable in history to be submitted to arbitration. The scope of arbitrability, however, differs from country to country. Following the trend of extending the scope of arbitrable matters and providing certainty to contractual parties, some commentators advocate a transnational approach of arbitrability,[73] which means that the tribunal should not apply national law, but should refer to international custom, usages and general principals of laws to decide arbitrability.[74] In practice, a tribunal should consider all matters arbitrable unless there is 'international public policy' against it.[75] In order to find out the 'international public policy', an arbitral tribunal might refer to the recent practice of courts and tribunals in one or more countries, no matter whether they are relevant to the dispute or arbitration.[76] This approach, however, may cause difficulty in practice because a state court may not wish to adopt the same approach, especially if a dispute is non-arbitrable in its domestic law due to the infringement of its public policy and the dispute has close connections to this country. Inconsistent practice between courts and tribunals may cause concurrent proceedings and conflict decisions.[77]

3 Matters subject to jurisdiction agreements

Although most countries accept that private parties have the freedom to decide competent courts to hear their disputes, the freedom only exists to handle private issues. As to other issues, where state power is involved, a country will wish to exercise its firm control over these subject matters which cannot be left for the free disposal of private parties. Choice of court agreements cannot have effect in the subject matters governed by exclusive jurisdiction. Some states also provide protections for weaker parties of contracts and prevent (or restrict) choice of court agreements in contracts with the inequality of bargaining power.

3.1 Exclusive jurisdiction

There is no international uniform concept of exclusive jurisdiction. However, compared to arbitrability, it is not as difficult to decide on the applicable law concerning exclusive jurisdiction. Exclusive jurisdiction is

73 Mistelis, 2009: 15; Lehmann, 2004: 766–768.

74 ICC Case No 4131 (1982); *Dow Chemical v Isover-Saint Gobain*, 110(4) J.D.I. 899 (1983), IX Y.B. Com. Arb. 131 (1984); ICC Case No 4381 (1986); ICC Case No 5065 (1986). Kovacas, 2012: s5.1.4.

75 Lehmann, 2004: 766–768.

76 Award in ICC Case No 4604 (1984), reprinted in 111 J. Droit Int'l 973 (1985); Award in ICC Case No 8423 (1994); Award in ICC Case No 4604 (1984). Referred to in Lehmann, 2004: 762–763.

77 Mistelis, 2009: 15.

classified as a question of procedure, and it is designated to protect the fundamental interest and sovereignty of a country. A court will apply the *lex fori* to decide whether a dispute is subject to its exclusive jurisdiction and will not consider the law of any other countries. Although exclusive jurisdiction differs from country to country, the common grounds to establish exclusive jurisdiction include the disposal of immoveable property, exercise of state administrative power, insolvency and matters concerning public registration, such as registration of IP rights and registration of companies.

Some countries have very broad exclusive jurisdiction. These countries usually consider jurisdiction an expression of state sovereignty and zealously protect such power. For example, Chinese law requires many matters that may be subject to party autonomy in other countries to be decided exclusively in Chinese courts. These matters include the performance of contracts for Chinese–foreign joint ventures, Chinese–foreign cooperative exploration and development of natural resources in China,[78] disputes concerning immoveable property,[79] disputes concerning harbour operation where the harbour is located in China[80] and succession, where the deceased had domicile in China upon his death or where the principal location of assets is in China.[81]

Disputes in relation to immoveable property

Countries assert exclusive jurisdiction over immoveable property located within their territories, and parties are deprived of the right to agree on jurisdiction governing disputes concerning immoveable property. Common law countries distinguish jurisdiction in *rem* from jurisdiction in *personan.*[82] Party autonomy on jurisdiction generally is only allowed in jurisdiction in *personan.*[83] Civil law countries also exclude party autonomy from dealing with disputes with object rights in *rem* in immoveable property.[84] From the perspective of the enforcement, a country has absolute and exclusive control of immoveable property located in its territory. A foreign court's decision relating to the disposal of land located in another country is considered an intervention of the state's sovereignty.[85] Most countries reserve exclusive jurisdiction over the immoveable property and exclude party autonomy from being used. As a result, international harmonization

78 Chinese Civil Procedure Law (Amended) 2012, Art 266.
79 Ibid., Art 33(1).
80 Ibid., Art 33(2).
81 Ibid., Art 33(3).
82 Clarkson and Hill, 2011: 60; Fawcett and Carruthers, 2008: 353–422; Hartley, 2009: 11–12.
83 Hartley, 2009: 15–16.
84 Chinese Civil Procedure Law 2012, Art 33; Brussels I Regulation, Art 22(1).
85 Hartley, 2003: 11.

of jurisdiction rules usually excludes immoveables from its scope and choice of court agreements shall not have effect.[86]

Disputes in relation to companies and legal persons

It is generally recognized that there are three types of actions in relation to companies or legal persons. The first relates to their existence, validity, creation and dissolution. The second relates to their internal affairs, between shareholders and between companies and shareholders. The third is between companies and third parties in relation to external affairs and transactions.[87] The creation and dissolution of legal persons is usually the result of exercise of sovereign power of a state. Allowing the court of any other country to decide on this issue consists of the review of the exercise of administration power of another country, which intervenes into state sovereignty.[88] The first type of claim, as a result, excludes the employment of choice of forum agreements. Choice of court agreements, however, can be safely used in the second and third types of actions in relation to companies or legal persons.

The People's Republic of China has provided extra restrictions to parties' choice of court agreements. Chinese people's courts have make reservations over a number of important matters which may not be subject to exclusive jurisdiction in many other countries. The Chinese people's court has exclusive jurisdiction over disputes concerning Sino-foreign joint venture contracts, Sino-foreign cooperative enterprise contracts and Sino-foreign cooperative exploration or development of natural resources contracts, which are performed in the territory of China. There have been criticisms over whether such restrictions are necessary or meet the requirements of international investment. It is true that China has the closest connections to these contracts, but this is not a reason to exclude party autonomy. The Chinese legislation aims to protect the interests of the Chinese party of these contracts—in particular, state-owned enterprises. Party autonomy will be excluded safely under the ground of public policy and the protection of fundamental national interest, instead of the interest of one of the parties. There is no sufficient reason to justify that any Sino-foreign joint venture or Sino-foreign cooperative enterprise contracts concern Chinese public and national interests to the extent that it is reasonable to exclude parties' freedom to choose a competent court. If the performance of the contract relates to the disposal of state property or natural resources, exclusive jurisdiction is granted anyway under the heading of immoveable property. It is thus suggested that there is no general need to exclude party autonomy from Sino-foreign joint venture

86 See e.g. Hague Convention 2005, Art 2(2)(i); Brussels I Regulation, Arts 22 and 23(1).
87 Kessedjian, 1997: para 28.
88 Hartley, 2003: 11.

and cooperative enterprise contracts all together. The proper legislation should recognize such choices in general, subject to exception of public policy.

Insolvency

Insolvency proceedings are administrative in nature and do not deal with the substantive rights and obligations. Insolvency procedures and any related rescue methods are not open to parties' choice of court. Insolvency is excluded from the Hague Choice of Court Convention.[89] In EU, insolvency is dealt with exclusively by the Insolvency Regulation 2000, which provides special jurisdiction rules overriding any inconsistent choice of court agreements.[90] However, if insolvency arises as an incidental issue to a dispute in question, the parties still can choose the competent court to govern their dispute.[91] An example is that the parties entered into a sale of goods contract containing a choice of court agreement and the seller went into bankruptcy. The buyer's restitution claim is the main cause of action, and the choice of court clause is valid though insolvency exists as an incidental question.[92]

Intellectual property rights disputes

Some countries have broader subject matter limitations on jurisdiction over foreign intellectual property rights. In English common law, for example, it is difficult for an English court to take jurisdiction over the creation, validity and infringement of foreign IP rights, including registered and unregistered trademark and patent, as well as copyrights.[93] This practice, however, is inconsistent with the international trend, under which IP claims are distinguished between claims in relation to state register and claims in relation to the private right between the parties. In most countries, the registration and validity of intellectual property rights is subject to exclusive jurisdiction and the parties could not agree on the competent court to hear the dispute.[94] It is because the trademark and patent are granted by the act of a country and only a sovereign state can decide the validity of such an action.[95] Disputes on license or infringement of IP rights are usually private matters between the parties and freely

89 Art 2(2)(e).

90 Council Regulation (EC) No 1346/2000 of 29 May 2000 on insolvency proceedings, [2000] OJ L160/1; Magnus and Mankowski, 2012: 451.

91 Magnus and Mankowski, 2012: 451.

92 Hartley, 2003: para 15; Magnus and Mankowski, 2012: 451.

93 *Tyburn Productions Ltd v Conan Doyle* [1991] Ch 75; *Apple Co v Apple Computer* [1992] FSR 431. Fawcett and Torremans, 1998: 43–45.

94 Schulz, 2002a: 13.

95 Schulz, 2002b: 12.

disposable without states' intervention. They can be subject to choice of court agreements.[96]

The Hague Choice of Court Convention, on the other hand, makes different distinction between copyrights and other intellectual property rights.[97] Copyrights usually do not need state registration and disposition. Copyrights and related rights, such as rights of performers, rights of record producers and rights of broadcasting companies, can be subject to jurisdiction agreements, even if the dispute is on the validity.[98] However, judgment on validity of copyright can only bind the parties of the dispute and will not have *in rem* effects to bind any third party.[99] As to other IP rights (patent, trademark, design, etc.), the parties cannot choose the competent court to hear the validity of these IP rights, but can choose jurisdiction to decide the contractual obligations arising out of the private disposal of the IP rights, such as paying royalties, and validity and enforcement of licensing agreements. If the defendant raises invalidity as a defence, the chosen court can decide it as an incidental question.[100] An important exclusion in the Hague Convention is the infringement of IP rights without contractual relationship between the parties.[101] In other words, only when a party infringes IP rights by breaching contracts, the choice of court agreement can apply. The choice of court agreement cannot cover pure tort claims for infringing IP rights, even if the agreement is entered into after disputes have arisen.

Competition disputes

There are different types of competition disputes. Disputes concerning 'unfair competition' include, for example, trademark infringement and passing off, defamation, misrepresentation, unconscionable contracts, etc. These actions can be classified as general tort or breach of contract and usually concern private right and obligations between the parties. There is no problem for the parties to choose a competent court. Other competition disputes, such as antitrust and anti-dumping, may require the exclusion of party autonomy. Such disputes usually involve the state authorities exercising administrative power. Some actions are criminal proceedings. Even if private proceedings might likely exist in rare cases, they concern the interest of the general public and are not freely disposable by the parties.[102]

96 Schulz, 2002a: 13; Schulz, 2002b: 12.

97 Art 2(2)(n) and (0). Hartley and Dogauchi, 2007: para 33.

98 Hartley and Dogauchi, 2007: para 73.

99 Ibid., para 34.

100 Ibid., paras 37–38. However, it is different from choosing a court to hear the validity of patent or trademark. The decision in the incidental question is not entitled for automatic recognition and enforcement pursuant to the Convention.

101 Art 2(2)(0); Hartley and Dogouchi, 2007: paras 79–82.

102 Hartley, 2003: 10.

3.2 Protecting weaker parties

Development of private international law in the late twentieth century demonstrates the introduction of value consideration to the original technical conflict rules. Protective jurisdiction has been established to protect the weaker parties in contracts with inequality of bargaining power, such as consumer contracts, employment contracts and insurance contracts. This trend originated from some European continental states,[103] but was followed later in the European harmonization of private international law.[104] Pursuant to the protective jurisdiction rules under the Brussels I Regulation, parties' choice of court agreements in consumer contracts are prima facie invalid unless such a choice can expand the consumer's option, the choice was concluded after disputes have arisen or the common domicile of both parties was chosen at the time of contracting.[105] The rule in protecting the weaker party does not completely exclude the adoption of choice of court agreements in deciding a competent court, but it largely limits the effectiveness of such a choice.

The rationale for the limitation is to protect the weaker party from disadvantaged bargaining power. It is believed that the stronger party can unilaterally insert a jurisdiction clause into a contract, choosing the court that is most convenient to itself, which usually is the domicile or habitual residence of the stronger party. The weaker party is placed in the take-it-or-leave-it position and usually enters into the contract without reading. Choice of court agreements, as a result, are not subject to authentic or genuine consent between the parties and should be unenforceable.[106]

The protective jurisdiction, however, is not universally adopted. In the USA, for example, common law jurisdiction rules apply equally to ordinary contracts and adhesive contracts. Under a controversial case, *Carnival Cruise Lines v Shute*,[107] the US court enforced a choice of court agreement in a cruise ticket against the consumer passenger. The same approach was adopted in *Ware Else & Ware Enterprises v Susan Ofstein*[108] and *Nowland v Hill-Rom*,[109] where the courts enforced jurisdiction agreements which required the employees to sue their employers out-of-state. These decisions are justified in terms of economic efficiency. Such jurisdiction agreements reduce commercial costs and risks, and the weaker parties also benefit from the reduced prices and, probably, job opportunities with higher wages.[110]

103 Jenard, 1979: 33; Schlosser, 1979: 117.
104 Brussels Convention, section 4; Brussels I Regulation, section 4. For general, see Tang, 2009: 6–8.
105 Art 17 of Brussels I.
106 Tang, 2009: 8–9.
107 *Carnival Cruise Lines v Shute* 499 US 585 (1991).
108 *Ware Else & Ware Enterprises v Susan Ofstein* 865 So 2d 1079 (Fla app 5 Dist 2003).
109 *Nowland v Hill-Rom* 2008 WL 1909217 (D Or 2008).
110 *Carnival Cruise Lines v Shute* 499 US 585, 594 (1991).

No consensus can be made on whether jurisdiction clauses should be restricted or excluded in contracts with the inequality of bargaining power. This is one of the issues which prevents the Hague Conference on Private International Law from adopting a fuller judgment convention covering consumer and employment contracts. Every state continues to use its domestic law to decide the subjective scope of choice of court agreements, i.e. whether they can be applied to contracts with the inequality of bargaining power.

4 Subject matter scope: comparing arbitration and jurisdiction clauses

It is easily taken for granted that the subject matter scope of arbitration and jurisdiction is the same. It is true that similar considerations have been given to decide what subject matters can be freely disposed by the parties. Restrictions to arbitrability and the subject matter scope of jurisdiction clauses include public policy, protection for third parties and involvement of state sovereign interest and administrative power. Bribery, fraud, intellectual property rights, antitrust and competition, insolvency, contracts involving weaker parties, etc. are controversial areas in both jurisdiction and arbitration agreements.

In general, the subject matter scope of arbitration agreements is broader than jurisdiction agreements. Development of arbitration in the past 50 years witnesses the relaxation of rules on arbitrability. Most countries are willing to limit the reach of state power and public policy, and allow party autonomy in wider areas. Arbitrators now could stretch their arms to areas that were traditionally non-arbitrable, including certain issues relating to bribery, corruption, competition and IP rights. There is, however, no such development in the area of jurisdiction agreements. All countries have exclusive jurisdiction, which excludes parties' choice of court. Some commentators suggest that arbitrability can be defined by referring to exclusive jurisdiction.[111] Some domestic law explicitly makes matters subject to exclusive jurisdiction non-arbitrable.[112] While a court reserves certain issues exclusively to its jurisdiction, it excludes party autonomy to opt for both another country's court and arbitration. However, the fact that a subject matter is within the range of exclusive jurisdiction of a particular country does not render this issue non-arbitrable. Arbitrability cannot always be referred from the concept of exclusive jurisdiction.[113] Exclusive jurisdiction sometimes is provided exclusively in deciding allocation of jurisdiction between courts. The legislator has no intention to

111 Poudret and Besson, 2007: 293.

112 German law, ZPO, s1030(3); Belgian Law, CJB, Art 1676(3); Swiss Law, CIA, Art 5; Poudret and Besson, 2007: 293–294.

113 Poudret and Besson, 2007: 294; Lazic, 2007: 6.

extend the rules to the scope of arbitration. An example is exclusive jurisdiction established in the Brussels I Regulation.[114] Although the Regulation provides exclusive jurisdiction in a number of disputes relating to the exclusion of jurisdiction agreements, this rule does not apply to arbitration.[115] In China, the Civil Procedure Law provides notoriously broad exclusive jurisdiction. The Chinese exclusive jurisdiction rules only exclude the parties' freedom to choose a foreign court to hear the specifically defined disputes,[116] but do not exclude the freedom to submit these disputes to arbitration. Article 305 of the '1992 Opinion' provides that the parties could not choose the court of any other countries for disputes subject to exclusive jurisdiction, except arbitration agreements. In other words, if the parties have chosen an arbitral tribunal, either seated in China or abroad, this choice is not invalid even if the subject matter is subject to exclusive jurisdiction. Furthermore, Article 3 of the Chinese Arbitration Law provides the following matters non-arbitrable, including marriage, adoption, guardianship, support, succession and administrative disputes,[117] which differs from exclusive jurisdiction. Contractual disputes arising out of Sino-foreign joint ventures, for example, are not subject to jurisdiction agreements but can be submitted to arbitration. In *Desputeaux v Éditions Chouette*,[118] the Supreme Court of Canada also ruled that the statutory provisions providing exclusive jurisdiction to the copyright dispute did not exclude arbitration.

114 Art 22.

115 Art 1(2)(d) excludes arbitration from the scope of the Brussels I Regulation. Poudret and Besson, 2007: 294.

116 Arts 33 and 266 of PRC Civil Procedure Law 2012.

117 Art 3, PRC Arbitration Law 1994.

118 Supreme Court, Canada, [2003] 1 SR. 178, 2003 SCC 17, as cited in UNCITRAL 2012 Digest of Case Law on the Model Law on International Commercial Arbitration, para 12.

5 Enforceability of dispute resolution agreements

1 Introduction

After a forum is satisfied that a valid jurisdiction or arbitration agreement is concluded by the parties to govern the dispute in question, the forum will move to consider the enforceability of this agreement. It is necessary to know that a valid dispute resolution clause does not mean it will be enforced by the forum. Validity decides whether an agreement meets the preliminary requirements of law to be legally sound. Enforceability, on the other hand, means what effect should be given to the legally sound agreement. The former refers mainly to contractual requirements of a dispute resolution clause, and the latter considers a country's policy to give party autonomy its binding effect. Enforcement of a dispute resolution agreement is exclusively the procedure issue of a court. Although different choice of law rules may apply to decide the validity of a dispute resolution agreement, enforceability or effectiveness of this agreement is governed exclusively by the *lex fori*.[1]

The enforceability of choice of forum clauses depends on many different elements. Usually, a valid arbitration agreement will be given its full effectiveness: a court will dismiss the case and refer the dispute to the arbitral tribunal. This effect has been clearly provided by the New York Convention and the UNCITRAL Model Law.[2] The effectiveness given to jurisdiction clauses, however, is uncertain. Not all jurisdiction clauses have the same effect as an arbitration agreement to derogate a non-chosen court from its jurisdiction. Furthermore, many countries, although accept-

1 Kahn-Freund, 1977: 834. Validity and enforceability are frequently confused and comingled in both practice and academic writings. Some issues do not strictly relate to the contractual concept on validity agreements, such as whether a conflicts clause could choose an unrelated court and whether the conflicts clause can be enforced in consumer contracts. These issues can be considered part of validity, or can be considered something relating to the enforceability. As a result, strict dichotomy between validity and enforceability is not necessary in practice. However, for the purpose of effective analysis, the book defines enforceability narrowly, which concerns the legal effect given by a court to a conflicts clause, which is not tainted in any way by preliminary conditions.

2 Art II.3, New York Convention; Art 8(1), Model Law.

ing that courts, if competent under the domestic law, should decline jurisdiction in favour of arbitration, do not grant the same rule to an exclusive foreign jurisdiction clause. In common law countries, a court chosen by the parties in a valid prorogation jurisdiction agreement may refuse to take jurisdiction if it is inappropriate to do so. The effectiveness of a jurisdiction clause thus depends on a lot of different factors: first, whether the jurisdiction clause is exclusive or non-exclusive; second, whether the court which is seized to enforce the clause is the chosen court or non-chosen court; third, whether the court has discretion in face of a valid jurisdiction agreement; fourth, whether there is any judicial cooperation between the seized court and the chosen court, or any other courts which have connections to the dispute or defendant.

This chapter compares the practice in major jurisdictions in the enforcement of arbitration and jurisdiction agreements. It aims to analyse why the different effectiveness is given to jurisdiction and arbitration agreements in national law and to explore how the effectiveness of jurisdiction clauses can be improved in the future.

2 Enforcement in China

2.1 Arbitration agreements

Legislation

Full effectiveness is given to arbitration agreements in China. China is a civil law country and traditionally refuses courts' discretion to decline jurisdiction. Under the traditional jurisprudence, all jurisdictional grounds and all possibilities for a court to decline jurisdiction shall be permitted by law.[3] The Chinese Civil Procedure Law has, in a few provisions, ascertained the derogation effect of an arbitration agreement to courts' jurisdiction. Article 124(2) provides that, if both parties have entered into arbitration agreements in writing, the claimant should not bring the action in court. Article 124(3) further provides that the court should refer the claimant to the other dispute resolution organ, if, according to law, the dispute should be decided by organs other than courts. This provision can also be interpreted as a provision to support the derogation power of an arbitration agreement. In addition, Article 271 provides rules for dealing with international arbitration, which provides that the parties can bring their dispute to the people's court only if there is no arbitration clause in their contracts or no arbitration agreement is concluded in writing after the

3 Art 111 of PRC Civil Procedure Law 2007 provides that a Chinese court 'must' hear a case if it has jurisdiction. This sentence is revised in the 2012 amendment but there is nothing to positively suggest that Chinese courts could use discretion to decline jurisdiction granted by law.

contract is concluded. If an arbitration agreement exists, the parties could not commence actions in the people's court. Besides the Civil Procedure Law, Article 5 of the PRC Arbitration Law 1994[4] also provides: 'If the parties have concluded an arbitration agreement and one party institutes an action in a people's court, the people's court shall not accept the case, unless the arbitration agreement is null and void.'

Chinese statutes are consistent in terms of the derogation effect of an arbitration agreement. This is a mandatory requirement for a Chinese court to decline jurisdiction where a valid arbitration agreement exists.

Challenging court's jurisdiction

Although a Chinese court is compelled to decline jurisdiction in face of a valid arbitration agreement, a Chinese court is not obliged to use its own motion to find out whether there is a valid arbitration agreement between the parties. If the claimant did not disclose the existence of an arbitration agreement to the court, the defendant must challenge court's jurisdiction by proving a valid arbitration agreement exists and covers the dispute in question. The reason is that the contractual parties have freedom to waive their rights under the arbitration agreement at any time. If the claimant commences an action in a people's court in breach of an arbitration agreement and the defendant simply appears to defend, the defendant has submitted to the court's jurisdiction.[5]

If the defendant wants to use the arbitration clause to challenge jurisdiction, the defendant must plea before the trial commences.[6] If the defendant does not raise the defence on time, the arbitration agreement is deemed to be repudiated. Establishing a time limit to challenge courts' jurisdiction is reasonable in that it could prevent wasting time and judicial resources.

It makes a difference if the defendant of a contract, where an arbitration clause exists, does not enter an appearance. The Supreme People's Court provides in its judicial direction that in this circumstance the people's courts should examine the validity of an arbitration agreement. If the arbitration agreement is valid, the court should decline jurisdiction.[7] It is clear that the Supreme People's Court aims to protect the effectiveness of an arbitration agreement and it imposes the duty to the court to examine *ex officio* the validity of an arbitration agreement. However, applying this direction depends on the condition that the court must have been given sufficient information prior to the hearing that there is an arbitration agreement

4 Adopted at the Ninth Meeting of the Standing Committee of the Eighth National People's Congress on 31 August 1994 and promulgated by Order No 31 of the President of the People's Republic of China on 31 August 1994.

5 PRC Civil Procedure Law, Art 127; PRC Arbitration Law, Art 26.

6 PRC Arbitration Law, Art 26.

7 Supreme People's Court, 'Response about how to handle the case where a party in a contract with an arbitration agreement fails to enter an appearance', (2008) No 3.

between the parties. If the claimant fails to disclose this fact, the court has no obligation to examine the likely existence of arbitration agreements.

Internal Report-and-Review procedure

Although a Chinese law requires Chinese courts to decline jurisdiction in hearing a dispute subject to an arbitration agreement, many Chinese courts have the tendency to expand their jurisdiction and ignore the parties' intention to submit disputes to arbitration. These courts would not blindly breach the law by taking jurisdiction regardless of a valid arbitration clause. The common approach taken by these courts is to rule an arbitration clause invalid before taking jurisdiction.[8] In order to protect the reasonable effectiveness of an arbitration agreement, the Supreme People's Court introduces the Internal Report-and-Review procedure to prevent local courts from unduly competing with the arbitral tribunal in jurisdiction.[9] The Intermediate People's Court has jurisdiction of the first instance to hear a case with foreign elements. If an Intermediate People's Court holds an international arbitration agreement to be invalid, before it can move to take jurisdiction, it must refer the decision to the High People's Court for a review. If the High People's Court overrules the decision, the Intermediate People's Court must decline jurisdiction and send the parties to arbitration. If the High People's Court affirms the decision, the High People's Court should refer the case to the Supreme People's Court for the second review. Only after the Supreme People's Court affirms the intermediate court's jurisdiction can this court continue the proceedings.[10]

The Internal Report-and-Review procedure is a special procedure only available in China. It aims to properly protect the enforcement of arbitration agreements and prevent protectionism in local courts. The procedure, however, is not a judicial process. It is rather an administrative procedure granting supervisory power to the court that has a higher hierarchy. The local intermediate court should, by its own motion, report the decision to the local High Court and voluntarily stay jurisdiction. If the local intermediate court fails to report, the higher court would not review

8 Many Chinese courts conducted a check of the validity and existence of an arbitration clause. E.g. *Liantai Photo-Voltaic* Jiangsu Province High People's Court (2009) No 179. Du, 2007: 157.

9 Supreme People's Court, 'Notice on Issues about the Handling of Cross-Border and Foreign Arbitration', (1995) No 18, Art 1.

10 Shanghai Municipal High People's Court Trial Committee, 'Opinions on Several Issues Relating to the Execution of "Arbitration Law of the People's Republic of China"', 3 January 2001, Article 8(2); Supreme People's Court, '*Liberia Liberia Power Shipping*, the claimant, and *China Chongqing Xinfu Food*, the respondent, on the dispute on jurisdiction in the contract for the carriage of goods by sea', [2006] No 26; 'Re asking for instruction about the validity of an arbitration agreement in *CECT and Korea Mobile, Shanghai Ausheng Investment* dispute on jurisdiction in Joint Venture Contract', [2006] No 19.

the lower court's jurisdiction, unless one of the parties appeal the lower court's decision.[11] For example, in *Ningxia Hebin Minzhu Electric Power v HK Qilong Industry*,[12] the Yinchuan Municipal Intermediate People's Court held the arbitration agreement invalid because one party of the arbitration agreement no longer existed. The intermediate court, however, did not report the order to the Ningxia High Court pursuant to the judicial direction. The resisting party had to appeal the order to the High Court. The High Court upheld the appeal by stating that the rights and obligations of the original party of the arbitration agreement were subrogated to the current defendant and the arbitration agreement was enforced.

One may wonder why the Internal Report-and-Review procedure is necessary if the party could achieve the same result by appeal. The reason is that the internal procedure could save litigation cost and is usually quicker.[13] Furthermore, the resisting party only has one chance to appeal an order.[14] If the High Court affirmed the intermediate court's decision that the arbitration agreement was invalid in an appeal, the resisting party has no further chance to appeal to the Supreme Court. In the Internal Report-and-Review procedure, even if the High Court approves the intermediate court's decision, the decision will be referred to the Supreme People's Court for a second review. In practice, although most referrals have been approved by the Supreme Court, there are also cases where both the intermediate and the High Courts have decided to take jurisdiction while the Supreme People's Court order the courts to decline jurisdiction to give effect to the arbitration agreement.[15] If the courts fail to voluntarily enforce the report-and-review procedure, the resisting party then loses the second chance provided in the Internal Report-and-Review procedure.

Furthermore, the procedure only applies where the local intermediate court take jurisdiction based on the ruling that the arbitration clause is invalid. It does not apply where the intermediate court simply takes jurisdiction without considering the existence and validity of an arbitration agreement. The consideration is that, if a local court simply ignores an arbitration agreement, this court would not have the sufficient knowledge or motion to refer the decision to the higher court. Taking jurisdiction in breach of an arbitration agreement in this situation can only be challenged by appeal.

11 Art 154 of the PRC Civil Procedure Law 2012.

12 Ningxia Province Yinchuan Municipal Intermediate People's Court, (2004) No 19, rev'd, Ningxia High People's Court, (2004) No 4.

13 Du, 2007: 159.

14 PRC Civil Procedure Law, Art 175.

15 E.g. *Hubei Province Import and Export Co, Hubei Donghu Disk Technology Ltd v Kangweike Technology (Chengdu)*, No 4 Civil Tribunal of the Supreme People's Court, [2004] No 34; *Inner Mongolia Zhicheng Mining Ltd v South Africa Huajin International Group Ltd*, No 4 Civil Tribunal of the Supreme People's Court, [2001] No 26.

It is also argued that the Internal Report-and-Review procedure increases the court's workload, especially the Supreme People's Court. Although the review system is supposed to be quick, in practice, delay is observed in the Supreme Court. In *China Pacific Insurance v Sunglide Maritime*,[16] for example, the referral and review took eight months. In *Zhangjiagang Electro v Best-Better Worldwide Ltd*,[17] the Supreme People's Court took 15 months to decide that the local court should not take jurisdiction. In other cases, the review procedure usually takes around 3–6 months.[18] It is also observed that the Supreme People's Court has taken increasing time to consider the referral. It is probably because more and more local courts now have proper understanding of the importance of arbitration agreements and the purpose of the Internal Report-and-Review procedure. As a result, more cases are reported voluntarily to the higher court. The increased case number has overloaded the Supreme People's Court. There is the worry that delays will become more and more severe in the future. Since the majority of cases that have been reported by the High Courts to the Supreme Court have been affirmed, there is doubt whether the 'double review' system is still necessary. The system could probably be simplified by a single review of the High Court. With the improved knowledge of the local court, the procedure may nevertheless be abolished in the future.

2.2 Jurisdiction agreements

In contrast to legislative provisions granting explicit derogation effect to arbitration agreements, no such clear effect is provided for jurisdiction agreements. As a result, in comparison with the enforcement of arbitration agreements, the enforcement of jurisdiction agreements in Chinese courts is problematic.[19]

Prorogation effect of jurisdiction agreements

There is not much difficulty for a court to accept prorogation effect of a valid jurisdiction clause. The PRC Civil Procedure Law 1991 provided the

16 No 4 Civil Tribunal of the Supreme People's Court, [2008] No 50.

17 No 4 Civil Tribunal of the Supreme People's Court, [2006] No 1.

18 *Dongguan ACE Medical Packaging*, No 4 Civil Tribunal of the Supreme People's Court, [2007] 45; *Rent Co v Zhongcheng Ningbo Import & Export*, No 4 Civil Tribunal of the Supreme People's Court, [2008] No 4; *Tianjing Goubuli Dumpling*, No 4 Civil Tribunal of the Supreme People's Court, [2007] No 37; *Bejing Ailisheng v Japan Sunglide*, No 4 Civil Tribunal of the Supreme People's Court, [2007] No 14; *Shenzhen Huahan v Xionghai*, No 4 Civil Tribunal of the Supreme People's Court, [2005] No 41; *Shengmei v Hangzhou Huangshun*, No 4 Civil Tribunal of the Supreme People's Court, [2005] No 4; *China People Insurance v Zhongcheng International Transport*, No 4 Civil Tribunal of the Supreme People's Court, [2004] No 39.

19 For more discussion, see in general, Tang, 2012b: 459–484.

parties in international contracts the right to choose a Chinese court to hear their dispute. The provision remains in the amended Civil Procedure Law in 2007 and 2012. Article 34 of the PRC Civil Procedure Law (Amended) of 2012 provides:

> Parties to a dispute over a contract or other property rights and interests may, through written agreement, choose the court of the place where the defendant has his domicile, where the contract is performed, where the contract is concluded, where the claimant has his domicile, where the subject matter is located, or other places which has practical connections with the dispute to exercise jurisdiction. Such a choice should not violate the provisions of this Law on jurisdiction by forum level and on exclusive jurisdiction.

As a result, the prorogation effect of a jurisdiction clause will be enforced if this jurisdiction clause is valid according to Chinese law and if it is consistent with the Chinese legislation on jurisdiction by forum level and on exclusive jurisdiction.[20] However, even if a Chinese jurisdiction clause violates the jurisdiction by forum level, it will not automatically invalidate such a clause. Chinese courts have taken a flexible approach to allow the claimant to vary the jurisdiction clause and make it consistent with the internal allocation of jurisdiction. For example, in *Xu v Yan*,[21] a Chinese resident and a Hong Kong citizen entered an exclusive jurisdiction agreement choosing the Fujian Province Quanzhou Municipal Intermediate People's Court. However, the dispute had no connections to Quanzhou City, which violated the requirement asking for the 'practical connections' between the dispute and the chosen court.[22] The claimant then sued in Fujian Province Zhangzhou City, which was a competent court under Article 241 of the Civil Procedure Law 2007 (Article 34 of CPL 2012).[23] The court took jurisdiction and treated the claimant's voluntary change of jurisdiction as acceptable. Although the claimant sued in a non-chosen court, it is the correct court in the chosen jurisdiction. If the Zhangzhou court refused jurisdiction and insisted the claimant sue in the chosen court, the chosen court would nevertheless transfer the case back to the Zhangzhou court. Zhangzhou court thus took jurisdiction which was

20 'Jurisdiction by forum level' is called *Ji Bie Guan Xia* in Chinese. It allocates jurisdiction within one territory to different levels of authorities, formed by the basic people's courts, Intermediate People's Court, High People's Court and Supreme People's Court.

21 Fujian Province High People's Court, (2010) No 78.

22 Art 34 of PRC CPL 2012 (Art 35 of CPL 2007).

23 Art 34 provides that a Chinese court can take jurisdiction over a dispute on contract or other property rights or interest against a non-domicile defendant, if the contract is concluded or performed in China, the subject matter is located in China, the defendant has enforceable property located in China, the defendant has a representative in the territory of China or the tort occurs in China.

considered an effective method and avoided extra procedural steps to transfer jurisdiction.

Furthermore, the Supreme People's Court makes the choice of a Chinese court compulsory. This is provided in the judicial interpretation entitled 'Summary of the Second National Conference on the Adjudication of Commercial and Maritime Cases with Foreign Elements' issued in 2005.[24] This interpretation means that, if a Chinese court is chosen in a valid jurisdiction clause, this court must take jurisdiction and cannot decline jurisdiction by any reasons—for example, there is another forum which is more appropriate to hear the dispute, the same cause of action is pending in another forum, the case has been heard and decided in another forum or the jurisdiction clause is non-exclusive in nature.

Derogation effect of jurisdiction agreements

More uncertainty, however, exists as to the derogation effect of a jurisdiction agreement.[25] The '2005 Summary' provides instead that, even if the parties agree in their contract that a foreign court has exclusive jurisdiction, this agreement could not exclude jurisdiction of other competent courts.[26] As a result, the derogation effect of a valid jurisdiction clause is not compulsory and the Supreme People's Court, at least in 2005, still recognizes the Chinese court's power to take jurisdiction irrespective of a valid jurisdiction clause granting exclusive jurisdiction to a foreign country.

Chinese courts, thus, have discretion as to whether to give the derogation effect to a foreign jurisdiction clause. The recent judicial practice shows that more and more Chinese courts recognize the importance of party autonomy and intend to decline jurisdiction in favour of a chosen foreign court. In *Lai v ABN AMRO Bank*,[27] the claimant was a private investor who entered into a contract out of his trade or profession. The contract was a standard contract unilaterally drafted by the bank and the claimant signed without proper understanding of contract terms. The jurisdiction clause was also an asymmetric clause, granting the bank the freedom to sue Lai in any competent court while the claimant could only sue the bank exclusively in Hong Kong. Unfortunately, there was no law to regulate unfair contract terms, or to protect consumers in adhesive contract. The only protection for the claimant is that the Chinese court would exercise discretion not to enforce the jurisdiction clause.

The courts held that a foreign exclusive jurisdiction should exclude jurisdiction of Chinese courts. The courts refused to exercise discretion but

24 Supreme People's Court, '2005 Summary', [2005] No 6, Art 11.

25 The existence of a foreign exclusive jurisdiction clause is not listed in Art 124 of PCL 2012.

26 [2005] No 6, Art 11.

27 *Lai v ABN AMRO Bank*, Shanghai Municipal High People's Court, (2010) No 49.

rather treated the exclusive jurisdiction clause as a compulsory requirement for the courts to decline jurisdiction. The Shanghai Municipal High People's Court confirmed the intermediate court's decision to decline jurisdiction in favour of Hong Kong, which was chosen in the parties' jurisdiction agreement.

Does it mean Chinese courts, in their practice, have avoided the judicial direction in the '2005 Summary' by giving foreign exclusive jurisdiction clauses full derogation effects? An empirical study has shown that most Chinese courts have voluntarily recognized the derogation effects of foreign exclusive jurisdiction clauses and declined jurisdiction to enforce party autonomy.[28] However, some Chinese courts still refuse to decline jurisdiction in favour of a chosen court. These cases can be separated into two categories: (1) the Chinese courts simply fail to respect party autonomy; (2) the Chinese courts have considered the necessity to enforce judgment and decide to take jurisdiction for the purpose of enforcement.

The first category is simply wrong and does not require further discussion. The second category, however, demonstrates the more fundamental reason limiting the proper functioning of party autonomy in Chinese courts. In international commercial practice, the parties want certainty, predictability and security. They enter into jurisdiction clauses to reduce litigation cost and risk, and they also want to have judgments eventually recognized and enforced. If the chosen court's judgment cannot be enforced, requiring the parties to sue in the chosen court would deprive judgment creditors their rights. The necessity of recognition and enforcement of judgments has been referred to as one of the most important elements that a Chinese court should consider when making discretion. If the judgments of the chosen court cannot be enforced in China, the Chinese court may take jurisdiction to hear the dispute regardless of the fact that the parties have chosen another forum.[29]

An example is *NKK (Japan) v Beijing Zhuangsheng*,[30] where a sale of goods contract between a Japanese company and a Chinese company included a clause submitting all disputes to Hong Kong to the exclusion of all other courts. Since at the time of dispute there was no judicial cooperation between China and Hong Kong, the Hong Kong judgments based on

28 *Yacheng Automobile Parts v Huifeng*, Jiangsu Province Wuxi Municipal Intermediate People's Court, (2006) No 23; *Sojitz v Xiao*, Shanghai Municipal High People's Court, (2004) No 72; *Wenzhou Light Article Industry v CMA (France)*, Fujian Province High People's Court, available at www.chinalawinfo.com, reference code: CLI.C.21767; *Junichirou Watanabe v Culture & Art Press*, Shanghai Municipal No 1 Intermediate People's Court, (2008) No 210.

29 Tang, 2012b: 459.

30 *NKK (Japan) v Beijing Zhuangsheng*, Beijing Municipality High Court, (2008) Gao Min Zhong Zi No 919.

the jurisdiction agreement cannot be enforced in China.[31] Considering the procedural efficiency and the importance to have judgments enforced, the Chinese court took jurisdiction irrespective of the choice of court agreement.[32]

Unfortunately, the grounds for Chinese courts to recognize and enforce foreign judgments are narrow, with no exception given to party autonomy, which means that even if the parties have chosen a foreign court, and this choice is valid under both Chinese law and the law of the chosen court, judgments based on the jurisdiction clause cannot be enforced in China in most cases. This provides Chinese courts with reasons to take jurisdiction irrespective of a valid jurisdiction clause choosing a foreign state, without judicial cooperation or reciprocity with China. Therefore, the enforcement of jurisdiction clauses in China is very complicated because it directly connects to the profound issue of recognition and enforcement of judgments. Without an improvement of law of recognition and enforcement of foreign judgments and without being more open and more ready to enter into international judicial cooperation, giving party autonomy the weight that it desires would not truly happen.[33]

2.3 Assessment

Chinese law and judicial practice has demonstrated great divergence in enforcing arbitration agreements and jurisdiction agreements. Chinese law has expressly granted arbitration agreements full enforceability and has ordered the Chinese courts to give up jurisdiction in favour of arbitral tribunals. The Supreme People's Court even introduced an Internal Report-and-Review procedure to ensure every local court has paid due respect to arbitration agreements. On the other hand, the enforcement of jurisdiction is very much in doubt. Although Chinese courts are required to recognize the prorogation effect of a jurisdiction clause choosing Chinese courts, they have discretion as to whether or not to recognize the derogation effect of a foreign jurisdiction clause. More importantly, sometimes it is improper for a Chinese court to enforce an exclusive foreign jurisdiction clause because judgments made pursuant to such a clause cannot be enforced in China.

31 Hong Kong–China judicial cooperation now exists. The Supreme People's Court and the Government of Hong Kong Special Administrative Region entered into the 'Arrangement on Reciprocal Recognition and Enforcement of Judgments in Civil and Commercial Matters by the Courts of the Mainland and of the Hong Kong Special Administrative Region' in 2006.

32 Another example is *Kwok & Yih Law Firm v Xiamen Huayang Color Printing Company*, Xiamen Municipality Intermediate People's Court, 13 August 2003.

33 For more on recognition and enforcement of judgments in China, see Ch 8. See also Tang, 2012b: 459.

The Chinese practice is a typical example of the important influence of international treaties in domestic law. China is one of the Contracting States of the New York Convention. Pursuant to the New York Convention, China has the treaty obligation to enforce valid arbitration agreements and to recognize and enforce arbitral awards made in a Contracting State. China later enacted the Arbitration Law 1994 and the Supreme People's Court published the judicial interpretation to fulfil Chinese treaty obligation to give effects to a valid arbitration agreement.

There is no international judicial cooperation in court judgments and choice of court agreements. Chinese courts have no treaty obligations to enforce choice of court agreements choosing another country. Furthermore, China has very narrow grounds to recognize and enforce foreign judgments. If Chinese courts take the possibility of recognition and enforcement of foreign judgments as one important element to exercise the Chinese-style *forum conveniens*, Chinese courts will refuse giving full effectiveness to a lot of jurisdiction clauses choosing foreign courts.[34] The Hague Convention of 2005 has not yet entered into force and China has not yet signed the Convention. Presumably, if China joins the Hague Convention, the enforcement dilemma in foreign jurisdiction agreement may be resolved. However, it still depends on the international acceptance of the Hague Convention. If the Hague Convention is as successful as the New York Convention and is accepted by most countries in the world, joining the Hague Convention will largely improve the current situation in China. Otherwise, the difficulty will continue to exist unless the domestic law in recognition and enforcement is fundamentally improved.

3 Enforcement in England

3.1 Enforcement of arbitration clause—statutory obligation

Pursuant to s9 of the Arbitration Act 1996, a party to an arbitration agreement may apply to the court to stay the court proceedings.[35] The time for application must be between taking the appropriate procedural step to acknowledge the proceedings and taking any step to answer the

34 See more discussion in Ch 8.

35 s9(1). *Aeroflot-Russian Airlines v Berezovsky*, [2012] EWHC 1610 (Ch); *Fiona Trust v Privalov* [2007] 1 All ER (Comm) 891; *Al-Naimi v Islamic Press Agency* [2000] 1 Lloyd's Rep 522; *Anglia Oil v Owners and/or Demise Charterers of the Marine Champion (The Marine Champion)* [2002] EWHC 2407 (Admlty); *Best Beat v Rossall*, [2006] EWHC 1494 (Ch); *Bovis Homes Ltd v Kendrick Construction Ltd* [2009] EWHC 1359 (TCC); *Downing v Al Tameer Establishment*, [2002] 2 All ER (Comm) 545; *El Nasharty v J Sainsbury Plc*, [2004] 1 All ER (Comm) 728; *Excalibur Ventures LLC v Texas Keystone Inc*, [2012] 1 All ER (Comm) 933.

substantive claim.[36] Any substantive response will be considered as a submission to the jurisdiction and waive of the arbitration agreement. If the resisting party applies for summary judgment from the English court, the application for a stay may be refused because the applicant is deemed to have accepted the court's jurisdiction. On the other hand, if the application for a summary judgment is made on the condition that the application for stay is failed, a stay may be granted.[37] The court, upon the application, 'shall grant a stay unless satisfied that the arbitration agreement is null and void, inoperative, or incapable of being performed'.[38] In other words, only a valid arbitration clause can be enforced and lead to the stay of court's proceedings.[39] The word 'shall' demonstrates that the court has no discretion but must recognize the derogation power of a valid arbitration clause. Furthermore, the court has no power to stay jurisdiction upon its own motion. Finally, the mandatory stay of jurisdiction applies to all types of arbitration agreements, regardless of the seat of arbitration.

English courts also clarify that the application can be made by both defendant and claimant acting in the counter-claim.[40] Questions may arise as to why the claimant, when bringing the claim in the court, is not deemed as repudiating an arbitration agreement and is allowed to raise the arbitration clause as a defence to the counter-claim. The possibility is that an arbitration claim does not cover the original claim but only the counter-claim. This, however, would not happen frequently in practice.

Furthermore, the proceedings that must be stayed are in respect of a matter which 'is to be referred to arbitration'. It, as a result, does not include the court's supervisory power of arbitration. If a party brings the court proceedings to issue an anti-suit injunction against another party suing in a foreign court, this action is not a matter covered by the arbitration agreement and should not be stayed under s9. Even if a party brings the court proceedings to review the existence and validity of an arbitration agreement, the court does not need to stay jurisdiction under s9. Section 9 of the Arbitration Act 1996, as a result, does not derogate a court from its power to 'supervise' arbitration or consider preliminary issues of an arbitration agreement.[41]

36 s9(3). *Capital Trust Investments Ltd v Radio Design TJ AB* [2001] 1 All ER (Comm) 1079; *Pitchers Ltd v Plaza (Queensbury) Ltd* [1940] 1 All ER 151; *Eagle Star Insurance Co Ltd v Yuval Insurance Co* [1978] 1 Lloyd's Rep. 357; *Patel (Jitendra) v Patel (Dilesh)* [2000] QB 551.

37 *Capital Trust Investments v Radio Design* [2001] 1 All ER (Comm) 1079.

38 s9(4). *Aeroflot-Russian Airlines v Berezovsky*, [2012] EWHC 1610 (Ch), para 104–112; *Ahad v Uddin*, [2005] EWCA Civ 883; *Albon v Naza Motor Trading Sdn Bhd*, [2007] 2 All ER 1075; *Cigna Life Insurance Co of Europe SA NV v Intercaser SA de Seguros y Reaseguros* [2002] 1 All ER (Comm) 235; *Collins (Contractors) Ltd v Baltic Quay Management (1994) Ltd* [2004] EWCA Civ 1757.

39 *Aeroflot-Russian Airlines v Berezovsky* [2012] EWHC 1610 (Ch), paras 104–112.

40 s9(1). *Nomihold Securities v Mobile Telesystems Finance SA* [2012] EWHC 130 (Comm).

41 For more details, see Fawcett and Carruthers, 2008: 450–455.

3.2 Enforcement of exclusive jurisdiction clause—common law discretion

The enforcement of exclusive jurisdiction clauses, however, is under discretion of a court. Although, after the cornerstone case *Eleftheria*, a valid jurisdiction clause will be held prima facie effective, the court still has discretion not to enforce it under specific circumstances.[42]

Prorogation effect

English common law preserves the discretion to determine the effect of a prorogation jurisdiction clause. Although it is relatively unusual for a chosen court to decline jurisdiction on the ground that it is more appropriate for a non-chosen forum to hear the case, the discretionary probability exists in theory. If the claimant brings proceedings in the court stimulated in the exclusive jurisdiction clause, the court will normally assert jurisdiction. Although the defendant can apply for a stay based on *forum non conveniens*, it is hard for the court to refuse jurisdiction, because the exclusive jurisdiction clause creates a prima facie case that the chosen forum is appropriate and the proceedings elsewhere are 'oppressive and vexatious'.[43] From this perspective, declining jurisdiction granted by a valid agreement may only have theoretic value without practical significance.

There is an argument that a jurisdiction clause may not be enforced if something unforeseeable at the time of contracting occurs.[44] However, it also depends on the effect of such unexpected facts. If the unexpected events only increase ordinary difficulties to the parties or increase litigation expenses at a reasonable level, there is no strong reason to avoid party autonomy. Only where such events make enforcement of the jurisdiction clause impractical may the court use discretion not to enforce the jurisdiction clause.

Derogation effect

The derogation effect of a foreign jurisdiction clause, however, is relatively easy to be ignored. In a few cases, English courts refused to stay jurisdiction

42 [1970] P 94.

43 *Seismic Shipping Inc & Anor v Total E & P UK Plc (The Western Regent)* [2005] 2 CLC 182; *Elektrim SA v Vivendi Universal SA* [2007] 2 Lloyd's Rep. 8; *Claxton Engineering Services Ltd v TXM Olaj-Es Gazkutato Kft* [2011] 2 All ER (Comm) 128; *Society of Lloyd's v White & Ors* [2000] CLC 961; *Donohue v Armco Inc* [2002] 1 All ER 749; *Sohio Supply Co v Gatoil (USA) Inc* [1989] 1 Lloyd's Rep. 588; *Star Reefers Pool Inc v JFC Group Co Ltd* [2012] 1 CLC 294.

44 *Beazley v Horizon Offshore Contractors* [2005] ILPr 11.

in favour of a foreign jurisdiction clause.[45] The courts usually consider the balance of private and public interest and conclude that, despite the jurisdiction clause designating a foreign court, English courts should be the more appropriate forum. In *The Fehmarn*,[46] a party brought the proceedings in England, though a Russian exclusive jurisdiction clause existed. The English court, however, took jurisdiction on the ground that England had closer connections to the dispute and the defendant would not object to submit to England if he could avoid giving security. In this case, the valid jurisdiction clause was departed from too lightly. Although the jurisdiction clause was contained in a standard form contract not subject to negotiation between the parties, it might not be the reason for the court to give it little weight, bearing in mind that both parties are sophisticated businessmen with equal bargaining power. There is no different treatment to standard form contracts and non-standard ones, except the *contra proferentem* rule applied to the interpretation of ambiguous terms. The possible explanation is that *The Fehmarn* was decided at the end of the 1950s, when the *Eleftheria* test was not provided. The court in *The Fehmarn* took a different approach to decide the effectiveness of a foreign jurisdiction clause.

In *Evans Marshall & Co. Ltd v Bertola S.A.*,[47] an English distributor (D1) and a Spanish wine producer entered into an exclusive distribution contract under which the English distributor was the sole agent to distribute the producer's wine in England. An exclusive jurisdiction clause was concluded providing Spanish courts jurisdiction. The producer later claimed that the performance of D1 was unsatisfactory and appointed another company (D2) as the agent to replace the distributor. D1 sued the producer and D2 as co-defendants in England, claiming conspiracy, breach of contract on the part of the producer and interference with performance of contract on the part of D2, and applied for injunction preventing the producer and D2 from selling wine in England. The English court, however, took jurisdiction regardless of the foreign exclusive jurisdiction clause. The reason given is that: the distribution dispute solely concerned England; the performance of D1 occurred in England exclusively; English witnesses were involved to testify D1's performance; proceedings would be slower in Spain and no interlocutory relief was available there. The approach is the same with *The Fehmarn* where ordinary connecting factors are considered and used to derogate from the jurisdiction clause. The only difference is that, in *Evans Marshall*, a third party to the jurisdiction clause was involved. If a dispute concerns the rights of a third party, who is not bound by the exclusive jurisdiction, and enforcing the jurisdiction

45 *Aratra Potato Co Ltd v Egyptian Navigation Co ('The El Amria')* [1981] Lloyd's Rep 119, CA; *Citi-march Ltd and Another v Neptune Orient Lines Ltd and Others* [1996] 1 WLR 1367; *The Athenee*, 11 Ll L Rep 6; *The Fehmarn* [1957] 1 WLR 815; *Mahavir Minerals Ltd v Cho Yang Shipping Co Ltd ('The MC Pearl')* [1997] CLC 794.

46 [1958] 1 WLR 159.

47 [1973] 1 WLR 349.

clause inevitably leads to split of proceedings and inconsistent result, a court may exercise its discretion not to enforce the jurisdiction clause. *Evans Marshall* only treats the third party interest as an ordinary factor.

After *The Eleftheria*,[48] the traditional approach to treat such a clause as only one factor in *forum non conveniens* is generally abandoned. English courts adopt the modern approach established in *The Eleftheria* to treat exclusive jurisdiction clauses prima facie effective unless the resisting party shows strong reasons proving contrary. The new approach greatly improves the effectiveness of a foreign exclusive jurisdiction clause. Many English courts have enforced a valid jurisdiction clause choosing a foreign court by refusing to issue a claim form out of jurisdiction or granting *forum non conveniens*.[49]

English courts, however, in a couple of cases continue to assert jurisdiction regardless of valid foreign jurisdiction clauses. In *Aratra Potato Co Ltd v Egyptian Navigation Co ('The El Amria')*,[50] the English Court of Appeal refused to decline jurisdiction in favour of the chosen court. The contract contained an exclusive jurisdiction clause choosing Egyptian courts and Egyptian law should apply. Nevertheless, the English court held that the disputed matter existed in England, the evidence was located in England and it would be impossible for an Egyptian court to understand the technical evidence, the parties could not obtain full and thorough investigation in Egypt and it was impossible to permit all witnesses to be fully heard in Egypt. The English court held that England was the more appropriate forum and the weight of the exclusive jurisdiction clause was overridden by other factors pointing to England. The same approach was also adopted by the Canadian court in *Anraj Fish Products Industries v Hyundai Merchant Marine Co Ltd*.[51] The Canadian court continued jurisdiction in breach of a valid jurisdiction clause choosing the Seoul Civil District Court (Korea). The court applied *The Eleftheria* and considered the location and availability of evidence and the litigation cost in both countries. Some witnesses would travel from France and some evidence was located in New York. Although the dispute had limited connections to Canada, evidence was more readily available there. It seems, however, the discretion has been applied too lightly in both cases. It is true that the parties may have made a choice of a court which is not the most convenient and inexpensive forum in the world. However, it is doubtful whether a court shall have the discretion to intervene. The parties' choice may be unreasonable or unwise, but as far as it is genuine and bona fide, and it does not affect the right of a third party or contradict public policy, there is no reason for the

48 [1970] P 94.

49 Fawcett and Carruthers, 2008: 444. *Mackender and Others v Feldia A. G.*, [1967] 2 QB 590; *Konkola Copper Mines Plc v Coromin* [2005] 1 CLC 1021.

50 *Aratra Potato Co Ltd v Egyptian Navigation Co ('The El Amria')* [1981] Lloyd's Rep 119, CA.

51 [2000] ILPr 717.

court to correct the choice. Permitting the parties to freely handle their business is the utmost goal of party autonomy.

The third party's interest and the necessity to consolidate proceedings are exceptional grounds used to depart from a valid jurisdiction clause.[52] In *Citi-March v Neptune Orient Lines*,[53] goods were damaged during shipping and the holder of the bill of lading sued the shipper and others responsible for storage in England. There was a clause in the bill of lading designating Singapore as the exclusive jurisdiction. The English court, however, refused to stay the proceedings based on the ground that this was a multi-defendant's litigation and the parties other than the shipper were not subject to the jurisdiction clause. Requiring the claimant to sue in Singapore under the jurisdiction clause would split proceedings and cause the risk of inconsistent decisions. Furthermore, evidence from the defendants not subject to the jurisdiction clause was important to decide liability. Suing in Singapore would prevent the claimant from getting the evidence. Therefore, strong causes were shown to depart from the jurisdiction clause. In *Mahavir Minerals v Cho Yang Shipping*,[54] the Queen's Bench Division (Admiralty Court) refused to enforce the Korean exclusive jurisdiction clause because it was considered necessary to concentrate all parties' disputes in one forum.

Time-bar in the chosen forum may also form a basis to avoid the enforcement of a valid foreign exclusive jurisdiction clause in England. However, English courts usually treat this factor with caution. The English courts should balance the policy of preventing a party from allowing time to run out in the chosen court and the policy not to deprive the claimant of his right to access to justice.[55] In *Citi-March v Neptune Orient Lines*, the court held that, if there was no strong cause showing English courts should not enforce a foreign jurisdiction clause, the claimant may rely on the time-bar of the chosen forum as far as he did not act unreasonably to allow the time to run out.[56] The unreasonableness is determined by all the circumstances, including the awareness of the time-bar, the explanation for the failure to preserve time and the appropriateness of the chosen forum in hearing the dispute.[57] If the claimant deliberately or negligently leaves the time to run out, the court will consider whether there are other strong causes in favour of English jurisdiction. If there are not, the English court will decline jurisdiction; if there are other strong causes, an explanation from the claimant is required.[58] However, it is unclear how much weight should be given to the explanation, and what if there is no legitimate

52 *Skype v Joltid*, [2011] ILPr 8., para 34.
53 [1996] 1 WLR 13367.
54 [1997] CLC 794.
55 *The Adolf Warski* [1976] 2 Lloyd's Rep 241 (CA), 112–113.
56 [1996] 1 WLR 1367, 1374C–F.
57 Ibid.
58 *Mahavir Minerals v Cho Yang Shipping*, 807.

explanation other than the claimant believes England is a more convenient or natural forum? In *Mahavir Minerals v Cho Yang Shipping*, the claimant did not commence proceedings in time in the chosen jurisdiction of South Korea. The court said that the failure was either deliberate strategy or oversight. No better explanation could be provided by the claimant. The English court took jurisdiction anyway, deciding there were strong causes in favour of English jurisdiction. Finally, English courts also have the power to stay jurisdiction in favour of the chosen forum on the condition that the other party waives the time-bar defence in the chosen jurisdiction.[59]

3.3 Enforcing jurisdiction agreements within the Brussels I Regulation

After the UK acceded to the Brussels Convention in 1979, the civil law approach in the Brussels I Regulation was applied to enforce jurisdiction agreements falling within the scope of the Brussels I Regulation. The Regulation applies where one of the parties has his or her domicile within one of the Member States and the parties have chosen one of the Member States to hear the dispute.[60] The Brussels I Regulation requires the chosen court to take jurisdiction. *Forum non conveniens* cannot be used to decline jurisdiction.[61] If both parties have their domiciles out of the Member States but have chosen the court of a Member State, the Brussels I Regulation does not require the chosen court to take jurisdiction, but demands non-chosen Member States to stay jurisdiction until jurisdiction is established by the chosen court.[62]

The distinction between EU and non-EU parties has generated criticism. There is no reason to leave uncertainty in enforcement of jurisdiction clauses by a Member State where parties in third parties are involved. Judgments resulting from such a jurisdiction clause also cannot be recognized and enforced in other Member States subject to the Regulation rules. The uncertainty has been recognized by the legislator and, in the Brussels I Recast, the uniform rules on enforcement have been extended to all jurisdiction clauses choosing a Member State, irrespective of the country of domicile of the parties.[63]

59 *Baghlaf Al Safer Factory Co BR for Industry Ltd v Pakistan National Shipping Co & Anor* [1998] CLC 716.

60 Art 23(1).

61 Case C-412/98, *Group Josi Reinsurance v Universal General Insurance* [2000] ECR I-5925; Case C-159/02, *Turner v Grovit* [2004] ECR I-3565.

62 Art 23(3).

63 Art 25(1) of the Brussels I Recast: 'If the parties, regardless of their domicile, have agreed that a court or the courts of a Member State are to have jurisdiction to settle any disputes which have arisen or which may arise in connection with a particular legal relationship, that court or those courts shall have jurisdiction...'

3.4 Assessment

In England, the effect and enforceability of an arbitration agreement is clearly stated in the statute, while the effectiveness of a valid jurisdiction clause in common law is uncertain. Discretion of a court is used in the latter instead of the former. The situation in jurisdiction clauses is much clearer in cases falling within the scope of the Brussels I Regulation, which establishes unambiguous duties for Member States to give full effectiveness to jurisdiction clauses. No discretion can be exercised in this scenario.

Certainty in jurisdiction agreements will be further improved after the Brussels I Recast enters into force, which extends the certain and predictable jurisdiction rules to all jurisdiction clauses choosing one of the Member States. Whenever English courts are chosen, the court must exercise jurisdiction and have no power to use discretion under the *Eleftheria.* When another Member State is chosen, the English court must decline jurisdiction and there is no room for it to assert jurisdiction for the purpose to achieve the end of justice. Common law rules can only be used where a non-EU Member State is chosen.

4 Enforcement in the USA

4.1 Enforcement of arbitration agreements

It has been observed by many commentators that US state courts traditionally held hostile attitudes towards arbitration agreements.[64] However, the Federal Arbitration Act (FAA) of 1925 established a policy in favour of the enforcement of an arbitration agreement.[65] The purpose of the FAA is to encourage the use of arbitration to reduce cost of litigation and to protect the commercial parties' freedom of contract.[66] The enforceability of an arbitration agreement is the same as all other contract terms and only subject to the contract theory.[67] In other words, after the court is satisfied that the arbitration agreement is valid, the court has no discretion not to enforce it. This rule pre-empts the law of individual states and guarantees the enforceability of arbitration agreements in the USA.[68] Arbitration agreements are enforced in claims in relation to statutory violation.[69]

64 Ritter, 2012: 44; Cunningham, 2012: 129; Crystal and Giannoni-Crystal, 2012: 238.

65 Ritter, 2012: 45; *Moses H. Cone Mem'l Hospital v Mercury Construction.*, 460 US 1, 24–25 (1983).

66 Crystal and Giannoni-Crystal, 2012: 238.

67 Cunningham, 2012: 129.

68 Ritter, 2012: 45; Crystal and Giannoni-Crystal, 2012: 240.

69 *Shearson/American Express Inc v McMahon,* 482 US 220, 226 (1987); Crystal and Giannoni-Crystal, 2012: 239.

Furthermore, US court practice demonstrates a distinction between domestic arbitration and international commercial arbitration. Although the courts also protect domestic arbitration, more flexibility and favour is given to international arbitration. The standard of arbitrability is relaxed in international arbitration, where the US Supreme Court upheld an arbitration agreement involving claims of fraud pursuant to the Securities Exchange Act of 1934.[70] There is argument that the implementation of the New York Convention contributes, at least partly, to the favourable attitudes towards international arbitration agreements.[71] The justification is that more uncertainties exist in international contracts than in domestic contracts caused by the relevance of different domestic law.[72] Arbitration agreements in international commercial contracts could produce predictability and, because it is reached with the mutual consent of the parties, it could prevent the possibility that the dispute is submitted to a forum hostile to the interest of one party.[73] This reason demonstrates the higher necessity to enforce arbitration agreements in international than in domestic disputes.

The enforcement of arbitration agreements is strengthened after the implementation of the New York Convention. It becomes a duty of US courts to enforce arbitration agreements and to recognize and enforce foreign arbitral awards falling within the scope of the New York Convention. Some commentators even argue that the US now has a strong culture in favour of arbitration and some judgments even turn hostile to litigation.[74] This is probably an overstatement. However, it is true that, unlike jurisdiction agreements, the enforcement of which is established by case law and the practice in each state is still inconsistent, the enforcement of arbitration clauses in the US shows consistency and certainty. The effectiveness of arbitration agreements is reassured by federal statutes and international treaties.[75] There is no evidence showing a US court could use discretion to refuse the enforcement of a valid arbitration agreement. Discretion, if it exists, should only rely on public policy, i.e. enforcing an arbitration agreement may harm US national interest. Even so, *Mitsubishi* still states that the court 'must weigh the concerns of American safety against a strong belief in the efficacy of arbitral procedures for the resolution of international commercial disputes and an equal commitment to the enforcement of freely negotiated choice of forum clauses'.[76] It is uncertain whether the New York Convention permits Contracting States

70 *Scherk v Alberto-Culver*, 417 US 506; Crystal and Giannoni-Crystal, 2012: 242.

71 Crystal and Giannoni-Crystal, 2012: 242.

72 *Scherk*, 417 US 506, 516.

73 Ibid.

74 Cunningham, 2012: 129; Siegel, 2006: 1139–1146. *AT&T Mobility v Vincent Concepcion et ux.* 131 S. Ct. 1740 (2011).

75 Crystal and Giannoni-Crystal, 2012: 246; *Mitsubishi*, 473 US 614, 636–640.

76 473 US 614, 630.

to refuse enforcing an arbitration agreement based on public policy, though it is clearly listed as a ground to refuse recognition and enforcement of arbitration awards.

4.2 Enforcement of jurisdiction agreements

Enforcement of jurisdiction agreements in the USA is generally based on common law. Pursuant to *Bremen*, a jurisdiction agreement must be enforced unless the opposing party can show that 'enforcement would be unreasonable and unjust', 'the clause was invalid for such reasons as fraud or overreaching' or enforcement is contrary to public policy.[77] In deciding whether enforcement is unreasonable, the court will consider whether the chosen court is 'seriously inconvenient for the trial of the action'.[78] 'Convenience' here includes the proximity between the chosen forum and the dispute, such as in a case where two Americans choose a foreign court to resolve essentially local disputes,[79] the remoteness is such a nature that the stronger party deprives the weaker party of his rights in an adhesive contract,[80] or the parties did not consider the particular dispute and thus made an unreasonable choice.[81] However, US court practice is very unclear as to whether the *Bremen* rule is reserved in US courts determining all disputes brought to the US courts, or the *Bremen* rule would be subject to the applicable law. The US court could apply the law of another country to decide the enforceability of choice of court clause.[82] The *Bremen* test replaces the ordinary *forum non conveniens* in deciding jurisdiction in cases where there are jurisdiction agreements.[83]

Enforcement of choice of court agreements is reinforced in *Carnival Cruise Lines v Shute*,[84] where a jurisdiction agreement in a standard contract between a carrier/company and a passenger/consumer was enforced. The Supreme Court did not accept the argument that the passenger had no opportunities to bargain, thereby rendering the jurisdiction clause unenforceable. The Supreme Court held that, first, the business had an interest to limit its commercial risk in terms of where to be sued; second, the jurisdiction provided certainty to both parties; third, the passenger probably received benefits by reduced fares associated with higher

77 *Bremen v Zapata Off-Shore*, 407 US 1, 15 (1972); Dubay, 2011: 15; Moberly, 2009: 275.

78 *Bremen*, 407 US 16.

79 *Bremen*, 407 US 17.

80 *Bremen*, 407 US 17.

81 *Bremen*, 407 US 17. Dubay, 2011: 15.

82 Dubay, 2011: 17.

83 *Pelleport Investors v Budco Quality Theatres*, 741 F.2d 273, 280 (9th Cir. 1984); *Aguas Lenders Recovery v Suez, S.A.*, 585 F.3d 696, 700 (2d Cir. 2009); *Evolution Online System v Koninklijke PTT Nederland*, 145 F.3d 505, 509–510 (2d Cir. 1998); cited in Dubay, 2011: 19–20. For more on *Bremen*, see Holt, 2009: 1913; Corsico, 2003: 1853; Marcus, 2008: 973; Moberly, 2009: 265; Brittain, Jr., 2001: 305.

84 *Carnival Cruise Lines, Inc. v Shute*, 499 US 585 (1991).

commercial safety; fourth, the clause was not induced by fraud or over-reaching; fifth, the chosen forum was the principal place of business and was not chosen for the purpose of preventing consumers from suing; and sixth, the consumer was informed of the existence of the clause and had the option to reject.[85] *Carnival Cruise Line* thus adopted the same test to adherent contracts and believed that discretion was enough to achieve fairness and justice in individual cases.

Although the US Federal Court has consistently followed the *Bremen* test to enforce a valid jurisdiction clause, US state courts use different standards when deciding enforceability of jurisdiction clauses.[86] In New York, for example, the choice of New York courts requires the jurisdiction agreement to be governed by New York law and the value of transaction to be above one million dollars.[87] The power to refuse enforcing a jurisdiction clause choosing US courts by *forum non conveniens* is still maintained by state courts.[88] Even though many state courts believe the opposing party has a strong burden to show the jurisdiction clause should not be enforced, they, at least, permit a valid jurisdiction clause to be set aside.[89]

Enforceability of a jurisdiction clause may also be denied if such a clause may prevent its party from participating in class action. It is true that a jurisdiction clause is not a class action waiver agreement. It, however, has the potential to prevent consumers from bringing class actions in another country. In *Doel v AOL*,[90] the parties entered into an exclusive jurisdiction clause choosing courts of Virginia. The plaintiffs brought the class action in California. The defendant did not defend the plaintiffs' right to bring class action, but asked for the court to enforce the jurisdiction clause, which was freely entered into between the parties. The Ninth Circuit refused the argument based on public policy. The jurisdiction agreement required all disputes to be heard by courts 'of' Virginia, instead of courts 'in' Virginia. It was interpreted as referring to state courts of Virginia, instead of the federal courts within Virginia. Since state courts of Virginia did not allow class actions, enforcing the jurisdiction clause

85 *Carnival Cruise Lines*, 499 US 585, 592–593. More on *Carnival Cruise Lines*, see Wright, 2011: 1625.

86 *Stewart Organization v Ricoh*, 487 US 22, 29 (1988). Dubay, 2011: 20–22; Moberly, 2009: 265.

87 New York General Obligations Law, s5–1402, as cited in Nygh, 1999: 16.

88 Nygh, 1999: 16; *May v US HIFU, LLC.*, 98 A.D.3d 1004, 951 N.Y.S.2d 163 (N.Y.A.D. 2 Dept., 2012); *Bumpus v Ward*, Ohio App. 5 Dist., 2012 (Oct 09, 2012); *In re Marriage of Ricard and Sahut*, 975 N.E.2d 1220 (Ill.App. 1 Dist., 2012).

89 *March USA v Hamby*, 28 Misc.3d 1214 (Sup. Ct., N.Y. County 2010); *Banco Ambrosiano v Artoc Bank and Trust*, 62 N.Y.2d 65 (1984); *National Union Fire v Source One Staffing*, 36 Misc.3d 1224(A) (N.Y.Supp., 2012); *K2M3, LLC v Cocoon Data Holding Pty. Ltd*, Not Reported in S.W.3d, 2012 WL 2469705 (Tex.App.-Corpus Christi, 2012); *RWI Acquisition LLC v Todd*, Not Reported in A.3d, 2012 WL 1955279 (Del.Ch., 2012). For the practice in Arizona, see Moberly and Lisenbee, 2010: 54; practice in Texas, see Yetter, 2010: 274.

90 2009 WL 103657 (9 Cir. Jan 16, 2009).

effectively prevented Californian consumers from exercising their rights to participate in class actions. The effect violated the public policy of California, in which the current action was brought.[91]

4.3 Assessment

The US practice distinguishes conflicts between states and international disputes, and upholds party autonomy more in the latter cases. In general, a policy to support party autonomy has been established. The difference is that the policy is enforced more readily in arbitration agreements than in jurisdiction agreements. The above discussion shows that jurisdiction and arbitration agreements have a similar history in the USA, and the US courts' attitude changes from hostility to support.[92] The difference exists in the reason for change. The change of attitude in arbitration agreements was initiated by the statutes and reinforced by treaty duties; the change in jurisdiction agreements was initiated by judgments. The different sources also show that enforcement of arbitration agreements is more certain and consistent in US courts, while the enforcement of jurisdiction agreements is uncertain, subject to courts' discretion. Although the *Bremen* test established criteria to decide the enforceability, there lacks consistent interpretation as to how the criteria should be interpreted. Questions arise as to what it meant by reasonableness, and when public policy can be used to refuse the enforcement of jurisdiction clauses.

5 Enforcement by and against the third party

5.1 General rule

It is also necessary to know that a common exception to the enforcement of a valid dispute resolution agreement is that it usually could not bind a third party. A third party does not enter into the agreement. If one of the parties, after disputes have arisen, applies to add a third party into the proceedings, where the action is brought under a jurisdiction clause which prorogates jurisdiction to an otherwise incompetent forum, the application could not be successful. The question as to which party is subject to the agreement is determined under the *lex fori*. In the US, the court will consider all the circumstances of case and the contract terms to interpret the meaning and scope of a dispute resolution clause. In *YA Global Investments v Cliff*,[93] the Superior Court of New Jersey held that a personal guarantor was a third party to the financing agreement between the guarantee

91 *Bremen v Zapata Off-Shore Co*, 407 US 1 (1972). See also *America Online v Superior Court of Alamed County*, 108 Cal. Rptr.2d 699 (Cal. App. 2001).

92 Crystal and Giannoni-Crystal, 2012: 247.

93 15 A.3d 857 (N.J.Super.A.D., 2011).

and the lender, even if the guarantor signed the agreement acknowledging its existence, because the body of the agreement implied that only the lender and the guarantee were parties to the agreement. The agreement signed by the guarantor has used clear language stating that it is a contract 'by and among' A and B, and the body also used the language 'the other party' in the singular term to demonstrate only two parties are bound by the agreement.[94] In *Asoma v SK Shipping*,[95] the court held that a charterer should be bound by the jurisdiction clause in charter party and will not be influenced by the bill of lading. In EU, the uniform interpretation is provided to determine the effect of a jurisdiction clause against a third party. Pursuant to a recent case, *Refcomp SpA v Axa Corporate Solutions Assurance SA*,[96] the ECJ decided that a jurisdiction clause concluded in the contract between the manufacturer and the buyer would not bind the third party who is the sub-buyer in the re-sale or chain contract. The same general principle applies to arbitration agreements. Arbitrators' power is solely originated from parties' consent and, as a result, arbitrators have no power to extend the arbitration agreement to a third party.[97]

However, a third party is bound by a dispute resolution clause if he takes over the rights and obligations of one of the original parties under the rule of subrogation,[98] expressly gives his consent to the clause,[99] has acquired benefit from express terms of the original contract[100] or has a close relationship with the original contract or with one of the original parties.[101]

5.2 Taking over the rights and obligations of the other party

It is a common practice that a jurisdiction or arbitration clause in a bill of lading binds the litigation activity of the holder even if it is a clause entered into by the carrier and the shipper. In *Tilly Russ*,[102] the ECJ decided that as far as the third party, by acquiring the bill of lading,

94 15 A.3d 862–863.

95 467 F.3d 817 (C.A.2 (N.Y.), 2006).

96 Case C-543/10, *Refcomp SpA v Axa Corporate Solutions Assurance SA*, unreported 7 February 2013. See comments in Note, 'Jurisdiction clause does not bind subsequent purchaser without his assent' (2013) 305 EU Focus 8.

97 Ambrose, 2001: 415, 415–416; Blackaby *et al.*, 2009: s1.112.

98 Brand and Herrup, 2008: 261; Gunerozbek, 2011: 279; Hartley and Dogauchi, 2007: paras 97, 142, 143 and 294; Hess *et al.*, 2007: paras 285–291; Hartley, 2009: 175; Ambrose, 2001: 416. Case C-387/98, *Coreck Maritime v Handelsveem*, [2000] ECR I-9337, para 22; Case 71/83, *Tilly Russ v Nova*, [1984] ECR 2417.

99 Case C-543/10, *Refcomp SpA v Axa Corporate Solutions Assurance SA*.

100 Contracts (Rights of Third Parties) Act 1999, section 1. Case 201/82, *Gerling v Amministrazione del Tesoro dello Stato* [1983] ECR 2503.

101 *Lu v Dryclean-USA of California*, 11 Cal.App.4th 1490 (Cal.App. 1 Dist. 1992).

102 Case 71/83, *Tilly Russ and Ernest Russ v NV Haven- & Vervoerbedrijf Nova and NV Goeminne Hout* [1984] ECR 2417.

succeeds to the shipper's rights and obligations, the jurisdiction clause will bind the third party. The holder is vested with all the rights and obligations mentioned in the bill of lading, including the jurisdiction agreement.[103] This is also expressly accepted in the UK Carriage of Goods by Sea Act 1992.[104]

A third party who is an assignee will also be bound by a jurisdiction clause concluded by its assignor.[105] In *Glencore International AG v Metro Trading International (No 1)* and *Metro Trading International v Itochu Petroleum (No 1)*,[106] multiple proceedings were brought by multiple parties. A seller entered into a sale of goods contract with some companies, which included an exclusive jurisdiction clause choosing England. After the seller went bankrupt, a receiver was appointed. A French bank that financed the seller's business commenced actions in France against the seller and other parties to recover the amounts due. The receiver brought the action in England in the name of the seller to recover payment of the purchase price from one of the buyers. This buyer joined the bank as a third party to ensure that they would be bound by the court's decision. Although the bank was an assignee of the seller, the bank claimed that it was a third party and did not know the existence of the exclusive jurisdiction clause. Under English law, an assignee cannot be better off than the assignor when taking over the latter's rights. The assignee must, in the same time, be bound by all the obligations that are originated from the contract together with the rights.[107] Since Article 17 of the Brussels Convention (same content of Art 23 of the Brussels I Regulation) applied to the dispute, the English court considered whether an assignee should be bound by the jurisdiction clause entered into by the assignor. The court believed that a third party in assignment had the same status as it did in a bill of lading.[108] The court also believed that requiring an assignee to be bound by the exclusive jurisdiction clause would not undermine the principles of prorogation jurisdiction under the Brussels Convention. The court states that:[109]

> The assignee of a debt, as a recipient of rights, but not of obligations, will always be the claimant in an action between himself and the debtor and the agreement will not therefore derogate from his right under the Convention to be sued in the courts of his own country of domicile when he is a defendant. For his part, the debtor has agreed to be sued in the chosen jurisdiction and has therefore agreed to any such derogation.

103 [1984] ECR 2417, para 25.
104 s2(1).
105 *Firswood Lea v Petra Bank*, [1996] CLC 608.
106 [2000] ILPr 358.
107 Ibid.
108 Case 71/83, *Tilly Russ* [1984] ECR 2417.
109 *Glencore International AG v Metro Trading International Inc*, 99.

The same applies to arbitration agreements. In *The Hari Bhum (No 2)*,[110] the insurer of the shipper settled the damage claim for losses and sued the insurer of the liable haulage company to recover the costs. The English court requires the claimant to bring the action in arbitration pursuant to the arbitration agreement in the original contract between the shipper and the haulage company because both insurance companies were treated as the assignees or transferees of the original contract parties.

5.3 Expressly granting the benefits to a third party

While bill of lading and assignment both vest the third party all the rights and obligations of the original contractor, the third party beneficiary in an insurance contract acquires its rights and obligations in the jurisdiction and arbitration clause by a different means. In *Gerling v Amministrazione del Tesoro dello Stato*,[111] there was a contract concluded between the insured and the insurer but expressly for the benefit of the third party beneficiary. The ECJ believed that the insurance contract was made for the benefit of the third party and gave him the right to rely on it to bring an action against the insurer. The insurer, when entered into the agreement, agreed to be sued by either the policy holder or the beneficiary according to the jurisdiction clause. As a result, the beneficiary, though not a party to the agreement, is totally entitled to sue the insurer according to the jurisdiction clause.

This practice is recognized by legislation in the UK Third Parties (Rights Against Insurers) Act 1930. In non-insurance cases, if a Himalaya clause is concluded to confer rights to the third parties, the courts will still hold the third parties bound by the dispute resolution agreement concluded in the original contract, treating the third parties as entering into the original contract.[112] More development exists in the Contracts (Third Parties) Act 1999, which provides that if the third party wants to enforce a contract term that confers him substantive rights subject to an arbitration clause in the original contract, the third party shall be treated as a party of the arbitration clause and be bound by the arbitration agreement.[113] The substantive benefit is a 'conditional' benefit subject to a procedural condition of submitting to arbitration.[114]

The same decision was held in the USA. In *Taag Linhas Aereas de Angola v Transamerica Airlines*,[115] the court held that a third party beneficiary of an

110 [2005] 1 CLC 376.

111 Case 201/82, *Gerling v Amministrazione del Tesoro dello Stato* [1983] ECR 2503.

112 Ambrose, 2001: 417.

113 s8(1).

114 *Fortress Value Recovery Fund v Blue Skye Special Opportunities Fund*, [2013] EWCA Civ 367, para 42 (per Lord Toulson).

115 915 F.2d 1351 (9th Cir 1990). See *Eric H Lu v Dryclean-USA of California*, 11 Cal.App.4th 1490 (Cal.App. 1 Dist. 1992).

insurance contract should be bound by the choice of court agreement in the contract because 'it is well-settled contract law that the scope of a third-party beneficiary's rights is defined by the contract'. This is justified as the third-party must have the knowledge of the contract and the jurisdiction clause therein and, as a result, must have reasonably foreseen the application of the jurisdiction clause in order to enforce his contractual rights.

5.4 Consent and knowledge of the third party

Where a third party has given consent or has knowledge of the dispute resolution clause, when taking over rights and obligations of an original party, there is no problem to bind the third party by the dispute resolution clause. In China, for example, the Supreme People's Court provided judicial direction that if the third party has taken over all, or part of, the rights and obligations of the original party of an arbitration agreement, the agreement is effective to the successor, unless the third party expressly objects to or has no factual or constructive knowledge of an arbitration agreement not written within their main contract.[116]

However, it is questionable as to whether a third party's consent or knowledge to the existence and content of the jurisdiction clause is mandatory before the clause can be enforced against him. In *Tilly Russ*, the ECJ made its decision solely on the legal effect of subrogation, namely the holder of the bill of lading acquired all the rights and obligations of the shipper as set out in it. ECJ specifically stated that the requirement of safeguard to the third party's intention was irrelevant.[117] In *Metro Trading*,[118] the court rejected the defendant assignee's argument that it did not have actual knowledge of the existence of the jurisdiction clause. The court believed that assignment was a straightforward procedure to transfer rights and obligations under a contract to another party. The third party thus completely takes the original party's shoes. The contract thus is enforceable between the third party and one of the original parties without extra test as to which obligations the third party was aware of. The binding effect originates from the legal consequence of the assignment and subrogation, instead of the consent to conclude each contract term by the third party. Substantive knowledge on the part of a third party is considered immaterial for the exclusive jurisdiction clause to bind the third party.

However, in other cases, the court has considered the knowledge of the third party and required at least constructive knowledge of the existence of the jurisdiction clause. In *Firswood Lea v Petra Bank*,[119] for example, when

116 'Arbitration Law Interpretation 2006', Art 9.
117 Para 24.
118 [2000] ILPr 358.
119 [1996] CLC 608.

justifying the decision to bind an assignee to a jurisdiction clause concluded by the assignor, Schiemann LJ considered the elements as follows: (1) the contract subject to assignment is the type of contract the benefit of which is frequently assigned; (2) the other contractual party suffers no advantage from being sued in the chosen court by a different claimant; (3) 'there would be nothing unreasonable in holding the assignee bound by a jurisdiction clause of which he had knowledge and which was clearly set out in the agreement the benefit of which has been assigned to him'.[120] The simple existence of a jurisdiction clause was not enough to bind the assignee, but there must be elements suggesting the assignee was aware of the existence of the jurisdiction clause. In *Gerling*, although it was the third party who relied on the jurisdiction clause, the ECJ still took the fact that the original contract party knew and was aware of the jurisdiction clause.

It is true that binding the holder of a bill of lading to a jurisdiction clause contained in it is a common practice and it is a custom not to require the holder to express its consent or to sign the agreement. However, it does not mean constructive knowledge is completely unnecessary for a dispute resolution clause to bind a third party. If two contractual parties have a long-term business relationship and have a dispute resolution clause binding them, without a written contract to clearly set the clause out, a third party subrogator will have no opportunity to know the existence of such a clause and will be prejudiced by the lack of knowledge. Although the actual knowledge is not required, the dispute resolution clause should at least be provided to the third party and be observable in the contract. Otherwise, there must be either common practice between the assignor, assignee and the other party, or common usage in trade and commerce, to support the constructive knowledge.

5.5 Close relationship with the third party

Where the third party has not taken over the original party's rights and obligations and is not expressly named in the original contract, it may still be bound by the dispute resolution agreement if it is closely related to the original contractual relationship or with one of the original parties. In *Lu v Dryclean-USA of California*,[121] the franchise agreement between the franchisee and franchiser included a jurisdiction agreement. The claimant later brought an action to rescind the franchise contract based on misrepresentation and tried to avoid the jurisdiction agreement by claiming two defendants did not sign the franchise contract and were not parties to the jurisdiction agreement. The court, however, held that the two defendants were closely connected to the franchise contract and they were alleged by the claimant to have participated in the misrepresentation. They were also

120 [1996] CLC 608, 618.
121 *Lu v Dryclean-USA of California*, 11 Cal.App.4th 1490 (Cal.App. 1 Dist. 1992).

alleged to be the alter ego of the franchiser. The third parties, thus, had close relationship with the contract and one of the parties.

A similar approach is applied in arbitration. In *Dow Chemical France v Isover (France)*,[122] the French tribunal pierced the corporate veil between the parent company, a US company and a French subsidiary in the same corporate group and took jurisdiction over all the relevant parties, though not all of them signed the arbitration agreement, since all the companies were involved and played substantive roles in the negotiation, conclusion and performance of one contract. In England, the English court also allows arbitration clauses to bind a closely related third party by relying on the doctrine of corporate veil, though the test standard is much higher in English common law.[123]

What relationships are considered close enough? They include parent–subsidy, director–company, principal–agent, successor–predecessor, controlling shareholder–company, guarantor–guarantee, and affiliated companies.[124] These relationships usually have the potential to make the related parties jointly liable for a specified obligation. The justification is that, if a jurisdiction clause does not bind a closely related third party, this situation may be abused by both original parties to escape a valid jurisdiction clause. The non-related original party may escape a valid jurisdiction clause by bringing actions against a closely related third party.[125] The related original party may also escape the clause by allowing the third party to bring actions instead. Furthermore, the close relationship makes the third party reasonably foresee it may be bound by the chosen court. Extending jurisdiction against them may not breach their expectation. Finally, according to the principle of mutuality, the third party that can foresee being bound by a jurisdiction clause is also entitled to enforce this clause positively against the other party.[126]

In *Venard v Jackson Hole Paragliding*,[127] the claimant signed agreements to obtain membership with the US Gliding and Paragliding Association (GPA), which submitted all disputes to the court of California. The claimant then suffered injury when attending paragliding training offered by a

122 (1984) IV Yearbook Commercial Arbitration 131.

123 See *Roussel-Uclaf v GD Searle Co* [1978] 1 Lloyd's Rep 225. Blackaby *et al.*, 2009: s2.45.

124 *Venard v Jackson Hole Paragliding* 292 P.3d 165, 172 (Wyo., 2013). *Medtronic, Inc. v Endologix, Inc.*, 530 F. Supp. 2d 1054, 1057 (D.Minn. 2008); *Marano Enters. v Z–Teca Rests., L.P.*, 254 F.3d 753, 757 (8th Cir. 2001)); *Cooper v Meridian Yachts, Ltd*, 575 F.3d 1151, 1170 (11th Cir. 2009); *Holland Am. Line, Inc. v Wartsila N. Am., Inc.*, 485 F.3d 450, 456 (9th Cir. 2007); *Lipcon v Underwriters at Lloyd's*, 148 F.3d 1285, 1299 (11th Cir. 1998). Blackaby *et al.*, 2009: s2.40, s2.49.

125 11 Cal.App.4th 1490, 1494.

126 *Venard v Jackson Hole Paragliding* 292 P.3d 165, 172; *Frietsch v Refco, Inc.*, 56 F.3d 825, 827–828 (7th Cir. Ill. 1995); *General Electric Co. v Siempelkamp GmbH & Co.*, 809 F. Supp. 1306, 1310 (S.D.Ohio 1993), aff'd, 29 F.3d 1095 (6th Cir. 1994); *Buffet Crampon S.A.S. v Schreiber & Keilwerth*, 2009 WL 3675807, 9, 2009 US Dist. (N.D.Ind. 2 November 2009).

127 292 P.3d 165 (Wyo., 2013).

paragliding company and brought action against the paragliding company in Wyoming. The defendant claimed that the jurisdiction clause should apply because they were also members of the same association. The defendant had relationship with one of the original parties to the contract, but this relationship is not close enough to make the defendant and the GPA share any liability. The court then refused the petition to allow the third party to enforce the jurisdiction agreement.

6 Conclusion

The recent development in international commerce and the wide acceptance of party autonomy determine the trend to favour dispute resolution agreements, including both jurisdiction and arbitration agreements. However, comparing jurisdiction and arbitration agreements, evidence shows that more effectiveness and respect is given to the parties' consent to submit their dispute to arbitration than to the court of another country. In the USA, UK and China, enforceability and effectiveness of arbitration agreements is established by clear and unambiguous statutory provisions. In order to protect the enforcement of arbitration agreements, China has even adopted a unique internal report and review scheme to ensure the better enforcement of arbitration agreements. In the US and England, the court has no discretion to take jurisdiction irrespective of a valid arbitration agreement. The common law doctrine of *forum conveniens* has no place in disputes involving arbitration agreements.

Comparatively, the enforcement of jurisdiction agreements is more uncertain. In all three countries, enforceability of jurisdiction agreements is not clearly expressed in statutes, with one exception to the Brussels I Regulation. Proper enforcement of a jurisdiction agreement requires the court to recognize both its prorogation power, by taking jurisdiction if it is the chosen court, and its derogation power, by declining jurisdiction if it is not chosen. While most courts now readily recognize the prorogation effect of a jurisdiction clause, some still hold a sceptical attitude against the derogation effect. It is probably because a court does not like its statutory power of jurisdiction to be ousted by private parties, and feels extremely uncomfortable to give up its power to a court with equal authority in another sovereign state. Although arbitration agreements also 'oust' a court's jurisdiction, the derogation power of arbitration agreements has been widely accepted. A court does not feel uneasy to let a private body take the power to decide private parties' dispute, considering it is in the best interest of commercial convenience to permit the parties free disposal of their disputes in arbitration.

In English and US law, enforceability of a jurisdiction clause is subject to common law, which establishes a basic test to assess the enforceability of such a clause but nevertheless lacks clearer guidance. Discretion is left to judges in making decisions on a case-by-case basis. Furthermore, the traditional common law doctrine of *forum non conveniens* still plays a role in disputes involving a choice of court agreement. Uncertainty remains an issue.

One of the most important reasons contributing to the difference is the existence of international treaty obligations in enforcing arbitration agreements. While most countries have ratified the New York Convention, they should fulfil their treaty obligations to give full effectiveness to arbitration agreements. The lack of the same obligations partially causes the uncertainty in enforcement of jurisdiction agreements. In England, for example, uncertainty remains in the traditional common law, but great certainty exists for cases covered in the regime of the Brussels I Regulation. It is reasonable to predict that if the Hague Choice of Court Convention is ratified by many countries, jurisdiction clauses will have enforceability not less than arbitration agreements.

Refusing the derogation effect of a jurisdiction clause usually stems from two reasons: state sovereignty and enforcement of judgments. As to the first reason, it is believed that the jurisdiction is based on an external expression of state sovereignty. Private parties may have autonomy to decide their own affairs, but they do not have the power to exclude states' jurisdiction they may otherwise have. Private parties cannot intervene into state sovereignty. In this sense, the derogation effect of a jurisdiction clause may be considered as something against public policy of the country which has jurisdiction in the absence of jurisdiction. Second, without judicial cooperation, decisions made pursuant to jurisdiction clauses cannot be enforced easily in the other country. If there is no chance for the judgment to be enforced and one party sued in the non-chosen country where enforcement will be sorted, the court may assert jurisdiction in breach of the exclusive jurisdiction clause based on the reason of easy enforcement of judgment.[128]

128 This is the case in China. In *NKK*, the court mainly based the decision to take jurisdiction on the ground that Hong Kong decisions could not be enforced in China Mainland.

6 Supporting party autonomy

Lis pendens, forum non conveniens and anti-suit injunctions

1 Introduction

Party autonomy is an effective instrument to resolve the problem of conflict of jurisdiction. In the ideal scenario, where all countries have the same set of rules in deciding the validity and enforceability of a jurisdiction agreement and all courts strictly follow these rules, the existence of a valid exclusive jurisdiction clause could diminish both positive and negative conflict of jurisdiction. The chosen court is the only competent one and must take jurisdiction pursuant to the agreement, while all non-chosen fora should decline jurisdiction. However, this ideal situation does not exist. Jurisdiction agreements, as a result, cannot completely end forum shopping or conflict of jurisdiction. The traditional instruments, such as *lis pendens*, *forum non conveniens* and anti-suit injunctions, continue to be applied in cases where an exclusive jurisdiction agreement exists.[1]

Conflict of jurisdiction may also exist between courts and arbitral tribunals. Compared to jurisdiction, there is better harmonization in international arbitration in the effectiveness of an arbitration agreement, but differences continue to exist in terms of existence and validity of arbitration agreements. There is the possibility that both an arbitral tribunal and a court assert jurisdiction to decide the subject matter and deliver different decisions. In arbitration, conflicts of jurisdiction may exist between the arbitral tribunal and the supervisory court, between the tribunal and a non-supervisory court, and between the supervisory and non-supervisory court. There is no rule of *lis pendens* relating to arbitration, but *forum non conveniens* and anti-suit/anti-arbitration injunctions are still available to handle the parallel proceedings arising out of arbitration.

1 See Tang, 2012a: 321.

2 *Lis pendens* and conflicts agreements

2.1 Lis pendens

Lis pendens means pending lawsuits in concurrent proceedings on the same or related matters.[2] It usually occurs where the claimant sues the defendant in one of the competent fora, while the defendant subsequently sues the claimant in another competent forum on the same subject matter.[3] Sometimes, the defendant sues the claimant in the second seized court on unidentical but related disputes, which also causes *lis pendens* in a broad sense.[4] In unusual cases, the same claimant may bring two proceedings in different courts.[5] *Lis pendens* can also occur at the enforcement stage, where one court has delivered judgment which is sought for enforcement by the claimant in another country, but the defendant brings an action on the same or related matter in a different forum. In all these cases, there will be more than one action existing concurrently.

It is not difficult to see why concurrent proceedings should be avoided. Concurrent proceedings would almost inevitably cause delay, expense and inconvenience to the parties, and waste judicial resources and public funds.[6] More problems would arise where irreconcilable judgments are given and both seek recognition and enforcement in the same country. This reason is recognized in the EU, which provides, in the Brussels I Regulation, that '(i)n the interests of the harmonious administration of justice it is necessary to minimise the possibility of concurrent proceedings and to ensure that irreconcilable judgments will not be given in two Member States'.[7] The problem in enforcing irreconcilable judgments is considered more severe among countries with judicial cooperation. Irreconcilable judgments and concurrent proceedings between Member States or Contracting States would undoubtedly affect mutual trust between countries. The *lis pendens* rule in countries with judicial cooperation requires the second seized court to stay jurisdiction in favour of the first one.[8] However, if there is no judicial cooperation facilitating sound administration of justice and reciprocal recognition and enforcement of judgments, the only consideration that may encourage a country to handle *lis pendens* is international comity and the practical concern of the waste of public recourses if the decision is not going to be enforced in another country. A country may not intend to avoid *lis pendens*, especially where the defendant has dis-

2 Clarkson and Hill, 2011: 114–122; Fawcett and Carruthers, 2008: 303ff.; Hartley, 2009: 237ff.

3 E.g. Art 27(1) of the Brussels I Regulation.

4 Art 28(1) of the Brussels I Regulation.

5 McLachlan, 2008: 227.

6 McLachlan, 2008: 216.

7 Recital 15 of the Brussels I Regulation.

8 Arts 27(1) and 28(1) of the Brussels I Regulation.

trainable property under the control of this country and judgments are likely to be enforced here.[9] Some countries believe jurisdiction is based on sovereignty and they would be reluctant to stay their jurisdiction or to interfere in other countries' jurisdiction to avoid concurrent proceedings.

2.2 **Lis pendens** *and jurisdiction agreements in civil law countries*

Using the chronological order to deal with concurrent proceedings is originated in civil law countries handling internal *lis pendens* between domestic courts.[10] For example, the PRC Civil Procedure Law provides that: if the plaintiff brings the lawsuit in two or more people's courts that have jurisdiction over the lawsuit, the people's court in which the case was first entertained shall have jurisdiction.[11] The reason for the adoption of *lis pendens* in the domestic context is to guarantee that only one competent domestic court should hear a dispute and no irreconcilable judgments should be provided in different domestic courts at the same hierarchic level of one country. However, extending domestic *lis pendens* to cross-border disputes is much more difficult. Almost no civil law countries expressly adopt the *lis pendens* rule in dealing with concurrent proceedings with other countries, unless required by treaty obligations.[12]

Lis pendens *and jurisdiction agreements in countries without judicial cooperation*

Civil law countries traditionally make jurisdiction compulsory and a court cannot refuse exercising jurisdiction unless expressly provided by legislation.[13] For example, although Chinese law accepts the *lis pendens* rule to combat conflict of jurisdiction between two Chinese courts, this rule is not equally applied in cross-border cases. The Supreme People's Court has, on more than one occasion, directed Chinese courts that the existence of the same proceedings in another country could not prevent a competent Chinese court from taking jurisdiction, unless provided otherwise by treaties.[14] It does not matter if the foreign court is seized first. In practice,

9 A typical example is the legal practice in China. Since Chinese courts have very narrow grounds to enforce foreign judgments, Chinese courts would not give consideration to *lis pendens* when taking jurisdiction.
10 Schlosser, 2000: 81; McLachlan, 2008: 270ff.
11 CPR Civil Procedure Law 2012, Art 35.
12 McLachlan, 2008: 271; Nuyts, 2007: 100.
13 Schlosser, 2000: 54.
14 Supreme People's Court, 'Summary of the Second National Conference on the Adjudication of Commercial and Maritime Cases with Foreign Elements', [2005] No 26, Art 10; Du, 2007; *Kwok & Yih Law Firm*, Xiamen Municipal Intermediate People's Court, 13 August 2003. Supreme People's Court, 'Opinions on Several Issues on the Implementation of the Civil Procedure Law of the People's Republic of China', [1992] No 22, Art 306.

Chinese courts rarely consider if a foreign action is pending on the same matter or if a foreign court has already given judgment on the issue in dispute.[15] Because the lack of judicial cooperation between China and most countries in recognition and enforcement of judgments, and because Chinese domestic law provides very narrow grounds to enforce a foreign judgment, Chinese law permits the party to bring the same action in China after a foreign court gives judgment, as far as the judgment cannot be enforced in Chinese courts.[16] Without judicial cooperation, most civil law countries will not voluntarily adopt *lis pendens* to stay their jurisdiction in favour of a first seized foreign court, or to expect a foreign court to stay its jurisdiction in favour of them.

A limited number of civil law countries, however, adopt *lis pendens* in cross-border cases with many extra conditions. For example, the Civil Code of Quebec provides that:

> (o)n the application of a party, a Québec authority may stay its ruling on an action brought before it if another action, between the same parties, based on the same facts and having the same object is pending before a foreign authority, provided that the latter action can result in a decision which may be recognized in Québec, or if such a decision has already been rendered by a foreign authority.[17]

However, the influence of an exclusive jurisdiction clause to *lis pendens* is unclear. It is very likely that these courts are more willing to give full effect to a jurisdiction clause than staying jurisdiction based on *lis pendens*. Once there is an exclusive jurisdiction clause, these courts, though accepting unilateral *lis pendens*, will not consider the concurrent proceedings any more, but will give the exclusive jurisdiction clauses a full effect.[18]

Unlike *lis pendens*, which is not unilaterally adopted by most civil law countries in cross-border disputes, many civil law countries expressly provide effects and enforceability to exclusive jurisdiction clauses. For example, the Civil Code of Quebec expressly provides that, although the court of Quebec might have jurisdiction based on one of the five

15 *Kwok & Yih Law Firm. Shanghai Saifeng International Trade v CICB Changzhou*, Jiangsu Province Changzhou Intermediate Court, (2006) No 26; *Jiangmen Xinhua Paper Mill v HK Tak Lee Metals & Paper*, Guangdong High Court, (1999) No 322.

16 Supreme Court, Opinion 1992, Art 318; *Russian National Orchestra Application on the Recognition of Judgments of English High Court*, Beijing Municipal No 2 Intermediate People's Court, (2004) No 928; *Zhuo v Nanjing Diansheng*, Jiangsu Province Nanjing Municipal Intermediate People's Court, (2004) No 7.

17 Art 3137.

18 See more discussion on the rule dealing with exclusive jurisdiction clauses in Quebec in the next paragraph.

jurisdictional grounds,[19] a Quebec court has no jurisdiction 'where the parties, by agreement, have chosen to submit all existing or future disputes between themselves relating to a specified legal relationship to a foreign authority'.[20] Germany, the Netherlands, Switzerland, Greece and Japan all demand the court to decline jurisdiction while there is a foreign exclusive jurisdiction clause.[21] Some countries do not have express statutory provisions demanding the enforcement of foreign exclusive jurisdiction clauses to the exclusion of competent domestic jurisdiction, but their courts provide interpretation to their law to the same effect. In Brazil, for example, Article 12 of the Introductory Law of the Civil Code provides that: 'Brazilian courts shall have jurisdiction in any case in which the defendant is domiciled here, or the contract must be performed in Brazil. (1) Only Brazilian courts are competent to hear cases involving real estate situated in Brazil.'[22] The Brazilian court interpreted it as meaning that jurisdiction granted in Article 12 of the Code can be derogated from by parties' intention to exclude its jurisdiction, except cases falling within subsection 1.[23] The Argentine court also interpreted its ordinary jurisdiction rules as default rules deciding the jurisdictional competence of Argentine courts 'in the absence of parties' agreement'.[24] Since most civil law countries accept the derogation effect of a jurisdiction clause but not *lis pendens*, courts in these countries will dismiss an action with a foreign jurisdiction clause without considering whether another court has taken the action first. For the same reason, these courts will exercise jurisdiction based on a jurisdiction clause regardless of whether concurrent proceedings exist with a foreign country.

There are also civil law countries which do not have clear legislation or judicial legislation to the enforceability of jurisdiction clauses. Uncertainty thus exists. For example, in China, different approaches have been adopted by courts. Some take jurisdiction regardless of the existence of a foreign exclusive jurisdiction clause;[25] others decline jurisdiction on the

19 Art 3148, (1) the defendant has his domicile or his residence in Québec; (2) the defendant is a legal person, is not domiciled in Québec but has an establishment in Québec, and the dispute relates to its activities in Québec; (3) a fault was committed in Québec, damage was suffered in Québec, an injurious act occurred in Québec or one of the obligations arising from a contract was to be performed in Québec; (4) the parties have by agreement submitted to it all existing or future disputes between themselves arising out of a specified legal relationship; (5) the defendant submits to its jurisdiction.

20 Art 3148.

21 Fawcett, 1995: 47–50.

22 Translation is acquired from Aballi, 1968: 203.

23 *Martinelli v Columbia*, 115 Achivo 319 (1955); Aballi, 1968: 202.

24 Aballi, 1968: 205.

25 *NKK (Japan) v Beijing Zhuangsheng*, Beijing Municipality High Court, (2008) Gao Min Zhong Zi No 919; *Kwok & Yih Law Firm v Xiamen Huayang Color Printing Company*, Xiamen Municipality Intermediate People's Court, 13 August 2003. Tang, 2012b: 459.

ground that such a clause exists.[26] It is questionable whether consideration might be given to *lis pendens* in certain circumstances when deciding whether a Chinese court would want to enforce the derogation agreement choosing another court. Since China does not expressly recognize the rule of *lis pendens* or the derogation effect of an exclusive jurisdiction clause, it causes great uncertainty and confusion in practice.

Lis pendens *and jurisdiction agreements in countries with judicial cooperation*

The civil law practice of *lis pendens* is adopted between countries with judicial cooperation to facilitate sound administration of justice in the treaty framework. A typical example is the Brussels I Regulation, which provides mandatory and absolute rule of *lis pendens*. Article 27 provides that

1. Where proceedings involving the same cause of action and between the same parties are brought in the courts of different Member States, any court other than the court first seised shall of its own motion stay its proceedings until such time as the jurisdiction of the court first seised is established.
2. Where the jurisdiction of the court first seised is established, any court other than the court first seised shall decline jurisdiction in favour of that court.

The rule is mechanical. It does not require the court to consider any substance or merit of its or other courts' jurisdiction grounds, but only consider which country is seized in a chronological order. This is an equivalent copy of internal rules in civil law countries when dealing with competing domestic courts. The question, however, arises as to whether *lis pendens* applies where the courts are seized to decide which court has jurisdiction instead of the substance of the claim, and where there is a jurisdiction clause granting all disputes, including the disputes on the validity and enforceability of this clause to the second seized court.[27] Under the current EU law, the second seized court must stay jurisdiction in favour of the first seized one, regardless of which court is chosen in an exclusive jurisdiction clause.[28] This approach has been criticized and the Brussels I Recast has adopted a negative *kompetenz-kompetenz* rule to exclude the

26 *Lai v ABN AMRO Bank*, Shanghai Municipal High People's Court, (2010) No 49; *Yacheng Automobile Parts v Huifeng*, Jiangsu Province Wuxi Municipal Intermediate People's Court, (2006) No 23; *Sojitz v Xiao*, Shanghai Municipal High People's Court, (2004) No 72; *Wenzhou Light Article Industry v CMA (France)*, Fujian Province High People's Court, available at www.chinalawinfo.com, reference code: CLI.C.21767; *Junichirou Watanabe v Culture & Art Press*, Shanghai Municipal No 1 Intermediate People's Court, (2008) No 210.

27 See Ch 7.

28 Case C-116/02 *Gasser v MISAT*, [2003] ECR 14693.

application of *lis pendens* in cases where an exclusive jurisdiction clause exists.[29]

It is believed by some commentators that, even with international judicial cooperation, *lis pendens* should not be a proper approach to deal with competing jurisdictions where an exclusive jurisdiction clause exists. It is believed better for legal certainty and contractual freedom to give the chosen court exclusive jurisdiction not only on substance but also on the existence, validity and enforceability of the jurisdiction clause. The Hague Convention 2005 does not provide any rules on *lis pendens.* It is presumed that the Convention rules on exclusive jurisdiction clauses require all chosen courts to exercise jurisdiction, all non-chosen courts to decline jurisdiction and only judgments of chosen courts should be recognized and enforced in other Member States. There is thus no need for *lis pendens* rules as the non-chosen court should not take jurisdiction in the first place. However, *lis pendens* can continue to exist under the scenario of the Hague Convention if a party sues in a non-chosen forum which, applying its domestic rule, decides that one party lacks capacity or that giving effect to the agreement would lead to a manifest injustice or be contrary to its public policy and decides to take jurisdiction;[30] or if two courts are chosen to decide the validity of the jurisdiction clause. The Hague Convention does not provide the rule as to which country should decide this issue and, as a result, any country seized by the parties could take jurisdiction to make the declaration. The Hague Convention does not require the chosen court to consider pending proceedings in any other courts either. The chosen court could directly take jurisdiction to decide the validity of a jurisdiction clause even if a non-chosen court has been seized to make a negative declaration.[31]

Lis pendens is an effective tool to deal with concurrent proceedings only between countries with judicial cooperation. Such a tool can operate effectively and appropriately only where certain rules are provided concerning its relationship with exclusive jurisdiction clauses. Two approaches exist: first, a strict mechanical *lis pendens* takes over jurisdiction clauses. That means the first seized court should always take jurisdiction to decide

29 Article 31(2) of the Brussels I Recast. For more discussion see Ch 7, s6.1. This rule was proposed in the Commission Recast Proposal in the Brussels I Regulation European Commission, 'Proposal for a Regulation of the European Parliament and of the Council on jurisdiction and the recognition and enforcement of judgments in civil and commercial matters (Recast)', ('Recast Proposal'), December 2010, COM(2010) 748 final, Art 32(2). It was later accepted in the amendment propositioned by the Denmark Presidency in 2012, see Council of the European Union, 'Proposal for a Regulation of the European Parliament and of the Council on jurisdiction and the recognition and enforcement of judgments in civil and commercial matters (Recast)—First Reading—General approach', ('Denmark Presidency Amendment') 10609/12 JUSTCIV 209 CODEC 1495 ADD 1, Brussels, 1 June 2012, Art 32(2). It is finally accepted in the Recast Regulation.

30 Art 6.

31 Kruger, 2006: 453.

its own jurisdiction while the second seized court, even if the chosen court in an exclusive jurisdiction clause, should always give priority to the first seized court to decide this issue. The second approach is that exclusive jurisdiction clauses should always take priority. That means, where there is an alleged exclusive jurisdiction clause in the contract, all non-chosen countries should stay jurisdiction and wait for the decision of the chosen country. The current trend is clear. More weight will be given to the parties' choice of court which overrides the mechanical certainty of the *lis pendens* rule.[32] In other words, the chosen court should take jurisdiction and all other courts should stay proceedings albeit first seized. This approach could prevent the parties from rushing to the court, forum shopping and initiating Italian Torpedo for the sole purpose of hampering the other party from suing in the chosen court.[33]

2.3 **Lis pendens** *and jurisdiction agreements in common law countries*

There is no chronological *lis pendens* rule in common law countries. *Lis pendens* is not treated as a stand-alone negative jurisdiction rule in common law countries, but as only one factor that a judge takes into account when deciding which country is a natural forum.[34] Since the jurisdictional philosophy of common law countries is to consider the ends of justice of an individual case, the relative time to seize the court is insignificant.[35] The concurrent proceedings in different countries are undesirable but it is only one factor to be considered when deciding if it is the end of justice to continue the proceedings, to stay the local proceedings or to restrain the foreign proceedings. If the local court is the natural forum, the concurrent proceedings would rarely justify the stay of jurisdiction. Especially if there is a jurisdiction clause choosing the local court, the English court will not exercise discretion to depart from party autonomy simply based on the ground that parallel proceedings exist.[36] Much weight is given to *lis pendens* if the foreign proceedings are having substantial progress and a judgment is expected to be delivered in a reasonable period of time.[37] Lord Goff said in *De Dampierre v De Dampeirre* that:[38]

> Genuine proceedings have been started and have not merely been started but have developed to the stage where they have had some

32 See the Recast Proposal and the Denmark Presidency Amendment of the Brussels I, Art 32(2).

33 See Ch 7.

34 McLachlan, 2008: 214; Fawcett, 1995: 29–31; *De Dampierre v De Dampierre* [1988] AC 92.

35 *EI Du Pont de Nemours v Agnew* [1987] 2 Lloyd's Rep 585, 589 (per Bingham LJ).

36 *The El Amria,* [1982] 2 Lloyd's Rep. 28; *Celltech R&D v Medimmune,* [2004] EWHC 1522 (Pat); *Breams Trustees v Upstream Downstream Simulation Services* [2004] EWHC 211 (Ch).

37 McLachlan, 2008: 313; Fawcett, 1995: 29.

38 [1988] AC 92 at 98.

> impact on the dispute between the parties, especially if such impact is likely to have a continuing effect, then this may be a relevant factor to be taken into account when considering whether the foreign jurisdiction provides the appropriate forum for the resolution of the dispute between the parties.

On the other hand, if foreign proceedings were not progressing well, with substantial difficulty in acquiring evidence or witnesses, less weight will be given to *lis pendens*.[39]

In the US, concurrent proceedings are also considered acceptable. In *Quaak*,[40] it is stated as an 'accepted proposition' to have parallel proceedings on the same in personam claim to take place simultaneously.[41] Even if a court has power to restrain a foreign action, the court must account for the presumption in favour of concurrent jurisdiction before issuing an injunction.[42]

Comparatively, the exclusive jurisdiction clause is a much more important factor in common law countries. Although commonwealth countries reserve discretion not to give effect to an exclusive choice of court clause, the starting point is that such a clause is prima facie effective unless strong causes are shown to the contrary.[43] In the USA, a jurisdiction clause shall be honoured unless: (1) the inclusion of the clause in the agreement was the product of fraud or overreaching; (2) the party wishing to repudiate the clause would effectively be deprived of his day in court were the clause enforced; (3) the law to be applied in the selected forum is fundamentally unfair; and (4) enforcement would contravene a strong

39 Fawcett, 1995: 29; *Arkwright Mutual Insurance v Bryanston Insurance* [1990] 2 Lloyd's Rep 70, 80.

40 361 F.3d 11 (1st Cir. 2004).

41 Ibid.

42 Ibid.

43 *The Eleftheria*, [1970] P 94; *The El Amria* [1981] 2 Lloyd's Rep 119 (CA); *Apple Computer v Apple Co* [1990] 2 NZLR 598; *The Vishva Apurva* [1992] 2 SLR 175 (CA); *Oneon Insurance v Moshe*, 17 PD 646 (1963); *Carvalho v Hull Blyth*, [1979] 3 All ER 280; *Trendtex Trading Co v Credit Suisse* [1980] QB 629; *Import Export Metro v Compania Sud Americana de Vapores SA*, [2003] 1 All ER (Comm) 703; *Citi-March Ltd v Neptune Orient Liens* [1996] 2 All ER 545; *Donohue v Armco* [2002] 1 All ER 749; *Konkola Copper Mines v Coromin* [2006] 2 All ER (Comm) 400; *Benarty v EG Thomson*, [1985] QB 325; *Alberta v Katanga Mining* [2009] 1 BCLC 189; *Sinochem International Oil v Mobil Sales*, [2000] 1 All ER (Comm) 758; Fawcett, 1995: 47.

public policy of the forum in which suit is brought.[44] Since stronger weight has been given to an exclusive jurisdiction clause than concurrent proceedings, a common law country usually enforces exclusive jurisdiction clauses without giving much consideration to *lis pendens*.

English courts have considered the interrelationship between *lis pendens* and exclusive jurisdiction clauses in a few cases, all treating exclusive jurisdiction clauses as more weighty factors. In *Dubai Islamic Bank v PSI Energy Holding*,[45] the parties entered into an agreement giving exclusive jurisdiction to England. The claimant brought an action in Bahrain instead where the defendant would dissipate its assets. The claimant subsequently brought the same action in England. The defendant applied for the English proceedings to be stayed based on the ground that Bahrain was first seized by the same claimant to hear the same action. It argued that the claimant was deemed to give up the exclusive jurisdiction clause and was estopped from relying on it and the concurrent proceedings gave rise to the risk of irreconcilable judgments on the same matter. The English court held that bringing the action in a non-chosen forum did not mean the claimant definitely repudiated the agreement. The Bahrain proceedings were sought for the reason of precautionary relief over assets which were not mutually exclusive to the English proceedings.[46] Furthermore, very strong reasons should be shown by the opposing party to depart from an exclusive jurisdiction clause. The judge considered the primary motive of the claimant to get protective relief following the advice of Bahraini lawyers was *bona fide*. The judge agreed the claimant's proposal that two proceedings should continue and the party should stay one procedure depending on which court made the first decision.

44 *M/S Bremen v Zapata Off-Shore*, 407 US 1 (1972); *Carnival v Shute; Cal-State Business v Ricoh* 12 Cal App 4th 1666 (Cal App 3 Dist 1993); *Reynolds-Naughton v Norwegian Cruise Line* 386 F3d 1 (Cal (Mass) 2004); *Lee v New Seaescape* 1998 WL 730873 (ND Cal 1998); *Stewart Organization, Inc. v Ricoh Corp.*, 108 S.Ct. 2239, (US Ala. 20 June 1988); *Scherk v Alberto-Culver Co.*, 417 US 506, (US Ill. 17 June 1974); *Huffington v T.C. Group*, 637 F.3d 18, (1st Cir. (Mass.) 25 February 2011); *Rafael Rodriguez Barril, Inc. v Conbraco Industries, Inc.*, 619 F.3d 90 (1st Cir.(Puerto Rico) 8 September 2010); *Royal Bed and Spring Co., Inc. v Famossul Industria e Comercio de Moveis Ltda.*, 906 F.2d 45 (1st Cir.(Puerto Rico) 26 June 1990); *Aguas Lenders Recovery Group v Suez, S.A.*, 585 F.3d 696(2nd Cir.(N.Y.) 23 October 2009); *Phillips v Audio Active Ltd*, 494 F.3d 378 (2nd Cir.(N.Y.) 24 July 2007); *Evolution Online Systems, Inc. v Koninklijke PTT Nederland N.V.*, 145 F.3d 505 (2nd Cir.(N.Y.) 27 May 1998); *New Moon Shipping Co., Ltd v MAN B & W Diesel AG*, 121 F.3d 24, (2nd Cir.(N.Y.) 18 June 1997); *Roby v Corporation of Lloyd's*, 996 F.2d 1353 (2nd Cir.(N.Y.) 2 June 1993); *Blanco v Banco Indus. de Venezuela, S.A.*, 997 F.2d 974 (2nd Cir.(N.Y.) 30 April 1993); *Jones v Weibrecht*, 901 F.2d 17 (2nd Cir.(N.Y.) 11 April 1990); *Red Bull Associates v Best Western Intern., Inc.*, 862 F.2d 963, (2nd Cir.(N.Y.) 29 November 1988).

45 [2011] EWHC 1019 (Comm).

46 *China National Foreign Trade Transportation v Evlogia Shipping (The Mihaios Xilas)* [1979] 1 WLR 1018; *Motor Oil Hellas (Corinth) Refiners SA v Shipping Co of India (The Kanchenjunga)* [1990] 1 Lloyd's Rep 391.

More importantly, some English courts give an English non-exclusive jurisdiction clause the same weight as an exclusive one and refuse to stay jurisdiction granted by even a non-exclusive jurisdiction clause to avoid parallel proceedings with another country. In *Highland Crusader Offshore Partners LLP v Deutsche Banke AG*,[47] Toulson LJ considered the relationship between *lis pendens* and a non-exclusive jurisdiction clause:[48]

> However undesirable it is that parallel proceedings may proceed and in theory result in conflicting judgment, whether and to what extent it happens in practice … is another matter. Experience suggests that when parallel cases continue to be fully fought after the initial jurisdiction battles the courts will do their best to use their management powers to prevent tactical obstructionism and to achieve a just and orderly disposal of the litigation, taking into account the progress of the parallel proceedings as may be appropriate.

In *Antec International v Biosafety USA*,[49] a distribution agreement was concluded where the English manufacturer would produce products in the UK which were distributed by the American distributer to the US. A non-exclusive jurisdiction was concluded to choose English courts. After the conclusion of the agreement, the English company became fully owned by a US company. The dispute arose and the claimant sued in England pursuant to the non-exclusive jurisdiction clause and the defendant argued that the US should be the natural forum and it would bring the proceedings against the American owner in the US. The English court, however, applied the same *Eleftheria* test, requiring the opposing party to show strong causes to relieve it from its bargain. The court expressly stated that the undesirability of parallel proceedings in this case was not a strong or compelling reason to do so. It is necessary to note that, in this case, the parallel proceedings did not even exist at the time of the plea and remained a possibility.

Of course, some English courts realized the difference between exclusive and non-exclusive jurisdiction clauses.[50] In *BP International v Energy Infrastructure Group*,[51] for example, Morison J stated:

> A non-exclusive jurisdiction clause in an agreement gives the parties a right to commence proceedings in this jurisdiction as to their respective rights and duties under the contract. The right to commence proceedings is not absolute. The Court retains discretion, and a

47 [2009] 2 Lloyd's Rep 617.
48 [2009] 2 Lloyd's Rep 617.
49 [2006] EWHC 47 (Comm).
50 *BP International v Energy Infrastructure Group*, [2003] EWHC 2924 (Comm).
51 Ibid., 552.

> significant factor in the balance is the existence of other proceedings in another jurisdiction, where there is a risk that those proceedings will overlap and potentially conflict with the proceedings in this country. There is a distinction, clearly, between an exclusive and a non-exclusive jurisdiction clause.

This statement expressly makes the concurrent proceedings in another country a significant factor in deciding whether to take jurisdiction granted by a non-exclusive jurisdiction clause. It also implies that *lis pendens*, comparatively, is not an important factor when making decisions in cases with an exclusive jurisdiction clause. Nevertheless, the court also stated that, if there were parallel proceedings between England, which was chosen in the non-exclusive jurisdiction clause, and Texas, which was a non-chosen court, the non-exclusive jurisdiction would make England the only sensible place for the whole litigation.[52] That means even if concurrent proceedings exist, they are insufficient to require a chosen court in a non-exclusive jurisdiction to stay jurisdiction. Other factors are required to support the stay of jurisdiction. The court stayed jurisdiction in the current case because the claimant submitted to the Texas jurisdiction before bringing the current proceedings. It was the submission, not the nature of the jurisdiction clause, which made the difference to the decision.

In many cases, a common law country not only continues jurisdiction regardless of concurrent proceedings in another country, but, if there is an exclusive jurisdiction clause giving the common law country jurisdiction, it will issue an anti-suit injunction to restrain a party from continuing jurisdiction in the other country, even if the other court is the first seized one.[53] However, such an injunction usually will be exercised with caution and only be granted if it could actually stop concurrent proceedings. In *Donohue v Armco*,[54] for example, the House of Lords confirmed that when considering whether an injunction could be issued the court should give effect to an exclusive jurisdiction clause unless very strong reasons were shown to the contrary. These strong reasons include the interest of both parties and the likelihood of parallel proceedings. However, in the current case, strong reasons have been found, as some foreign defendants could not be the joint defendants in English courts under the exclusive jurisdiction clause or under English rules for service out of jurisdiction. If an injunction was granted, concurrent proceedings were likely to exist in England and New York. The court refused to grant an injunction for the

52 Ibid., para 25.

53 *Society of Lloyd's v White (No 2)*, [2002] ILPr 11; *Beazley v Horizon Offshore Contractors, Inc*, [2005] ILPr 11; *Samengo-Turner v J&H Marsh & McLennan (Services) Ltd* [2007] EWCA Civ 723; *OT Africa Line Ltd v Hijazy & Anor*, [2001] CLC 148; *Donohue v Armco Inc*, [2002] 1 All ER 749; *Bank of New York Mellon v GV Films Ltd*, [2010] 1 Lloyd's Rep. 365.

54 [2002] 1 All ER (Comm) 749.

reason that it was better to have a single action in New York. It is necessary to know that higher test standard exists for a court to issue an anti-suit injunction than to decline jurisdiction. The existence of concurrent proceedings in a non-chosen forum does not mean the foreign proceedings are vexatious and oppressive for the injunction to be issued.[55] But permitting the foreign proceedings to run does not mean English courts would stay its own jurisdiction granted by a jurisdiction clause to avoid *lis pendens.*

2.4 **Lis pendens** ***and arbitration agreements***

No law has provided the *lis pendens* rule to tackle the parallel proceedings between an arbitral tribunal and a court. Parallel proceedings on substantive matters of disputes between arbitral tribunals and courts, however, are rare. Most states adopt a compulsory rule to handle the relationship between courts and arbitral tribunals. If there is no concern on the jurisdiction of an arbitral tribunal, a court is obliged to decline jurisdiction in favour of arbitration. This rule exists in the New York Convention, which all Contracting States of the Convention have the treaty obligation to follow. Article II(3) of the New York Convention reads: 'The court of a Contracting State, when seized of an action in a matter in respect of which the parties have made an agreement within the meaning of this article, shall, at the request of one of the parties, refer the parties to arbitration…'. In other words, regardless of whether the court or an arbitral tribunal is seized first, a court should use its own motion to decline jurisdiction in favour of the chosen tribunal. In common law countries, although courts usually will give effects to an exclusive jurisdiction clause, discretion is reserved for courts to rule exceptionally. However, there is usually a statutory requirement for a court to decline jurisdiction in face of a valid arbitration agreement, giving effects to Article II(3) of the New York Convention.[56] As a result, there is not much need to adopt the *lis pendens* rule to establish the way to manage the relationship of parallel proceedings between courts and tribunals.[57]

However, parallel proceedings between arbitral tribunals and courts may exist in deciding the validity and scope of an arbitration agreement.[58] While one party questions the validity of an arbitration agreement in courts and another in the designated tribunal, there will be parallel proceedings and there will not be the *lis pendens* rule to tackle the situation. No country has granted an arbitral tribunal unfettered power to examine its own jurisdiction; a court's supervision on this issue is usually available before, during or after the arbitral procedure. The difference exists in the

55 *Deutsche Bank v Highland Crusader Offshore Partner,* [2010] 1 WLR 1023.
56 See e.g. Section 9 of the Arbitration Act 1996 (UK).
57 McLachlan *et al.*, 2010: 83.
58 *Claxton Engineering Services Limited v Tam Olaj-Es Gazkutato* [2011] EWHC 345.

level and extent of review and intervention by courts.[59] Compelling a court to stay jurisdiction in favour of an arbitral tribunal simply because it is first seized in time is fundamentally contrary to the basic arbitration principle accepted worldwide. Second, an arbitral tribunal is granted the power to decide its own jurisdiction based on the doctrine of *kompetenz-kompetenz*. UNCITRAL Model Law has provided that, while the issue is pending in court, an arbitral procedure does not need to be suspended.[60] Furthermore, UNCITRAL Model Law also accepts the concurrent proceedings between an arbitral tribunal and a court in substantive issues. Article 8 of the Model Law provides that if a court is seized to hear disputes subject to a valid arbitration agreement, the court should refer the parties to arbitration,[61] and before the court does so, an arbitration procedure can be commenced or continued without the necessity to wait for the court's decision.[62] If a non-supervisory court holds the arbitral agreement void and takes jurisdiction, arbitral proceedings still can be commenced or continued.[63]

It is possible that both the tribunal and the court are seized to decide the validity of an arbitration agreement and arrive at different decisions. Concurrent proceedings on the substance are likely to occur. An individual state will use legislation to decide the priority of the conflicts decisions. In China, for example, the Arbitration Law permits the questions on the validity of an arbitration clause to be brought to either the tribunal or the people's court. However, if different decisions are reached, the court's ruling should prevail.[64] If there is no dispute on the preliminary issues of an arbitration agreement, the court is required to stay jurisdiction in favour of the arbitral tribunal. In general, there are usually different principles in dealing with parallel proceedings between tribunals and courts than between two civil courts. The *lis pendens* rule has no place in the arbitration scenario.

Lis pendens, however, can be used to deal with concurrent proceedings between two courts in deciding issues relating to arbitration. Ordinary rules applying to concurrent proceedings between different courts shall equally apply here. In the European Union, where judicial cooperation imposes the rule of *lis pendens*, it applies to two courts' proceedings even if they concern an arbitration agreement. Strict chronological order still applies. Which court can continue to decide this matter depends on which

59 See in general, Moses, 2012: 91–95.

60 Art 16(3), Art 8.

61 Art 8(1).

62 Art 8(2).

63 Arts 8(1) and (2). *SPP v Egypt*, (1985) 3 ICSID Reports 129 (ICSID suspended proceedings in favour of French litigation based on comity instead of *lis pendens*); e.g. Art 186 of the Swiss Law of International Private Law.

64 PRC Arbitration Law 1994, Art 20.

court is seized first.[65] The *lis pendens* claim may also arise where a court is seized to decide the merit of the case, while another court is requested to recognize and enforce arbitral awards on the same issue.[66]

3 Anti-suit injunctions and dispute resolution agreements

3.1 Anti-suit injunctions in concurrent proceedings

One powerful instrument used by common law countries to protect the effectiveness of exclusive jurisdiction clauses and to prevent concurrent proceedings is anti-suit injunctions. It is a court order restraining a party from commencing or pursuing legal proceedings in a foreign country.[67] Civil law countries usually consider anti-suit injunctions an improper intervention of another country's sovereignty, that every sovereign state should have sufficient competence to decide its own jurisdiction independently. Although common law countries believe an injunction is directed to the litigating party instead of the foreign court,[68] anti-suit junction is usually used with particular caution[69] and only when it could serve the ends of justice.[70] In the USA, an anti-suit injunction can be granted if the foreign proceedings: (1) frustrate a policy of the forum issuing the injunction; (2) are vexatious or oppressive; (3) threaten the issuing court's in rem or quasi in rem jurisdiction; or (4) prejudice other equitable considerations.[71]

The biggest concern of an anti-suit injunction is the potential violation of international comity. The issue of comity is fully discussed by Lord Goff in *Airbus v Patel*,[72] which concerns an air crash that occurred in India. Two of the deceased passengers were British and their families sued the manufacturer in Texas. At the time, Texas did not adopt the doctrine of *forum non conveniens* and Airbus could not seek a stay of proceedings. Airbus sought an injunction from the English court, restraining the appellants

65 Case C-185/07, *Allianz SpA v West Tankers* [2009] ECR I-663.

66 *Sovarex SA v Romero Alvarez SA*, [2011] EWHC 1661 (Comm).

67 For more information, see Fawcett and Carruthers, 2008: 455–457; Clarkson and Hill, 2011: 152f.

68 Hartley, 2009: 222. *Bushby v Munday* (1821) 5 Madd. 297, 307; *Société Nationale Industrielle Aerospatiale v Lee Kui Jak* [1987] AC 871, 892.

69 *Cohen v Rothfield* [1919] 1 KB 410; *Castanho v Brown & Root*, [1981] AC 557, 573.

70 *Bushby v Munday* (1821) 5 Madd. 297, 307; *Carron Iron Co. v Maclaren* (1855) 5 H Cas 416, 453; *Castanho v Brown & Root (U.K.) Ltd* [1981] AC 557; *British Airways Board v Laker Airways Ltd* [1985] AC 58, 81; *Société Nationale Industrielle Aerospatiale v Lee Kui Jak* [1987] AC 871, 892.

71 *Re Unterweser Reederei Gmbh*, 428 F.2d 888, 896 (5th Cir. 1970), aff'd, 446 F.2d 907 (1971); *M/S Bremen v Zapata Off-Shore*, 407 US.1 (1971); *Triton Container International v Di Gregorio Navegacao LTDA*, 440 F.3d 1137, 1138 (9th Cir., 2006); *Seattle Totems*, 652 F.2d, 855; *Gallo v Andina*, 446 F.3d 984, 990.

72 [1999] 1 AC 119.

from continuing with their action in Texas on the grounds that pursuit of that action by the appellants would be contrary to justice and/or vexatious or oppressive. It was remarked by Lord Goff that:

> before an anti-suit injunction can properly be granted by an English court…, comity requires that the English forum should have a sufficient interest in, or connection with, the matter in question to justify the indirect interference with the foreign court which an anti-suit injunction entails.[73]

However, exceptions can be made 'where the conduct of the foreign state exercising jurisdiction is such as to deprive it of the respect normally required by comity'.[74] US judges also follow the same line. In *Seattle Totems Hockey Club v National Hockey League*,[75] the court confirmed that:

> A federal district court with jurisdiction over the parties has the power to enjoin them from proceeding with an action in the courts of a foreign country, although the power should be used sparingly. The issue is not one of jurisdiction, but one of comity.

Under English case law, comity overrides the procedural benefit in avoiding concurrent proceedings when a court decides whether to grant an anti-suit injunction. Since 'parallel proceedings in different jurisdictions are not of themselves regarded as unacceptable' in England,[76] the English court will not directly use the injunction to stop the foreign action from processing alongside the English one. Even if the English court is held to be the natural forum, an injunction cannot be issued on this ground alone.[77] Where concurrent proceedings are brought by the same claimant both in England and abroad,[78] English courts usually permit the claimant to elect which proceedings to continue and will grant the injunction only if the foreign action is vexatious or oppressive.[79] However, the stage of each trial will be taken into account. If the English proceedings are processing properly, bringing another suit in a foreign country will be restrained.[80] It is fair to say, although the mechanism of anti-suit

73 [1999] 1 AC 119, 138.

74 [1999] 1 AC 119, 140.

75 652 F.2d 852 (9th Cir. 1981), 855.

76 *Airbus Case*, 132–133, per Lord Goff; *Gredit Suisse First Boston v MLC* [1999] 1 All ER (Comm) 237, 257; *Royal Bank of Canada v Cooperative Centrale* [2004] 2 All ER (Comm) 847.

77 *Aerospatiale Case* [1987] AC 871; *Deutsche Bank*, [2010] 1 WLR 1023, 1037.

78 *Société Nationale Industrielle Aerospatiale*, 893.

79 *McHenry v Lewis* (1882) 22 Ch.D 397; *Peruvian Guano v Bockwoldt* (1883) 23 Ch.D 225; *Société Nationale Industrielle Aerospatiale*, 893.

80 *Royal Bank of Canada*, [2004] 2 All ER (Comm) 847, 860–861.

injunctions can be used to prevent concurrent proceedings, the existence of parallel proceedings alone is not a weighty factor for English courts to grant anti-suit injunctions.[81]

3.2 Anti-suit injunctions in support of jurisdiction and arbitration clauses

General principle

Although *lis pendens* is not an important factor for a court to grant an anti-suit injunction, the existence of a valid exclusive jurisdiction or arbitration clause brings a prima facie case for the injunction to be granted. English courts believe a person has the right to sue, or the obligation to be sued, in any competent forum unless special factors restrain this right or the obligation. An exclusive jurisdiction clause or an arbitration clause shows that a person gives promise to be bound. Enforcing this clause will restrain a person's right and obligation that he might otherwise have.[82] A dispute resolution agreement with the derogation feature creates a prima facie case that the chosen forum is more appropriate than any other fora and gives the parties the obligation not to bring the disputes in a non-chosen forum.

English courts are more ready to issue anti-suit injunctions where a party brings proceedings abroad in breach of an exclusive jurisdiction clause or arbitration clause.[83] Where there is no such clause, the court may require higher standards to be satisfied in order not to infringe international comity. If there is an exclusive dispute resolution clause, it is a prima facie case to restrain foreign actions and the court has an 'inherent power' to do so without specifically considering the requirement of comity.[84] This

81 In the USA, concurrent proceedings are relevant factors to use anti-suit injunctions. The first step a US court will take is to consider whether the parties and issues in parallel proceedings are the same, and whether the first action is dispositive of the action to be restrained. *Sun World v Lizarazu Olivarria*, 804 F. Supp. 1264, 1267 (E.D.Cal. 1992); *Paramedics Electromedicina Comercial, Ltd v GE Medical Sys. Info. Techs., Inc.*, 369 F.3d 645, 652 (2d Cir. 2004); *Quaak v Klynveld Peat Marwick Goerdeler Bedrijfsrevisoren*, 361 F.3d 11, 18 (1st Cir. 2004); Bermann, 1990: 626.

82 *Turner v Grovit*, [2002] CLC 463 (per Lord Hobhouse), para 25.

83 Fawcett and Carruthers, 2008: 470–475; *Oceanconnect UK Ltd & Anor v Angara Maritime Ltd* [2010] 2 CLC 448.

84 *Aggeliki Charis Compania Maritima SA v Pagnan SpA (The Angelic Grace)* [1995] 1 Lloyd's Rep 87; Fawcett and Carruthers, 2008: 474.

principle applies to both arbitration and exclusive jurisdiction agreements.[85] It was observed by Toulson LJ in *Deutcsche Bank* that:[86]

> An injunction to enforce an exclusive jurisdiction clause governed by English law is not regarded as a breach of comity, because it merely requires a party to honour his contract. In other cases, the principle of comity requires the court to recognise that, in deciding questions of weight to be attached to different factors, different judges operating under different legal systems with different legal policies may legitimately arrive at different answers, without occasioning a breach of customary international law or manifest injustice, and that in such circumstances it is not for an English court to arrogate to itself the decision how a foreign court should determine the matter. The stronger the connection of the foreign court with the parties and the subject matter of the dispute, the stronger the argument against intervention.

It implies that an exclusive jurisdiction clause choosing English courts gives English courts inherent power to restrain foreign proceedings in breach of the agreement.[87] An injunction granted in such cases does not bring any challenges to comity in the view of English courts. English courts do not need to consider other connecting factors such as natural forum, subject matter and the connections between a foreign country with the dispute. An injunction is simply a tool to force a party to obey its promise.

From the perspective of other countries, however, this is not the case. Although there are exclusive jurisdiction agreements or arbitration agreements, a non-chosen court still considers it is completely within its sovereignty to decide its own jurisdiction. Although the English courts may issue a restraining order in the name of requiring a party to honour his contract, the order has the functioning of: (1) deciding the jurisdiction or arbitration clause is valid and enforceable under English law, including its private international law; and (2) stopping the foreign proceedings from

85 *Mackender v Feldia AG* [1967] 2 QB 590; *Unterweser Reederei GmbH v Zapata Off-Shore Co (The Chaparral)* [1968] 2 Lloyd's Rep 158; *The Eleftheria* [1970] P 94; *DSV Silo- und Verwaltungsgesellschaft mbH v Owners of the Sennar and 13 Other Ships (The Sennar (No 2))* [1985] 1 WLR 490; *British Aerospace Plc v Dee Howard Co* [1993] 1 Lloyd's Rep 368; *Continental Bank NA v Aeakos Compania Naviera SA and Others* [1994] 1 WLR 588; *Akai Pty Ltd v People's Insurance Co Ltd* [1998] 1 Lloyd's Rep 90; *Donohue v Armco* [2002] 1 All ER 749; *Deutcsche Bank* [2010] 1 WLR 1023.

86 [2010] 1 WLR 1023, 1036–1037.

87 *Mackender v Feldia AG* [1967] 2 QB 590; *Unterweser Reederei GmbH v Zapata Off-Shore Co (The Chaparral)* [1968] 2 Lloyd's Rep 158; *The Eleftheria* [1970] P 94; *DSV Silo- und Verwaltungsgesellschaft mbH v Owners of the Sennar and 13 Other Ships (The Sennar (No 2))* [1985] 1 WLR 490; *British Aerospace Plc v Dee Howard Co* [1993] 1 Lloyd's Rep 368; *Continental Bank NA v Aeakos Compania Naviera SA and Others* [1994] 1 WLR 588; *Aggeliki Charis Compania Maritima SA v Pagnan SpA (The Angelic Grace)* [1995] 1 Lloyd's Rep 87; and *Akai Pty Ltd v People's Insurance Co Ltd* [1998] 1 Lloyd's Rep 90.

being commenced or continuing. By issuing the injunction, the English court does not need to consider whether the non-chosen forum, according to its domestic law, would honour the jurisdiction or arbitration clause. It is hard to say how this is not an intervention.

Because of the comity controversy, many courts in practice will not rely solely on the existence of jurisdiction or arbitration agreements, but would prefer to find other grounds to support the decision of issuing an injunction. In *Royal Bank of Scotland v Hicks*,[88] the English court restrained the proceedings subject to an English exclusive jurisdiction clause from continuing in Texas. The court held that the applicant had the right to have the claim heard in England pursuant to the jurisdiction clause and foreign proceedings would be 'extremely inconvenient'. However, the court went on to consider the connections between the claim and the foreign court and the intention to bring the foreign action. The court concluded that the claim had no real connections with Texas, as assets were located in England, duties concerned were governed by English law and disputes were about English directors' duty to English companies. The party that brought the action in Texas aimed to seek punitive damages in a jurisdiction without connections to the dispute, which was oppressive. The court granted an injunction based not only on the party's right to enforce a jurisdiction clause, but also on other factors that prove the foreign proceedings oppressive.

Exceptional grounds

The existence of an English exclusive jurisdiction clause usually shows a prima facie case to sue in England, unless the resisting party could demonstrate to the contrary by showing strong, sometimes exceptional, reasons.[89] Exceptional grounds might exist where: (1) the interests of third parties are involved;[90] or (2) part of the claims are not subject to the jurisdiction clause.[91] In order to avoid inconsistent decisions made in different jurisdictions, it is accepted that claims against multi-defendants or multi-claims would better be consolidated and decided in one trial.

It has been stated before that a third party is generally not bound by a jurisdiction clause, with a few exceptions.[92] However, complicated disputes

88 [2011] EWHC 287 (Ch).

89 *The Eleftheria*, [1970] P 94.

90 *Evans Marshall and Co Ltd v Bertola SA and Another* [1973] 1 WLR 349; *Aratra Potato Co Ltd v Egyptian Navigation Co (The El Amria)* [1981] 2 Lloyd's Rep 119; *Halifax Overseas Freighters Ltd v Rasno Export (The Pine Hill)* [1958] 2 Lloyd's Rep 146; *Taunton-Collins v Cromie* [1964] 1 WLR 633; *Citi-March Ltd v Neptune Orient Lines Ltd* [1996] 1 WLR 1367; *Mahavir Minerals Ltd v Cho Yang Shipping Co Ltd (The M C Pearl)* [1997] 1 Lloyd's Rep 566; *Bouygues Offshore SA v Caspian Shipping Co* [1998] 2 Lloyd's Rep 461; *Donohue v Armco* [2002] 1 All ER 749.

91 *Crédit Suisse First Boston (Europe) Ltd v MLC (Bermuda) Ltd* [1999] 1 All ER (Comm) 237.

92 See Ch 5, section 5.

frequently arise in cross-border commercial transactions, where third parties' interests are involved in the dispute between the contractual parties who are subject to the jurisdiction clause. An anti-suit injunction to restrain foreign proceedings may be refused if the third parties could not be sued in the chosen forum as joiners and granting an injunction is likely to cause concurrent proceedings.

In *Donohue v Armco*,[93] three New York companies transferred their assets into a new company. The New York companies then sold the share of the new company under a sale and purchase agreement to four companies as the buyers. In all these agreements, there were exclusive jurisdiction clauses choosing English courts. The three New York companies that directly entered the transaction agreement and two other companies in the same group later brought actions in New York against the purchasers and their executives who took part in the negotiation as well as the companies of two of them on fraud and the breach of fiduciary duty. One defendant applied the anti-suit injunction from the English court to restrain the New York proceedings and applied to join all other defendants as claimants in the English action. The House of Lords held that the jurisdiction clause only bound its direct parties, i.e. the buyers of the company could be joined in English proceedings, but not others. Pursuant to the jurisdiction agreements, the applicant and the buyers could sue the three New York companies in England; the proceedings between the New York companies and other defendants in the New York proceedings could not be brought in English courts. The executives who negotiated the transaction and their respective companies were not parties to the jurisdiction agreements and could not benefit from the agreements. If the three New York companies are properly brought to English jurisdiction, English courts are only entitled to hear the disputes between them and the buyers. The court held that if the interests of third parties meant that other proceedings would continue anyway with the risk of irreconcilable judgments, the court should balance the right of a contractual party to bring the action in the chosen court and the right of another party to continue actions against third parties in the other country. In this dispute, the actions between all the defendants and two New York companies which are not direct parties in the contracts could not be brought in England. An injunction should be refused.

Donohue shows a scenario where A and B enter into an exclusive jurisdiction clause and A and C sue B and D in a non-chosen forum, which has jurisdiction over all defendants. In such circumstances, B could not acquire an injunction restraining proceedings between A and B in the non-chosen forum. Although A was bound by the jurisdiction clause, such obligations exist between neither A and D, nor between C and B/D. If the chosen court has jurisdiction over the whole disputes in other grounds

93 [2002] 1 All ER 749.

and all parties could be properly joined in the jurisdiction, an injunction could be considered. Otherwise, taking the dispute as a whole, considering all the parties' interest and the likelihood of parallel proceedings, an injunction should not be used to enforce an exclusive jurisdiction agreement.[94]

Sometimes, two parties enter into a jurisdiction clause to submit certain disputes to the chosen forum, but not others. If a party claims on matters not subject to the jurisdiction clause, a court cannot use anti-suit injunctions based on the reason to enforce the jurisdiction clause. An example is *Credit Suisse First Boston v MLC*;[95] the buyer purchased Russian bonds through its US investment manager from the seller's US agent. The contract was concluded and transactions took place in New York. There was an exclusive jurisdiction clause choosing English courts to cover claims arising 'out of or in connection with' the agreement. After the Russian government announced a moratorium on the repayment of foreign debt, the buyer failed to pay the price under its contract. The seller sued for the balance under the contract in England while the buyer sued in New York alleging misrepresentation, non-disclosure and fraud on the part of the seller. The seller applied for an anti-suit injunction from the English court. The English court held that the claims in New York were not all covered by the jurisdiction clause. The court only issued an injunction to restrain claims covered by the jurisdiction clause.

Compared to *Donahue*, *Credit Suisse* clearly leads to parallel proceedings. The buyer would continue actions in New York against the buyer on issues outside the scope of the jurisdiction clause, while the buyer could bring actions in England for those claims covered by the clause. More importantly, because those claims are related, it is undesirable in terms of both economy and procedure efficiency to have two trials continued in to countries. The result of *Credit Suisse* is not pragmatic and it is hard to say it is better for the ends of justice to require two proceedings going on in two countries.

US practice

Although without consensus,[96] some US courts have shown intention to adopt the same approach to give effectiveness to an exclusive jurisdiction or arbitration agreement. In the US, courts adopt a two-threshold test in deciding whether to issue an anti-suit injunction: (1) the parties must be the same in parallel proceedings and the resolution of the case in the current court is dispositive of the other action; if satisfied, (2) the court

94 See comments, Tett, 2003: 7; Bramley, 2002: 3.

95 [1999] CLC 579.

96 It is argued that the permission to grant anti-suit injunctions is not clearly settled in the US. *Albemarle Corp. v AstraZeneca UK Ltd* 2009 WL 902348, 6 (DSC 2009).

could use discretion to consider whether the foreign action frustrates the current court's domestic policy, is vexatious or oppressive, treats its jurisdiction *in rem*, prejudices equitable considerations, or causes delay, inconvenience, expense, inconsistency or race to judgment.[97] US courts do not adopt different criteria for cases with an exclusive jurisdiction or arbitration agreement. In *Stolt Tankers*,[98] for example, the same criteria have been provided in deciding whether an anti-suit injunction should be granted to support a New York arbitration clause by restraining Brazilian proceedings. The court considered the two thresholds in term. After being satisfied the first threshold was met, the court considered the five elements in the second threshold to make discretion. It was held that permitting Brazilian proceedings to continue frustrates the policy of the New York forum, namely the policy to promote arbitration. The Brazilian court would apply different laws, which causes different results if two proceedings continued, and the potential divergence could provoke rush to the forum. Equitable considerations include the prevention of forum shopping and rush to the court. Parallel proceedings would cause inconvenience, cost, inconsistency and race to the judgment.[99] Since arbitration agreements aim to provide the effective solution to disputes and to prevent extra costs and inconvenience, compelling the party that is bound by the agreement to arbitration while permitting a foreign action to continue is contrary to parties' purpose and expectation. An injunction is thus issued.

Gallo v Andina[100] is a leading case where the US Court of Appeals issued an anti-suit injunction to support an exclusive jurisdiction clause. Gallo, a Californian company, entered into a distribution contract with the distributor, an Ecuadorian company. The contract contained an exclusive jurisdiction clause choosing Californian courts. The distributor, however, sued in Ecuador on their dispute, and the Californian manufacturer applied to the court for an injunction to be issued. The court considered the criteria to issue an anti-suit injunction, one of which is that the foreign litigation would frustrate the policy of the local forum.[101] The court accepted the argument that jurisdiction clauses have gained widespread acceptance in the US,[102] and a strong policy in favour of the enforcement of jurisdiction clauses has been established by the US Supreme Court.[103] Jurisdiction

97 *China Trade v MV Choong Yong*, 837 F.2d 33, 35 (2d Cir. 1987); *Paramedics Electromedicina Comercial v GE Medical System Information* 369 F.3d 645, 652 (C.A.2(NY) 2004); *Stolt Tankers BV v Allianz Seguros, S.A* WL 2436662 (S.D.N.Y. 2011); *Umbro Int'l Inc. v Japan Professional Football League*, 1997 WL 33378853 (D.S.C. 2 October 1997); *In re Unterweser Reederei Gmbh*, 428 F.2d 888, 890 (5th Cir. 1970), *rev'd* on *other grounds*, 407 US 1, 92 S.Ct. 1907, 32 L.Ed.2d 513 (1972).

98 Ibid.

99 Ibid., 5.

100 446 F.3d 984 (C.A.9(Cal.) 2006.

101 *Seattle Totems*, 652 F.2d 855; *Re Unterweser Reederei*, 428 F.2d 896.

102 *Gallo*, 992.

103 Ibid.

clauses are increasingly used in cross-border business transactions, providing certainty and reducing transaction costs and risks.[104] There has been a strong claim in the US that a valid jurisdiction agreement should be enforced in the absence of strong reasons against enforcement.[105] Foreign proceedings in breach of an exclusive jurisdiction clause thus frustrate Californian policy to enforce validity jurisdiction agreements and an anti-suit injunction should be issued as the only way to enforce this agreement.[106]

Although these courts do not adopt a specific approach to support party autonomy by anti-suit injunctions, the thresholds, however, are relatively easy to be achieved in cases where there is an arbitration or exclusive jurisdiction agreement. First of all, it is US national policy to promote arbitration and to enforce a choice of court agreement. Any actions brought in foreign courts in breach of such an agreement frustrate this national policy.[107] Even a threat to bring such an action frustrates US policy.[108] Second, if a party has signed an agreement to promise submitting all disputes to a particular court or to arbitration and later brings claims to a non-chosen court, this action is done in prima facie bad faith.[109] Third, if foreign proceedings are commenced, it usually will lead to cost and inconvenience and will be more so if parallel proceedings exist because of the breach of agreement.[110] Fourth, it is always an equitable consideration to deter forum shopping and the most serious form of forum shopping is suing in an inappropriate forum in breach of agreement.[111] It seems that an anti-suit injunction will usually be granted in support of a dispute resolution agreement applying the ordinary thresholds.[112]

US courts, when issuing anti-suit injunctions in support of parties' agreements, also consider the impact on international comity.[113] Although US courts accept that anti-suit injunctions may generate comity concerns, they also believe that comity in international jurisdiction and judgments is not an absolute obligation.[114] Comity will not be negatively affected if

104 Ibid.

105 Ibid.

106 *Gallo*, 992. Force, 2011: 441ff.

107 *Amaprop v Indiabulls Financial Services*, WL 1050988, 5 (S.D.N.Y. 2010); *Mitsubishi Motors Corp. v Soler Chrysler–Plymouth, Inc.*, 473 US 614, 638–640, 105 S.Ct. 3346, 87 L.Ed.2d 444 (1985); *Arciniaga v General Motors Corp.*, 460 F.3d 231, 234 (2d Cir. 2006); *Ibeto Petrochemical Industries, Ltd v M/T 'Beffen'* 2010 WL 1050988 (S.D.N.Y. 2010); *Applied Medical Distribution Corp. v Surgical Co. BV* 587 F.3d 909 (C.A.9 (Cal) 2009); *Gallo v Andina; Seattle Totems*; *Re Unterweser Reederei.*

108 *Amaprop v Indiabulls Financial Services*, 5.

109 *Amaprop*, ibid., 6.

110 *Amaprop*, ibid., 6–7; *Storm*, 28; *Stolt Tankers*, 5.

111 *Suchodolksi Assoc., Inc. v Cardell Fin. Corp*, 2006 WL 3327625, 2.

112 *LAIF X SPRL*, 199.

113 *Gallo*, 446 F.3d at 994; *Applied Medical v Surgical*, 919.

114 *Asvesta v Petroutsas*, 580 F.3d 1000, 1010–1011 (9th Cir. 2009); *Applied Medical v Surgical*, 920.

parties are private parties, parties enter into a dispute resolution agreement to resolve private matters and the agreement is freely negotiated after exhaustive, arm-length, fairly-conducted negotiation.[115]

However, although by applying the standard test an injunction in support of a dispute resolution agreement usually can meet the required criteria, a court may refuse to enjoin foreign proceedings but permit parallel proceedings to continue based on the reason of necessity. Some courts believe injunctions should be issued in 'the rarest of cases'[116] and they should consider 'whether an injunction is necessary to protect the jurisdiction of a federal court or if allowing the foreign litigation to continue would allow a party to evade the forum's important policies'.[117] In *Answers in Genesis of Kentucky v Greation Ministries Intern*,[118] the Federal Court refused to issue an injunction against Australian proceedings but compelled the parties to arbitrate in Kentucky. The court's reason was that an injunction was unnecessary. An injunction usually should be granted to prevent a party from intentionally evading his dispute resolution agreement and bringing vexatious and oppressive foreign proceedings to frustrate the other party.[119] The court did not believe the Australian proceedings were commenced in bad faith with the intention to evade the arbitration agreement based on two reasons: first, Australia is a Contracting State of the New York Convention and it is obliged to refer the parties to arbitration;[120] and second, when the US court was seized to compel arbitration, the Australian proceedings were suspended.[121] The US court had confidence that, after the US decision was made, the parties would have clearer knowledge as to how to proceed. It was not necessary to issue an injunction at this stage and an application for injunction could be renewed after the Australian proceedings restarted in breach of the agreement.[122]

In the USA, the court has no discretion to issue an anti-suit injunction if a foreign action involves the interest of a third party or a claim which is not subject to the arbitration or jurisdiction agreement. An anti-suit injunction can only be granted if the parties in the foreign action are the

115 *Gallo*, 446 F.3d at 994; *Applied Medical v Surgical*, 920.

116 *Gau Shan Co., Ltd v Bankers Trust Co* 956 F.2d 1349, 1351 (C.A.6(Tenn) 1992); *Answers in Genesis of Kentucky, Inc. v Creation Ministries Intern., Ltd* 556 F.3d 459, 471 (C.A.6(Ky) 2009).

117 *Answers in Genesis of Kentucky*, 471; *Gau Shan Co., Ltd*, 1357.

118 556 F.3d 459 (C.A.6(Ky) 2009).

119 *Int'l Equity Invs., Inc. v Opportunity Equity Partners Ltd*, 441 F. Supp. 2d 552, 563 (S.D.N.Y. 2006); *Quaak v Klynveld Peat Marwick Goerdeler Bedrijfsrevisoren*, 361 F.3d 11, 20 (1st Cir. 2004); *Software AG, Inc. v Consist Software Solutions, Inc.*, 2008 WL 563449, 24 (S.D.N.Y. 21 February 2008); *A.P. Moller-Maersk A/S v Ocean Express Miami*, 590 F. Supp. 2d 526 (S.D.N.Y. 2008).

120 556 F.3d 471.

121 556 F.3d 471–472.

122 556 F.3d 472.

same and the cause of actions in the arbitration is dispositive of foreign action.[123] The result is usually the same with English tests where the involvement of third parties and other causes of actions are issues for the court to take discretion to make exception to the general principle in favour of issuing an injunction to support exclusive jurisdiction and arbitration agreements. The difficulty with the US approach, however, is that the court cannot use discretion to rule exceptionally at all if a third party interest is involved. In practice, there may be cases where it is better for the end of justice to restrain the foreign action even if a third party is involved in that action—for example, the third party is brought in the action for the sole purpose to frustrate the anti-suit injunction.

3.3 Anti-suit injunction: party autonomy versus statutory jurisdiction

What if there is a statutory requirement that grants exclusive jurisdiction to a country and invalidates a jurisdiction clause? An anti-suit injunction in this case could be used to restrain the party from suing in the chosen court, though the domestic law of the chosen court does not have such a restriction and the chosen court would assert jurisdiction under the agreement. In *Samengo-Turner v J&H Marsh & McLennan (Services) Ltd*,[124] an English domiciliary was employed as the company's reinsurance broker by an English company which provided services to a group company in New York. After the English broker decided to work for the English company's competitor, the New York group brought proceedings in New York to require the broker to repay the incentive award received during employment under a bonus agreement. The bonus agreement included an exclusive jurisdiction clause choosing New York courts. The English broker sued in the English court, claiming that the New York action was brought under an employment contract. According to Article 20 of the Brussels I Regulation, the action against the employee domiciled in a Member State should be brought in the courts of their domicile.[125]

The New York court asserted jurisdiction granted by the exclusive jurisdiction clause. The clause was invalid under Article 21 of the Brussels I Regulation, which states that the protective jurisdiction can only be departed from by a jurisdiction agreement which is entered into after the dispute has arisen, or which provides the employee more options to sue. However, the Brussels I Regulation could not bind New York courts. The English court was thus required to consider a difficult question: whether

123 *Abbott Laboratories v Qiagen Gaithersburg, Inc.* 2010 WL 1539952, 4 (N.D.Ill, 2010); *E. & J. Gallo Winery v Andina Licores S.A.*, 446 F.3d 984, 991 (9th Cir. 2006); *Lyman v Greater Boston Radio, Inc.*, 2010 WL 2557831, 6 (E.D.Mich. 21 June 2010).

124 [2007] ILPr 52.

125 Art 20(1) An employer may bring proceedings only in the courts in the Member State in which the employee is domiciled.

the court should issue an anti-suit injunction restraining proceedings in New York. The court recognized that the standard for such an injunction to be granted is high, especially where the proceedings that the applicant sought to restrain were brought in a highly reputed court in a friendly foreign country.[126] Furthermore, there was an exclusive jurisdiction clause choosing New York courts. Although the clause was invalid under the Brussels I Regulation, it is valid and enforceable under New York law, and in English common law.

Turckey LJ refused to accept that protective jurisdiction mandated by statute created the same strong ground as an exclusive jurisdiction clause in terms of issuing an injunction restraining foreign proceedings.[127] Where there is an exclusive jurisdiction clause, granting an injunction is to demand the parties to keep their contractual obligation; where protective jurisdiction is granted by statute, there is no such reason and the court shall simply consider the traditional criteria to decide the ends of justice.

However, the court eventually decided to grant an injunction based on the reasonable expectation. The New York company should expect to be subject to the jurisdiction of a Member State where its employee had his domicile when entering into the contract; the employee also had expected to be protected by the statute in terms of jurisdiction.[128] This decision is controversial, as expectation of both parties alone has never been used to justify issuing an anti-suit injunction. Expectation means the likelihood of knowledge of the parties, but it is different from their consent of being subject to the particular jurisdiction only. Furthermore, there is nothing to suggest that the New York proceedings were vexatious or oppressive and it is doubtful whether the decision has properly taken comity into consideration. The only possible justification is the ends of justice. The reason to establish protective jurisdiction in employment contracts is to protect an employee from being abused by his employer in terms of weaker litigating and bargaining power. The existence of an exclusive jurisdiction clause in an employment contract cannot necessarily mean the employee has any chance to consult on, negotiate or challenge this clause. The inequality of litigating power between an individual and a multinational company also suggests that justice could not be done if an employee is required to enter an appearance in a foreign trial. However, if this is the justification for issuing an anti-suit injunction against a country chosen in an exclusive jurisdiction clause, the court should consider all the circumstances of a case to decide the real status of the employee and the background of the employment contract, as well as the cause of action. Only the statutory compulsory jurisdiction with the purpose to protect the weaker party should not be a weighty consideration.

126 Para 40.
127 Para 41.
128 Para 44.

Different decisions, however, are made where there is an exclusive jurisdiction clause choosing English courts, which is unenforceable under the compulsory statute of a non-chosen country. In *OT Africa Line v Magic Sportswear Corp*,[129] a bill of lading included an exclusive jurisdiction clause choosing England. Where disputes had arisen, one party sued in Canada where the bill of lading was made, and according to Canadian Marine Liability Act 2001, claims under the bill of lading could be brought in Canada regardless of any jurisdiction clause. The English court applied English choice of law to decide the effectiveness of the jurisdiction clause. Since English law was the applicable law, the Canadian legislation was irrelevant for the English courts to decide whether England was the convenient forum pursuant to the jurisdiction clause. As to Canadian jurisdiction, the Canadian statute was not a sufficient exceptional ground to justify waiving the parties of their agreement. The Court of Appeal finally issued an anti-suit injunction to keep the parties to their bargain.[130]

It is necessary to distinguish *Samengo-Turner* and *OT Africa Line*, concerning the interplay between an exclusive jurisdiction clause and a statute that exempts the binding effect of the clause. In *Samengo-Turner*, the jurisdiction clause is ineffective in England because exclusive jurisdiction is granted to English courts, while in *OT Africa*, the jurisdiction clause continues to be effective in terms of prorogation but not derogation. The Canadian jurisdiction is not compulsory or exclusive, as the parties 'could' sue in Canada regardless of a foreign exclusive jurisdiction clause, instead of 'should' sue in Canada. This is the reason why the exclusive jurisdiction clause is disregarded in the former but not the latter case.

More weight will be given to statutory exclusive jurisdiction. For example, the parties' choice of court could not violate jurisdiction relating to special subject matter that a country will assert under any circumstances. A court has strong public policy and control power in this case, which is not departed from by party autonomy. For example, if the parties have entered into a foreign exclusive jurisdiction clause in deciding the right relating to immoveable property located in the local country, the local court, if seized, certainly will issue an injunction restraining foreign action relating to the jurisdiction clause. On the other hand, if the parties entered into an exclusive jurisdiction clause choosing the English court to decide disputes relating to land located in another country, which is subject to the exclusive jurisdiction of that country, the English court will stay jurisdiction instead of enforcing the exclusive jurisdiction agreement.

129 [2005] 1 CLC 923.

130 For the effect of jurisdiction clauses in the Canadian statute, see Michell, 2002: 476.

3.4 Enforcing an anti-suit injunction order

Civil law countries are usually not equipped with anti-suit injunctions to restrain foreign proceedings. As a result, most civil law countries hold a sceptical view against anti-suit injunctions restraining proceedings in the local courts. However, it is not rare to find a civil law country enforcing an injunction order against its own proceedings in order to enforce an exclusive jurisdiction clause.

French courts traditionally refused to enforce anti-suit injunctions against French proceedings, considering it as infringing the sovereignty of France and contrary to French public policy.[131] The position, however, is relaxed in cases where an injunction is issued to enforce an exclusive jurisdiction clause. The French court enforced an injunction order issued by a US court in *In Zone Brands International v In Zone Brands Europe*.[132] The contract concluded between a French company and a US company contained an exclusive jurisdiction clause choosing Georgian courts. After disputes had arisen, the French party sued in France in breach of the agreement. The Georgian court issued an anti-suit injunction preventing the French party from continuing the French proceedings. The US party applied for the injunction order to be recognized and enforced in France, which was upheld by the French court. The French court did not believe such an injunction was an infringement of French sovereignty but agreed that the parties should be bound by their agreement and the injunction only aimed to enforce the agreement freely entered into between the parties.[133]

German courts, however, take a very different approach. In a German case, the Oberlandesgericht (Regional Court of Appeal) of Dusseldorf refused to serve the respondent the anti-suit injunction granted by the English High Court,[134] preventing the respondent from continuing proceedings in German courts in breach of an arbitration agreement choosing the London Court of International Arbitration. The German court believed the injunction infringed the German jurisdiction because the German court, representing a state's sovereignty, has the power to decide if jurisdiction should be taken alone, and no instruction should be taken from a foreign court.[135] The German court refused the justification provided by English courts that the injunction was granted against the respondent instead of a foreign court because no court proceedings can be pursued without a claimant's cooperation. In the German court's view,

131 *Stoltzenberg*, Cass 1ere civ. 30 June 2004, Rev crit DIP (2004) 815. See also Perreau-Saussine, 2010: 524.

132 Cass Civ 1, 14 October 2009, n 08–16369.

133 Ibid. Michell, 2002: 476. French courts also used anti-suit injunctions restraining proceedings abroad. See *Banque Worms v Brachot* (Cass. 1re civ., 11 November 2002).

134 *Re the Enforcement of an English Anti-suit Injunction* (Case 3 VA 11/95) (Oberlandesgericht, Dusseldorf) [1997] ILPr 320.

135 Para 14.

an injunction restraining the claimant from using the German court directly influenced the court's work and is equivalent to an injunction directed to the court.[136] An instruction as to how a party should act in a foreign court also amounts to an infringement to the procedural law of that country. No exception is granted to support party autonomy.

It is true that the justification based on to whom the injunction is directed only has theoretic value. No matter to whom the injunction is granted, it has the effect of restricting the exercise of jurisdiction of a foreign country.[137]

3.5 Anti-arbitration injunction

It has been discussed in the previous chapter that a court can issue anti-arbitration injunctions restraining the parties from continuing arbitration procedures.[138] This injunction is usually granted at the preliminary stage to deny the jurisdiction of the arbitration tribunal,[139] and English courts usually only grant this injunction where there is a good arguable case that the arbitration agreement does not exist between the parties at all.[140] However, a court can also issue an anti-arbitration injunction enjoining arbitral tribunals to rule on the merit of the case even though there is no argument on the existence of a binding arbitration agreement between the parties.

An anti-arbitration injunction may be sought where there are concurrent proceedings between an arbitral tribunal and a court in related issues. In *Intermet FZCO v Ansol*,[141] the applicant entered into a loan agreement with a Swiss arbitration agreement. After the borrower defaulted on payment, the lender alleged the borrower deceived it into the contract and commenced arbitration proceedings, claiming damages for breach of contract. The lender subsequently brought a court action against the borrower and other responsible parties not subject to arbitration for fraud and sought repayment of the loan. The applicant claimed that the two actions involved similar factual basis, similar witnesses and evidence, which led to substantial increase in cost, duplication of work and probably inconsistent findings;[142] it was desirable to have one forum to decide all claims against all defendants together, which could not be achieved by

136 Para 16.

137 *LAIF X SPARL v Axtel*, 390 F.3d 194, 199 (2d Cir. 2004).

138 Ch 3, section 3.2.

139 *Weissfisch v Julius* [2006] 1 CLC 424; *Excalibur* [2011] EWHC 1624 (Comm); *Albon v Naza* [2007] 2 C.L.C 782; *Claxton Engineering Services v TXM Olaj-es Gazkutato Kft* [2011] 2 All ER (Comm) 128.

140 *Excalibur* [2011] EWHC 1624 (Comm); *Albon v Naza* [2007] 2 C.L.C 782; *Claxton Engineering Services* [2011] 2 All ER (Comm) 128.

141 [2007] EWHC 26 (Comm).

142 Para 22.

arbitration as some defendants are not party to the arbitration agreement;[143] the arbitration was brought in an oppressive and vexatious manner with the intention of adding additional burden to the borrower.[144]

A party may also apply for injunction in cases where there are parallel arbitral proceedings in related actions. In *Jarvis & Sons Ltd v Blue Circle Dartford Estates,*[145] A and B entered into a contract for sale of goods and agreed on arbitration in tribunal X. A then contracted for C to manufacture the goods and agreed disputes to be arbitrated in tribunal Y. Upon the alleged defective quality of the goods, B commenced proceedings against A in tribunal X, while A brought proceedings against C in tribunal Y. C then applied for a court to issue an injunction against arbitration commenced in Y based on the grounds that parallel proceedings in related issues existed in two tribunals. In *Elektrim SA v Vivendi Universal SA & Ors,*[146] A and B entered into a contract providing all disputes are submitted to arbitration in tribunal X. After the dispute had arisen, A and B negotiated a settlement and in the settlement agreement there was another arbitration clause pointing to tribunal Y. Where A refused to enforce the settlement, B commenced two arbitral procedures against A, one for the original contractual dispute in tribunal X and another for the enforceability of the settlement agreement in tribunal Y.

In considering whether an anti-arbitration injunction should be granted, the court should answer the following questions: (1) is the court competent to issue an anti-arbitration injunction? (2) Could an anti-arbitration injunction be issued even if the jurisdiction of the arbitral tribunal is not in question? (3) What test should be adopted for a court to exercise its discretion? As to the first question, although the Arbitration Act 1996 does not provide express permission for a court to intervene by injunctions before an arbitral award is made, the English courts have power to issue an anti-arbitration injunction pursuant to s37 of the Senior Courts Act 1981.[147]

The second and third questions are considered in *Jarvis & Sons Ltd v Blue Circle Dartford Estates,*[148] which introduced four principles in granting anti-arbitration injunctions and which clearly recognized the possibility to grant such injunctions preventing arbitral tribunals from hearing the case as to its merit. The four principles are:[149]

143 Ibid.
144 Ibid.
145 *Jarvis & Sons Ltd v Blue Circle Dartford Estates,* [2008] Bus LR D25.
146 [2007] 1 CLC 227.
147 *Elektrim SA v Vivendi Universal SA & Ors.*
148 [2008] Bus LR D25.
149 Para 40.

(i) The court's power under section 37 of the Senior Courts Act 1981 to grant injunctions includes a power to grant an injunction to restrain an arbitration from proceeding.
(ii) That power may be exercised if two conditions are satisfied, namely: (a) the injunction does not cause injustice to the claimant in the arbitration, and (b) the continuance of the arbitration would be oppressive, vexatious, unconscionable or an abuse of process.
(iii) The court's discretion to grant such an injunction is now only exercised very sparingly and with due regard to the principles upon which the Arbitration Act 1996 is expressly based.
(iv) Delay by the party applying for an injunction is material to the court's exercise of discretion and may in some cases be fatal to the application.

The factor of delay was also emphasized in an earlier case, *Intermet FZCO v Ansol*, where the English court refused to grant an anti-arbitration injunction, because of the delay for the application and the manner in which the arbitration procedure was commenced.[150] The court held that an injunction was inappropriate if the application was brought too late and the foreign proceedings were well-advanced.[151] Furthermore, the lenders commenced arbitration procedures without oppressive intention based on their contractual rights.[152]

However, issuing an anti-arbitration injunction is a controversial matter and is never free from sceptical views of commentators. Although an anti-arbitration injunction at the preliminary stage in deciding jurisdiction may properly survive the question of the New York Convention, an injunction granted where jurisdiction of an arbitral tribunal is properly established is different. Such an injunction infringes the fundamental principle of the New York Convention and is contrary to the international commercial arbitration custom. Although in principle a court reserves the power to issue an injunction to restrain foreign proceedings pursuant to a foreign exclusive jurisdiction clause, the situation is very different in arbitration, where there are treaty obligations and in many countries statutory restrictions preventing a court from intervening in this way.[153]

150 Paras 24–26.
151 Para 24.
152 Paras 27–30.
153 For more on anti-arbitration injunction, see Tang 2012c: 589ff.

4 Stay of jurisdiction and dispute resolution agreements

4.1 Forum non conveniens *and jurisdiction agreements*

Forum non conveniens is an old common law doctrine. After a court is satisfied that it has jurisdiction to hear a cross-border dispute, the court may not exercise jurisdiction because it is more appropriate for another forum to hear the case in the interest of justice. When exercising discretion under the doctrine of *forum non conveniens*, a court usually considers the balance of private interest and public interest,[154] the intention of the parties,[155] the convenience and cost of trial,[156] the closest connection between a dispute and a forum[157] and the ends of justice.[158]

The relationship between *forum non conveniens* and jurisdiction agreements is confusing. Although common law countries preserve their discretion to enforce jurisdiction agreements, they usually hold the policy of contract freedom and give effectiveness to such agreements in most circumstances. Different approaches are used by different countries, different courts in one country and even different judges in the same court to decide the effectiveness of a jurisdiction clause. Some treat jurisdiction agreements as a factor considered in *forum non conveniens* and some believe the normal *forum non conveniens* consideration should not apply to jurisdiction agreements which can be directly enforced, while others believe that, although jurisdiction clauses are prima facie enforceable, strong reasons could still apply to refute their effectiveness.[159] The relevance, weight and status of jurisdiction clauses in *forum non conveniens* are never clear.

154 This approach is mainly used in the US, where the balance of public interest and private interest should be considered. See US cases: *Piper v Reynor*, 454 US 235; *Baumgart v Fairchild Aircraft* (1993) 981 F.2d 824 (US 5th Circuit of Appeals); *Stangvik v Shiley Inc* (1991) 54 Cal.3d 744. Cf. English cases: *Spiliada v Cansulex* [1987] AC 460; *Lubbe v Cape Plc* [2000] 1 WLR 1545; Fawcett and Carruthers, 2008: 439–440; Peel, 2001: 187.

155 *The Eleftheria*, [1970] P 94; *Donohue v Armco* [2002] 1 All ER 749; *Spiliada v Cansulex*; *British Aerospace v Dee Howard* [1993] 1 Lloyd's Rep 368; *Sabah Shipyard (Pakistan) Ltd v Islamic Republic of Pakistan* [2004] 1 CLC 149; *National Westminster Bank v Utrecht-America Finance Co* [2001] CLC 1372; *UBS AG & Anor v HSH Nordbank AG* [2009] 1 CLC 934. Fawcett and Carruthers, 2008: 443–454.

156 *Arkwright Mutual Insurance Co. v Bryanstan Insurance Co. Ltd and Others* [1990] 3 WLR 705; *Credit Chimique v James Scott Engineering Group Ltd* 1979 S.C. 406; *Ace Insurance SA-NV v Zurich Insurance Co & Anor* [2001] CLC 526; *Innovia Films Ltd v Frito-Lay North America*, [2012] EWHC 790 (Pat), para 42; *Amin Rasheed Shipping Corporation v Kuwait Insurance Co.* [1984] AC 50.

157 *Connelly v RTZ Corporation Plc & Ors*, [1997] CLC 1357; *Eastern Power Ltd v Azienda Comunale Energia e Ambiente*, [2001] ILPr 6; *Travelers Casualty & Surety Co of Canada v Sun Life Assurance Co of Canada (UK) Ltd*, [2007] Lloyd's Rep IR 619; *Barclays Bank Plc v Homan*, [1992] B 757; *Deutsche Bank AG v Highland Crusader Offshore Partners LP*, [2010] 1 WLR 1023.

158 *Lubbe v Cape Plc* [2000] 1 WLR 1545; *Spiliada Maritime Corp v Cansulex*, [1987] AC 460; *Lennon v Scottish Daily Record & Sunday Mail Ltd*, [2004] EWHC 359 (QB); *Connelly v RTZ*.

159 For case examples, see footnotes 164–166 below.

In the US, for example, some courts take the approach that a jurisdiction agreement will normally be enforced and f*orum non conveniens* usually does not apply unless the jurisdiction clause is held invalid by the court.[160] That means once there is a valid foreign exclusive jurisdiction clause, a US court should dismiss jurisdiction. In England and many commonwealth countries, jurisdiction clauses are prima facie enforceable unless the defendant can prove strong reasons to the contrary.[161] In some early English cases, an exclusive jurisdiction clause is only one factor to consider in the decision to stay jurisdiction.[162] This approach is not applied in modern practice.

Although divergence exists, there are a few things in common. First, more weight is given to choice of court agreements worldwide. Decisions to treat an exclusive jurisdiction clause as one ordinary factor in *forum non conveniens/forum conveniens* existed only in early decisions and are generally abandoned by most courts in the world.[163] It is remarked by Lewison J that:[164]

> the standard considerations that arise in arguments about *forum non conveniens* should be given little weight in the face of an exclusive jurisdiction clause where the parties have chosen the courts of a neutral territory in the context of an agreement with world-wide application. Otherwise the exclusive jurisdiction clause would be deprived of its intended effect. Indeed, the more 'neutral' the chosen forum was the less the importance the parties must have placed on the convenience of the forum for any particular dispute. If the standard considerations that arise in arguments about *forum non conveniens* were to be given full weight, they would almost always trump the parties' deliberate selection of a neutral forum.

Second, although many courts accept that, in theory, same effectiveness should be given to a jurisdiction clause choosing the local forum and foreign country, a court is more willing to give prorogation effect to a local jurisdiction clause than giving derogation effect to a foreign jurisdiction clause.[165] In other words, if there is a jurisdiction clause choosing the local

160 *AAR International v Nimeias Enterprises S.A.*, 250 F.3d 510, 524–525 (7th Cir.), cert. denied. 534 US 995 (2001).

161 *The Eleftheria.*

162 *Cargo Lately Laden on Board The Fehmarn (Owners) v Fehmarn (Owners) (The Fehmarn)* [1958] 1 WLR 159.

163 *Animal Film, LLC v D.E.J. Productions; Stangvik*, 54 Cal.3d at 751; *Bechtel v Industrial Indem* (1978) 86 Cal.App.3d 45, 51–53.

164 *Skype v Joltid*, [2011] ILPr 8, para 33.

165 The English courts have struck down foreign exclusive jurisdiction clauses in a few cases; see, e.g. *The Hollandia* [1983] 1 AC 565; *Aratra Potato v Egyptian Navigation (The El Amria)* [1981] 2 Lloyd's Rep 119; *Citi-march Ltd and Another v Neptune Orient Lines Ltd* [1996] 1 WLR 1367.

court, it is very difficult for the court to stay jurisdiction in favour of a more appropriate forum abroad; on the other hand, if there is an exclusive jurisdiction clause choosing a foreign country, a court is more ready to take jurisdiction instead and to refuse to use *forum non conveniens* to enforce this jurisdiction clause.

A few words may be necessary on the development of *forum non conveniens* in China. China is a civil law country but it has adopted very basic discretion to decline jurisdiction based on 'convenience'.[166] Factors considered in the Chinese version of *forum non conveniens* are based on the factual connections between the dispute and the forum, the location of the witnesses and evidence, the location of the disposable assets of the defendant, the potential enforcement of the judgments, etc.[167] The choice of a foreign jurisdiction nonetheless is not a consideration in the Chinese version of *forum non conveniens.*[168] On the other hand, the choice of a Chinese court is conclusive to exclude the exercise of discretion under *forum non conveniens.*[169] The discriminatory treatment of Chinese and foreign jurisdiction clauses shows the tendency to guard Chinese jurisdiction as part of judicial sovereignty continues to exist.[170]

4.2 Enforcing exclusive jurisdiction agreements

In most cases, a court will enforce jurisdiction agreements in the absence of invalidity and injustice. Ordinary *forum non conveniens/forum conveniens* usually does not apply in such circumstances.[171] A large amount of cases can be found where a common law court enforced the jurisdiction clause and refused to exercise discretion to depart from it.[172] In England and other commonwealth countries, although in principle, strong reasons could persuade a court to depart from a jurisdiction clause, these reasons

166 Supreme People's Court, 'Answers to Questions Arising out of Trial Practice of Commercial and Maritime Cases with Foreign Elements 2004'. A Chinese version is available at www.lawtime.cn/info/maoyi/myzc/20081217111.html, answer 7; Supreme People's Court, 'Summary of the Second National Conference on the Adjudication of Commercial and Maritime Cases with Foreign Elements 2005', Fa Fa [2005] No 6, Art 11. *Dongpeng Trade v HK Bank of East Asia, Selected Cases of People's Courts* (People's Court Publisher, 1996), 143; *Sumitomo Bank v Xinhua*, Supreme Court, (1999) Jing Zhong Zi No 194.

167 Supreme People's Court, 'Summary 2005', Art 11.

168 Ibid., Art 11(3).

169 Ibid., Art 11(3).

170 For discussion on Chinese *forum non conveniens*, see Du, 2007: 152; Li and Liu, 2008: 68; Tu, 2012: 341.

171 *Yes To v Hur*, 2011 WL 902297 (N.D.Cal., 2011).

172 *National Westminster Bank Plc v Utrecht-America Finance Co* [2001] CLC 1372; *J.P. Morgan Securities Asia Private Limited v Malaysian Newsprint Industries* [2002] ILPr 17; *Ultisol Transport Contractors Ltd v Bouygues Offshore SA & Ors* [1998] CLC 1526; *Hamed El Chiaty & Co. (T/A Travco Nile Cruise Lines) v The Thomas Cook Group* [1994] ILPr 367; *Middle Eastern Oil v National Bank of Abu Dhabi* [2008] All ER (D) 285.

should be something more than what are predictable at the time of contracting. Legitimate reasons include circumstances that change after the conclusion of the contract, that cannot be reasonably foreseeable by both parties[173] and that make the enforcement of the agreement impractical or impossible. The court may also consider the necessity to avoid inconsistent decisions and split of proceedings, public policy, and political, race, gender or religious reasons that may prevent a party from acquiring a fair hearing. The resisting party should prove these facts beyond simple possibility, suspicion or likelihood. Clear and cogent evidence is required to support such allegations.[174]

In the USA, some courts use the terminology of 'mandatory forum-selection clauses' to refer to exclusive jurisdiction clauses. An exclusive jurisdiction clause can only be challenged if it is the product of fraud or overreaching, enforcement would effectively deprive defendants of their day in court or enforcement would contravene a strong public policy of the forum.[175] The standard *forum non conveniens* consideration cannot be used to dismiss an action where a valid jurisdiction clause exists.[176]

4.3 Stay of jurisdiction in breach of local exclusive jurisdiction clauses

It is hard to find a case where a court stay jurisdiction in breach of exclusive jurisdiction clauses choosing the local court. In China, the Supreme Court has provided judicial direction that jurisdiction cannot be stayed if there is a valid jurisdiction clause, either exclusive or not, choosing Chinese courts.[177] In practice, many Chinese courts would not consider staying jurisdiction until they were satisfied that there was no choice of court agreement choosing Chinese courts.[178]

In England, although a court sometimes would stay jurisdiction designated in a non-exclusive jurisdiction clause to avoid concurrent proceedings,[179] staying jurisdiction where exclusive jurisdiction is conferred to the local court is extremely unusual. Any objects foreseeable at the time of contracting or any factors pointing to a natural forum are not

173 *Import Export Metro Ltd v Compania Sud Americana De Vapores SA* [2003] EWHC 11.

174 *Middle Eastern Oil*, [2008] EWHC 895 (Comm), para 24.

175 *M/S Bremen v Zapata Off-Shore*, 407 US 1 (1972); *Richards v Lloyd's of London* 135 F.3d 1289, 12294 (9th Cir. 1998); *Yes To v Hur.*

176 *Yes To v Hur; Piper Aircraft v Reyno* (1981) 454 US 235, 219; *Yavuz v 61 MM*, 576 F.3d 1166 (10th Cir. 2009), 1171.

177 Supreme People's Court, 'Summary 2005', Art 11(3). *Forum non conveniens* is adopted in judicial practice at an experimental stage.

178 *Baron Motorcycles Inc v Awell Logistics Group, Inc*, Ningbo Maritime Court, (2008) Yong Hai Fa Shang Chu Zi No 277, the court referred to the lack of a jurisdiction clause choosing China as one of the factors supporting the use of *forum non conveniens* to decline jurisdiction; *Jaten Electronic v Smartech Electronic*, Shanghai Municipality No 1 Intermediate People's Court, (2009) Hu Yi Zhong Min Wu (Shang) Chu Zi No 51.

179 *Bas Capital Funding Corporation & Ors v Medfinco Ltd* [2003] EWHC 1798 (Ch).

weighty factors to support departing from a jurisdiction clause. The resisting party must provide reasons that suing in the local forum is not good to reach the ends of justice. It is unlikely that a defendant could successfully argue in an English court that the English judicial system is independent, or he cannot receive fair trial for political or other reasons.

In *Horn Linie Gmbh v Panamericana Formas e Impresos SA*,[180] the parties chose English courts as the exclusive forum to hear their disputes arising out of a contract for the carriage of cargo to and for delivery in Columbia. The contract had no connections with England, which was a neutral forum. The defendant claimed that, although England was chosen in the clause, English courts should stay jurisdiction under *forum non conveniens* because Columbia law prohibited the choice of forum in such a contract, and any jurisdiction clauses would be contrary to the public policy of Columbia. However, Morison J believed that party autonomy should not be overridden by public policy of Columbia in this case. Since the defendant had given his consent while knowing the Columbian law, the defendant freely accepted the governance of English courts and was estoppeled from claiming that honouring the agreement would cause him to offend Columbian public policy.[181]

One reason that may be accepted to depart from a local exclusive jurisdiction clause is the necessity to avoid splitting proceedings and inconsistent decisions. In *Donahue*, the House of Lords decided to apply the exception by refusing to issue an anti-suit injunction to restrain US proceedings subject to a valid English exclusive jurisdiction clause because the third parties not subject to the clause were parties in the US trial and part of the proceedings involving the third parties could not be restrained. Restraining US proceedings would cause parallel proceedings in related matters. However, it is also necessary to recognize that staying forum proceedings is different from restraining a foreign action. More stringent rules apply in anti-suit injunctions where the maintenance of international comity is always an issue that a court needs to bear in mind. The court may refuse to restrain foreign proceedings because of the concern of splitting proceedings but this may not be a reason for a court to stay domestic jurisdiction, especially if there is an exclusive jurisdiction clause choosing the local forum.

4.4 Staying jurisdiction in favour of arbitration agreements

Usually, a court has treaty or statutory obligation to decline jurisdiction in favour of an arbitration agreement. Staying jurisdiction in favour of a valid arbitration agreement is a statutory duty which is compulsory not discretionary. *Forum non conveniens* is irrelevant in supporting arbitration

180 [2006] 2 All ER (Comm) 924.
181 Para 20.

agreements in judicial practice.[182] In a multi-party litigation, where only some parties are subject to an arbitration agreement, the court is not obligated to stay jurisdiction over parties not subject to arbitration, unless by exercising discretion, a stay of jurisdiction is in the interest of justice.[183] In *Reichhold Norway ASA v Goldman Sachs International*,[184] a buyer of a subsidiary company claimed that the financial adviser of the parent company committed misrepresentation. The sales agreement was subject to Norwegian arbitration. The buyer commenced arbitration proceedings in Norway against the financial adviser and commenced proceedings in the English court against the parent company for alleged responsibility for the misrepresentation. The parent company applied for a stay of English jurisdiction. The English court recognized that staying English proceedings in light of related arbitration proceedings between different parties in another country would only be granted in exceptional cases if there were compelling reasons to do so. In the current case, the arbitration results would affect the court's decision. The success in arbitration would prevent the claimant from claiming further remedies against the parent company.

In *Mabey & Johnson v Danos*,[185] an English manufacturer entered into a representation agreement with a Jamaican company which acted as the former's agent in connection with the supply of products to a Jamaican project. The representation agreement provided that all disputes arising out of the agreement should be submitted to arbitration. Where the Jamaican company engaged in an alleged conspiracy and fraud with its director, the English manufacturer sued both the agent and the director in the English court. The agent invoked the arbitration clause and requested the English court to stay jurisdiction under s9 of the Arbitration Act 1996. The agent's director applied for a stay of proceedings on the reason that he would also be involved in the arbitration though he was not a direct party, because he was the director of the defendant agent. If both court and arbitral proceedings continued, the director would be involved in two proceedings in England.

The English court, however, refused the director's application. It was the agent, probably with the director's instruction, who invocated the arbitration clause preventing court proceedings from continuing. The agent's action fragmented the proceedings and caused parallel proceedings between the court and the tribunal. The director was not entitled to take advantage of the arbitration shield and could not base his argument on the fact that fragment of proceedings was not good for the end of

182 Park, 1995: 201.
183 Joseph, 2005: para 11.46.
184 [2000] 1 WLR 173.
185 [2007] EWHC 1095 (Ch).

justice because the agent, under the direction of the director, applied for the proceedings to be fragmented.[186]

5 Conclusion

Party autonomy in deciding jurisdiction is a useful method to avoid uncertainty brought about by conflicts of jurisdiction, but it may lose its effectiveness without proper instruments to protect its enforceability. The civil law approach of *lis pendens* is not an instrument to enforce a valid dispute resolution clause. It is based on the chronological order, requiring the second seized court to give priority to the first seized one without considering the effectiveness of party autonomy. In cases, it is even a tool easily abused by the party that aims to escape from a freely entered contract to the detriment of another party. *Lis pendens* also has no role to play in supporting arbitration agreements.

The available procedural tools that could provide real and effective protection to dispute resolution agreements are anti-suit injunctions and *forum non conveniens*. A country usually adopts either both of these tools or neither of them. If a country only has the former but not the latter, it has taken an ambitious approach to compete with other countries for jurisdiction, which certainly violates international comity; a country adopting only the latter restrains itself but cannot properly protect its citizens against deliberate breach of dispute resolution clauses and the inappropriate grasp of jurisdiction of other countries. If used properly and in an ideal context, conflicts of jurisdictions usually can be managed within a reasonable level and dispute resolution clauses can be enforced and acquire the greatest effectiveness.

However, an ideal world does not exist. The exercise of *forum non conveniens* and anti-suit injunctions is inevitably affected by a lot of factors other than strict conflict of laws consideration, such as comity with another country and enforceability of judgments. Divergence exists for the application of these approaches in different countries. Even within one country, discretion and flexible criteria make the application uncertain. Divergence, flexibility and inconsistent application of discretion inevitably lead to different judgments. In an international context, it still means that forum shopping and conflict of jurisdiction cannot be completely avoided and the certainty brought about by jurisdiction and arbitration agreements is diminished.

186 Para 37.

7 Autonomy and supporting measures in Europe[1]

1 Introduction

The previous chapter shows that there are various instruments to protect party autonomy. This chapter examines the effect of these instruments in the regime where judicial cooperation exists. Applying common law measures to support jurisdiction and arbitration agreements is challenged in the European Union. EU jurisdiction rules are harmonized in the Brussels I Regulation. Since the majority of the EU Member States are civil law countries, the European jurisdiction rules follow the civil law tradition and greatly restrict the discretionary power of a court.[2] The Brussels I Regulation does not provide any express terms to incorporate *forum non conveniens* and anti-suit injunctions in its regime. Instead, the civil law concept of *lis pendens* has been adopted.[3] The ECJ has demonstrated a clear attitude in a number of cases that these common law instruments cannot be used within the Brussels regime.[4] This restriction not only applies to jurisdiction agreements, but also extends to arbitration agreements.

2 *Lis pendens* and jurisdiction agreements

2.1 *Conflict of two doctrines in the Brussels I Regulation*

Under the Brussels I Regulation, the court of a Member State second seized shall, by its own motion, stay proceedings in favour of the court of a Member State first seized in deciding the same cause of action between

1 This chapter is a revised and extended version of the article entitled 'Conflicts of Jurisdiction and Party Autonomy in EU' by the author, published first in (2012) 59 LIX Netherlands International Law Review 321.

2 When the original six Contracting States negotiated the Brussels Convention in 1968, none of them were common law countries. The latter accession of the UK and Ireland could not vary the civil-law basis on which the Convention was based. See von Mehren, 2002; Hartley, 2005.

3 Arts 27 and 28. Case C-116/02 *Gasser* v *MISAT*, [2003] ECR 14693.

4 *Turner v Grovit*, ibid.; Case C-185/07, *Allianz SpA v West Tankers* [2009] ECR I-663; Case C-281/02, *Owusu v Jackson* [2005] ECR I-1383.

the same parties,[5] and should decline jurisdiction if the first seized court has established jurisdiction.[6] The court of the Member State second seized may stay its proceedings in favour of the first seized Member State in related actions,[7] which are so closely connected that it is expedient to hear and determine them together to avoid the risk of irreconcilable judgments resulting from separate proceedings.[8]

This rule does not require the court to consider such issues as procedural efficiency, natural forum, litigation cost and convenience to both parties. Questions arise where there is an exclusive jurisdiction agreement falling within the framework of the Brussels I Regulation choosing one of the Member States.[9] Conflicts arise where the claimant brings the dispute to the first seized Member State in breach of an exclusive jurisdiction clause and the other party subsequently brings the same action in another Member State which is chosen in the agreement. The rule of *lis pendens* requires the second seized court (chosen forum) to stay jurisdiction in favour of the first seized one (non-chosen forum), while the doctrine of party autonomy requires the non-chosen forum (the first seized court) to decline jurisdiction in favour of the chosen forum (the second seized court). Even if the second seized court stays jurisdiction in favour of the first seized one, the first seized court usually should decline jurisdiction after confirming the jurisdiction clause is valid and exclusive.[10] However, there is a risk that the first seized court may nevertheless decide the jurisdiction clause invalid according to a different interpretation of substantive validity, which is not uniformly provided by the Brussels I Regulation.[11]

5 Art 27(1) Brussels I.
6 Art 27(2) Brussels I.
7 Art 28(1) Brussels I.
8 Art 28(3) Brussels I.
9 Art 23(1) Brussels I Regulation.
10 Art 23(1) Brussels I Regulation.
11 Art 23(1) Brussels I Regulation only provides uniform rules on formal validity of a jurisdiction clause. Some ECJ cases suggest that formal validity is sufficient to ensure authentic consent of the parties, see Case C-159/97 *Transporti Castelletti Spedizioni International SpA v Hugo Trumpy SpA*, [1997] ECR I-1587, paras 49 and 51; Case C-106/95 *MSG v Les Gravieres Rhenanes Sarl* [1997] ECR I-911, para 15; Case C-378/98 *Coreck Maritime GmbH v Handelsvee BV* [2000] ECR I-9337, para 13. However, this suggestion is clearly incorrect because formal validity cannot cover issues where parties totally understand the existence of a jurisdiction clause but signed because of fraud, duress or undue influence. Others suggest that national law, including choice of law of each Member State, can be used to decide material validity. See Hess *et al.*, 2007: para 377; Austrian case, 7 Ob 320/00k, ZfRV 2001/71 = RdW2001/678; 7 Ob 38/01s, RdW 2001/676 = ÖRZ-EÜ 2001/70 =ZfRV 2001/63 = ecolex 2002, 420 = ELF 2001, 431; 5 Ob 130/02g. 'National Report Austria (Oberhammer/Domej)', Study JLS/C4/2005/03, http://ec.europa.eu/civiljustice/news/docs/study_bxl1_austria.pdf, accessed 28 January 2012. Since inconsistency exists, it is likely that inconsistent decisions may be made depending on which court is seized to decide validity of a jurisdiction clause.

2.2 Contract priority versus procedure priority

Contract priority: English approach prior to Gasser

Before the ECJ provided an answer to the relationship between party autonomy and *lis pendens*, the English court considered the same issue but reached a decision completely different from the ECJ. In *Continental Bank v Aeakos*,[12] the bank, which was domiciled in Illinois, had its seat and centre of administration in Chicago and had business in Greece, entered into a loan agreement with some ship companies registered in Panama. The contract contained an exclusive jurisdiction clause choosing English courts and a choice of law clause choosing English law. After the disputes arose, however, the companies sued the bank in Greece. The bank applied for injunctions from the English court and subsequently brought the second action in England claiming sums allegedly due from the debtors under the loan agreement. The English court refused to stay jurisdiction in favour of the first seized court. The reason was contractual freedom. The English court did not consider there was necessity to strictly apply *lis pendens* where there was a valid choice of court agreement. The only issue that mattered was that both parties had entered into a valid exclusive jurisdiction agreement and should be bound by it. The protection provided by the exclusive jurisdiction clause to the bank was a consideration required by the bank in exchange for the loan, and the bank did not give up and waive its right not to be sued in any other countries granted by the jurisdiction clause. The companies promised to be bound by the jurisdiction clause and there was no reason for them to evade this promise. The English court then continued to hear the case pursuant to the jurisdiction clause and granted an anti-suit injunction to restrain the Greek proceedings from continuing on behalf of the bank.[13] The 'contract priority' approach is adopted. This approach focuses on enforcing parties' agreement. It is, however, rather unilateral. It does not require the Member State to consider the fact that the same proceedings are pending in another Member State; neither does it require the other Member State to give up jurisdiction. Adopting this approach will cause parallel proceedings, unless the court issues an anti-suit injunction to restrain another country's proceedings at the same time.

Intermediate approach: AG opinion in Gasser

The ECJ was seized to answer the same question in *Gasser v MISAT*.[14] In this case, an Austrian company, Gasser, and an Italian company, MISAT,

12 *Continental Bank NA v Aeakos Compania Naviera SA and Others*, [1994] 1 WLR 588. Followed by *O.T. Africa Line Limited v Fayad Hijazy*, [2002] ILPr 18.

13 The decision to issue anti-suit injunctions is also challenged by the ECJ in the Brussels I scheme. See section 4 for anti-suit injunctions.

14 Case C-116/02 *Gasser v MISAT*, [2003] ECR 14693.

entered into a contract for the sale of goods, without choice of court agreements. Subsequent invoices sent by Gasser contained an exclusive jurisdiction clause choosing Austria courts, which were duly paid by MISAT. After disputes arose, MISAT brought an action in Italy for a declaration of termination of contract; Gasser subsequently sued in Austria based on the jurisdiction clause. MISAT claimed that the court first seized was Italy and Austrian court's proceedings were barred by *lis pendens.*

As it has been ruled in *Benincasa v Dentalkit,*[15] a jurisdiction clause is severable and independent from the main contract. The dispute on the invalidity or termination of the main contract does not prevent the chosen court from taking jurisdiction to hear the dispute.[16] The chosen court has the prorogation jurisdiction to decide its own competence under the doctrine of *kompetenz-kompetenz* even if the dispute is about the invalidity of the jurisdiction clause.[17] However, the Brussels I Regulation does not prevent a non-chosen Member State from taking jurisdiction to decide the validity of a jurisdiction clause.[18] The key question is whether the second seized court must, with no exception, give priority to the first seized court, even if such a stay is made in breach of an exclusive jurisdiction clause.

Advocate General P Leger believed that the purpose of the *lis pendens* rule is to prevent parallel proceedings in different Member States and to avoid irreconcilable judgments.[19] This rule, however, can be derogated from where the second seized court has exclusive jurisdiction to hear the case under Article 22 of the Brussels I Regulation,[20] which grants *in rem* jurisdiction to a court based on the exclusive state control. AG Leger considered the principle might be extended to circumstances in which the second seized court had exclusive jurisdiction under an exclusive jurisdiction clause.[21] The chosen court in an exclusive jurisdiction clause is

15 Case C-269/95 [1997] ECR I-3767. Case C-18/02 *Danmarks Rederiforening v LO Landsorganisationen i Sverige,* [2004] ECR I-1417; *Skype Technologies SA v Joltid Ltd,* [2011] ILPr 8; *Knorr-Bremse Systems for Commercial Vehicles Ltd v Haldex Brake Products GmbH,* [2008] 2 All ER (Comm) 448.

16 For comments on the doctrine of separability, see Harris, 1998: 279; Force, 2011: 401; Rosen, 1994: 599.

17 This is the doctrine of *kompetenz-kompetenz,* which means a forum has the competence to decide its own competence. Rosen, 1994; Fraterman, 2011: 913–914; Inoue, 2006: 178; McLachlan, 2008: 233–234; Walt, 1999: 375–376. *Mackender v Feldia AG.* [1967] 2QB 590 (the English court decided the validity of a Belgium jurisdiction clause); *Dubai Electricity v Islamic Republic of Iran Shipping Lines (The Iran Vojdan),* [1984] 2 Lloyd's Rep 380 (the English court decided whether a German jurisdiction clause was valid under German law); *Trendtex Trading v Credit Suisse,* [1980] QB 628 (the English court decided whether to stay jurisdiction in favour of an exclusive Geneva jurisdiction clause and whether the clause was valid).

18 Article 23(1) only provides that the chosen court has jurisdiction. It does not say which court should decide the validity of the exclusive jurisdiction clause.

19 [2005] 1 All ER (Comm) 538, para 44.

20 Ibid., para 48.

21 Ibid., para 48.

designed by the parties to be exclusive.[22] Although the exclusivity of a chosen court in an exclusive jurisdiction clause is acquired from party autonomy, while the exclusivity of a jurisdiction *in rem* stems from state sovereignty, the practical nature of the exclusivity is comparable. Both grant jurisdiction to one country to the exclusion of other states.

AG Leger also considered practical advantages to require priority to be given to a court that has exclusive jurisdiction. On the one hand, requiring the second seized chosen court to decline jurisdiction in favour of the first seized one undermines the effectiveness and certainty of the prorogation jurisdiction.[23] On the other hand, requiring all non-chosen courts to give priority to the chosen court could reduce inconsistent decisions.[24] The answer to the validity of a jurisdiction clause largely depends on which country makes decision. If any first seized courts could make this decision, the result largely depends on in which court the claimant brings the action.

AG Leger's justification is not completely based on contractual freedom. It is a combination of contractual freedom and procedure certainty. AG Leger recognizes the effect of an exclusive jurisdiction clause granted by the parties and admitted that the parties have the power to grant the chosen country 'exclusive jurisdiction' to the equivalent effect of exclusive jurisdiction designated by Article 22 of the Brussels I Regulation. At the same time, he also considered the legal certainty and uniform decision which is achievable by providing priority to party autonomy.

Procedure priority: ECJ decision in Gasser

The Advocate General's opinion, however, was not accepted by the ECJ, which adopted a 'procedure priority' approach. The ECJ emphasized the fundamental object of the *lis pendens* rule to prevent parallel proceedings. In order to tackle parallel proceedings promptly, the rule of *lis pendens* should be interpreted broadly to cover all situations.[25] *Lis pendens* applies without distinction between different grounds on which jurisdiction is based.[26] Before the first seized court declines jurisdiction, the second seized court could, under no circumstances, examine jurisdiction of either the first seized court[27] or the second seized one.[28]

Another practical justification of the ECJ approach is that, although the parties entered into a jurisdiction clause, both of them may agree to change it or not to invoke it at a later stage. Sometimes the intention to

22 Ibid., paras 57, 58–61.
23 Ibid., paras 57, 62–71.
24 Ibid., paras 57, 72–82.
25 Case C-116/02 *Gasser v MISAT*, [2003] ECR 14693, para 41.
26 *Gasser v MISAT*, ibid., para 43.
27 Ibid., para 44.
28 Ibid., para 48.

repudiate the agreement is demonstrated impliedly by the fact that the claimant sues in a non-chosen forum and the defendant submits to that forum.[29] The defendant always has the freedom to enter an appearance before the non-chosen forum.[30] As a result, the existence of a jurisdiction clause is not conclusive and legal certainty cannot be served by requiring any non-chosen courts to decline jurisdiction straightforwardly.

Furthermore, the ECJ distinguishes exclusive jurisdiction acquired under mandatory European law[31] and exclusivity acquired under exclusive jurisdiction clauses.[32] Exclusive jurisdiction under the mandatory European law is comprehensive and conclusive. In contrast, the Brussels I Regulation grants exclusive jurisdiction to the chosen court in an exclusive choice of court agreement to decide disputes subject to the agreement, but it does not grant the same level of exclusivity for the chosen court to decide the existence and validity of the jurisdiction clause.[33] The negative *kompetenz-kompetenz* is not accepted in the EU.[34] Since the chosen court has no exclusive jurisdiction in deciding its own jurisdiction, it cannot preclude the application of the *lis pendens* rule between Member States.

The procedure priority approach strictly follows the chronological order to prevent concurrent proceedings. The approach does not give much weight to party autonomy or the reasonable expectation of the parties. The intention of the parties is held inconclusive because it was variable and the right granted by it waiveable. Procedure certainty, thus, overweighs contractual certainty.

Contract priority versus procedure priority: assessing the Gasser decision

The procedure priority approach is criticized by commentators, mostly in England, as being an 'absolute refusal to consider the requirements of reasonableness',[35] while many European lawyers believe the *Gasser* approach to be legitimate.[36] It is because, under the civil law tradition, the court's duty is to apply the law according to how it is legislated. The wording of Article 27 does not provide any leeway to exclusive jurisdiction

29 Ibid., para 49.
30 Ibid., para 49.
31 Art 22 Brussels I Regulation.
32 Art 23 Brussels I Regulation.
33 *Gasser v MISAT, supra* n. 41, para 49.
34 *Kompetenz-kompetenz* permits the chosen court to decide its own jurisdiction, while a negative *kompetenz-kompetenz* doctrine precludes non-chosen courts in an exclusive jurisdiction clause from deciding the existence and validity of the jurisdiction clause. The same position exists in the Hague Convention 2005, where any non-chosen court can also decide the preliminary issue of an exclusive jurisdiction clause.
35 Fentiman, 2006: 304. For other criticisms, see Hartley, 2005: 827.
36 Steinle and Vasilliades, 2010: 570; Blobel and Spath, 2005: 532.

clauses. Furthermore, Article 23 does not state anywhere that it shall override the *lis pendens* rule of the Regulation.

However, it is doubtful whether the rigid literal interpretation could achieve the ends of justice and serve the purposes of the Brussels I Regulation in facilitating the sound administration of justice.[37] First of all, requiring the second seized court that has been designated by an exclusive jurisdiction agreement to stay jurisdiction in favour of the first seized court is not the only way to prevent concurrent proceedings or irreconcilable judgments. In certain circumstances, it is more appropriate to require any other courts to stay jurisdiction in favour of the court that might have exclusive jurisdiction. The exclusive jurisdiction can be acquired by exclusive jurisdiction rules[38] or by party autonomy.[39] Second, one object of the Brussels I Regulation is certainty and predictability.[40] Allowing any first seized court the priority to decide the validity of a jurisdiction clause could hamper certainty because the Member States use different national law, including domestic private international law, to decide material validity of a jurisdiction clause under the current scheme of Brussels I Regulation.[41] It has been observed by Pfeiffer that:

> As for now, the law of some Member States refers to the *lex fori* (since choice-of-forum agreements constitute a procedural contract) whereas others refer to the *lex causae*. Whilst divergence as such does not necessarily cause harmful effects, the situation may be different here because—due to different choice-of-law rules and, as a consequence, differences in the applicable law—jurisdictional agreements may be considered valid in one Member State whereas they are considered invalid in another.[42]

The greatest concern, from commercial sectors and practitioners, is that one of the contractual parties subject to a valid exclusive jurisdiction clause could bring proceedings for a negative declaration in a non-chosen Member State, which bars proceedings that would be duly brought in the chosen Member State. This practice would cause delay to the legitimate action. The delay lasts as long as the proceedings in the non-chosen court would take.[43] A party that is meant to lose in the substance of a claim could abuse the system by bringing procedural harassment to the other party and postponing the legitimate litigation. The ECJ, however, believes that the tactics with the intention of delaying proceedings in the competent

37 Recital 12 Brussels I.

38 Such as jurisdiction *in rem*. See Art 22 Brussels I Regulation.

39 Art 23 Brussels I Regulation.

40 Recital 11: 'The rules of jurisdiction must be highly predictable . . .'.

41 See *supra* n. 27.

42 'Heidelberg Report', *supra* n. 27, para 377.

43 Mance, 2004: 357.

court are not enough to question the broad application of *lis pendens* in the Brussels I Regulation.[44] This conclusion is unfortunate and clearly contrary to commercial soundness. A serious delay has the practical effect of hampering a party's right to access to justice. Legal proceedings in some Member States are extremely slow. In Italy, for example, the court took ten years to decide it had no jurisdiction in a notorious case, *Trasporti Castelletti v Hugo Trumpy*,[45] where a standard, normal choice of court clause was concluded without anything unusual.[46] Even if, under the Brussels I Regulation, the Italian court must eventually decline jurisdiction in favour of the chosen forum, the excessive delay is undesirable.[47] The party that is facing a losing litigation could abuse the process, by bringing a negative declaration claim in Italy first. Even if he would lose eventually, he could keep the proceedings going for years and block actions in other states.

The *Gasser* approach would also encourage parties to 'rush to the court'. Regardless of the merit of their claim, and regardless of the possibility to negotiate and settle the dispute out of courts, one party needs to commence the action as quickly as possible and before the action brought by another party. This is, certainly, another side effect to the commercial world.

Furthermore, the procedure priority approach adopted by *Gasser* has inherent inconsistency. The *Gasser* decision permits any Member States, chosen or not, to decide the effectiveness of a jurisdiction clause once seized by the party if they are competent under default jurisdiction rules.[48] Although the ECJ justifies the decision primarily based on the interest in having clear and effective procedure, the approach to permit the non-chosen forum to decide the validity of jurisdiction itself causes uncertainty and creates procedural barriers to prevent legitimate proceedings. It is hard to say how the *Gasser* approach as a whole could promote procedure efficiency.

Narrowing the application of Gasser

The *Gasser* decision gives the long-debated issue a definitive answer. Although it was harshly criticized, it was followed by Member States in

44 Case C-116/02 [2003] ECR 14693, para 53.

45 See the Corte di Cassazione (Italy) decision in [1998] ILPr 216 and the ECJ decision in Case C-159/97 [1999] ECR I-1597.

46 See, in general, Hartley, 2009: 255.

47 Hartley, 2009: 255; Simons and Calabresi-Scholz, 2007; Sifakis, 2006: 307–312; Hueske, 2009: 433; Clarke, 2007: 105 and 124; Kulpers, 2009: 1510–1516.

48 Steinle and Vasilliades, 2010: 571; Brand, 2009b: 376; Rainer, 2009: 441.

later cases.[49] However, English courts could try to provide a narrower interpretation to what the 'same' and 'related' action is to avoid the rigid effect of *Gasser*. In *JP Morgan Europe Ltd v Primacom AG*,[50] for example, an English bank and some German companies entered into a loan agreement providing English courts exclusive jurisdiction. The German companies, after defaulting payment, brought an action in Germany in breach of the jurisdiction clause claiming the loan agreement was unenforceable. The bank brought three proceedings in England seeking (1) injunction preventing the German companies from disposing of assets, (2) disclosure of a financial report, and (3) declaration that the loan agreement was valid. The German companies applied to stay English jurisdiction based on *Gasser*.

The English court held that, in principle, the German court should find it had no jurisdiction to hear the dispute. However, if the actions in the two countries were the 'same', the English court should stay jurisdiction until the German court made decisions on its jurisdiction—it was expected that the German court should decline jurisdiction eventually. Although three proceedings were brought in England, only the declaration proceedings were the same as the action in Germany. The English court should stay jurisdiction on this issue. The other two proceedings on the disclosure and injunction were not the 'same' or 'related' with the German proceedings because they were not going to bring forward irreconcilable judgments. The English court then continued jurisdiction on hearing these two issues.

In *Underwriting Members of Lloyd's Syndicate v Sinco SA*,[51] three English companies and a Greek company entered into contracts with an exclusive jurisdiction clause choosing English courts. After disputes arose, the English companies commenced the action against the Greek company in England in breach of contract. After issuing the claim form but before serving it on the defendant, the defendant brought proceedings in Greece

49 *J v P*, [2007] EWHC 704 (Fam); *Irish Response Ltd v Direct Beauty Products*, [2011] EWHC 37 (QB); *Trademark Licensing Co Ltd v Leofelis SA*, [2010] ILPr 16; *Catalyst Investment Group Ltd v Lewinsohn*, [2010] 2 WLR 839; *National Navigation Co v Endesa Generacion SA (The Wadi Sudr)*, [2009] 1 Lloyd's Rep 666; *Underwriting Members of Lloyd's Syndicate 980 for 1999, 2000, 2001, 2002, 2003, 2004 and 2005 v Sinco SA*, [2009] 1 All ER (Comm) 272; *Goshawk Dedicated Ltd v Life Receivables Ireland Ltd*, [2008] ILPr 50; *Phillips v Symes (A Bankrupt)*, [2008] 2 All ER 537; *Czech Republic v European Media Ventures SA*, [2008] 1 All ER (Comm) 531; *Jurisdiction in the Case of a Sale Involving the Carriage of Goods, Re (5 U 99/07)*, [2010] ILPr 29; *Kolden Holdings Ltd v Rodette Commerce Ltd*, [2007] 4 All ER 62; *Jacobs & Turner Ltd v Celsius Sarl*, [2007] SLT 722; *Lloyd's Syndicate 457 v Shifco (Somali High Seas International Fishing Co)*, [2009] ILPr 18; *Orams v Apostolides*, [2007] 1 WLR 241; *Phillips v Symes (A Bankrupt)*, [2006] 1 WLR 2598; *Advent Capital Plc v GN Ellinas Imports-Exports Ltd*, [2006] 1 All ER (Comm) 81; *OT Africa Line Ltd v Magic Sportswear Corp.*, [2006] 1 All ER (Comm) 32; *Through Transport Mutual Insurance Association (Eurasia) Ltd v New India Assurance Co Ltd (The Hari Bhum) (No 2)*, [2005] 2 Lloyd's Rep 378; *Speed Investments Ltd v Formula One Holdings Ltd (No 2)*, [2005] 1 WLR 1936.

50 [2005] 1 CLC 493.

51 [2008] 2 CLC 187.

against the English companies based on tort, arguing the jurisdiction clause did not cover tort claim, and the jurisdiction clause was contrary to mandatory rules of Greek law. The English companies then applied to add a claim in English proceedings that the Greek company had breached the exclusive English jurisdiction clause by suing in Greece. The Greek company applied for a stay of action on the basis that the same cause of action was brought in Greece first.

The proceedings in England were about the breach of contract and jurisdiction clause; the action in Greece was on tort and the challenge to the English jurisdiction clause. The English court considered whether, in deciding if there were concurrent proceedings existing in Article 27, the court should look at the whole action, or individual claims in the action. It was true that the contract claim and the tort claim arising out of the contract were not the same or related actions.[52] If the court considered two proceedings as a whole and decided whether the 'central or essential issues' in the two actions were the same or related,[53] the English and Greek proceedings concerned different matters.[54] If the court looked at each individual claim, the English claim on the breach of exclusive jurisdiction clause and the Greek claim on the non-application of the jurisdiction clause were the same.[55] The court second seized to decide this issue should stay jurisdiction.

Both approaches were accepted in English precedents.[56] However, the judge in the current case adopted the whole proceedings approach and refused to treat the jurisdiction clause as a separate claim. One reason probably is that the challenge on the jurisdiction of the court is not a claim on the substance. This challenge arises in most actions where the parties have brought disputes in two different courts. The consideration of whether parallel proceedings exist in the same action only requires the court to consider the 'substantive claim'. If there is more than one

52 Ibid., para 50.

53 Ibid., para 41, citing *Evialis SA v SIAT* [2003], 2 Lloyd's Rep 377.

54 *Underwriting Members of Lloyd's Syndicate*, *supra* n. 67, para 50.

55 Ibid., paras 31–52.

56 There are ECJ decisions supporting the splitting of actions and applying *lis pendens* to each individual claim, see Case C-405/92 *Owners of Cargo v Owners of the Maciej Ratij (The Tarty)*, [1994] ECR I-5439 (the second seized court stayed proceedings between the same parties in the first action, but continued with action between parties not involved in the first action); *Bank of Tokyo-Mitsubishi Ltd v Baskan Gida Sanayi Pazarlama AS*, [2004] 2 Lloyd's Rep 395 (the English court stayed action on contractual claims because the proceedings for a negative declaration of contractual obligations were pending in Italy, but the claim on tort continued). Others argued the splitting approach complicated the situation and was impractical. See *Grupo Torras SA v Al-Sabah (No 1)* [1995] 1 Lloyd's Rep 374, p. 419, per Mance J; *Evialis SA v SIAT* [2003] 2 Lloyd's Rep 377, para 130, per Smith J (the words 'actions' and 'proceedings' refer to the action as a whole, instead of separate claims in one action); *Continental Bank v Aeakos* [1994] 1 WLR 588, per Gatehouse J (the existence of one same claim on both actions was not enough to make the court stay jurisdiction in Art 21 Brussels Convention [now Art 27 Brussels I Regulation]).

substantive claim in each action, the court could split the case and decide whether to stay proceedings on each claim separately. If the substantive claims are completely different in two proceedings, and the only thing in common is the courts are asked to examine the jurisdiction of itself and the other, requiring the second court to stay jurisdiction is not justifiable. The reason, however, is weak. Irreconcilable decisions can exist on validity of a jurisdiction clause. This decision, nevertheless, may demonstrate the reluctance of the English courts to apply the European rules to deny the effect of an English jurisdiction clause. By providing a specific interpretation, the English court has limited the application of *Gasser*.

2.3 Jurisdiction clauses concluded by parties domiciled outside the Member States

The current situation in Europe, pursuant to the ECJ case law, resolves conflicts of jurisdiction between the Member States by granting priority to the first seized court over the chosen court. The same order, however, does not apply where both parties of a jurisdiction clause are domiciled outside the Member States.[57] Article 23(3) provides that if both parties have their domiciles in third countries, and choose a court located within a Member State, all other Member States must stay jurisdiction until the chosen court makes its decision.[58] Clearly, exclusive jurisdiction is given to the chosen court in deciding the validity and effectiveness of a jurisdiction clause. The negative *kompetenz-kompetenz* is adopted in the context where neither parties have domicile within the Member States.

It is uncertain why the European law-maker adopts negative *kompetenz-kompetenz* for jurisdiction clauses concluded by none EU domicidiaries, but permits any competent court to take jurisdiction to decide the enforceability of a jurisdiction clause concluded by at least one EU party. One explanation is that the law-maker considers Article 23(1) provides full and complete rules on deciding enforceability of a jurisdiction clause. This provides a presumption that no matter which Member State is seized to hear this issue, the decision might be the same.[59] There is, thus, not much harm to apply the strict rule of *lis pendens* to ensure proper judicial cooperation between Member States. When both parties are domiciled in a third country, the harmonized formal validity rules included in Article 23(1) do not apply.[60] As a result, the effectiveness of a jurisdiction clause

57 See Art 23(3) Brussels I.

58 Art 23(3): 'Where such an agreement is concluded by parties, none of whom is domiciled in a Member State, the courts of other Member States shall have no jurisdiction over their disputes unless the court or courts chosen have declined jurisdiction.'

59 Although this is not true, see *supra* n. 27 and text accompanying n. 57–58.

60 Article 23(1) provides that it applies to the jurisdiction clause concluded by the parties, 'one or more of whom is domiciled in a Member State'. Magnus and Mankowski, 2007: 391; Layton and Mercer, 2004: para 20.101.

varies from country to country. A non-chosen Member State, if seized, is competent to use its domestic law to decide the validity and enforceability of this jurisdiction clause,[61] and would likely give decisions different from the chosen Member State and from other non-chosen Member States, which lead to conflict between different Member States and undermine the commercial purpose of the contractual parties.

This explanation, however, is not accepted by other commentators. Many writers hold the view that if a jurisdiction clause wants to acquire the derogation power as mentioned in Article 23(3), it must meet the uniform formal requirements in Article 23(1).[62] This is supported, first, by the expression of Article 23(3) using 'such an agreement', which may refer to an agreement defined in Article 23(1).[63] Second, the agreement in Article 23(3) affects the jurisdictional power of non-chosen Member States. It is not unreasonable to expect the harmonized Union requirements on formal validity to be satisfied. If such an interpretation is accepted by the ECJ, it is hard to justify the different treatment to jurisdiction clauses concluded by parties domiciled outside the Member States and by parties at least one of whom is domiciled within the Member States.

The negative *kompetenz-kompetenz* in deciding validity and enforceability of jurisdiction clauses achieves the aim of certainty and predictability and helps to provide good case management between Member States. Since the negative *kompetenz-kompetenz* is already adopted by the Brussels I Regulation to deal with the conflict of jurisdiction between Member States in cases where both parties have their domiciles in the third countries, there are sufficient reasons to extend the doctrine to cases involving jurisdiction clauses within the scope of the Brussels I Regulation.[64]

3 *Forum non conveniens* in the Brussels I Regulation

3.1 Owusu v Jackson

Forum non conveniens is a traditional common law doctrine permitting a court to take discretion not to exercise jurisdiction that it otherwise has on the basis that there is another, more appropriate forum available and it is in the interest of justice to let that forum hear the dispute.[65] *Forum non*

61 Art 4(1) Brussels I.

62 'Schlosser Report', 1979: para 177; Clarkson and Hill, 2011: 78.

63 Magnus and Mankowski, 2007: 391.

64 This option is accepted by the European Commission in the Proposal for the Brussels I (Recast). See *infra* section 5.

65 *Spiliada Maritime v Cansulex*, [1987] AC 460; *Cherney v Deripaska*, [2008] EWHC 1530 (Comm); *Dornoch Ltd v Mauritius Union Assurance Co Ltd*, [2006] Lloyd's Rep IR 127; *Lubbe v Cape Plc*, [2000] 1 WLR 1545; *Connelly v RTZ Corp Plc (No 1)*, [1996] QB 361; Collins *et al.*, 2006: Ch 12, Sections 1 and 2; Gray, 2009: 207; Slater, 1988: 554; Kennett, 1995: 552; Blair, 1929: 1; Stein, 1985: 781.

conveniens has its particular functioning in cases involving a jurisdiction clause.[66] It is also a common law tradition that a court reserves discretion to decide whether it will give effects to a valid jurisdiction clause.[67] According to *The Eleftheria*,[68] an exclusive jurisdiction clause is prima facie enforceable, unless there are strong causes shown to the contrary. If there is a local jurisdiction clause, common law countries are reluctant to use *forum non conveniens* to stay its jurisdiction unless something unexpected at the stage of contracting justifies evading the jurisdiction clause;[69] if there is a foreign exclusive jurisdiction clause, common law countries should stay jurisdiction unless strong reasons show justice cannot be done in the chosen forum.[70]

Applying *forum non conveniens* in the Brussels scheme is questioned by *Owusu v Jackson*.[71] *Owusu v Jackson* is not a case relating to jurisdiction agreements, but it might have widespread effects which would influence the enforcement of jurisdiction agreements within and even beyond the Brussels I Regulation. Owusu, a British national domiciled in the UK, entered into a contract with Jackson, another domiciliary in England, to rent the latter's holiday villa located in Jamaica, a non-EU country. Owusu suffered injury during the holiday and sued Jackson for breach of contract and several Jamaican companies managing the villa for tort. It is clear that Jamaica, where the accident occurred and evidence was more easily accessible, should be the more appropriate forum to hear the case. In an English precedent, *Harrods (Ruenos Aires)*,[72] the English Court of Appeal suggested that the court of a Member State could stay jurisdiction under the Brussels regime in favour of a third country. Applying this decision, an English court could stay jurisdiction granted by Article 2(1) of the Brussels I Regulation by using *forum non conveniens* in favour of Jamaica.

66 *The Eleftheria*, [1970] P 94; *Skype v Joltid*, [2011] ILPr 8, para 33; *Yes To v Hur*, 2011 WL 902297 (N.D.Cal., 2011).

67 Although common law countries preserve their discretion to enforce jurisdiction agreements, they usually hold the policy of contract freedom and give effectiveness to such agreements in most circumstances.

68 [1970] P 94; *Anraj Fish Products Industries Ltd v Hyundai Merchant Marine Co Ltd*, [2000] ILPr 717; *Aratra Potato Co Ltd v Egyptian Navigation Co (The El Amria)*, [1981] 2 Lloyd's Rep. 119.

69 *National Westminster Bank Plc v Utrecht-America Finance Co*, [2001] CLC 1372; *J.P. Morgan Securities Asia Private Limited v Malaysian Newsprint Industries*, [2002] ILPr 17; *Ultisol Transport Contractors Ltd v Bouygues Offshore SA & Ors*, [1998] CLC 1526; *Hamed El Chiaty & Co. (T/A Travco Nile Cruise Lines) v The Thomas Cook Group*, [1994] ILPr 367; *Middle Eastern Oil v National Bank of Abu Dhabi*, [2008] All ER (D) 285.

70 *The Fehmarn*, [1958] 1 WLR 159; *Evans Marshall & Co. Ltd v Bertola S.A.*, [1973] 1 WLR 349; *Citi-March v Neptune Orient Lines*, [1996] 1 WLR 13367.

71 Case C-281/02, *Owusu v Jackson* [2005] ECR I-1383. For a full introduction of the case see, Palser, 2006: 32.

72 [1992] Ch 72. *Haji-Ioannou v Frangos*, [1999] 2 Lloyd's Rep 337, CA; *Ace Insurance v Zurich Insurance*, [2001] 1 Lloyd's Rep 618. Compare *Lubb v Cape*, [2000] 4 All ER 268.

The ECJ decided that Article 2 of the Brussels Convention, which grants jurisdiction to the domicile of the defendant, is mandatory in nature and cannot be derogated from by any national law except derogation laid down by the Convention.[73] It is a common understanding that *forum non conveniens* is not accepted either expressly or impliedly within the system of the Brussels Convention.[74] Furthermore, one major object of the Brussels jurisdiction rules is to establish certainty in cross-border civil disputes,[75] which could be undermined by *forum non conveniens* and the discretion-based approach. Third, the ECJ strengthened the purpose of Article 2, which follows the traditional doctrine of *actor sequitur forum rei*, to protect defendants and by making it reasonably foreseeable in which potential forum he may be sued.[76] Furthermore, using *forum non conveniens* would cause delay.[77] Fifth, allowing *forum non conveniens* in the Brussels context would affect the uniform application of the rules of jurisdiction within the regime, especially when this doctrine is recognized only in a limited number of Contracting States.[78]

It is uncertain whether the effect of *Owusu v Jackson* will be limited in the particular case where a Member State's jurisdiction is granted by Article 2 of the Brussels I Regulation, or it extends to all other occasions where the jurisdiction of a Member State is granted by any grounds of the Brussels I Regulation. The ECJ is very careful not to give a definite answer to the question. When being asked whether the application of *forum non conveniens* is precluded in all cases or only in certain circumstances, the court refused to give 'advisory opinions on general or hypothetical questions'.[79] This very important question is thus left unanswered. It leaves a lot of uncertainty and confusion in later courts' decisions.

3.2 Stay of jurisdiction in favour of a chosen third country in a jurisdiction clause

In the Brussels I Regulation, courts in a Member State do not need to use *forum non conveniens* to stay jurisdiction in favour of the chosen court in another Member State. Article 23(1) of the Brussels I Regulation grants jurisdiction to the chosen court of a valid exclusive jurisdiction clause and

73 Case C-281/02 *Owusu v Jackson*, [2005] ECR I-1383, para 37.
74 Ibid., para 37.
75 Ibid., paras 38–39; Case C-440/97 *GIE Groupe Concorde and Others*, [1999] ECR I-6307, para 23; Case C-256/00 *Besix* [2002] ECR I-1699, para 24.
76 *Owusu v Jackson*, para 42.
77 *Owusu v Jackson*, para 42.
78 *Owusu v Jackson*, para 43.
79 *Owusu v Jackson*, para 50. Case C-314/96 *Djabali*, [1998] ECR I-1149, para 19; Case C-318/00 *Bacardi-Martini and Cellier des Dauphins*, [2003] ECR I-905, para 42; Joined Cases C-480/00 to C-482/00, C-484/00, C-489/00 to C-491/00 and C-497/00 to C-499/00 *Azienda Agricola Ettore Ribaldi and Others*, [2004] ECR I-0000, para 72.

a non-chosen Member State has no jurisdiction. A court could simply decide that it has no jurisdiction under the Regulation than staying jurisdiction under *forum non conveniens.*[80]

A different story exists if an exclusive jurisdiction clause chooses a non-Member State. Article 23(1) does not apply to this jurisdiction clause and an English court cannot claim that it has no jurisdiction under Article 23(1). If the English jurisdiction is based on common law (e.g. the defendant has domicile abroad), the case is totally out of the reach of the Brussels I Regulation and there is no European interest involved. The English court is entitled to stay jurisdiction by using *forum non conveniens.* However, if the English jurisdiction is based on the Brussels I Regulation—for example, the defendant is domiciled in England—the *Owusu* restriction is relevant. Could an English court stay jurisdiction in favour of the chosen non-Member State if England has jurisdiction under the Brussels I Regulation?

An answer is given in *Konkola Copper Mines v Coromin,*[81] where England had jurisdiction under Article 2 of the Brussels I Regulation and the dispute was subject to a valid exclusive jurisdiction clause designating Zambia, which was also the natural forum to hear the case. The Queen's Bench Division distinguished the *Owusu* case by holding that a different approach should be adopted in a case with exclusive jurisdiction clauses.[82] Colman J intended to keep the influence of *Owusu v Jackson* strictly within its own context, where the defendant is domiciled in a Member State, a non-Member State is a natural forum and there is no jurisdiction clause involved. In the *Owusu* case, there is nothing in the Convention/Regulation to support the English court to stay jurisdiction, but if there is an exclusive jurisdiction clause choosing a third country, though it is not subject to the Brussels I Regulation, Article 23 of the Regulation suggests a general policy to give effectiveness to the valid jurisdiction clause.[83]

Support can also be found in the Schlosser Report, which provided that:

> In cases where parties agree to bring their disputes before the courts of a State which is not a party to the 1968 Convention there is obviously nothing in the 1968 Convention to prevent such courts from declaring themselves competent, if their law recognizes the validity of such an agreement. The only question is whether and, if so, in what form such agreements are capable of depriving Community courts of jurisdiction which is stated by the 1968 Convention to be exclusive or

80 *Rawlinson & Hunter Trustees SA v Kaupthing Bank HF and another,* [2011] EWHC 566 (Comm).

81 [2005] 2 All ER, aff'm in [2006] 1 All ER (Comm) 437.

82 This point was not challenged in the appeal.

83 *Konkola Copper Mines v Coromin,* [2005] 2 All ER, para 89.

> concurrent.... If a court within the Community is applied to despite such an agreement, its decision on the validity of the agreement depriving it of jurisdiction must be taken in accordance with its own *lex fori*. In so far as the local rules of conflict of laws support the authority of provisions of foreign law, the latter will apply. If, when these tests are applied, the agreement is found to be invalid, then the jurisdictional provisions of the 1968 Convention become applicable.[84]

It means where there is a jurisdiction clause choosing a third country, a Member State will not use the Brussels I Regulation uniform jurisdiction rules, but shall use the *lex fori* to decide whether the jurisdiction clause is valid. The European law is thus irrelevant.[85]

3.3 Stay of jurisdiction granted by Article 23(1)

Although the ECJ did not answer whether *Owusu* should extend to jurisdiction granted by provisions other than Article 2, exclusive jurisdiction in Article 22 and jurisdiction granted by exclusive jurisdiction clauses in Article 23(1) have higher hierarchy than Article 2. If a court based on Article 2 cannot stay jurisdiction, the discretionary power is certainly lost in Articles 22 and 23(1). If an exclusive jurisdiction clause exists under Article 23(1), a court cannot use *forum non conveniens* to stay jurisdiction in favour of a more appropriate third country, even if permitting the third country to hear the dispute is better for the ends of justice.[86] In *Skype v Joltid*,[87] the English High Court was asked to consider the parallel proceedings between England and the US. A valid English exclusive jurisdiction clause existed in the license agreement. Skype sued in the English court claiming invalid termination of contract on the part of Joltid, while Joltid brought an action against Skype, investors and other parties in the US, which was the place of registration of the copyright in the source code allegedly breached. Although there was an exclusive jurisdiction clause choosing the English courts, the case involved interests of third parties, and the US was the only place where all claims could be heard.[88] The English court extended the decision in *Owusu v Jackson* to Article 23 and held that the English court could not stay jurisdiction under *forum non conveniens* if it has jurisdiction pursuant to Article 23 of the Brussels I

84 'Schlosser Report', *supra* n. 78, Art 176.

85 See also *Winnetka Trading v Julius Baer International* [2009] Bus.L.R. 1006.

86 An argument as to whether *Owusu v Jackson* extends to jurisdictional grounds other than Art 2. Palser, 2006, *supra* n. 138, 37.

87 [2011] ILPr 8.

88 *Donohue v Armco*, [2001] UKHL 64; Tett, 2003: 7; Bramley, 2002: 3.

Regulation.[89] On the other hand, the court could not restrain the defendant from bringing proceedings against the third parties to the contract in the US.[90] The court had to give up the goal to keep a single forum for the whole claim but decide whether to issue an injunction only for claims between the parties subject to the exclusive jurisdiction clause.[91] An injunction was granted restraining proceedings against Skype from continuing in the US, but left other claims unaffected.[92] The result is a fragment of proceedings, where part of the proceedings continued in England while a related part in the US.

3.4 Stay jurisdiction under Article 23(3) of the Brussels I Regulation

What if both parties have their domiciles outside any Member States but choose jurisdiction of England? Could the English court apply the traditional *forum non conveniens* approach to stay jurisdiction granted by the clause?

The prorogation jurisdiction in Article 23(1) of Brussels I applies only to situations where at least one party has its domicile within the EU and a Member State is chosen in the jurisdiction clause.[93] It shows that, where both parties have domiciles outside the Member States, the Member State chosen in the jurisdiction clause should use its national rule to decide the validity and enforceability of the jurisdiction clause. Article 23(3) does not provide a positive rule for a court to decide whether or not a jurisdiction clause is valid or enforceable. Instead it only provides a conflicts rule to handle the likelihood of competing jurisdiction between different Member States in a case where two third-country parties choose a Member State to hear their disputes. Article 23(3) requires all non-chosen Member States to wait until the chosen forum makes decisions. It gives priority to the chosen forum in order to avoid the possible concurrent proceedings

89 *Skype*, [2011] ILPr 8, para 22. *Equitas v Allstate Insurance*, [2009] 1 All ER (Comm) 1137, para 64; *Gomez v Gomez-Monch Vives*, [2008] EWHC 259 (Ch), para 112; *CAN Insurance v Office Depot International*, [2005] EWHC 456 (Comm), para 26; Collins *et al.*, 2006: paras 12.124 and 12.127.

90 *Skype v Joltid*, paras 34–35; *Donohue v Armco Inc.*, para 27; *Rimpacific Navigation Inc v Daehan Shipbuilding Co Ltd*, [2010] 2 All ER (Comm) 814; *Markel International Co Ltd v Craft (The Norseman)*, [2007] Lloyd's Rep IR 403; *OT Africa Line Ltd v Magic Sportswear Corp*, [2006] 1 All ER (Comm) 32; *Society of Lloyd's v White (No 2)*, [2002] ILPr 11.

91 *Skype*, para 35. *Morgan Stanley v China Haisheng Juice* [2009] EWHC 2409 (Comm); *Credit Suisse First Boston (Europe) Ltd v MLC (Bermuda) Ltd* [1999] 1 Lloyd's Rep. 767.

92 Compare: *Donohue v Armco; Dubai Islamic Bank PJSC v PSI Energy Holding Co BSC*, [2011] EWHC 1019 (Comm); *USB v HSH Nordbank AG*, [2010] 1 All ER (Comm) 727; *Deutsche Bank AG v Highland Grusader Offshore Partners*, [2009] 2 Lloyd's Rep 61; *Middle Eastern Oil v National Bank of Abu Dhabi*, [2009] 1 Lloyd's Rep 251; *Winnetka Trading Corp v Julius Baer International Ltd*, [2009] 2 All ER (Comm) 735; *Konkola Copper Mines Plc v Coromin Ltd*, [2006] 2 All ER (Comm) 400; *Cadre* v *Astra Asigurari*, [2006] 1 Lloyd's Rep 560.

93 Art 23(1). *Supra* section 2.3.

and irreconcilable decisions. However, it does not say whether the chosen Member State could take jurisdiction or not. Logically, since the chosen Member State is entitled to use any domestic rules to decide its jurisdiction in such a circumstance and to decide its jurisdiction without worrying about the mutual trust, Union judicial cooperation and Union jurisdiction rules, *forum non conveniens*, as part of the domestic law, should be legitimate to use. English courts, thus, are entitled to use *forum non conveniens* to stay jurisdiction conferred to it by two third-country parties.[94]

3.5 Enforcing anti-suit injunctions from a third country

What if a party that has commenced or is prepared to commence proceedings in a Member State is enjoined from doing so by an anti-suit injunction from a third country, such as the US, and the other party applies to the enjoined Member State to enforce the order? Would the EU Member State recognize and enforce the injunction and stay forum proceedings?

To some Member States, which traditionally refuse to enforce anti-suit injunctions from foreign countries, *Owusu v Jackson* does not introduce anything new. An injunction, ordered from a third country, is unenforceable and certainly cannot influence jurisdiction based on the Brussels I Regulation.[95] For other countries, such as the UK and Ireland, an anti-suit injunction traditionally can be enforced if it satisfies the normal recognition and enforcement criteria. A 2008 French decision also enforced a US anti-suit injunction in support of an exclusive jurisdiction clause choosing Georgia against French proceedings brought under French national law.[96] The problem is whether an injunction that might be otherwise enforceable in a Member State cannot be enforced if the court of this Member State has jurisdiction granted by one of the provisions in the Brussels I Regulation. For example, an English company and a US company concluded a contract conferring US courts exclusive jurisdiction. When the US company sued the English company in breach of contract in England, the English court had jurisdiction under Article 2(1) of the Brussels I Regulation.[97] Suppose the US court issued an anti-suit injunction, would the injunction be enforced in England? Could the English court stay jurisdiction granted under Article 2 of the Brussels I Regulation?

94 Palser, 2006, *supra* n. 138, 37. However, compare *Equitas Ltd v Allstate Insurance Co*, [2007] 2 Lloyd's Rep 138, para 64, where the court equalizes the effect of Arts 23(3) and 23(1) and applied *Owusu v Jackson* to Art 23(3).

95 A German court even refused to serve an anti-suit injunction to the party. See *Phillip Alexander Securities Ltd v Bamberger & Ors*, [1997] ILPr 73 at 104, C.A.; Wilson, 1997: 426.

96 *In Zone Brands International v In Zone Brands Europe*, Cass Civ 1e're, 14 October 2009, nx 08–16369.

97 Art 2(1) of the Brussels I Regulation: 'Subject to this Regulation, persons domiciled in a Member State shall, whatever their nationality, be sued in the courts of that Member State.'

Enforcing a third-country judgment is exclusively governed by national law and is immune from the influence of the Union harmonization.[98] Although domestic criteria vary largely between Member States, there is one thing in common: a foreign judgment infringing public policy of the forum cannot be enforced. If enforcing anti-suit injunctions from a third country requires the stay of jurisdiction granted in the Brussels I Regulation, the exercise which, according to *Owusu*, is compulsory, the consequence could be considered as contrary to public policy as against European law. A Member State, as a result, is not allowed to stay jurisdiction under the Brussels I Regulation as a response to a third-country anti-suit injunction.

4 Anti-suit injunctions and jurisdiction clauses in Europe

4.1 Introduction

Anti-suit injunction is a traditional common law instrument preventing a party from commencing or continuing proceedings in another forum.[99] The most difficult task in applying anti-suit injunctions is to balance the need for the ends of justice and international comity.[100] Since anti-suit injunctions bring about the risk of infringement of another country's sovereignty, they are used with particular caution.[101] A court may be more

98 The Brussels I Regulation only established rules facilitating free movement of judgments between Member States. Art 34 (recognition of foreign judgments) and Art 38 (enforcement of foreign judgments) both clarify that the rules only apply to judgments delivered in a Member State.

99 *Airbus Industrie GIE v Patel*, [1999] 1 AC 119 (HL); *British Airways Board v Laker Airways Ltd*, [1985] AC 58; *General Star International Indemnity Ltd v Stirling Cooke Brown Reinsurance Brokers Ltd*, [2003] EWHC 3 (Comm); *Shell International Petroleum Co Ltd v Coral Oil Co Ltd (No 2)*, [1999] 2 Lloyd's Rep. 606; *Trendtex Trading Corp v Credit Suisse*, [1982] 1 AC 565; *South Carolina Insurance Co v Assurantie Maatshappij De Zeven Provincien NV*, [1987] AC 24; Wilson, 1997: 424; Bramley, 2002: 3; Asariotis, 1999: 447.

100 *Barclays Bank Plc v Homan*, [1992] BCC 757; *Akai Pty Ltd v People's Insurance Co Ltd*, [1998] 1 Lloyd's Rep 90; *Alfred C Toepfer International GmbH v Société Cargill France*, [1998] 1 Lloyd's Rep 379; *Airbus Industrie GIE v Patel; National Westminster Bank Plc v Utrecht-America Finance Co*, [2001] 3 All ER 733; *Glencore International AG v Metro Trading International Inc. (No 3)*, [2002] 2 All ER (Comm) 1; *Sabah Shipyard (Pakistan) Ltd v Pakistan*, [2003] 2 Lloyd's Rep 571; *American International Specialty Lines Insurance Co v Abbott Laboratories*, [2003] 1 Lloyd's Rep 267; *Noble Assurance Co v Gerling-Konzern General Insurance Co*, [2007] 1 CLC 85; *Samengo-Turner v J&H Marsh & McLennan (Services) Ltd*, [2007] 2 All ER (Comm) 813; *Standard Bank Plc v Agrinvest International*, [2008] 1 Lloyd's Rep 532; *Deutsche Bank AG v Highland Crusader Offshore Partners*, [2010] 1 WLR 1023; *Oceanconnect UK Ltd v Angara Maritime Ltd*, [2011] 1 All ER (Comm) 193.

101 *Oceanconnect UK Ltd & Anor v Angara Maritime Ltd*, [2010] 2 CLC 448, para 42; *Highland Crusader Offshore Partners LP & Ors v Deutsche Bank AG*, [2009] 2 CLC 45, para 61; *Law Debenture Trust Corp Plc v Concord Trust*, [2007] EWHC 2255 (Ch), para 24; *Société Nationale Industrielle Aerospatiale v Lee Kui Jak*, [1987] AC 871, 892; *Donohue v Armco*, [2001] UKHL 64, para 19.

willing to grant an anti-suit injunction in cases where there is a valid exclusive jurisdiction clause and the foreign action is brought in breach of the agreement. It is easier to satisfy the court that an action brought in breach of the parties' agreement has infringed the other party's contractual and equitable right, is brought with bad faith and is thus oppressive and vexatious.[102]

The use of anti-suit injunctions within a regime where judicial cooperation and mutual trust exist is more controversial. On the one hand, if granting an injunction to enforce a valid jurisdiction clause has nothing to do with international comity but is only a tool to keep the parties to their promise,[103] an injunction issued within the EU should not be a problem, because the purpose of issuing an injunction is the same—enforcing contractual obligations. On the other hand, where mutual trust exists, there is an argument that no one should review another country's jurisdiction.[104] In *Overseas Union Insurance v New Hampshire Insurance*,[105] it was held that a Member State could not use anti-suit injunctions to restrain the jurisdiction of the second seized Member State. It is questionable as to whether injunctions can be used where a court does not review the other country's jurisdiction but only enforces an exclusive jurisdiction agreement.

Before the ECJ delivered the decision on *Turner v Grovit*, English courts did not hesitate to issue anti-suit injunctions against proceedings in another Member State in support of an exclusive jurisdiction clause.[106] In *Continental Bank v Aeakos*,[107] the parties entered into a loan contract containing a jurisdiction clause requiring the borrower to sue the lender exclusively in England. After the dispute arose, the borrower sued the lender in Greece and an anti-suit injunction was issued. The lender's lawyer submitted that the English court should trust the Greek courts on deciding their jurisdiction by providing evidence proving the Greek court

102 *Oceanconnect UK Ltd & Anor v Angara Maritime Ltd*, [2010] 2 CLC 448; *Barclays Bank v Homan*, [1993] BCLC 680, 686–688; *Deutsche Bank*, [2010] 1 WLR 1023, 1036–1037.

103 *Mackender v Feldia AG*, [1967] 2 QB 590; *Unterweser Reederei GmbH v Zapata Off-Shore Co (The Chaparral)*, [1968] 2 Lloyd's Rep 158; *The Eleftheria*, [1970] P 94; *DSV Silo- und Verwaltungsgesellschaft mbH v Owners of the Sennar and 13 Other Ships (The Sennar (No 2))*, [1985] 1 WLR 490; *British Aerospace Plc v Dee Howard Co*, [1993] 1 Lloyd's Rep 368; *Continental Bank NA v Aeakos Compania Naviera SA and Others*, [1994] 1 WLR 588; *Aggeliki Charis Compania Maritima SA v Pagnan SpA (The Angelic Grace)*, [1995] 1 Lloyd's Rep 87; *Akai Pty Ltd v People's Insurance Co Ltd*, [1998] 1 Lloyd's Rep 90.

104 *Oceanfix International Limited v AGIP Kazakhstan North Caspian Operating Company*, 2009 WL 908173, para 64; *Turner v Grovit*, paras 25–26; *West Tankers*, para 26.

105 Case 351/89 [1991] ECR I-3317.

106 E.g. *Continental Bank v Aeakos*, [1994] 1 WLR 588; *OT Africa Line Ltd v Hijazy (The Kribi) (No 1)*, [2001] 1 Lloyd's Rep 76; *Gilkes v Venizelos ANESA*, [2000] ILPr 487; *Glencore International AG v Metro Trading International Inc (No 1)*, [1999] 2 All ER (Comm) 899; *Navigation Maritime Bulgare v Rustal Trading Ltd (The Ivan Zagubanski)*, [2002] 1 Lloyd's Rep 106; *Ocarina Marine Ltd v Marcard Stein & Co*, [1994] 2 Lloyd's Rep 524.

107 [1994] 1 WLR 588.

might assume jurisdiction regardless of a valid jurisdiction clause.[108] The English court believed that, without an injunction, the lender would persist in the breach of contract to infringe the right of the borrower and the Greek proceedings were vexatious and oppressive.[109]

The English court considered the special circumstances of the case and believed that the only effective remedy for the borrower was an injunction. The court also gave reasons why it did not trust the Greek court to decide on its own jurisdiction, because evidence proved the Greek court would continue the proceedings that were vexatious to the borrower and that might violate the ends of justice. The English court, however, did not consider the fact that both courts took jurisdiction under the judgment convention, which required the Contracting States to trust each other.[110]

4.2 Turner v Grovit

Turner v Grovit[111] is a milestone case, in which the ECJ gave guidance on the compatibility of the anti-suit injunction in the European Community for the first time. Turner was a British national domiciled in England who was recruited by a Spanish group of companies and worked in Madrid. He later returned to England and commenced proceedings against his ex-employer for unfair dismissal. English courts had jurisdiction under Section 5 of the Brussels I Regulation as England was the place where the employee had his domicile. The employee commenced proceedings in Spain against Turner for breach of contract and claimed losses resulting from Turner's professional conduct. Turner subsequently applied for an injunction restraining the employers from continuing the action in Spain. In the view of the English Court of Appeal, the Spanish proceedings were commenced for 'no purpose other than to harass and oppress a party who is already a litigant here ... and fall to be condemned as abusive as a matter of elementary principle'.[112] An injunction was granted. However, following the referral by the House of Lords, the ECJ ruled that the Brussels Convention (now the Brussels I Regulation) precludes a court of a Contracting State from granting an anti-suit injunction to prohibit a party from commencing or continuing proceedings in another Contracting

108 The Greek Court might interpret the clause differently from England or the court would consider the borrower's early cooperation as submission. In Greek civil procedure law, a defendant could not challenge jurisdiction without filing a defence on the merits.

109 See comments in Hartley, 1994; Chatterjee, 1995: 334; Bell, 1994: 204; Briggs, 1994: 158; Rogerson, 1994: 241; Hartley, 2002: 139; Berg, 2002: 117.

110 More comments in Merrett, 2006: 315; Hartley, 2005.

111 Case C-159/02 [2004] ECR I-3565. See Kruger, 2004: 1030; Williams, 2006: 4.

112 [2000] I QB 345.

State, even if the restrained proceedings were commenced with bad faith of this party.[113]

The decision is not surprising as it is in line with the common position of the ECJ to uphold the community interest and stick to the basic principle of mutual trust.[114] It also shows the lack of understanding and the general sceptical and negative attitude of the ECJ against the common law instrument of anti-suit injunctions.[115] It is commented that no sufficient voices from the common law countries were heard because the *Turner* decision was made with no British or Irish in the 11 judges.[116] It is also necessary to recognize that only two Member States out of 27 have common law tradition and the Brussels regime is established by following the civil law philosophy.[117] The discretion-based common law approach conflicts with the rule-based civil law tradition.[118] Although some discretion-based elements are adopted in some civil law countries,[119] it does not mean common law approaches can be easily accepted in a regime dominated by civil law countries.

However, it is doubtful whether anti-suit injunctions certainly violate mutual trust. Mutual trust exists more internally between different states of one country than internationally between different sovereignties that have concluded judicial cooperation treaties. Nevertheless, anti-suit injunctions are frequently used between different legal regions of one country.[120] One wonders why one region should not wait and trust the other of the same country to make decision. The answer lies in the practical needs. Waiting on the other legal district of the same country to make decision causes delay and, sometimes, unreasonable cost to the party whose right has been infringed. In certain circumstances, the law requires

113 Case C-159/02 [2004] ECR I-3565. See comments in Blanke, 2004: 261; Dickinson, 2004: 273; Mourre and Lahlou, 2004: 538; Hare, 2004: 570; Robert-Tissot, 2005: 1496; Nurmela, 2005: 115; Blobel and Spath, 2005, *supra* n. 52; Hartley, 2005, *supra* n. 10.

114 Briggs, 2004: 530; Clarke, 2007: 101–129; Blobel and Spath, 2005: 1030–1040.

115 Briggs, 2004: 530.

116 Briggs, 2004: 530.

117 From 1 January 2007, the EU had 27 Member States, but only the UK and Ireland have the common law tradition.

118 Lenaerts, 2010: 286–287; Clarke, 2007: 109; Hartley, 2005.

119 For example, France granted anti-suit injunctions in a 2002 case. See Briggs, 2004: 530.

120 For example, in *In re Wanzer Ltd*, [1891] 1 Ch 305, the English court granted an injunction restraining Scottish proceedings. In other cases, the courts accepted England had power to restrain Scottish proceedings, though injunctions were not granted for other reasons: *Cohen v Rothfield*, [1919] 1 KB 410; *Walter Baine Grieve v Marion Jack Tasker*, [1906] AC 132; *Bland v Low*, [1894] 1 Ch 147; *In re Dynamics Corporation of America*, [1973] 1 WLR 63, 68 (obiter). In the USA, anti-suit injunctions are issued between sister states. E.g. *John G. and Marie Stella Kenedy Memorial Foundation v Fernandez*, 315 S.W.3d 512 (Tex., 2010); *Davis Intern., LLC v New Start Group Corp.* 367 Fed.Appx. 334 (C.A.3 (Del.), 2010); *Freddie Records, Inc. v Ayala*, Not Reported in S.W.3d, 2009 WL 3135790 (Tex.App.-Corpus Christi, 2009); *Withem v Deison*, Not Reported in S.W.3d, 2009 WL 2045322(Tex.App.-Beaumont, 2009).

speedy measures. An anti-suit injunction is speedy, effective and can be granted with relatively low cost.[121] An injunction is thus tolerated in countries with different legal regions and no one challenges the application of this instrument on the basis that there should be mutual trust within a country. The pure assertion of mutual trust is not enough to justify the abandonment of anti-suit injunctions. A more realistic explanation for the ECJ decision probably is that only two Member States have been equipped of anti-suit injunctions, which creates imbalance between the Member States. There is a concern that, once the injunction is permitted in the European Union, British and Irish courts have more procedural advantages than their neighbours, which could only rely on the Union rules to protect their jurisdiction.[122]

It is also argued that anti-suit injunctions conflict with the aim to achieve certainty and predictability within the Brussels regime.[123] A party may not bring an action under the established rules of the Brussels I Regulation but have to worry whether an injunction based on flexible criteria will be issued by another court.[124] It is thus unpredictable as to which court will eventually take jurisdiction. This argument may stand in cases without party autonomy. Where an exclusive jurisdiction clause exists, enforcing the agreement is the most certain and predictable result for both parties, while allowing any of them to breach the agreement by relying on any other jurisdictional grounds causes uncertainty.[125]

English courts try to justify that anti-suit injunctions are compatible with the Brussels I Regulation. It is argued by Lord Hobhouse that anti-suit injunction is a matter of procedure instead of a matter of jurisdiction rules.[126] The Brussels I Regulation harmonizes jurisdiction rules and provides uniform interpretation to it, and no Member State can rely on its own jurisdiction rules or interpretation in issues that are covered by the Brussels I Regulation.[127] However, the Brussels I Regulation does not influence the domestic procedure of each Member State. After deciding jurisdiction by relying on jurisdiction rules of the Brussels I Regulation, a Member State should be allowed to use its domestic procedural law for the

121 Chavier, 1990: 259; Wilson, 2004: 772–773; Nurmela, 2005: 141.

122 Ambrose, 2003: 412–413.

123 Ambrose, 2003: 412.

124 Ambrose, 2003: 409; Whincop, 2000: 70.

125 Clarke, 2007: 128; Tan, 2005: 643.

126 *Overseas Union v New Hampshire*, [1992] QB 434, para 30.

127 Case 9/77 *Bavaria Fluggesellschaft Schwabe & Co. KG and Germanair Bedarfsluftfahrt GmbH & Co. KG v Eurocontrol*, [1977] ECR 1517, para 4; Case C-115/88 *Reichert and others v Dresdner Bank*, [1990] ECR I-27; Case C-214/89 *Powell Duffryn Plc v Wolfgang Petereit*, [1992] ECR I-1745, para 11; Case C-440/97 *GIE Groupe Concorde and Others v The Master of the Vessel 'Suhadiwarno Panjan' and Others*, [1999] ECR I-6307, para 10; Case C150/77 *Société Bertrand v Paul Ott KG*, [1978] ECR 1431; Case C-26/91 *Jakob Handte & Co GmbH v Traitements Mecano-Chimiques des Surfaces SA (TMCS)*, [1992] ECR I-3967; Case C-269/95 *Benincasa v Dentalkit*, [1997] ECR I-3767, para 33.

purpose of procedure. If an anti-suit injunction is classified as procedure, it is outside the Brussels I Regulation and could be maintained. However, the distinction between jurisdiction and procedure is not clear cut,[128] and it is even more so in the common law system. In England, there is no separate statute on jurisdiction rules and civil procedure rules; civil jurisdiction and procedural matters are all included in the Civil Procedure Rules.[129] Furthermore, anti-suit injunction is hardly pure procedure which has nothing to do with substantive jurisdiction. It, by its nature, restrains foreign proceedings from being commenced or continuing.[130] When considering whether to grant it, a court will review the jurisdiction of another county where the enjoined proceedings occur.[131] In most cases, a court decides to take jurisdiction at the same time as granting an injunction.[132] It is hard to classify anti-suit injunctions as pure procedural instruments which are irrelevant to jurisdiction.

4.3 Impact of **Turner v Grovit** *in jurisdiction agreements*

Although *Turner* was not a case concerning jurisdiction agreements, the language used in the ECJ decision is broad enough to prevent an injunction from being used in any circumstances where a case falls within the scope of the Brussels I Regulation. It demonstrates that the existence of a jurisdiction clause is no exception. This decision is commented as '"system" prevails over practicality'[133] and '(p)rotecting the interests of States prevails over doing justice to individuals'.[134] It would be worse where a valid exclusive jurisdiction clause is involved.[135]

Combined with *Gasser v MISAT*, the current status of jurisdiction clauses in the EU is very uncertain. The two decisions of ECJ demonstrate that effectiveness will be given to a valid jurisdiction clause only if it does not challenge the Union interest and mutual trust between the Member

128 For a general account of jurisdiction and procedure, see Haycraft and Polozola, 1998: 459; Makynen, 1981: 396; Snyckers, 1997: 657; Buchanan, 1974: 673.

129 Available at www.justice.gov.uk/guidance/courts-and-tribunals/courts/procedure-rules/civil/index.htm, accessed on 28 July 2011.

130 Ambrose, 2003: 412.

131 Ambrose, 2003: 412.

132 Ambrose, 2003: 412.

133 Hartley, 2009: 822.

134 Ibid.

135 The *Turner* decision was confirmed and applied in cases where there was an arbitration agreement. In Case C-185/07 *West Tankers v Allianz SpA (the Front Comor)* [2009] ECR I-663, the existence of an arbitration agreement cannot permit an English court from issuing an anti-suit injunction to prevent the Italian court from taking jurisdiction to decide the validity of an arbitration agreement. The ECJ claims that the validity of an arbitration agreement is within the scope of the Brussels I Regulation despite Article 1.2(d), which excludes arbitration from the Regulation.

States.[136] Where a party brings proceedings in a Member State in breach of a valid exclusive jurisdiction clause with the sole purpose of oppressing the other party and to restrain the other party from bringing legitimate proceedings in the chosen forum, as far as the proceedings were brought first, the chosen forum must stay jurisdiction and trust the first seized non-chosen forum to make its decision.[137] Furthermore, the chosen forum could not use any injunction order to restrain the party with bad faith from doing so.[138] Finally, the judgments made in breach of the jurisdiction clause should be enforced in all other Member States, including the chosen forum.[139]

However, since *Turner* is based on mutual trust and no intervention in the decision of the court of a Member State to decide its own jurisdiction, an injunction might still be allowed prior to any courts being seized.[140] This could happen if a party threatens to sue in another country in breach of its agreement without actually commencing the proceedings.[141] It is right to consider that no country's sovereignty is infringed since no court is seized. However, granting an injunction before any courts are seized still amounts to the review of other states' jurisdiction.[142] Finally, if a party applied in English courts under an English jurisdiction clause for an injunction restraining any potential actions that might be subsequently brought in a non-chosen Member State, England is the forum first seized. Any non-chosen Member States shall stay jurisdiction in favour of the English court in deciding the enforceability of the jurisdiction clause.[143] There is no need to grant any injunction in the circumstances. The best option for the contractual party, in the context of the European Union, is not to apply for an anti-suit injunction but to commence proceedings on the substance of the case, or simply apply for a declaratory relief, as soon as possible. The more effective *lis pendens* rule will prevent all other Member States from attending the same action,[144] and the judgment or the declaration on the validity of the jurisdiction clause should be recognized and enforced by all other Member States.[145]

136 *Gasser v MISAT, supra* n. 41; *Turner v Grovit, supra* n. 13; *West Tankers v Allianz SpA,* ibid.
137 *Gasser v MISAT,* ibid.
138 *Turner v Grovit, supra* n. 13; *West Tankers v Allianz SpA, supra* n. 141.
139 Arts 33, 38 Brussels I. The four grounds for the court of a Member State to refuse recognition and enforcement of another Member State's decision does not include the improperly taking of jurisdiction. See Art 34. Hartley, 2009: 822.
140 Briggs, 2004: 531.
141 Ibid., 531.
142 Ibid., 531.
143 *Gasser v MISAT, supra* n. 41.
144 Art 27(1) Brussels I. *Gasser v MISAT, supra* n. 41.
145 Arts 33 and 38 Brussels I.

4.4 What if jurisdiction of a Member State is granted by domestic law?

Could injunction be used where the proceedings of another Member State were based on domestic law instead of the Brussels I Regulation? For example, the defendant is a New York domiciliary and the exclusive jurisdiction chooses the English court. Where dispute has arisen, the claimant sued in France instead, based on French Civil Procedure Law.[146] Since the French jurisdiction is not based on the Brussels I Regulation but national law, could the English court issue an anti-suit injunction restraining the claimant from continuing the French action?

The wording of *Turner v Grovit* is very broad and does not specify whether the jurisdiction basis of the enjoined state is relevant. Taking a broad view, anti-suit injunctions are prohibited completely between Member States in order to protect mutual trust, regardless of the jurisdictional ground of the court the action in which is restrained. However, it is fair to claim that mutual trust and judicial cooperation in civil and commercial matters is rooted in the Brussels regime. If a country receives jurisdiction from its national law, restraining this action is not a review of the other country's jurisdiction under the Brussels regime. Furthermore, the Brussels I Regulation does not require a Member State to trust the other in deciding jurisdiction under its domestic law. Since the jurisdiction basis is outside the Brussels regime, granting injunctions in such a case does not affect certainty and predictability of the regime nor the uniform application of the Union jurisdiction rules. However, a likely counter-argument is that Article 4 of the Brussels I Regulation permits a Member State to apply the national law in certain circumstances. Applying the national law, as a result, is also part of the Regulation. Furthermore, the mutual trust exists beyond the jurisdiction rules of the Regulation and between Member States in all areas where judicial cooperation is maintained.[147] For example, the Member States are required to mutually recognize and enforce each other's judgment regardless of jurisdictional grounds, which shows the extension of mutual trust into national jurisdiction basis.

4.5 Anti-suit injunctions and a third country

Could the UK and Ireland continue to use anti-suit injunctions to restrain proceedings in a third country? In *Skype v Joltid*,[148] the English court decided whether the English court could, after *Turner v Grovit*, issue an anti-suit injunction restraining US proceedings. The court considered that the effect of *Turner v Grovit* should be limited within the range of the European Union, where Member States are all part of the internal market

146 Where the defendant is domiciled in a third country, jurisdiction of a Member State is decided by national law under Art 4 of the Brussels I Regulation.

147 Ambrose, 2003, *supra* n. 104, at pp. 421–422.

148 *Skype v Joltid*, [2011] ILPr 8.

and where mutual trust exists. *Turner v Grovit* said nothing to prohibit an injunction from being used to restrain proceedings in a third country, where there is no Union interest or mutual trust.[149]

5 Anti-suit injunctions and arbitration agreements in the EU

Anti-suit injunctions are also used frequently by English courts to protect arbitration proceedings taking place in London, which provide advantages to London as a popular seat of international commercial arbitration.[150] After *Turner v Grovit*, the status of anti-suit injunctions in enforcing arbitration agreements is unclear. On the one hand, the ECJ has announced that anti-suit injunctions are incompatible with the Brussels I Regulation. On the other hand, Article 1(2)(d) of the Brussels I Regulation excludes arbitration from its scope. It is arguable that, when an anti-suit injunction is granted to enforce arbitration agreements, such an injunction is out of the scope of the Brussels I Regulation and escapes the effect of *Turner v Grovit*. This question is answered in the ECJ decision in *West Tankers v Allianz SpA ('The Front Comor')*.[151]

5.1 Situations before Front Comor

Article 71 of the Brussels I Regulation provides that this Regulation will not prejudice the treaty obligations of Member States under other international conventions in matters relating to jurisdiction, recognition and enforcement of judgments. In the EU, all Member States are Contracting States of the New York Convention, and the Council of Europe was preparing a European Convention on uniform law of arbitration. In order to avoid conflicts between the Brussels regime and the New York Convention and the future European Convention on arbitration, the European lawmakers decided to exclude arbitration from the Brussels regime.[152]

However, in practice, the request for clearer interpretation of Article 1(2)(d) has never faded away. This provision refers to 'arbitration', which is a very broad term, including arbitration proceedings, the validity of arbitration agreements, and courts supervision and intervention of arbitration. The Schlosser Report takes a broad view by stating that: 'A judgment determining whether an arbitration agreement is valid or not, or, because it is invalid, ordering the parties not to continue the arbitration proceedings, is not covered by the 1968 Convention.'[153] According to this interpretation, if a court approves the validity of an arbitration agreement and restrains

149 *Turner v Grovit*, *supra* n. 41, paras 26–28.
150 Steinbruck, 2007: 358.
151 Case C-185/07 *West Tankers Inc v Allianz SpA (The Front Comor)* [2009] ECR I-663.
152 Jenard, 1979: 13.
153 Schlosser, 1979: 93.

court proceedings, this order is not covered in the scope of the Brussels I Regulation and should be free from the effect of the *Turner* decision.

This issue was first considered in *Marc Rich v Societa Italiano Impianti*.[154] Marc Rich, a Swiss company, and Impianti, an Italian company, entered into an agreement for the sale of crude oil. Their contract included an agreement providing any disputes should be resolved by three arbitrators in London, one to be appointed by each party and the third to be appointed by the two chosen arbitrators. After disputes arose, Impianti commenced litigation in Italy denying liability. Marc Rich then commenced arbitration proceedings in London. Upon the refusal to participate and appoint an arbitrator by Impianti, Marc Rich applied to the English High Court to appoint an arbitrator pursuant to s10(3) of the Arbitration Act 1950 and served a summon on Impianti. Impianti argued that the English jurisdiction should be stayed because the dispute was on the existence of an arbitration agreement, which fell within the Brussels Convention. Since the Italian court was seized to decide this issue, the English court should stay jurisdiction pursuant to the *lis pendens* rule of the Brussels Convention.

There are a few issues that the ECJ needs to consider. First, whether the exclusion of 'arbitration' in the Brussels Convention refers to the arbitration procedure, or it covers court proceedings in which the 'subject matter' is arbitration. The ECJ stated that, since the New York Convention covered not only the recognition and enforcement of foreign arbitral awards, but also rules relating to arbitration agreements, the Brussels Convention intended to 'exclude arbitration in its entirety, including proceedings brought before national courts'.[155] The ECJ held that the procedure to appoint an arbitrator by the English court is part of arbitration proceedings and should be excluded from the Brussels Convention. An English court, thus, has jurisdiction to appoint an arbitrator pursuant to its domestic law.[156] The ECJ clearly took a broad view to exclude not only arbitration proceedings but arbitration-related court proceedings, or proceedings ancillary to arbitration, such as the appointment or dismissal of arbitrators, the fixing of the place of arbitration or the extension of the time limit for making awards,[157] from the scope of the Brussels Convention.

Second, even if the procedure to appoint an arbitrator is part of arbitration procedure, before an English court can appoint an arbitrator, the court must be satisfied that the arbitration agreement exists and is valid. Impianti further argued that the existence and validity of an arbitration agreement were not part of arbitration procedure and should be included in the Brussels I Regulation. Impianti argued that the Brussels Convention

154 Case C-190/89, *Marc Rich v Societa Italiano Impianti* [1991] ECR I-3855. For more on this case, see Munro, 1992: 116; Hartley, 1991: 529; Illmer and Naumann, 2007: 147; Kaye, 1993: 359.

155 Para 18.

156 Para 19.

157 Case C-391/95, *Van Uden Maritime BV v Deco-Line* [1998] ECR I-7091, para 32.

only excluded proceedings where arbitration was the principal issue. If arbitration was raised as an incidental question, the whole proceedings should still be covered by the Brussels Convention. Otherwise, a party could easily escape the Brussels Convention by arguing the existence of arbitration agreements in any cases.[158] This argument was rejected by the ECJ. By looking at the 'subject matter' of the court proceedings, if the proceedings were out of the scope of the Brussels Convention, even though the existence of an arbitration agreement should be determined as the preliminary issue, it could not be distinguished from the whole proceedings and should be excluded from the Convention.[159] Determining the nature of the procedure by the existence of a preliminary issue would cause uncertainty.[160] The ECJ finally decided that 'the exclusion provided for therein extends to litigation pending before a national court concerning the appointment of an arbitrator, even if the existence or validity of an arbitration agreement is a preliminary issue in that litigation'.[161]

Marc Rich demonstrates that arbitration itself and court proceedings relating to arbitration are both excluded from the Brussels Convention. If a court is seized to exercise its supervision power over arbitration, such as appointing an arbitrator, extending time for beginning arbitral proceedings, removing arbitrators, etc., even if the court has to decide the validity and existence of an arbitration agreement as the preliminary issue, this cannot bring the court proceedings within the scope of the Brussels Convention. The whole proceedings fall out of the Brussels regime all together. *Marc Rich*, however, does not reverse the Schlosser Report. It does not say whether the existence and validity of arbitration agreements, standing alone, is a matter for the Brussels Convention. It also does not expressly decide whether certain interim or protective measures, such as an anti-suit injunction in support of arbitration, are also excluded from the scope of the Brussels Convention and thus allowed.

The relationship between arbitration and the Brussels Convention was addressed in *Van Uden Maritime BV v Deco-Line*[162] years later. Van Uden, a Dutch company, and Deco-Line, a German company, entered into a charter hire agreement, including an arbitration clause. Upon the failure to pay, Van Uden commenced the arbitration proceedings in the Netherlands pursuant to the arbitration clause, and applied to the Dutch court for interim relief. The ECJ states that interim proceedings are not ancillary to arbitration proceedings. They are ordered in parallel to arbitration proceedings as measures of support. The status of interim proceedings should be considered 'not by their own nature but by the nature of the right which they

158 Paras 22–23.

159 Para 26.

160 Para 27.

161 Para 29.

162 Case C-391/95, *Van Uden Maritime BV v Deco-Line* [1998] ECR I-7091. Rodger, 1999: 199; Hartley, 1999: 674.

serve to protect'.[163] If an application is made to restrain court proceedings in another Member State in support of a valid arbitration agreement, the right that the interim proceedings serve to protect is the right to determine the dispute by arbitration. In other words, arbitration is the subject matter of anti-suit injunctions in support of arbitration. Reading the decision together with *Marc Rich*, anti-suit injunctions issued in support of arbitration should be excluded from the scope of the Brussels regime.

5.2 West Tankers v Allianz SpA (Front Comor)

Front Comor is a cornerstone case that has finally answered the question of whether anti-suit injunctions can be used in support of arbitration agreements within the EU. In this case, a vessel, 'Front Comor', owned by the West Tankers, collided with a jetty in Italy. The Charter Party contained an arbitration clause submitting disputes to the arbitration body in London. The insurance company of the jetty sued West Tankers in Italy. West Tankers applied an interim injunction from the English court to restrain the insurer from continuing the Italian proceedings.

The English High Court held that *Turner* applied to anti-suit injunctions against a Member State from taking jurisdiction under the Brussels I Regulation. Since arbitration is excluded from the Brussels I Regulation, jurisdiction in deciding the validity of an arbitration agreement is excluded from the scope of Brussels I. Where a Member State has taken jurisdiction to decide the validity of an arbitration agreement, it can issue anti-suit injunctions in support of the agreement based on its finding where the *Turner* decision is irrelevant. The New York Convention required a court seized in breach of an arbitration agreement to refer parties back to arbitration, which granted this court jurisdiction in determining its jurisdiction. Furthermore, the New York Convention does not preclude any court from reviewing jurisdiction of any other Contracting State. The English court, as a result, could decide the validity of an arbitration agreement as the supervisory court and could issue an anti-suit injunction after ascertaining the validity of the arbitration agreement.

The House of Lords also supported granting anti-suit injunctions. Three reasons were provided. First, the exclusion in Article 1(2)(d) was interpreted broadly by the ECJ in *Marc Rich & Co AG v Società Italiana Impianti*, which suggests that the exclusion applies not only to arbitral proceedings, but also to court proceedings where the subject matter is arbitration.[164] The subject matter is arbitration if the proceedings serve to protect the right to have the dispute determined by arbitration.[165]

163 *Van Uden*, para 33; Case C-261/90 *Reichert and Kockler v Dresdner Bank* [1992] ECR I-2149, para 32.

164 [2007] UKHL 4, para 13.

165 *Van Uden Maritime BV v Deco-Line*, para 33.

Furthermore, the basic principle of the Brussels I Regulation, i.e. *maxim actor sequitur forum rei*, is fundamentally unsuitable to arbitration, where party autonomy plays the substantive and fundamental role.[166] The House of Lords supported the argument that all issues relating to arbitration, including validity of arbitration agreements, standing alone, are excluded from the scope of the Brussels I Regulation. Second, the House of Lords believes the importance of arbitration in commercial practice requires effective tools to protect party autonomy and arbitration agreements.[167] Anti-suit injunctions are important and valuable in promoting legal certainty and reducing the conflicts of jurisdiction between courts and arbitration tribunals. They also protect certainty and expectation of the parties.[168] Third, the House of Lords also considers that anti-suit injunctions bring the advantage to London arbitral tribunals as an attraction to parties in the commercial world.[169] If the EU prevents EU Member States from adopting anti-suit injunctions to protect arbitration as an industry, it will make London arbitration worse off and lose the competitiveness compared to those non-EU states which are also famous arbitration centres and which are equipped with anti-suit injunctions.[170]

Regardless of the argument supporting using anti-suit injunctions in protecting arbitration agreements, the ECJ made a decision not surprising to most, which followed the line of *Turner* by prohibiting anti-suit injunctions from being used between Member States. The ECJ provided that, even if arbitration and related court proceedings are excluded from the scope of the Brussels I Regulation, those proceedings may undermine the effectiveness of the Brussels I Regulation and should not be allowed.[171] The objective of the Regulation is to unify rules of jurisdictions and to facilitate the free movement of decisions. Although an anti-suit injunction in support of arbitration is out of the scope of Brussels I, it prevents another Member State from exercising jurisdiction conferred on it by Brussels I.[172] It also permits a Member State to review another Member State's jurisdiction held pursuant to the Brussels I Regulation. Furthermore, an anti-suit injunction between Member States is against the principle of mutual trust on which the Brussels I Regulation is based. Anti-suit

166 [2007] UKHL 4, para 12.
167 [2007] UKHL 4, para 17.
168 [2007] UKHL 4, para 19.
169 [2007] UKHL 4, para 20. 'Whether the parties should submit themselves to such a jurisdiction by choosing this country as the seat of their arbitration is … entirely a matter for them. The courts are there to serve the business community rather than the other way round. No one is obliged to choose London. The existence of the jurisdiction to restrain proceedings in breach of an arbitration agreement clearly does not deter parties to commercial agreements. On the contrary, it may be regarded as one of the advantages which the chosen seat of arbitration has to offer.'
170 [2007] UKHL 4, paras 20–21.
171 [2009] ECR I-663, para 24.
172 [2009] ECR I-663, para 24.

injunction, in such circumstances, is still against the purpose and principle of Brussels I and should not be allowed.[173]

The ECJ decision is based primarily on the policy of mutual trust and the philosophy of the European judicial cooperation. The ECJ does not consider in detail the question of whether a court's jurisdiction to grant anti-suit injunctions to support arbitration, by its nature, is within or outside the scope of the Brussels I. Instead, the ECJ is concerned much more with the effect such injunctions may have on the Member States and the European jurisdiction regime as a whole. If jurisdiction of the proceedings against which the anti-suit injunction is issued is granted under the Brussels I Regulation, the anti-suit injunction affects jurisdiction in Brussels I and is contrary to the purpose of the Brussels I Regulation.

5.3 Criticism of the **Front Comor** *decision*

The *Front Comor* decision raises rigorous criticisms and debates. Many criticize the reasoning itself, which is said to be over-simplified.[174] Although the ECJ accepts that, following the past ECJ case law, *Marc Rich* and *Van Uden*, a logical conclusion is that anti-suit injunctions in support of arbitration are excluded from the scope of Brussels I, it quickly concludes that such proceedings should nonetheless be covered by Brussels I because of its effects on the functioning of Brussels I.[175] There is insufficient justification for this conclusion and there is no explanation as to why the ECJ adopts the 'effect' test over the 'subject matter' test adopted in the previous judgments.

Further, there is still no official answer as to whether proceedings deciding the existence and validity of arbitration agreements are excluded from the scope of the Brussels I Regulation. If they are, anti-suit injunctions against the court proceedings of a Member State for a declaration on the preliminary issue should be allowed, because the latter is also out of the scope of the Brussels I Regulation. The 'effect' argument cannot stand in such a circumstance. However, the other line of the decision concerns the mutual trust between Member States and such 'mutual trust' shall exist within the EU regime irrespective of the Brussels I Regulation. Whether anti-suit injunctions would be completed banned between EU Member States is a question for the future.

In addition, the decision may well affect an arbitral tribunal's jurisdiction to issue anti-suit injunctions. Arbitrators can issue anti-suit injunctions and they do not acquire jurisdiction to do so from the Brussels I Regulation. The injunction, however, has the effect of influencing jurisdiction of the court of a Member State under the Brussels I Regulation. In *Eco*

173 [2009] ECR I-663, paras 28–31.
174 See, for example, Layton, 2009.
175 *Front Comor*, [2009] ECR I-663, paras 22–26.

Swiss,[176] the ECJ decided that arbitrators sitting in a Member State are bound to apply EU law. Following the lines of reasoning in *Front Comor* and *Eco Swiss*, there is the risk that the EU arbitrators' power may also be restrained.

Most concerns arise from the arbitration business. London is one of the most popular arbitration seats in the world, given its location, language advantages, advanced commercial law and the great support of arbitration by English courts.[177] Among these advantages, anti-suit injunction in protecting English arbitration is a strong instrument to give confidence to businessmen choosing the English seat, because they have the assurance that no one can easily ignore the arbitration agreement.[178] The consideration to protect London arbitration as an industry is one of the reasons that the House of Lords adopted in its support of anti-suit injunctions.[179] However, some commentators believe most negative comments from English lawyers are 'overreactions'.[180] Although anti-suit injunctions play an important and effective role, it is hard to argue that the ban of anti-suit injunctions would directly bring great adverse impact on London's standing as a popular arbitration seat, which acquires its international recognition based on many other reasons.[181] There are other equally popular seats for international commercial arbitration, such as Paris, Vienna, Zurich, Stockholm, Geneva, etc., where there is no common practice to issue anti-suit injunctions in protecting arbitration.[182] Furthermore, anti-suit injunctions can still be used against torpedo proceedings outside of the EU.[183] Arbitration between EU parties constitutes a small proportion of London arbitration. It is suggested that the strong negative effects in London as an arbitration centre are exaggerated.[184]

English practitioners are also concerned with the encouragement of 'Italian Torpedo' in arbitration. Torpedo action in a strong sense means that, if a contracting party deliberately commences court proceedings in breach of an arbitration agreement, the court of other Member States or an arbitral tribunal cannot decide the same or related issued between the parties until the first seized court declines jurisdiction. This type of torpedo action will cause considerable delays to the other party.[185] This type of torpedo action, however, can hardly be an effective bar in

176 Case C-126/97 *Eco Swiss China Time Ltd v Benetton International NV* [1999] ECR I-3055.
177 Materna, 2011: 576.
178 Materna, 2011: 576.
179 *West Tankers v RAS* [2007] UKHL 4 (HOL), paras 21 (per Lord Steyn) and 28 (per Lord Mance).
180 Materna, 2011: 575.
181 Dutson and Howarth, 2009: 337–338; Qureshi, 2009: 24; Materna, 2011: 583; Illmer and Naumann, 2007: 147; Peel, 2009: 365; Steinbruck, 2007: 372.
182 Dutson and Howarth, 2009: 337–338; Materna, 2011: 584.
183 *Shashoua v Sharma* [2009] EWHC 957 (Comm).
184 Dutson and Howarth, 2009: 338.
185 Materna, 2011: 577–578.

arbitration because the rule of *lis pendens* does not apply to arbitration proceedings. Even if the court of a Member State is seized to decide a dispute subject to an alleged arbitration agreement, it cannot prevent the arbitral tribunal seated in another Member State from commencing arbitral proceedings. In *CMA v Hyundai*,[186] the arbitral tribunal and the English court both held that they were not bound by the French court judgment which was made on the substance of the dispute in breach of an arbitration agreement.[187] The only possible barrier is that the supervisory court of the arbitral tribunal cannot take jurisdiction to declare the arbitration agreement is valid, which might be included in the Brussels I Regulation. However, the *Front Comor* decision does not necessary lead to the conclusion that the decision on validity of an arbitration agreement is within the Brussels I Regulation. This issue remains open. Further, pursuant to the *Marc Rich* decision, if the supervisory court makes any order to support arbitration, such as appointing an arbitrator or summoning the other party, the *lis pendens* rule of the Brussels I Regulation is irrelevant as the court proceedings in arbitration are excluded from the Regulation.

Torpedo actions in a weak sense, however, may exist in arbitration, which will not effectively bar the legitimate proceedings, but may cause unnecessary burden, cost, inconvenience and oppression. Where the parties have entered into an arbitration agreement choosing a European tribunal, a party may select another EU Member State for a declaration that the arbitration agreement is invalid or does not exist, in order to disturb the arbitration proceedings or to have the arbitral awards set aside.[188] Although an arbitral tribunal is not bound to stay jurisdiction until the foreign court declines jurisdiction, the judicial proceedings may interrupt arbitral proceedings.[189] Parallel proceedings may exist.[190] It is admitted that the parallel proceedings between arbitration and litigation are not ideal.[191] It increases dispute resolution costs and causes potential irreconcilable decisions. There is the worry that the ban of anti-suit injunctions may make arbitration more expensive than litigation in the EU, caused by parallel proceedings.[192] The parties may lose faith in choosing not only London tribunals, but also arbitral tribunals in Europe, fearing that another party may bring action in the court of other Member States.[193]

186 [2008] EWHC (Comm) 2791.

187 Materna, 2011: 580.

188 Kim, 2011: 590.

189 Dutson and Howarth, 2009: 337; Tang, 2012c: 589.

190 Dutson and Howarth, 2009: 337; James and Lambert, 2006: 40; Cremades and Madalena, 2008: 507.

191 Harris, 2009.

192 In particular, the *Front Comor* decision may also ban anti-suit injunctions issued by arbitral tribunals sitting in the EU. Parallel proceedings cannot exist in litigation in the EU because of the *lis pendens* rule.

193 Dutson and Howarth, 2009: 337.

In particular, the decision may give psychological impact to encourage parties to use tactics to avoid normal proceedings. More difficulties exist if irreconcilable decisions are made by courts and arbitral tribunals. Pursuant to the Brussels I Regulation, Member States have the duty to recognize and enforce each other's judgments. Pursuant to the New York Convention, on the other hand, Member States also have treaty obligations to recognize and enforce arbitral awards falling in the scope of the New York Convention. Member States may also endorse arbitral awards in judgments, and recognition and enforcement of judgments fall within the scope of the Brussels I Regulation. A court may refuse to enforce any judgment if it is irreconcilable with domestic judgments in the related matter or judgments of another country which have already been recognized and enforced.

5.4 Manoeuvre around **Front Comor**

Based on *Front Comor*, commentators suggest alternative strategies to minimize the negative commercial impact of this case. First, the parties could apply to a court to obtain a decision on jurisdiction as soon as they can. If one party brought the action in a court of another Member State, the other party can still commence an action for such declaration and, hopefully, can receive judgments earlier than any judgments in foreign proceedings. The early judgment on this issue can be used as a guard to prevent recognition and enforcement.[194] Second, the other party can apply for a stay of jurisdiction of court proceedings in breach of the arbitration agreement pursuant to Article II(3) of the New York Convention.[195] Third, the other party can commence the arbitration process irrespective of the on-going foreign court proceedings.[196] In principle, an arbitral award may be obtained more quickly than court judgments and can be enforced under the New York Convention.[197] Fourth, the other party may apply for declaratory relief and claim damages for breach of the arbitration agreement.[198]

After the ECJ decision in *Front Comor*, the Italian court has taken jurisdiction, free of any restraint and injunction, to decide the parties' rights and obligations of the dispute subject to the London arbitration agreement. The next episode of the case is *West Tankers 2012*,[199] which concerns whether a declaratory award made by the London arbitral tribunal that the claimant is not liable may be entered as a judgment under s66 of the Arbitration Act 1996. Declaratory awards are arbitral awards declaring the

194 Arts 34(3) and 43(3). Dutson and Howarth, 2009: 343–344.
195 Dutson and Howarth, 2009: 344.
196 Ibid., 344.
197 Ibid., 344.
198 Ibid., 344.
199 *West Tankers v Allianz SpA (The Front Comor)* [2012] EWCA Civ 27.

respective rights of the parties without requiring performance from either party.[200] S66(2) of the Arbitration Act 1996 provides that: 'Where leave is so given, judgment may be entered in terms of the award.'

The English court recognized that the court normally would not grant such a leave to turn a declaratory order into judgment.[201] However, the court understood the reason why the claimant made such an application. The claimant hoped that, after the negative declaration was made concerning English judgments, it could prevent the enforcement of future judgments delivered by the Italian courts holding them liable.[202] Regardless of the argument that a declaratory award cannot be 'enforced' as such, the English court took a liberal approach and concluded that 'enforcement' should be interpreted broadly and the declaratory award could be enforced.[203]

Could the arbitral awards be directly recognized in Italy pursuant to the New York Convention? In the context of *Front Comor*, the possibility is that the Italian court might refuse recognition of the awards pursuant to Article V of the New York Convention.[204] If the award was entered as judgment, pursuant to the Brussels I Regulation, Italian courts should recognize this judgment unless it is 'manifestly' contrary to public policy or it is irreconcilable with a judgment made in Italy.

It is remarked by some commentators that this case 'affirmed an important practical way around the non-availability of anti-suit injunctions where courts elsewhere within the European Union have already been seized'.[205] Since a declaratory award could be entered as a judgment, such a declaration can be acquired at a relatively early stage, before any potential judgment made in the EU court in breach of the arbitration agreement.[206] This consequence can undermine the benefit of torpedo actions.[207]

The negative declaration is also used in *National Navigation v Endesa (The Wadi Sudr)*.[208] The parties entered into an arbitration clause for London. After disputes arose, one party commenced proceedings in Spain and another subsequently brought arbitration proceedings in London seeking a negative declaration. The latter also commenced proceedings in the English court to apply for a declaration that the dispute should be

200 Zadkovich and Roberts, 2012: 52.
201 West Tankers 2012, [2012] EWCA Civ 27, para 6.
202 Ibid., para 12.
203 Ibid., para 36.
204 Art V of the New York Convention provides that a Contracting State may refuse recognition and enforcement of an arbitral award within the Convention if the agreement is invalid, or recognition and enforcement would be contrary to the public policy of the recognition country.
205 Zadkovich and Roberts, 2012: 55.
206 Ibid., 55.
207 Ibid., 55.
208 *The Wadi Sudr* [2010] 1 Lloyd's Rep 193.

referred to a London tribunal and that the English court was not going to recognize Spanish judgment. Before the English court had made the decision, the Spanish court, applying Spanish law, ruled that the arbitration clause was not concluded and the parties should not bring the dispute to London arbitration.

The English Court of Appeal held that the Spanish judgment on the non-existence of an arbitration agreement fell within the scope of the Brussels I Regulation. This judgment should be recognized by the English court under Article 33 of the Brussels I Regulation. The English court could not rely on public policy to refuse the enforcement of the Spanish court decision because the application of different applicable laws was not a ground to generate public policy.

6 Brussels I Recast

The European jurisprudence demonstrates a clear departure from the common law tradition in tackling conflicts of jurisdiction and parallel proceedings. Arguably, the civil law tradition provides certainty and is easier to apply in practice. However, the certainty is achieved with a cost of justice in individual cases. Pursuant to Article 73 of the Brussels I Regulation, the Commission conducted a review of the functioning of the Brussels I Regulation since 2007. In 2007, a general study commissioned by the Commission on the application and functioning of the Brussels I Regulation in Member States was published by the University of Heidelberg.[209] Based on the general study, a Report and a Green Paper were published by the European Commission in 2009.[210] After considering 130 responses to the Green Paper, empirical data on the impact,[211] conferences and expert meetings, a Recast Proposal was published at the end of 2010.[212]

209 Hess *et al.*, 2007.

210 In 2009, the European Commission published a report entitled 'Report on the Review of Council Regulation (EC) No 44/2001 on Jurisdiction and the Recognition and Enforcement of Judgments in Civil and Commercial Matters', Brussels, 21 April 2009, COM(2009) 174 final and a consultation paper entitled 'Green Paper on the Review of Council Regulation (EC) No 44/2001 on Jurisdiction and the Recognition and Enforcement of Judgments in Civil and Commercial Matters', Brussels, 21 April 2009, COM(2009) 175 final.

211 Study on Data Collection and Impact Analysis Certain Aspects of a Possible Revision of Council Regulation No 44/2001 on Jurisdiction and the Recognition and Enforcement of Judgments in civil and Commercial matters, conducted by the Centre for Strategy and Evaluation Services (CSES), 2010, available at http://ec.europa.eu/justice/doc_centre/civil/studies/doc_civil_studies_en.htm; Study to Evaluate the Impact of a Possible Ratification by the European Community of the 2005 Hague Convention on Choice of Court Agreements conducted by GHK, 2007, available at http://ec.europa.eu/dgs/justice_home/evaluation/dg_coordination_evaluation_annexe_en.htm.

212 European Commission, 'Proposal for a Regulation of the European Parliament and of the Council on Jurisdiction and the Recognition and Enforcement of Judgments in Civil and Commercial Matters (Recast)', COM(2010) 748 final.

Subject to a few substantive amendments, the Recast Brussels I,[213] based on the Recast Proposal, was approved by the Council of the European Union. The Recast Brussels I is expected to enter into force on 10 January 2015,[214] and applies in all Member States, including UK and Denmark.[215]

6.1 Jurisdiction agreements

The European Commission recognized that the *Gasser* decision opens the door for the abuse of process by one party who wants to escape from the agreement, which is entered into freely, by seizing the court of a non-chosen Member State for the sole purpose of jeopardizing the proceedings in the chosen court.[216] In its consultation paper, the European Commission considered three approaches. The first is not to apply the *lis pendens* rule to the court chosen in an exclusive jurisdiction clause.[217] However, without any rule to decide the priority of two competing courts in the concurrent proceedings, this approach will only lead to uncertainty, parallel proceedings and irreconcilable judgments.[218] The second approach gives the chosen court in an exclusive jurisdiction clause the priority to decide its jurisdiction in all cases and to abolish the strict *lis pendens* rule in these cases.[219] The weakness is that it might prejudice the party resisting the jurisdiction clause if such a clause is invalid or does not exist.[220] The third option is to maintain the current rule on *lis pendens*, but to require the concerned courts to conduct direct dialogue and impose a deadline for the first seized court to decide jurisdiction in a reasonable time.[221] Besides, the Commission also considered supplementary approaches, such as granting damages to penalize the breach of jurisdiction clauses as contract terms,[222] abolishing the *lis pendens* rule in cases where parallel proceedings exist between actions on the substance and

213 Regulation on Jurisdiction and the Recognition and Enforcement of Judgments in Civil and Commercial Matters (Recast), [2012] OJ L 351/1.

214 Art 81 of the Brussels I Recast.

215 Agreement between the European Community and the Kingdom of Denmark on jurisdiction and the recognition and enforcement of judgments in civil and commercial matters, OJ 2013 L 79/4; the Council of the European Union, 'Recast of the Brussels I Regulation: towards Easier and faster circulation of judgments in civil and commercial matters within the EU', 6 December 2012, 16599/12, PRESSE 483, www.consilium.europa.eu/uedocs/cms_data/docs/pressdata/en/jha/134071.pdf, accessed on 4 January 2013. Recital 40 and 41 of the Brussels I Recast.

216 Commission Report, 6.

217 Green Paper, 5.

218 Ibid., 6.

219 Ibid., 6.

220 Ibid., 6.

221 Ibid., 6.

222 Ibid., 6.

actions seeking negative declaratory relief,[223] and prescribing standard jurisdiction clauses to expedite decisions.[224]

Based on consultation and responses from stakeholders, the European Commission published a Recast Proposal on the Brussels I Regulation.[225] The Commission stated in the proposal that one of the main objects for the reform is to enhance the effectiveness of choice of court agreements. The proposal provides two amendments: (1) providing harmonized choice of law to decide material validity of jurisdiction clauses, and (2) adopting the negative *kompetenz-kompetenz* rule granting the chosen court exclusive jurisdiction to decide the validity of an exclusive choice of court clause.[226] The final Recast Regulation is very similar to the Recast Proposal in terms of jurisdiction agreements.

The Recast Regulation first of all provides a uniform choice of law rule to decide the material validity of jurisdiction clauses. Article 25(1) provides that the chosen court of a jurisdiction clause shall have jurisdiction 'unless the agreement is null and void as to its substance under the law of that Member State'.[227] It means that domestic law of the chosen court will be systematically applied to decide the material validity of the jurisdiction clause regardless of which court is seized by the claimant to decide this issue. With completely uniformed law in deciding validity of jurisdiction clauses,[228] uniform decisions are expected from all Member States. Even if a non-chosen forum is allowed to decide the validity of a jurisdiction clause, it is likely to decline jurisdiction as far as the jurisdiction clause is valid pursuant to the law of the chosen forum.[229]

It seems that uniform results can be reached after the harmonization of the applicable law in deciding validity of jurisdiction clauses, i.e. the non-chosen court is expected to decline jurisdiction anyway. Does it mean no further reform is necessary to vary the *Gasser* decision, provided that harmonized rules apply to decide the validity of a jurisdiction clause? The answer is negative. The purpose of an exclusive jurisdiction clause is to grant jurisdiction to only one court with the parties' voluntary and free consent. This ultimate certainty will be undermined by the fact that the party could freely go to a non-chosen court to challenge the validity of this clause. There is a presumption that the parties, as commercially

223 Ibid., 6.

224 Ibid., 6.

225 European Commission, 'Proposal for a Regulation of the European Parliament and of the Council on Jurisdiction and the Recognition and Enforcement of Judgments in Civil and Commercial Matters (Recast)', December 2010, COM(2010) 748 final.

226 'Recast Proposal', para 3.1.3.

227 See also, Recast Brussels I, recital 20.

228 This includes uniform substantive law on formal validity and uniform choice of law rules in substantive validity. See Recast Brussels I, Art 25(1).

229 Art 23(1) of the Brussels I Regulation; Steinle and Vasilliades, 2010: 570.

experienced persons,[230] should have the intention to submit 'all' disputes, including the challenges on the validity of an exclusive jurisdiction clause, to the chosen forum. Certainty provided by an exclusive jurisdiction clause means the parties, when dealing with each other, would have no worry about the possibility that one day they are brought to a different forum. The certainty is prejudiced where any non-chosen court is permitted to hear the challenge on the validity of an exclusive jurisdiction clause. The introduction of a uniform applicable law to material validity of jurisdiction clauses is welcome, but it cannot replace the necessity to establish a sound system to deal with the conflict of jurisdiction between different Member States.

As a result, special revisions have been made to the interrelationship between *lis pendens* and jurisdiction clauses, which are particularly necessary and important. The new recital 22 states that:

> in order to enhance the effectiveness of exclusive choice-of-court agreements and to avoid abusive litigation tactics, it is necessary to provide for an exception to the general lis pendens rule in order to deal satisfactorily with a particular situation in which concurrent proceedings may arise. This is the situation where a court not designated in an exclusive choice-of-court agreement has been seised of proceedings and the designated court is seised subsequently of proceedings involving the same cause of action and between the same parties. In such a case, the court first seised should be required to stay its proceedings as soon as the designated court has been seised and until such time as the latter court declares that it has no jurisdiction under the exclusive choice-of-court agreement. This is to ensure that, in such a situation, the designated court has priority to decide on the validity of the agreement and on the extent to which the agreement applies to the dispute pending before it. The designated court should be able to proceed irrespective of whether the non-designated court has already decided on the stay of proceedings.

Pursuant to the recital, Article 31(2) of the Recast Regulation provides that:

> where a court of a Member State on which an agreement as referred to in Article 25 confers exclusive jurisdiction is seised, any court of another Member State shall stay the proceedings until such time as the court seised on the basis of the agreement declares that it has no jurisdiction under the agreement.

230 Exclusive jurisdiction agreements in contracts with inequality bargaining power, such as consumer contracts, are generally not allowed in the Brussels I Regulation. See section 4, Brussels I.

This revision is laudable because it could effectively prevent concurrent proceedings and provide an easy way for a court to make prompt decisions. It provides certainty to the parties and can properly protect party autonomy and parties' reasonable expectation.

It is true that the suggested approach is not perfect in that it may cause unfairness to the resisting party in an invalid choice of court agreement. If the other party inserted the jurisdiction clause without the authentic consent from the resisting party and the domestic law of the chosen court does not invalidate such a jurisdiction clause, the resisting party would have no other defence but to conduct proceedings in the chosen forum.

It is necessary to note that the Commission's Recast Proposal has provided a guideline for communication and coordination between Member States to achieve procedural efficiency and administration of justice. Proposed Article 29 provides the *lis pendens* rules. Article 29(2) provides that, if the second seized court stays jurisdiction under *lis pendens*, the first seized court shall establish jurisdiction within six months except where exceptional circumstances make this impossible.[231] Other seized courts should require the first seized court to provide information as to when the jurisdiction of the first seized court can be established.[232] This provision, however, is deleted in the final version of the Recast Regulation. It is probably because the communication and the six-month requirement impose unwanted pressure on the courts of Member States and affect the domestic legal system which should be in tact from the Regulation.

The Recast Regulation also clarifies the situation where the third country's interest is involved. It deletes the distinguished treatments to jurisdiction clauses concluded by both parties domiciled outside the Member States and jurisdiction clauses concluded by parties at least one of which is domiciled within the Member States. It provides the harmonized rules for any jurisdiction clauses choosing the court of one of the Member States, regardless of the parties' domicile. It improves the functioning of the Regulation in the international context and removes the uncertainty caused by the different interpretation to the current Article 23(3). Second, the Recast Regulation suggests the extension of *lis pendens* to concurrent proceedings between a Member State and a third country. This, however, requires closer scrutiny. Article 33(1) provides that a Member State may stay proceedings if a third country is the first seized and a stay is necessary in the interest of justice. The interest of justice can be established if the third country which is first seized is also a chosen court in a jurisdiction clause. However, the negative *kompetenz-kompetenz* rule applies only between EU Member States.[233] If a third country is chosen in an exclusive jurisdiction clause, a Member State does not need to stay proceedings. A third

231 Art 29(2), 'Recast Proposal'.
232 Ibid.
233 'Recast Proposal', Art 23(1).

country does not need to stay jurisdiction in favour of a chosen Member State either.[234] Finally, if a Member State has exclusive jurisdiction under a jurisdiction clause, while a third country is seized first in time, the new rule seems to suggest that the Member State is allowed to stay jurisdiction in favour of the non-chosen third state in exceptional cases for the purpose of sound administration of justice,[235] while the chosen state has no discretion to stay jurisdiction in favour of another Member State. Different treatment, again, has been provided to handle the conflict of jurisdiction within and outside the EU. It is thus concluded that the Recast Regulation in general could help to enhance the effectiveness of choice of court agreements and improve the function of the Regulation in the international context. However, there is still room for further improvement.

6.2 Arbitration

The interrelationship between arbitration and jurisdiction has been brought to the attention of the EU law-maker. It is one of the topics within the review of the Brussels I Regulation. The European Commission has recognized (correctly) that, although arbitration is excluded from the scope of the Brussels I Regulation in order to keep the system compatible with the New York Convention, it enables the parties to bring actions subject to arbitration to the court which 'may effectively undermine the arbitration agreement and create a situation of inefficient parallel court proceedings which may lead to irreconcilable resolutions of the dispute'.[236]

In the Green Paper on the Brussels I Regulation, the European Commission suggests that full effect and respect should be given to arbitration agreements and the Brussels I Regulation should leave the operation of the New York Convention unaffected. The Brussels I Regulation should prevent parallel proceedings between court actions and arbitration proceedings, subject to some issues relating to arbitration being addressed in the Regulation.[237] The Green Paper suggests a partial deletion of the exclusion of arbitration from the Regulation and inserting a special jurisdiction rule regulating jurisdiction of courts in taking jurisdiction to support arbitration proceedings.[238] The Regulation will also apply in courts' proceedings to issue provisional measures to protect arbitration, such as freezing orders. The court judgments in the validity and existence of arbitral awards, merging or setting aside arbitral awards, can be recognized and enforced in other Member States under the Regulation.[239] In particular, the Green Paper proposes methods to deal with the relationship between arbitral tribunals and courts

234 Because the Brussels I regime would not bind any third country.
235 Recast Brussels I, Art 33(1).
236 'Recast Proposal'.
237 Green Paper, 8.
238 Ibid., 9.
239 Ibid., 9.

in deciding the validity of an arbitration clause. The approach is to give priority to the supervisory court of arbitration.[240] The Green Paper also proposes a rule to refuse recognition and enforcement of judgments from a Member State if it is irreconcilable with an arbitral award enforceable under the New York Convention. Alternatively, the arbitral awards can be enforced freely within the EU after it is certified by the supervisory court.[241]

The Recast Proposal continues to exclude arbitration from its scope. Such exclusion is broad in that it excludes not only arbitral procedure but all issues in relation to arbitration from the proposed scheme, including 'the form, existence, validity or effects of arbitration agreements, the powers of the arbitrators, the procedure before arbitral tribunals, and the validity, annulment, and recognition and enforcement of arbitral awards'.[242] The Recast Proposal also includes a rule dealing with the relationship between arbitration and court proceedings. It does not provide a complete negative *kompetenz-kompetenz* rule to exclude all courts the power to decide the preliminary issues of an arbitration agreement. It, however, grants priority to the supervisory court of arbitration in case of conflicts. If the seat of the arbitration is in a Member State, once the supervisory court or the arbitral tribunal is seized to decide, either as a primary or an incidental question, the validity and effect of the arbitration agreement, the court in any other Member State where jurisdiction is contested on the basis of the existence of arbitration agreements should stay jurisdiction. The proposal, however, does not completely prevent a non-supervisory court from deciding the validity of an arbitration agreement. If the defendant contests jurisdiction based on the existence of a valid arbitration agreement without commencing proceedings in the supervisory court or arbitral tribunal, the non-seated court can continue proceedings to decide the preliminary issues relating to arbitration.

The seat priority, however, is deleted in the final version of the Recast Brussels I. The text of the Recast Regulation only includes the same exclusion provision as the old Article 1(2)(d), which excludes arbitration from its scope. Only Recital 12 provides some useful guidance in relation to arbitration, which reads:

> This Regulation should not apply to arbitration. Nothing in this Regulation should prevent the courts of a Member State, when seized of an action in a matter in respect of which the parties have entered into an arbitration agreement, from referring the parties to arbitration, from staying or dismissing the proceedings, or from examining whether the arbitration agreement is null and void, inoperative or incapable of being performed, in accordance with their national law.

240 Ibid., 9.
241 Ibid., 9.
242 Recital 11.

> A ruling given by a court of a Member State as to whether or not an arbitration agreement is null and void, inoperative or incapable of being performed should not be subject to the rules of recognition and enforcement laid down in this Regulation, regardless of whether the court decided on this as a principal issue or as an incidental question.
>
> On the other hand, where a court of a Member State, exercising jurisdiction under this Regulation or under national law, has determined that an arbitration agreement is null and void, inoperative or incapable of being performed, this should not preclude that court's judgment on the substance of the matter from being recognised or, as the case may be, enforced in accordance with this Regulation. This should be without prejudice to the competence of the courts of the Member States to decide on the recognition and enforcement of arbitral awards in accordance with the Convention on the Recognition and Enforcement of Foreign Arbitral Awards, done at New York on 10 June 1958 ('the 1958 New York Convention'), which takes precedence over this Regulation.
>
> This Regulation should not apply to any action or ancillary proceedings relating to, in particular, the establishment of an arbitral tribunal, the powers of arbitrators, the conduct of an arbitration procedure or any other aspects of such a procedure, nor to any action or judgment concerning the annulment, review, appeal, recognition or enforcement of an arbitral award.

This recital provides three important rules: first, the courts of any Member States have the competence to decide the validity of arbitration agreements according to their national law.[243] In other words, the Regulation does not resolve the conflict of jurisdiction in terms of arbitration agreements. There is no *lis pendens* rule in favour of the first seized court, or seat priority rule in favour of the supervisory court. There is even no rule giving priority to arbitral tribunals. The Regulation simply leaves this issue to be decided by the national law or international conventions.

Second, the ruling on the validity of an arbitration agreement is not subject to the recognition and enforcement of the Regulation. It means that even if a non-seated court rules the arbitration agreement invalid, it cannot bar a seated court from making a different ruling on the same issue. Further, other Member States are not obliged to recognize and enforce any court's ruling on the validity of arbitration agreements. This issue is completely excluded from the scope of the Regulation.

Third, if the court determines that an arbitration agreement is null and void, this should not preclude that court's judgment on the substance of the matter from being recognized and enforced within the Regulation.[244]

243 Recital 12.
244 Ibid.

The other Member State, at the same time, can also decide the recognition and enforcement to arbitral awards pursuant to the New York Convention, which takes precedence over the Recast Brussels I.[245] This works to deal with irreconcilable decisions resulting from the conflicts of jurisdiction. While a non-seated court can decide the validity of an arbitration agreement and does not need to give precedence to the supervisory court or tribunal, and no *lis pendens* rule applies while a court is asked to decide the validity of an arbitration agreement, the possibility is that more than one court or tribunal may proceed to decide the validity of an arbitration agreement. While the non-seated court rules the arbitration clause invalid, it will move on to give judgment to the merit. This judgment is enforceable under the Recast Regulation. However, if an arbitral tribunal also makes an award on the same matter, the enforcement court could enforce the award pursuant to the New York Convention. Although the recital does not clearly state whether the judgment or the award takes priority, the term 'without prejudice to' shows that the New York Convention shall take priority. In other words, if awards are made which are enforceable pursuant to the New York Convention, the court should enforce the awards instead of an irreconcilable judgment under the Brussels I Regulation. The problem here is: what if a non-seated court decides the merit earlier and the application has been made in the enforcement court? Shall the enforcement court enforce the judgment pursuant to the Regulation or shall the court wait while knowing the arbitral proceedings on the same merit is on-going? If the court has already recognized the judgment, and another party applies for the recognition and enforcement of an irreconcilable award, would recognition be refused based on public policy of the forum, i.e. it is against public policy to recognize an award which is contrary to the irreconcilable judgment that has already been recognized in this country? Fortunately, this situation may not exist very often in practice because arbitration usually is quicker than litigation.

All these rules are understood as means to maintain a sound relationship between the Regulation and other international conventions in the field of arbitration. If there is international law establishing judicial cooperation in the field of arbitration, the Regulation is reluctant to influence the Member States in these regards. However, can the Regulation keep clear of arbitration at all? The answer probably is negative. Although Regulation jurisdiction rules are not applicable to the validity of arbitration agreements,[246] they continue to apply if the courts of a Member State are seized to decide substance of a dispute allegedly submitted to arbitration.

245 Recital 12.

246 The second paragraph of the recital says that the decision on the validity of an arbitration agreement is not subject to the recognition and enforcement in the Regulation. It shows that validity of an arbitration agreement is completely excluded from the Regulation. The Regulation jurisdiction rules shall not apply either.

Arbitration, raised as a preliminary and incidental question, would not affect a court from taking jurisdiction under the Regulation over the merit of a dispute. The court then will consider the validity of arbitration agreements under the remit of this jurisdiction. Although it would not preclude parallel proceedings, at least the *lis pendens* rule would not apply to arbitration agreements, i.e. if the supervisory court is seized second to decide the validity of the arbitration agreement, the court does not need to stay jurisdiction in favour of the non-seat court.

8 Recognition and enforcement of judgments and awards

1 Introduction

Party autonomy should also be respected at the recognition and enforcement stage. The final outcome of any dispute resolution methods is to have the decision enforced. Otherwise, the whole procedure has no practical value to the parties and constitutes a complete waste of time and money. Unfortunately, effective recognition and enforcement require the cooperation of other jurisdictions. If a country fully respects party autonomy and enforces all valid jurisdiction or arbitration agreements, while the enforcement country does not have the same policy to give effects to party autonomy, judgments made by the country of origin will not be enforced. This will, in return, cause the country of origin to doubt its policy supporting a valid dispute resolution clause and may make this country refuse to give effects to party autonomy in cases where judgments may hardly be enforced in the place of enforcement. On the other hand, if the enforcement country adopts a strong policy to refuse enforcement of judgments made in breach of a valid jurisdiction or arbitration clause, it may not affect the law and practice in another country but may make parties reluctant to breach a freely agreed dispute resolution clause. In the current law, recognition and enforcement of arbitral awards are relatively straightforward and certain given the successful enforcement of the New York Convention. Comparatively, recognition and enforcement of judgments are more problematic.

2 Recognition and enforcement of arbitral awards

The New York Convention harmonized the rule in recognition and enforcement of arbitral awards made by the tribunal seated in a foreign country. Pursuant to Article III, each Contracting State 'shall' recognize and enforce foreign arbitral awards granted in another contracting country. The procedure of recognition and enforcement should follow the domestic law of the requested country, and the state cannot impose higher fees or more onerous conditions to enforce foreign awards than domestic awards. The policy is well received in many Contracting States. For example, US courts consider it an often stated federal policy in favour of the enforcement of arbitral awards.[1] In order to improve efficient enforcement of Convention awards, China promulgated the Fee Regulation, requiring decisions on recognition and enforcement to be made within two months and enforcement to be completed within six months after decision.[2]

The New York Convention also provides exceptions upon which recognition and enforcement can be refused. In total, seven refusal grounds are provided, five of which must be pleaded by the opposing party, while two of which can be relied on by the court using its own motion.[3] The enforcement of arbitral awards will be rejected if the opposing party could establish a party is incapable or the arbitration agreement is invalid, the defendant is not informed properly or the arbitral proceedings are not conducted fairly, the arbitrators exceed authority, the arbitral tribunal or the procedure is not composed according to the parties agreement, and the awards are not yet binding.[4] Enforcement may be refused if the court finds the arbitral awards are contrary to public policy or the subject matter is non-arbitrable.[5] The New York Convention is implemented in most countries in the world, and the rules on the recognition and enforcement apply in all the Contracting States of the Convention.

National practice, however, differs in the interpretation of these refusal grounds, especially the most controversial ground of public policy.[6] The concept of public policy is vague and varies widely between different countries. Some countries tend to use public policy more often than others to refuse recognition and enforcement of foreign arbitral awards, which makes the enforcement of arbitral awards more difficult in some countries than in others.

2.1 Public policy

English approach

In England, enforcement of arbitral awards cannot be refused simply because it infringes English law.[7] There is a high threshold to plea the

1 *Moses H. Cone Mem'l Hospital v Mercury Construction.*, 460 US 1, 24 (1983); *Whirlpool v Philips*, 848 F. Supp. 474, 478 (S.D.N.Y. 1994); *Shearson v McMahon*, 482 US 220 (1987).

2 Regulations of the Supreme People's Court Regarding the Issue of Fees and Investigation Periods for the Recognition and Enforcement of Foreign Arbitral Awards (promulgated by the Supreme People's Court, 14 November 1998, effective 21November 1998). Souza, 2006: 1333.

3 Art V.

4 Art V.1.

5 Art V.2.

6 Art V.2(b).

7 Fawcett and Carruthers, 2008: 658.

defence of public policy in order to deny the enforceability of arbitral awards.[8] Public policy should be used with 'extreme caution',[9] and cannot 'furnish an open-ended escape route for refusing enforcement of New York Convention awards'.[10] It can only be used to maintain the 'fair and orderly administration of justice'.[11]

Public policy will be upheld if the awards enforce an illicit contract in the place of performance. In *Soleimany v Soleimany*,[12] the English Court of Appeal held that arbitral awards will not be enforced in England if the arbitrators, by applying the law of another country, uphold the illicit transactions performed in a friendly neighbour country. In *R v V*,[13] however, the arbitral award was enforced, even if the purchase of personal influence was contrary to English law. The reason is that the contract was performed in Libya and valid under the law of performance.

While a contract is obtained by, or aims to facilitate, an illicit act, such as corruption and bribery, enforcing this contract is against public policy of English law. However, public policy used to rebut an arbitral award should be 'international public policy'. English courts then must balance two competing policies, namely the policy to fight against corruption and the policy to keep finality of arbitral awards. In *Westacre Investments v Jugoimport-SDPR Holdings*,[14] it was held that, although commercial bribery was contrary to public policy, it was not strong enough to override the finality of arbitral awards. Although the English court would invalidate the contract if it is the trial court, the English court had to enforce the arbitral award. The same decision was also made in *Omnium de Traitement et de Valorisation SA v Hilmarton Ltd*,[15] where the English court enforced another arbitral award which allegedly facilitated payment of bribes. The English court, again, stated that the concern was not whether the underlying contract could be enforced, but whether the arbitral award could be enforced. A different standard as to public policy, thus, applies.

Public policy defence can also be triggered if the awards are acquired by fraud, such as perjury. However, fresh evidence, which is not available at the time of arbitration with reasonable diligence, is required.[16] Public policy defence cannot be used if it may reopen an argument that was raised and considered in arbitration.[17] Furthermore, the alleged fraud should contribute 'in a substantive way' for the claimant to obtain the

8 *Nomihold Securities v Mobile Telesystems Finance SA*, [2011] EWHC 2143 (Comm), para 55.
9 *IPCO (Nigeria) Ltd v Nigerian National Petroleum Co* [2005] 2 Lloyd's Rep 326, para 13
10 *IPCO (Nigeria) Ltd*, ibid., para 13.
11 Ibid., para 13.
12 [1998] 3 WLR 811.
13 [2008] EWHC 1531 (Comm), [2009] 1 Lloyd's Rep 97.
14 [1999] 3 W.L.R 811.
15 [1999] 2 Lloyd's Rep. 222.
16 *Nomihold Securities*, para 77; *Ladd v Marshall*, [1954] 1 WLR 1489.
17 *Nomihold Securities*, para 55.

awards.[18] Because of the high threshold, although public policy defence was raised occasionally in English courts, it was rarely upheld.

Under the influence of the EU, recognition and enforcement of an arbitral award will be refused in England if the award is inconsistent with EU public policy. For example, the EU Treaty provided that an arbitral award shall not be recognized and enforced in a Member State if the award enforces a contract facilitating anti-competition activities, including fixed prices, market control, share markets or sources of supply, cartel, discriminatory pricing and tying.[19] Protecting competition is EU public policy and a uniform EU definition has been provided as to what activities are against EU policy. English courts, as a result, should enforce the EU law and refuse recognizing and enforcing arbitral awards on these grounds.

US approach

The US also considers that broad construction of public policy 'would vitiate the Convention's basic effort to remove pre-existing obstacles to enforcement'[20] and interprets public policy as the 'most basic notions of morality and justice'.[21] The narrow definition makes public policy defence hardly succeed in practice. In *Changzhou AMEC Eastern Tools and Equipments v Eastern Tools & Equipment*,[22] the California District Court said it 'has not found any case in which a district court has declined to confirm a foreign arbitral award under Article V(2)(b) based on a defense of duress'.[23] Arbitrators' errors in applying law, legal reasoning or manifest disregard of law,[24] inconsistent testimony,[25] economic sanctions and diplomat relations,[26] and existence of restrictive trade clause[27] are not enough to reach the level of public policy to refuse recognition and

18 *Nomihold Securities*, para 64.

19 Arts 101 and 102 TFEU.

20 *Parsons & Whittemore Overseas Co. v Société General de L'industrie du Papier*, 508 F.2d 969, 974 (2d Cir. 1974).

21 *Parsons & Whittemore Overseas Co*, ibid.; *Ameropa AG v Havi Ocean Co. LLC*, 2011 WL 570130, 2 (S.D.N.Y. 16 February 2011); *Ministry of Def. and Support for the Armed Forces of the Islamic Republic of Iran v Cubic Def. Sys.*, 665 F.3d 1091, 1097 (9th Cir. 2011).

22 Not reported in F. Supp. 2d, (C.D.Cal., 2012).

23 Ibid., 11.

24 *SEI Societa Esplosivi Industriali SpA v L-3 Fuzing and Ordnance Systems, Inc.*, 843 F. Supp. 2d 509 (D.Del.,2012); *Karaha Bodas Co., LLC v Perusahaan Pertambangan Minyak Dan Gas Bumi Negara*, 364 F.3d 274, 306 (5th Cir. 2004); *Banco de Seguros del Estado v Mutual Marine Office, Inc.*, 344 F.3d 255, 264 (2d Cir. 2003); *M & C Corp. v Erwin Behr GmbH & Co., KG*, 87 F.3d 844, 851 n. 2 (6th Cir. 1996).

25 *Waterside Ocean Navigation Co. v International Navigation Ltd*, 737 F.2d 150 (2d Cir. 1984). McLaughlin and Genevro, 1986: 261–262.

26 *Parsons v Whittemore*, (1974) 508 F.2D 2nd Cir. 969.

27 *La Société Nationale v Shaheen Natural Resources Co.*, 585 F. Supp. 57 (S.D.N.Y. 1983), aff'd, 733 F.2d 260 (2d Cir.), cert. denied, 469 US 883 (1984).

enforcement of arbitral awards. For example, in *Waterside Ocean Navigation Co*, the disputed arbitral award was made based on inconsistent testimony but the court ruled that since the arbitral tribunal was aware of the inconsistent testimony and no perjury was made, the award was not against public policy.[28]

Public policy defence, however, will be upheld if the procedural irregularity exists. For example, arbitrators fail to disclose connections with one party.[29] Escalated interest rate was a good reason to support public policy defence in at least one US case.[30] Duress or unconscionableness, if established, could form a basis to refuse enforcement of foreign awards under the New York Convention.[31] Some US courts extend duress and unconscionableness to all requirements to conclude a valid arbitration agreement, including fraud, mistake and duress.[32] This probably overlaps with the validity requirement for arbitration agreements. If an arbitration agreement was concluded under duress or was unconscionable under the US law as the law of the enforcement forum, enforcement could be denied under V(1)(a).

Chinese approach

Public policy defence is rephrased as 'public interest' (*gong gong li yi*) in Chinese legislation.[33] It is argued by some commentators that the meaning of public interest can be significantly broader than what intends to be public policy in the New York Convention.[34] It may include 'not only adopted rules, expressed state commitments and social morality, but also less transparent state interests and unstable short-term policies'.[35] The Chinese version of 'public policy' indeed shows the emphasis of government policies and political means, which is contrary to the original purpose or intention of the New York Convention. There is the worry that Chinese courts may refuse recognition and enforcement of foreign awards made against an important employer in China, a state company or an essential economic body.[36] Examples can be found in *Dongfeng Garments*

28 McLaughlin and Genevro, 1986: 262.

29 *Fertilizer Co of India v IDI Management, Inc.*, 517 Supp. 948, 955 (S.D. Ohio, 1981), reh'g denied, 530 F. Supp 542 (S.D. Ohio 1982); McLaughlin and Genevro: 1986: 262.

30 *Laminoirs-Trefileries-Cableries de Lens v Southwire Co.*, 484 F. Supp. 1063 (N.D. Ga. 1980). McLaughlin and Genevro: 1986: 262.

31 *Transmarine Seaways Corp. v Marc Rich & Co. A. G.*, 480 F. Supp. 352, 358 (S.D.N.Y. 1979). McLaughlin and Genevro: 1986: 262.

32 *Chloe Z Fishing Co. v Odyssey Re (London) Ltd*, 109 F. Supp. 2d 1236, 1259 (S.D.Cal. 2000); *DiMercurio v Sphere Drake Ins. PLC*, 202 F.3d 71, 79 (1st Cir. 2000).

33 Art 71, PRC Arbitration Act 1994; PRC Civil Procedure Law (2012 amendment), Art 274.

34 Pien, 2007: 594.

35 Zhang, 1999: 476; Souza, 2006: 1329.

36 Pien, 2007: 595.

Factory of Kaifeng City v Henan Garments Import and Export,[37] where the local court refused to enforce an award against a company which was a major player in the local economy because of the worry that the awards might 'seriously harm the economic influence of the State ... and adversely affect the foreign trade order of the State'.[38]

The broad and ambiguous interpretation of public policy in Chinese law has been widely criticized. It is suggested that the Chinese judge should have a better understanding of the nature of international arbitration and the need of international commerce. The reason that foreign arbitral awards may put a major company in financial difficulty or lead to the loss of employment cannot be a valid defence.[39] Fortunately, commentators have observed that the recent practice in China shows signs of improvement.[40] For example, the Stockholm Chamber of Commerce ordered a Chinese state-owned company to repay a debt to the Japanese company. The Chinese company raised the public policy defence based on the ground that the repayment had not been approved by the State Administration on Foreign Exchange (SAFE). The Supreme People's Court held that, although approval of the SAFE was compulsory for sending foreign currency out of China, the alleged breach of the administrative regulation did not naturally mean infringement of public policy.[41] Furthermore, according to an unverified statement of the deputy Chief Justice in a public speech, Chinese courts did not invoke public policy defence during 2000–2008.[42] Ironically, two months after the speech, the Supreme People's Court refused enforcement of an arbitral award on the public policy ground.[43] In this case, a Chinese company and three foreign companies entered into a joint venture contract, including an arbitration agreement. Later, a leasing dispute arose between the Chinese company and the joint venture and the dispute was brought to and decided by the ICC Paris in favour of the joint venture. The Chinese court, however, held that the arbitration agreement only bound the contractual parties, i.e. the Chinese company and the three foreign companies, but not the Chinese company and the joint venture, which was a separate new entity in law. The Chinese court, thus, has jurisdiction over the dispute. By taking jurisdiction, the arbitral tribunal has violated Chinese sovereignty and, thus,

37 Zhengzhou Intermediate People's Ct., 28 September 1992. Cited in Pien, 2007: 595. This award is not a foreign award but foreign-related award, which was made by a CIETAC with foreign parties involved.

38 Pien, 2007: 595. The decision was overruled by the Supreme Court.

39 Inoue, 2006: 189.

40 Greenberg *et al.*, 2011: 465.

41 Chen and Howes, 2009.

42 Wan, 2008.

43 www.chinanews.com.cn/cj/cyzh/news/2008/07-16/1314096.shtml (accessed on 30 July 2013).

infringed Chinese public policy.[44] This case is clear evidence that 'public policy' was lightly invoked in the Chinese court. Even if the arbitral tribunal had no jurisdiction in deciding the dispute, this might only fall under the grounds of Article V(c), i.e. the award deals with a different issue and does not fall within the arbitration agreement. The lack of jurisdiction of a tribunal may not be considered strong enough to breach 'international public policy'. It is thus argued that, although Chinese judges realize the importance of supporting international arbitration and only apply public policy with great precaution,[45] there is still a long way to go.

3 Recognition and enforcement of judgments—national law

3.1 English law

Recognition and enforcement of foreign judgments in England fall into three categories. The first type of judgment falls within the scope of the Brussels I Regulation and enforcement should follow the rule of Brussels I. The Brussels I Regulation establishes clear rules facilitating easy recognition and enforcement of foreign judgments with limited exceptions, which will be discussed later.[46] The second refers to judgments obtained in Commonwealth countries of states with bilateral recognition and enforcement treaties in the UK.[47] These treaties establish grounds similar to the Brussels I Regulation, in order to help effective recognition and enforcement of judgments in the UK. Recognition and enforcement, however, may be refused if the country of origin has no jurisdiction under English law, the defendant was not properly noticed or served and did not appear, the judgment was obtained by fraud, the enforcement would be contrary to English public policy or the party making application has no standing.[48]

The third type of judgment is obtained in the country without any judgment treaty with the UK. Enforcement of judgments shall be decided pursuant to common law. English common law does not require reciprocity between states, nor does it depend on comity.[49] English common law considers that the foreign judgments create a debt and the judgment debtor has the obligation to perform.[50] In order to enforce the foreign judgments, the English court should be satisfied the judgment is conclusive

44 Chen and Howes, 2009.
45 Wan, 2008.
46 See s4.1.
47 Administration of Justice Act 1920; Foreign Judgments (Reciprocal Enforcement) Act 1933.
48 Section 4 of the 1933 Foreign Judgments (Reciprocal Enforcement) Act.
49 Hartley, 2009: 344.
50 Hartley, 2009: 344, citing *Williams v Jones*, (1845) 13 M & W 628.

and final, it is monetary and does not involve penalty payment to a state organ, and the court of origin has jurisdiction pursuant to English private international law.[51] However, foreign courts' jurisdiction is determined by narrower grounds than deciding English courts' jurisdiction at the trial stage. The foreign court should either take jurisdiction upon the defendant's submission or have sufficient connection with the judgment debtor.[52] The ground is narrow because the connection between the cause of action and the foreign court is not a ground to recognize and enforce foreign judgments.[53] However, the ground of submission is interpreted broadly to include the conclusion of a valid choice of court clause.[54] Furthermore, if the foreign court takes jurisdiction in breach of a valid jurisdiction or arbitration agreement, the judgment may not be enforced in England.[55] Finally, even if all the above requirements are satisfied, enforcement of foreign judgments can be refused. The defendant could raise a few valid grounds to prevent the enforcement of foreign judgments, including the denial of a fair trial,[56] the existence of procedural fraud[57] and the contrary to public policy of England.

Foreign judgments obtained pursuant to a valid jurisdiction agreement may be enforced in England in accordance with the common law. The explicit provision preventing enforcement of foreign judgments made in breach of a valid jurisdiction clause may be helpful to urge the claimant to sue in the chosen court, if the judgment is likely to be enforced in England. In general, the conditions to recognize and enforce foreign judgments are not stringent. Foreign monetary judgments may be enforced in England as a matter of principle. The common law approach, however, requires discretion to be taken in individual cases, and uncertainty, thus, continues to exist.

3.2 US law

The US is not party to any bilateral or multilateral treaties facilitating reciprocal recognition and enforcement of foreign judgments. There is also no federal law on recognizing and enforcing foreign judgments in the US either. In an ancient case, *Hilton v Guyot*,[58] the Supreme Court expressed the view that a foreign judgment only has effect in its own territory, but the US court may give effect to foreign judgments based on

51 Fentiman, 2010: para 18.10; Clarkson and Hill, 2011: 174.
52 Clarkson and Hill, 2011: 164–165.
53 Hartley, 2009: 354.
54 Hartley, 2009: 354.
55 Section 32, the Jurisdiction and Judgments Act 1982. See Briggs, 2008: 355–357.
56 Fentiman, 2010: paras 18.25–18.29.
57 E.g. the claimant withheld evidence or the witness committed perjury. See Fentiman, 2010: para 18.30.
58 159 US 113 (1895).

comity and due process. If the foreign proceedings are fair and regular, the foreign courts are competent, the foreign judicial system can provide 'impartial administration to justice' and there is nothing to show prejudice or fraud, the US court may enforce the foreign judgment under the doctrine of comity.[59] Although the Supreme Court further imposed the requirement of reciprocity,[60] the reciprocal requirement is no longer good law in Federal courts.[61]

Hilton, however, did not provide guidance as to the standard to enforce foreign judgments. Since there is no uniform legislation on recognition and enforcement of judgments, the issue is largely left to each state to decide.[62] Some states have adopted the Uniform Foreign Money-Judgments Recognition Act 1962 or 2005, and others continue to use the common law in deciding recognition and enforcement of foreign judgments.[63] Although these state laws share certain similarities, they are far from identical.[64] State law allows courts to recognize and enforce foreign judgments pursuant to comity. Most states exclude the requirement of reciprocity as a condition; some states still make it a discretion of the court. Georgia and Massachusetts make reciprocity a mandatory ground to recognize and enforce foreign judgments.[65] The doctrine of reciprocity, however, is not applied as stringently as in Chinese law.[66] If the opposing party proves that the country of origin has no way to enforce US judgments, recognition and enforcement may be refused. It does not require a case precedence in the country of origin, under which the US judgment has been enforced.[67] The purpose of introducing the reciprocity requirement is not to make recognition and enforcement difficult in the USA, but to encourage or urge foreign countries to recognize and enforce US judgments.[68]

US courts generally take a liberal approach to recognizing and enforcing foreign judgments. Although as a matter of principle, most foreign monetary judgments can then be recognized and enforced in US courts, recognition and enforcement may be refused if the foreign proceedings lack due process[69]—for instance, the court of origin does not provide

59 159 US 202–203.
60 Brand, 1991: 258–262.
61 *Erie Railroad v Tompkins*, 304 US 64 (1938); Brand, 2012: 3; Brand, 1991: 263–265.
62 Luthin, 2008: 117; Brand, 2012: 2; *Restatement (Second) of Conflict of Laws*, s98.
63 Brand, 2012: 7.
64 Ibid., 6–9.
65 Ibid., 11.
66 See subsection 3.3 below.
67 Brand, 2012: 12; Luthin, 2008: 117–118; *Direction Der Disconto-Gesellschaft v United States Steel Corp.*, 300 F. 741, 747 (D.N.Y. 1924).
68 Luthin, 2008: 117–118.
69 *British Midland Airways Ltd (BMA) v Int'l Travel, Inc.*, 497 F.2d 869 (9th Cir. 1974).

impartial tribunals,[70] the court of origin has no jurisdiction,[71] the defendant is not properly served and has no chance to defend himself,[72] the foreign judgment is obtained by fraud[73] and enforcement will infringe US public policy.[74]

Foreign judgments made pursuant to a valid jurisdiction clause, as a result, should be able to be enforced in most US states, unless one of the refusal grounds exists. The difficulty is that US practice differs between each state, and the common law procedure in some states provides uncertainty. Applying for a judgment recognized in the USA is not straightforward and convenient in the view of many litigants. Furthermore, it is argued by Brand that breaching a valid jurisdiction agreement may make foreign judgments hard to enforce in the US.[75] Breaching a valid jurisdiction agreement questions the jurisdiction of the country of origin, and contradicts the principle established by *Berman*. If this is the case, it may encourage the parties to perform their jurisdiction agreements, especially where judgments are likely to be enforced in the US. However, there is uncertainty on this. First, the country of origin may not lack jurisdiction under its domestic law, though jurisdiction is taken in breach of the jurisdiction agreement, e.g. taking jurisdiction probably is better for the end of justice. Second, taking jurisdiction in breach of a jurisdiction agreement may not equalize to the lack of due process. It is thus submitted that suing in the court of origin in breach of a valid jurisdiction clause may not amount to a reason for the US court to refuse recognizing and enforcing the judgments.

3.3 Chinese law

China is one of the countries where very restrictive grounds have been provided to recognize and enforce foreign judgments. Foreign judgments can only be recognized and enforced in China if the judgment-rendering country and China have entered into bilateral/multilateral treaties, or if the reciprocal relationships exist. Article 282 of the PRC Civil Procedure Law (Amended) 2012 provides:

70 *Bank Melli Iran v Pahlavi*, 58 F.3d 1406 (9th Cir. 1995); *Bridgeway v Citibank*, 201 F. 3d 134 (2d Cir. 2000); Brand, 2012: 14.

71 Brand, 2012: 18–19; *Society of Lloyd's v Byrens*, 2003 US Dist. LEXIS 26719 (S.D. Cal. 29 May 2003); Luthin, 2008: 133.

72 *Corporacion Salvadorena de Calzado v Injection Footwear Corp.*, 533 F. Supp. 290 (S.D. Fla. 1982); Brand, 2012: 20.

73 *Laufer v Westminster Brokers, Ltd*, 532 A.2d 130 (D.C. App. 1987); *De La Mata v Am. Life. Ins. Co.*, 771 F. Supp. 1375, 1377–1390 (D. Del. 1991); Brand, 2012: 20–21.

74 *Somportex Ltd v Phila. Chewing Gum Corp.*, 453 F.2d 435, 443 (3d Cir. 1971), cert. denied, 405 US 1017 (1972); *Bachchan v India Abroad Publications*, 585 N.Y.S.2d 661 (Sup. Ct. 1992); Brand, 2012: 21–23.

75 Brand, 2012: 23; 2005 Recognition Act § 4(c)(5); 1962 Recognition Act § 4(b)(5).

> In the case of an application or request for recognition and enforcement of a legally effective judgment or written order of a foreign court, the people's court shall, after examining it in accordance with the international treaties concluded or acceded to by the People's Republic of China or with the principle of reciprocity and arriving at the conclusion that it does not contradict the primary principles of the law of the People's Republic of China nor violates State sovereignty, security and social and public interest of the country, recognize the validity of the judgment or written order.

It is clear that the existence of a jurisdiction clause is not one of the grounds for a Chinese court to recognize and enforce foreign judgments. Since the condition for a Chinese court to enforce foreign judgments is very restrictive, most foreign judgments could not be recognized and enforced in China. According to the information published by the PRC Ministry of Foreign Affairs in 2010, China had entered into judicial cooperation treaties to recognize and enforce civil judgments with around 30 countries,[76] four of which have not yet entered into force.[77] China has not entered into treaties with most of its important trade partners, such as Germany, the USA and Japan. Furthermore, the principle of reciprocity is defined very strictly in China. China would not recognize a foreign judgment if the foreign court might in principle recognize the Chinese judgment but has not done so yet in practice. There must be existing authority in the foreign country that has recognized Chinese judgments in precedence.[78] Furthermore, even if the foreign court had recognized Chinese judgments before, the judgment creditor must prove to the Chinese court that the judgment in application is the same type, and if it is made in China it would be equally recognized and enforced in the foreign country according to the precedent.[79] As a result, although the USA and Germany have recognized Chinese judgments before, it is not a guarantee that their judgments can certainly be recognized in China.[80] If the parties have chosen one of those courts the judgments of which could not be recognized and enforced in China, and the judgment creditor has all its assets located in China, enforcing the jurisdiction clause undoubtedly creates

76 See the website of the PRC Ministry of Foreign Affairs, www.mfa.gov.cn/chn/gxh/zlb/tyfg/, accessed on 1 May 2012.

77 Belgium, Argentina, Kuwait and Peru.

78 Supreme People's Court, 'Re whether the People's Courts should recognize and enforce the Judgment given by the Japanese Court in Payment of Debts', [1995] No 17; *NKK (Japan) v Beijing Zhuangsheng*, Beijing Municipality High Court, (2008) No 919; *RNO v Beijing International Music Festival Society*, Beijing Intermediate Court (2004) No 928.

79 Zhang *et al.*, 2010.

80 US courts recognized the judgment made by the Hubei Province High People's Court in *Hubei Gezhouba Sanlian Industrial & Hubei Pinghu Cruise v Robinson Helicopter Co, Inc*, 06–01798 (C.D. 2009).

difficulties for the judgment creditor and it is hard to say it is in the interest of justice for the Chinese court to decline jurisdiction in favour of the chosen court.

Furthermore, while the foreign judgment cannot be recognized and enforced in China, the judgment creditor could bring the same cause of action in China. This is provided in the '1992 Opinion' of the Supreme People's Court, Article 318 of which provides:

> If the party applied to the competent intermediate court of the People's Republic of China for recognition and enforcement of foreign judgments or rulings, if the country where the foreign court is located and the People's Republic of China have not concluded or acceded to international treaties, or formed the relation of reciprocity, the applicant could sue in the People's Court for the competent People's Court to make judgment for enforcement.

It means that if the Chinese court, when facing a valid foreign jurisdiction clause, declines jurisdiction and directs the parties to the chosen forum, after the chosen forum makes judgment in favour of the claimant, the claimant must sue in the Chinese court to make judgment for enforcement. The difficulty for a Chinese court to recognize and enforce foreign judgments causes tremendous disadvantages for the business of international commerce. It hampers not only international comity but also party autonomy. Even if the parties freely enter into a valid agreement to submit all their disputes to another country, the judgment cannot be enforced in China. If the defendant has assets located exclusively in China, it is irrational for the claimant to bring the action in the chosen court. If the claimant follows the choice of court agreement, the claimant will bring the same action in China in order to enforce the judgment at the enforcement state. It will lead to duplicate litigation, which increases litigation costs for both parties, wastes public resources and causes delay.[81] The most rational choice, as a result, is for the claimant to breach the choice of court agreement and to sue the defendant in China.

4 Recognition and enforcement of judgments—Brussels I Regulation

4.1 Current scheme

The Brussels I Regulation provides a straightforward and simple scheme to recognize and enforce judgments between Member States. A judgment within the scope of the Brussels I Regulation 'shall be recognised in the

81 *NKK (Japan) v Beijing Zhuangsheng*, Beijing Municipality High Court, (2008) No 919; *RNO v Beijing International Music Festival Society*, Beijing Intermediate Court (2004) No 928.

other Member States without any special procedure being required'.[82] All judgments that can be recognized should be enforced, regardless of whether the judgment is final or monetary.[83] Limited defences to recognition and enforcement exist though. These include public policy, irregular proceedings and irreconcilable judgments.[84] Public policy is ambiguous and shall be interpreted by the national court of each Member State according to its own concept and culture. However, within the framework of Brussels I, the interpretation of public policy is more restrictive than national law. The requirement of mutual trust and reciprocity requires the public policy defence to be used in exceptional circumstances.[85] Public policy defence can be invoked if the judgment is rendered by fraud, or the enforcement could contradict an important rule of law in the enforcement state.[86]

The generous recognition and enforcement conditions impose no problem in enforcing judgments made pursuant to jurisdiction agreements. At least, the parties will not be reluctant to enter into jurisdiction agreements worrying about the potential enforcement. The problem lies in the fact that whether the original court is competent is not a ground to refuse recognition and enforcement of judgments, unless the dispute falls within the scope of the protective jurisdiction for consumers, insureds and employees.[87] As a result, the requested country must enforce judgments of the original court, even if the original court takes jurisdiction in breach of a jurisdiction clause.[88] Public policy defence, however, cannot be used if the trial court fails to enforce a dispute resolution agreement, which is valid in the view of the enforcement country.[89] A potentially relevant ground is that the judgment cannot be enforced if it is irreconcilable with an earlier judgment in the enforcement state or other Member State.[90] If the chosen court made decision pursuant to the jurisdiction agreement, or the chosen court or other Member State ruled on the validity of the jurisdiction agreement, the judgment made in breach of the jurisdiction clause may be irreconcilable with earlier judgments.[91] However, the *lis pendens* rule and the *Gasser v MISAT* decision may prevent this situation from happening.[92] Since the current Brussels I Regulation does not fully harmonize validity requirements for a jurisdiction clause, it is likely that

82 Art 33.
83 Clarkson and Hill, 2011: 193.
84 Art 34, Brussels I Regulation.
85 Fawcett and Carruthers, 2008: 612.
86 Fawcett and Carruthers, 2008: 612–613.
87 Art 35, Brussels I; Case C-7/98, *Krombach v Bamberski* [2000] ECR I-1935.
88 Hartley, 2009: 337.
89 *The Wadi Sudr* [2010] 1 Lloyd's Rep 193; Clarkson and Hill, 2011: 196; Fawcett and Carruthers, 2008: 628–630.
90 Art 34(3) and (4), Brussels I.
91 Hartley, 2009: 337.
92 Ibid.

the trial court and the enforcement court would reach different conclusions. This enforcement ground provides opportunities for the party to breach its agreement and to have the judgments enforced. The status will be improved in the Brussels I Recast, where the non-chosen court cannot take jurisdiction until the chosen court proceeds to decline the enforcement of the jurisdiction clause.

4.2 Brussels I Recast—abolition of exequatur

The Brussels I Recast adopts important reforms to the recognition and enforcement of judgments by abolishing *exequatur*. *Exequatur* is the procedure to make declaration of enforceability before judgments can be enforced. Any party could appeal against the declaration at this stage. This is the current procedure in the Brussels I Regulation.[93] *Exequatur* procedure has two functions: declaration of enforceability and marginal inspection of the foreign judgment.[94] In the Commission's Brussels I Recast Proposal, it is argued that the mutual trust and judicial cooperation between Member States 'has reached a degree of maturity which permits the move towards a simpler, less costly, and more automatic system of circulation of judgments, removing the existing formalities among Member States'.[95] It is also argued that the enforcement of foreign judgments falling in the regime of the Brussels I Regulation is 'almost always' successful.[96] A survey shows the success rate of *exequatur* application is over 90 per cent.[97] According to the Brussels I Recast, a judgment given in a Member State can be enforced in another Member State without the need for a declaration of enforceability.[98] The defendant's right is protected by the requirement of fair trial and the public policy exemption.[99] Abolishing *exequatur* procedure could simplify the procedure for recognition and enforcement of judgments and reduce costs and time for EU businesses to assert rights abroad.[100]

93 Arts 38–43, Brussels I.
94 Kramer, 2011: 635.
95 European Commission, 'Proposal for a Regulation on Jurisdiction and the Recognition and Enforcement of Judgments in Civil and Commercial Matters (Recast)' (Commission's Recast Proposal), COM(2010) 748 final, para 3.11.
96 Green Paper on Brussels I, 2009: 2.
97 Centre for Strategy and Evaluation Services, 2010.
98 Art 39 of the Brussels I Recast.
99 Brussels I Recast, Art 45(1). Public policy and fair trial also includes the requirement of Art 47 of the EU Charter on Fundamental Rights; see Recast Proposal, para 3.11.
100 European Commission, 'Green Paper on the Review of Council Regulation (EC) No 44/2001 on Jurisdiction and the Recognition and Enforcement of Judgments in Civil and Commercial Matters' COM(2009) 175 final, para 1.

5 Recognition and enforcement of judgments—international scheme

The Hague Choice of Court Convention 2005 establishes an international framework to facilitate the effective recognition and enforcement of judgments made pursuant to an exclusive jurisdiction agreement. Denial of recognition and enforcement can only be based on the grounds listed in the Convention. In other words, state parties cannot use domestic law or discretion to refuse enforcing a judgment that falls within the scope of the Convention.

Upon the application for recognition and enforcement, the requested court should be bound by the fact found by the court of origin and should not review the merit of the judgment.[101] Recognition or enforcement may be refused in case of invalidity of judgment agreements, incapacity of a party, lack of natural justice, fraud, public policy infringement and irreconcilability with other judgments.[102] Recognition and enforcement can also be refused if the judgment is on a matter excluded from the scope of the Convention, the judgment is based on a finding on the excluded matter[103] or the judgment grants exemplary or punitive damages which are not available in the requested country.[104] Furthermore, judicial settlement proved by the court chosen in the exclusive jurisdiction clause can be recognized and enforced in the same manner.[105] The Convention permits the requested court to use domestic procedure to recognize and enforce judgments. The only requirement is that the court should act 'expeditiously'.[106]

The Convention further permits the state to make a declaration that its court will not recognize or enforce judgments made by the chosen court which has no objective connections with the dispute.[107] The state can also declare that its court will not recognize and enforce judgments made by the chosen court while all relevant elements are located in the requested state.[108] These are two further limitations to the recognition and enforcement of judgments. The Hague Convention does not make it a preliminary requirement for the chosen court to have connections with the dispute. It also allows the parties to choose a court to decide a purely domestic matter. This is consistent with the lax tendency in applying party autonomy in international commerce. Parties are allowed to choose a neutral third country to adjudicate their disputes. However, if some states

101 Art 8(2).
102 Art 9.
103 Art 10.
104 Art 11.
105 Art 12.
106 Art 14.
107 Art 19.
108 Art 20.

have made such declarations, these can clearly prevent the parties from choosing a neutral court or from subjecting a purely domestic claim to the court of another country. Although such choices may be ruled valid by the chosen state, judgments may not be enforced.

6 Conclusion

Jurisdiction and arbitration agreements only have actual benefits if judgments and awards made in pursuant to the dispute resolution agreements can be eventually recognized and enforced. The above study demonstrated that recognition and enforcement are relatively certain in the region with proper judicial cooperation. Examples are the New York Convention and the Brussels I Regulation. The difficulty of recognition and enforcement of foreign judgments in the scenario without judicial cooperation is obvious. The difficulty of recognizing and enforcing judgments made pursuant to a valid foreign jurisdiction clause would lead to the difficulty in granting full effectiveness to a valid foreign jurisdiction clause. A typical example is China, where recognizing foreign judgments is particularly difficult even if the foreign court takes jurisdiction in accordance to a valid jurisdiction clause. Judicial cooperation in terms of enforcement of party autonomy agreements is necessary; cooperation in the enforcement of judgments and awards is no less important.

Although the New York Convention has provided straightforward rules in enforcing foreign arbitral awards, which greatly contribute to the success of international commercial arbitration, diversity still exists between Contracting States when interpreting and applying refusal grounds in practice. Uncertainty largely exists in the public policy defence, which is a vague concept. In general, there is common understanding that public policy defence should be used with caution and should be interpreted very narrowly to cover only 'international public policy'. The difficulty is that there is still no consensus on what international public policy is. Although not completely identical, the UK and USA have adopted a restrictive rule to prevent public policy defence from being used too lightly. This includes both a narrow definition to what 'international public policy' is and procedural restriction to allow a court to reopen a substantive issue considered in arbitration. Compared to the UK and USA, public policy defence is used relevantly easily in China. It is submitted that reasonable discretion should be left to each Contracting State of the New York Convention. The flexibility is one reason for the success of the New York Convention. However, some guidance may be necessary to avoid too easy an application of the refusal ground in order to protect the purpose of the New York Convention.

9 International convention in jurisdiction and arbitration agreements

A comparative study

1 Introduction

In order to improve certainty and predictability, commercial efficiency and procedural effectiveness, international organizations and governments work together to build international conventions to establish judicial cooperation in jurisdiction and arbitration agreements. Global cooperation and harmonization in the field of arbitration is more successful than in jurisdiction. Cooperation in arbitration agreement has existed since 1959, with the enforcement of the New York Convention 1958. The UNCITRAL also published model laws and uniform rules on international arbitration, to establish further harmonization and certainty. Comparatively, there is no international instrument on jurisdiction agreements in force. The Brussels I Regulation only applies within the EU Member States and has limited effects at the international level. The Hague Choice of Court Convention 2005 has only been signed by the EU, USA and Mexico and ratified by Mexico. It is hoped that once the Convention is entered into force and ratified by a large number of countries, it can become the litigation equivalent of the New York Convention. This chapter provides an overview of basic international frameworks on judicial cooperation and harmonization in jurisdiction and arbitration agreements. It then compares the New York Convention and international harmonization in arbitration agreements and the Hague Choice of Court Convention to predict whether the original purpose of the Hague Convention 2005 is achievable in the future.

2 International framework on arbitration agreements

2.1 New York Convention

The New York Convention on the Recognition and Enforcement of Foreign Arbitration Awards was adopted by the United Nations Conference on International Commercial Arbitration in 1958. The New York Convention has two features: (1) to improve enforceability of a valid arbitration agreement by urging a court to refer disputes to arbitration unless the arbitration clause is found invalid or inoperative; (2) to facilitate effective enforcement of arbitral awards between Contracting States. The detailed provisions of the New York Convention have been discussed in previous chapters and will be compared with the Hague Choice of Court Convention in section 4 below.

Since the New York Convention was established more than 50 years ago, many of its provisions may be considered too simple or dated from today's perspective. The New York Convention 1958 does not provide much fundamental harmonization of preliminary rules on arbitration agreements, including their existence, formal and substantive validity. It does not provide any judicial cooperation between the courts and arbitral tribunals of Contracting States to prevent concurrent proceedings and irreconcilable judgments either. All of these issues are left to the domestic law of each Contracting State. It only provides the basic requirements and rules for the recognition and enforcement of arbitral awards that fall in the scope of the Convention. Regardless of these gaps, the Convention works rather successfully in commercial practice. Since 144 countries are party to the New York Convention, resolving disputes in arbitration can almost guarantee the global movement of arbitral awards.

2.2 UNCITRAL Model Law

Further to the New York Convention, the UNCITRAL has published model law and arbitration rules, which aim to reduce uncertainty caused by the inadequacy and disparity of domestic law on the validity and enforceability of arbitration agreements, arbitral procedure and the relationship between courts and tribunals.[1] The inadequacy and disparity cause uncertainty to the parties and may frustrate the functioning of arbitration as an effective dispute resolution method in international commerce.[2] The Model Law is specifically tailored to suit the requirement of international commercial arbitration. It provides a fairly flexible unified law in deciding formal validity of an arbitration agreement,[3] and emphasizes the enforceability of arbitration agreements by requiring a court to refer the parties to arbitration when finding a valid arbitration agreement,[4] adopting *kompetenz-kompetenz* doctrine to allow an arbitral tribunal to rule its own jurisdiction,[5] and permitting an arbitral tribunal to continue jurisdiction where the court is seized to make decision.[6] The Model Law basi-

1 Explanatory Note by the UNCITRAL secretariat on the 1985 Model Law on International Commercial Arbitration as amended in 2006, paras 6 and 7.

2 Ibid.

3 Art 7.

4 Art 8(1).

5 Art 16.

6 Art 8(2).

cally copies the New York Convention in rules relating to recognition and enforcement of arbitral awards[7] and provides the same refusal grounds for a court to set aside arbitral awards.[8] Furthermore, the Model Law also provides uniform rules on the choice of law for the substance of the dispute,[9] the composition of arbitral tribunals,[10] the conduct of arbitral proceedings,[11] interim measures and preliminary measures.[12] Although without mandatory requirements, many countries have incorporated the Model Law or the arbitration rules in their domestic law, or have revised their domestic law to reflect the international trend in arbitration.[13] The Model Law, however, still leaves the most controversial issue untouched, which is the law applicable to substantive validity of an arbitration agreement.

2.3 UNCITRAL arbitration rules

The UNCITRAL also published the Arbitration Rules (revised in 2010). The rules further harmonize the composition of the arbitral tribunal, the conduct of arbitral proceedings and giving awards. Parties could agree to opt in to the Arbitration Rules and to have the rules apply to their arbitral proceedings. Further consistency and certainty is provided. The Arbitration Rules, however, do not provide conflicts rules concerning validity and enforcement of arbitration agreements.

3 Judicial cooperation on jurisdiction agreements—regional and international scheme

3.1 Brussels I Regulation

If any cross-border regional cooperation is included in international cooperation, the cooperation in jurisdiction agreements is very successful in the region of the European Union. The Brussels I Regulation has harmonized all jurisdiction rules, not only choice of court agreements, in civil and commercial matters between Member States, and facilitated the free movement of judgments falling within the scope of the Regulation between Member States. Uniform formal validity rules are provided, and the Regulation requires effectiveness to be given to a jurisdiction

7 Ch VIII.
8 Ch VII.
9 Art 28.
10 Ch III.
11 Ch V.
12 Ch IV.
13 The UNCITRAL Model Law has been implemented in domestic legislation of 66 countries; see status at www.uncitral.org/uncitral/en/uncitral_texts/arbitration/1985Model_arbitration_status.html (accessed on 18 April 2013).

agreement. The Regulation has a few fall-backs though. First, it says nothing about how to decide substantive validity of a jurisdiction clause, which causes inconsistent practices in Member States. Second, it does not expressly state whether the same formal validity rules should apply to jurisdiction agreements concluded by the parties, both domiciled out of the EU. Third, the existing ECJ case law suggests that where a non-chosen Member State is seized first in time to hear a dispute subject to an alleged jurisdiction agreement, the chosen Member State must stay jurisdiction until the first seized court declines jurisdiction.

The status of the enforceability of jurisdiction clauses is strengthened by the improved rules in the Brussels I Recast, which will enter into force from 10 January 2015. The Brussels I Recast primarily follows the rules in the Brussels I Regulation, with three important improvements. First, it provides uniform choice of law rules to decide substantive validity of a jurisdiction clause. Second, it explicitly provides the doctrine of separability applying to jurisdiction clauses. Third, it removes the previous narrow scope of application and applies to all jurisdiction agreements choosing one of the Member States. Fourth, it provides party autonomy a superior status over *lis pendens*, and requires a non-chosen state to stay jurisdiction in deciding the existence and validity of a jurisdiction clause if a chosen state is also seized to decide this matter, irrespective of which court is seized first.

The regional harmonization proves successful and has helped the proposed objective of facilitating the free movement of judgments, improving certainty and predictability and facilitating sound administration of justice within the EU regime. The rules applying to jurisdiction clauses have been borrowed and used in the Hague Choice of Court Convention. The fact that the Brussels rule is regional in nature may prevent broader benefits in the international context. Different treatments exist in enforcement of jurisdiction clauses between Member States, and enforcing them between Member States and third countries. The *status quo* can only be improved if worldwide harmonization is adopted.

3.2 Hague Choice of Court Convention

Compared to the regional cooperation, there is no international convention on jurisdiction clauses in force. The Hague Choice of Court Convention was adopted on 30 June 2005 by the Hague Conference on Private International Law in the Twentieth Session. It will enter into force after three months of the deposition of the second instrument of ratification of the Convention.[14] It is a double convention, which means that it provides both jurisdiction rules and rules for the recognition and enforcement of judgments.[15] The first part of the Convention concerns the validity and

14 Art 31(1).
15 Brand, 2009a: 23–24.

enforceability of choice of court agreements. If a choice of court agreement is valid, its prorogation and derogation power must be recognized by the chosen court and non-chosen court. The second part concerns recognition and enforcement of judgments made pursuant to a choice of court agreement. The Convention requires that all Contracting States should recognize and enforce the judgment made by the chosen Contracting State, unless one of the seven refusal grounds exists. The general structure of the Convention is the same as the New York Convention.[16]

The jurisdiction rule concerning validity is similar to that in the Brussels I Regulation. It provides three basic rules, i.e. presumed exclusivity, flexible formal validity and separability. A jurisdiction agreement choosing one of the Contracting States is deemed exclusive, unless the parties state otherwise.[17] A jurisdiction clause is formally valid if it is 'in writing' or concluded or documented 'by any other means of communication', as far as subsequent reference is possible.[18] Furthermore, the invalidity of the underlying contract would not directly lead to the invalidity of the choice of court agreement.[19] It means that the dispute on the validity of the main contract can be brought to the chosen court. Furthermore, the Hague Convention uniform choice of law rules are provided for substantive validity in general and for capacity of a party in particular.[20]

In terms of enforceability of jurisdiction clauses, the Hague Convention provides straightforward rules which require the chosen court to take jurisdiction and the non-chosen court to decline jurisdiction. In this perspective, the Hague Convention is clearer than the Brussels I Regulation, which does not expressly require a non-chosen Member State to decline jurisdiction in favour of a chosen Member State.[21] It also clearly excludes the application of *forum non conveniens* and *lis pendens* in the context of the Hague Convention.[22] The Hague Convention, however, does not exclude the use of anti-suit injunctions.[23]

In terms of recognition and enforcement of judgments, the Hague Convention requires a Contracting State to recognize and enforce judgments made by the court of another Contracting State, which is chosen in an exclusive jurisdiction clause, unless the clause is held invalid or a party is incapable pursuant to the law of the requested court, procedural irregularity exists, the judgment is manifestly contrary to the public policy of the request court and enforcement is irreconcilable with an earlier judgment.[24]

16 Nanda and Pansuis, 2012: s20.26.
17 Art 3(b).
18 Art 3(c).
19 Art 3(d).
20 Arts 5(1) and 6(a)(b).
21 Art 23(1).
22 Art 5(2).
23 Art 7.
24 Art 9.

4 Comparative study of the Hague Convention and New York Convention

The Hague Convention is similar to the New York Convention in two basic principles. First, party autonomy is respected. Both conventions recognize the enforceability of jurisdiction and arbitration agreements and recognize their derogation and prorogation power. Second, the judgments or awards made pursuant to the Conventions should be recognized and enforced in other Contracting States. Third, recognition and enforcement can be refused based on limited exceptions. However, it does not mean the Hague Convention is a complete mirror image of the New York Convention. Important differences exist that may affect the parties' expectation and may determine the parties' choice of different dispute resolution methods.

4.1 Chosen and non-chosen fora

The New York Convention addresses the power to take jurisdiction and to recognize and enforce arbitral awards by the courts of each Member State. In other words, it only 'targets' courts which are non-chosen by the parties. The New York Convention does not concern the functioning and competence of arbitral tribunals. It does not require a tribunal to take jurisdiction and does not establish conditions when jurisdiction can or should be declined by an arbitral tribunal. If a court, pursuant to the New York Convention, refers the parties to arbitration,[25] this Convention does not guarantee the chosen tribunal definitely would take jurisdiction;[26] if a court, pursuant to its own private international law, declares an arbitration agreement invalid,[27] the Convention does not prevent the chosen tribunal from taking jurisdiction.

The Hague Convention, on the other hand, tries to regulate both the chosen and non-chosen Contracting State. Both chosen and non-chosen states have treaty obligations to take and decline jurisdiction. This is a means to prevent potential concurrent proceedings or negative conflicts of jurisdiction, where no country takes jurisdiction. Concurrent proceedings, however, are still likely to exist in the Hague Convention, especially at the preliminary stage, where both chosen and non-chosen states are seized to decide the validity of a jurisdiction clause. A non-chosen state is not required to stay the proceedings until the chosen state has made the decision, and there is no *lis pendens* rule to give priority to the first seized court to make this decision. It is, thus, possible that both courts have proceeded to give rulings on the preliminary issue. If the decisions are

25 New York Convention, Art II.3.

26 Although in practice declining jurisdiction in such circumstances would be extremely rare.

27 New York Convention, Art II.3; see section 4.3 below.

different, parallel proceedings may continue to exist as to the substance of the claim.

4.2 Scope of application

The New York Convention does not define its scope. It applies to disputes 'in respect of a defined legal relationship, whether contractual or not, concerning a subject matter capable of settlement by arbitration'.[28] It does not provide a list, exhaustive or not, of the 'defined legal relationship'; nor does it provide guidance as to what subject matters are arbitrable. This is, again, left to the law of each forum.

The Hague Convention has clearly established its scope of application. The Convention does not apply to consumer contracts,[29] employment contracts,[30] disputes on the status and capacity of a natural person,[31] family law matters,[32] some company law issues,[33] some matters relating to shipping and transport,[34] competition matters,[35] some tort claims,[36] some IP claims[37] and validity of entries in public registers.[38] Besides, Article 21 of the Convention permits a Contracting State to make declaration to exclude specific subject matters from the scope of the Convention. This declaration must be made with caution and should not be broader than necessary or be ambiguous. This exception is inserted in order to attract support from more states, which may traditionally intend to extend exclusive jurisdiction to more subject matters. Examples can be found in the exclusive jurisdiction in China covering Chinese–foreign joint venture contracts.[39] The Convention also requires the declaration to be reciprocal, i.e. other Contracting States do not need to enforce judgments falling within the scope of declaration of the state.[40]

It is likely that the scope of the New York Convention is broader, especially in light of the current liberal trend on arbitrality. Many issues that are excluded from the Hague Convention, such as competition matters, IP

28 New York Convention, Art II.1.
29 Hague Choice of Court Convention, Art 2(1)(a).
30 Art 2(1)(b).
31 Art 2(2)(a).
32 Maintenance (Art 2(2)(b)), matrimonial property (Art 2(2)(c)), wills and succession (Art 2(2)(d)).
33 Insolvency (Art 2(2)(e)), validity nullity or dissolution of legal persons (Art 2(2)(m)).
34 Carriage of passengers and goods (Art 2(2)(f)), marine pollution, limitation of liability for marine claims, general average and emergency towage and salvage (Art 2(2)(g)).
35 Art 2(2)(h).
36 Nuclear damage (Art 2(2)(i)), personal injury of a natural person (Art 2(2)(j)), damage to tangible property (art 2(2)(k)).
37 Validity and infringement of IP rights (Art 2(2)(n)).
38 Art 2(2)(p).
39 Tu, 2007: 347.
40 Art 21(2).

claims, carriage contracts and consumer contracts, are considered arbitrable under the law of many countries. However, the absence of clarification also causes uncertainty. Since the concept of arbitrality differs between country to country, and the standard may be applied differently between tribunals and courts, the parties cannot simply rely on the New York Convention to predict the consequence of their arbitration agreements, especially when they submit unconventional disputes or controversial matters to arbitration. A dispute that has been held arbitrable by the supervisory court or the tribunal may be considered unarbitrable by the enforcement court, where recognition and enforcement might be refused.

4.3 Grounds to refuse enforceability of a dispute resolution clause

Validity of forum selection clauses

Under the New York Convention, an arbitration agreement can be disregarded by a court at the trial stage if the clause is found to be 'null and void'.[41] The determination of the validity of an arbitration agreement, however, is left to the private international law of each court.[42] The result will become unpredictable because it depends on in which court or tribunal the party submits this issue.

The Hague Convention, on the other hand, provides clear rules determining the validity of a choice of court agreement. First, a simple rule is established in terms of formal validity, to validate all agreements 'in writing' or concluded or documented 'by other means of communication which renders information accessible so as to be usable for subsequent reference'.[43] The court should use its own law, including choice of law, to decide the substantive validity of a jurisdiction clause.[44] Although it does not mean the substantive law of the chosen court must apply, it makes the result reasonably predictable even if the law of the chosen court may refer to the substantive law of another country.[45] Greater certainty exists in the Hague Convention on the issue of validity.

Incapacity

The New York Convention does not list incapacity as one ground under which the court can refuse enforcing an arbitration agreement. However, it is hard to imagine a court may require the parties to bring the dispute to arbitration if it finds one of the parties is incapable of concluding an

41 Art II.3.
42 Brand, 2009a: 31.
43 Hague Convention, Art 3(c).
44 Hague Convention, Arts 5(1), 6(a) and 9(a); Hartley and Dogauchi, 2007: para 125.
45 Hartley and Dogauchi, 2007: para 125.

arbitration agreement under its law. It is possible that arbitration agreements are held invalid if incapacity is found. It is uncertain, however, which law applies to determine incapacity.

In the Hague Convention, on the other hand, incapacity is an explicit ground used by a non-chosen court to refuse enforcing a jurisdiction clause. Incapacity is determined under the law of the chosen court, as it falls within the scope of invalidity.[46] The non-chosen court, however, can also use its own law to invalidate an agreement if a party is capable under the law of the chosen court, but incapable under the law of this seized, non-chosen court.[47] In other words, a jurisdiction clause will not be enforced by a non-chosen court if a party is incapable under either the law of the chosen court or the law of this seized court.

Impossibility to perform

The New York Convention does not allow a court to refuse enforcing arbitration agreements at the jurisdictional stage not only based on invalidity, but also because the arbitration agreement is 'inoperative or incapable of being performed'.[48] Again, there is no explanation as to when a clause is considered 'inoperative or incapable of being performed' and whether the inoperativeness is due to the reasons other than the parties. It is possible that, if the tribunal refuses jurisdiction, the chosen tribunal no longer exists or the parties have made an ambiguous choice which cannot be properly construed or understood, a court can take jurisdiction irrespective of an arbitration agreement. In *Paczy v Haendler & Natermann GmbH*,[49] the claimant argued that the arbitration agreement was incapable of performing because the claimant had financial difficulty and could not bring the disputes to arbitration. The court rejected this argument saying that the mere difficulty of one party does not exempt the parties from their legal obligations. The Hague Convention provides similar exceptions which allow a non-chosen court to take jurisdiction if the agreement cannot reasonably be performed for exceptional reasons by the parties' chosen court, or the chosen court decides not to hear the case.[50]

Additional grounds in the Hague Convention—public policy

The Hague Convention also provides an additional ground under which enforceability of a validity jurisdiction clause may be refused.[51] A non-chosen court can continue jurisdiction irrespective of a valid jurisdiction

46 Ibid., para 150.
47 Art 6(b); Hartley and Dogauchi, 2007: para 150.
48 New York Convention, Art II.1.
49 [1981] RSR 250.
50 Hague Convention, Art 6(3).
51 Brand, 2009a: 32.

clause, if enforcing the clause may lead to manifest injustice or would be manifestly contrary to the public policy of the seized court.[52] This exception is strong and could override the applicable law governing the validity of a jurisdiction clause. In other words, even if the law of the chosen court considers a jurisdiction clause valid and takes jurisdiction, a non-chosen court can still take jurisdiction by holding the jurisdiction clause unenforceable because, for example, it is concluded under duress, undue influence, or it is the result of bribery or corruption, in accordance to the law and policy of this non-chosen court.

The public policy exception causes uncertainty to the enforcement of jurisdiction agreements. Public policy or injustice in relation to jurisdiction clauses usually concerns substantive validity of a jurisdiction clause. Although uniform choice of law is provided to decide the substantive validity of a jurisdiction clause, the exceptional ground provides non-chosen courts a leeway to apply its own law. It may lead to parallel proceedings where two countries have different laws determining substantive validity of a jurisdiction clause. However, concerning the difficulty in reaching a compromise in the question of substantive validity, this ground at least permits every country to avoid the strict application of the Convention based on its own public policy. The protection of the national interest is one reason that compromise can finally be reached and the Convention might have a greater chance to be ratified by more states in the future.

4.4 Refusal of recognition and enforcement

Both the New York Convention and the Hague Convention permit the enforcement court to refuse recognition and enforcement of arbitral awards or judgments. The refusal grounds in both Conventions share some similarity, but more diversity exists.

Invalidity of forum selection clauses

The invalidity of a forum selection clause is a valid ground of refusal in both Conventions. Both Conventions also provide uniform choice of law rules to decide validity at this stage. The New York Convention provides that the invalidity can be decided under the law chosen by the parties. In the absence of the chosen law, it shall be governed by the law of the seat where the arbitral award is made.[53] The Hague Convention subjects the validity to the law of the chosen court.[54]

The Hague Convention clearly excludes the possibility that the parties might have chosen a law to govern the substance of a jurisdiction clause.

52 Hague Convention, Art 6(3).
53 New York Convention, Art V.1(a).
54 Art 9(a).

There is no reason why such a choice is not allowed. This seems to be a limitation to party autonomy. The New York Convention, on the other hand, grants more weight to party autonomy. It is also unclear why the New York Convention does not provide the same choice of law rules to decide the validity of an arbitration clause at the jurisdictional stage. However, in practice many courts or tribunals have adopted the same rule to decide validity of an arbitration clause when it is seized to hear the dispute, for the purpose of consistent decisions[55] or issuing an enforceable award.[56]

Incapacity of a party

Both Conventions allow the refusal to be based on the incapacity of a party. The New York Convention applies the law applying to the person concerned.[57] The Hague Convention applies the law of the requested state.[58] Since capacity also falls within the scope of validity, the law applying to validity shall also apply. In other words, the requested state shall check capacity of the party under both the law of the chosen state and the law of the requested state and may reject enforcement if the party is found incapable under either law.[59]

Reading the provision of the Hague Convention on capacity in the jurisdictional stage, one may argue that the law applying to capacity is too complicated. In total, the law of three countries might be relevant. If a chosen court uses its law to hold a jurisdiction clause valid and continues jurisdiction, a non-chosen court might, upon the request of a rejecting party, continue jurisdiction by holding a party incapable at the time of contracting. The enforcing court might refuse to enforce the judgment made by the chosen court if the party is also held incapable pursuant to the law of the enforcing court. The complexity is caused by the difficulty to unify choice of law in relation to capacity.[60]

Procedure irregularity

Both Conventions allow refusal if the requested award or judgment is made under procedure irregularity—for example, the defendant has not been notified in sufficient time.[61] The Hague Convention also includes

55 A court may not want concurrent jurisdictions between itself and an arbitral tribunal. Many countries have taken this into account and add the same choice of law rules in their domestic arbitration law to guide their courts.
56 An arbitral tribunal would wish its awards to be enforced.
57 Art V.1(a).
58 Art 9(b).
59 Hartley and Dogauchi, 2007: para 184.
60 Ibid., para 184.
61 Hague Convention, Art 9(c); New York Convention, Art V.1(b).

'fraud'.[62] Examples include bribing judges or witnesses, concealing evidence or providing wrong information.[63] Furthermore, the Hague Convention also put procedural fairness as part of public policy and permits recognition being refused on this ground.

Public policy

Recognition and enforcement can also be refused if a judgment or award is manifestly contrary to public policy of the requested court.[64] The word 'manifestly' implies that public policy can only be relied on in exceptional grounds and only 'fundamental' or 'international' public policy can trigger this ground. It aims to prevent a contracting court from easily relying on public policy, which is a rather ambiguous concept, to avoid its treaty obligations.

Final and enforceable judgment

A judgment or an award can only be recognized and enforced if it is final and enforceable in the state where it is made. This request is the same in both Conventions. The Hague Convention provides that a 'judgment can only be enforced if it has effect in the State of origin, and shall be enforced only if it is enforceable in the State of origin'.[65] The New York Convention says an award may not be enforced if it is not binding or has been set aside or suspended by the supervisory court.[66]

Inconsistent decisions

Under the Hague Convention, a judgment may not be enforced if it is inconsistent with a judgment given in the requested state between the same parties,[67] or it is inconsistent with an earlier judgment given in another state between the same parties on the same cause of action which can be enforced in the requested state.[68] The second situation may exist if a non-Contracting State gives judgments earlier and there is a bilateral treaty between this state and the requested state, or if a non-chosen Contracting State takes jurisdiction based on the incapacity of a party, and this judgment meets the criteria for recognition and enforcement of the requested country.

62 Art 9(d).
63 Hartley and Dogauchi, 2007: para 188.
64 Hague Convention, Art 9(e); New York Convention, Art V.2(b).
65 Art 8(3).
66 Art V.1(d).
67 Art 9(f).
68 Art 9(g).

The New York Convention, however, does not include this ground. Usually, there will not be parallel arbitral proceedings deciding the same issues between the same parties. However, concurrent proceedings between arbitration and litigation are not rare. A non-supervisory court and an arbitral tribunal may decide arbitrability, validity and capacity differently, and both continue jurisdiction. Enforcement of arbitral awards should be refused if the court decision is given first and has been recognized in the requested court. However, refusal under such a circumstance may be based on the public policy ground, i.e. enforcing irreconcilable decisions is contrary to public policy.

The scope of party autonomy

The New York Convention provides more refusal grounds strictly based on party autonomy. Arbitral tribunals receive their authority from the parties' agreement. Arbitrators should only act within the mandate and follow the parties' instruction. An arbitral award may not be enforced if the award deals with a matter beyond the scope of the arbitration clause, or the composition of the tribunal or the procedure is not in accordance with the agreement of the parties (or, in the absence of which, the law of the seat).[69]

Neutral forum

The Hague Convention permits the state to make declaration that its court will not recognize and enforce judgments of a chosen court which has no objective connections with the dispute,[70] or the dispute is a purely domestic matter.[71] This requirement cannot be imposed to arbitration which is boasted for its neutrality. The choice of neutral forum is clearly favoured in international commerce, while the parties may not feel comfortable to subject the dispute to the forum that has connections with either of them. However, it is recognized that some courts may not permit the parties to prorogate to a non-related court, or to derogate from their jurisdictions for purely domestic affairs. The additional ground aims to receive support from those countries that have adopted the relatively restrictive view towards choice of court agreements.

4.5 Conclusion

Although the Hague Convention and the New York Convention share the same principles and the main concepts, they have more differences than

69 Art V.1(c) and (d).
70 Art 19.
71 Art 20.

similarities in detailed rules. In general, the Hague Convention is bigger in volume, more detailed and more complicated, with more carefully unified rules. The New York Convention is succinct and simple, leaving more flexibility to the Contracting States and the parties. Furthermore, the Hague Convention provides more limitations to party autonomy, which is demonstrated by the stricter scope, the grounds to question the enforceability of the jurisdiction clause and the grounds to refuse recognition and enforcement. Party autonomy and contractual freedom are respected more in the New York Convention.

This difference is not surprising. In terms of the detailed rules, the Hague Convention was established in 2005, about 50 years after the adoption of the New York Convention. The four decades of enforcement of the New York Convention exposes the weakness of the Convention, including the uncertainty and inconsistent decision in deciding an arbitration agreement. This weakness is addressed in the Hague Convention. In terms of party autonomy, it plays a much heavier role in arbitration than litigation. Courts are state organs, acquire authority from the sovereign state and serve as a state or public agent. Arbitral tribunals are private bodies, acquire power from parties' consent and serve the parties' commercial needs. Without party autonomy, a court can still assume jurisdiction and authority from a state, but an arbitral tribunal will lose its foundation to perform. There is no doubt that party autonomy has been given more protection in arbitration.

5 The future of the Hague Convention

If, in the past and at the moment, the popularity of arbitration over litigation in international commercial disputes is largely caused by the easy enforcement of arbitration agreements and arbitral awards, the possible future enforcement of the Hague Convention 2005 will reduce such difference and make the parties select their dispute resolution methods more cautiously, based primarily on the different nature of the dispute resolution methods.[72]

However, would countries be enthusiastic in signing and ratifying the Hague Convention? It is eight years since the completion of the Hague Convention. It has only been signed by Mexico, the USA and the EU, and only ratified by Mexico. This is not an impressive figure, compared to the New York Convention which received 24 signatures in the same year of its conclusion.[73] Other successful conventions also receive a relatively large amount of support fairly quickly, such as the UN Convention of

72 Brand, 2009a: 24.

73 Argentina, Belarus, Belgium, Bulgaria, Costa Rica, Ecuador, El Salvador, Finland, France, Germany, India, Israel, Jordan, Luxembourg, Monaco, Netherlands, Pakistan, Philippines, Poland, Russian Federation, Sri Lanka, Sweden, Switzerland, Ukraine.

International Sale of Goods 1980 (18 signatures in the first year) and the Warsaw Convention (21 signatures in the first year). There is the worry that the Hague Convention is 'in danger of dying a slow death for lack of interest'.[74] However, the fact that the USA and EU, two of the biggest economic bodies, have signed the Convention and are willing to be bound by it in the future may be encouraging. It is obvious that the two economic units consider it is in the domestic interest to have their judgments recognized and enforced in other countries and vice versa. The possible future ratification by the EU also means the application of the Convention in all EU Member States. From this perspective, there is the reasonable perspective for the Convention to have a greater influence than it appears to have had.[75] In many countries, the attitude of governments is ambiguous though. In China, the Mainland and Hong Kong have entered into an Arrangement on Reciprocal Recognition and Enforcement of Judgments in Civil and Commercial Matters, signed on 14 July 2006. The content of the arrangement primarily mirrors the content of the Hague Choice of Court Convention. This can be interpreted as a 'test application' of the Hague Convention between two regions within China. The successful application of the arrangement may encourage China to ratify or access the Convention in the future. However, in 2012, Chinese legislative body the Standing Committee of the Eleventh National People's Congress (NPC) approved the amendment to the Chinese Civil Procedure Law in the twenty-eighth meeting on 31 August 2012. The amended law entered into force on 1 January 2013. This amendment does not take into account the rules on choice of court agreements and recognition and enforcement of judgments made pursuant to such agreements in the Hague Convention.[76] It certainly does not mean the Chinese government does not attempt to become a Contracting State of the Hague Convention at all. Article 282 states that the people's court will decide recognition and enforcement of foreign judgment according to its treaty obligations or the principle of reciprocity. Although the rule is narrow, it can be properly complied with alongside the Hague Convention. There is no legal barrier for China to implement the Hague Convention.

Compared with governments, the attitude of many academic writers, professional bodies and commercial organizations is much clearer. Most advocate and support the implementation of the Hague Convention, believing it will promote national interest, improve cross-border transactions and relationships, increase commercial confidence, strengthen relationships with other countries and improve comity. The response from most US practitioners and academics is supportive—in a survey carried out by the ABA, over 98 per cent of respondents believed the Convention

74 Woodward, 2008: 657.
75 Lipe and Tyler, 2010: 38.
76 See, e.g., Art 281.

would help their practice.[77] A similar positive view is also shared by European legislators and commentators.[78] There are criticisms, of course, on some features of the Convention.[79] However, this does not prevent them from believing that joining the Convention would bring more benefits to their countries as a whole.[80]

The Hague Choice of Court Convention is not perfect, but it is a stable instrument, aiming to reach compromise and smooth disagreements between different countries and receiving the widest ratification and support. Academic writers also realize that small imperfectness in terms of theory will not hamper a state from ratifying the Convention, which is finally down to a political decision. Whether a government is willing to ratify this Convention depends on the follows: (1) would the Convention differ fundamentally or tremendously from the current national law? (2) Would the ratification cause great uncertainty and difficulty in the country's domestic legal culture and tradition? (3) Are other countries ratifying this Convention the close trade partners of this country? (4) Would national interests be protected if judgments in other countries are recognized and enforced pursuant to the Convention?

Among all these questions, the fourth one is the most fundamental. Although most academic writers have analysed this issue and explained that there would not be any real harm in theory, most authorities prefer to take a safe position. The advantage of ratifying the Hague Convention is not obvious by far and there is no empirical evidence showing it works effectively for other countries. Most countries would wish to wait until the practical effectiveness is proven by the enforcement of the Convention between other countries. In general, this situation may bring one to a vicious circle. The effective enforcement depends on the popularity, while the popularity also depends on the effective enforcement.[81]

Even if the Hague Convention is ratified by many countries in the world, it does not guarantee that jurisdiction agreements will acquire the same popularity as arbitration agreements in international commerce. Compared to adjudication, arbitration as a dispute resolution procedure has unique advantages, such as neutrality, confidentiality, higher level of autonomy, procedural efficiency and appropriateness to resolve disputes

77 American Bar Association, 'Recommendation, adopted by the House of Delegates', 7–8 August 2006, http://apps.americanbar.org/intlaw/policy/investment/hcca0806.pdf, accessed on 21 January 2013, 2.

78 See European Commission, 'Proposal for a Council Decision on the Signing by the European Community of the Convention on Choice of Court Agreements', Brussels 5 September 2008 COM (2008), 538; Hartley, 2006: 414; Schulz, 2005: 1, cited in Garnett, 2009: fn 62.

79 Garnett, 2009: fn 64–67 and accompanied text and p. 180.

80 Australia: Garnett, 2009: 180; China: Tu, 2007: 347; Canada: Black, 2007: para 95; India: Rashid, 2005.

81 Adler, 2012: 40A.

with states or state-owned entities as a party. The most the Hague Convention can do is lead the parties to make a sound choice between adjudication and arbitration based on the nature and procedural advantages of these two types of dispute resolution methods in the absence of the worry that favourable decisions cannot be enforced in other countries in the world.[82]

82 Brand, 2009a: 23–24.

Bibliography

Aballi, A., 'Comparative developments in the law of choice of forum' (1968) 1 New York University Journal of International Law and Politics 178.

Adler, M.H., 'Figueiredo v Peru: A step backward for arbitration enforcement' (2012) 32 Northwest Journal of International and Business Ambassador 38A.

Ahmed, M., 'Implied compulsory mediation' (2012) 31 Civil Justice Quarterly 151.

Ambrose, C., 'When can a third party enforce an arbitration clause?' [2001] Journal of Business Law 415.

Ambrose, C., 'Can anti-suit injunctions survive European Community law?' (2003) 52 ICLQ 401.

Asariotis, R., 'Anti-suit injunctions for breach of a choice of forum agreement' (1999) 19 Yearbook of European Law 447.

Bell, A.S., 'Anti-suit injunctions and the Brussels Convention' (1994) 110 Law Quarterly Review 204.

Berg, A., 'Rethinking English jurisdiction clauses' (2002) 17 Butterworths Journal of International Banking and Financial Law 117.

Berger, M., 'Arbitration and arbitrability: Toward an expectation model' (2004) 56 Baylor Law Review 753.

Bermann, G.A., 'The use of anti-suit injunctions in international litigation' (1990) 28 Columbia Journal of Transnational Law 589.

Black, V., 'The Hague Choice of Court Convention and the common law' (2007) Uniform Law Conference of Canada, Civil Section, available at http://ssrn.com/abstract=2116549, accessed on 21 January 2013.

Blackaby, N., Partasides, C., Redfern, A., Hunter, M. (eds.), *Redfern and Hunter on International Arbitration* (5th ed., OUP, 2009).

Blair, P., 'Doctrine of *forum non conveniens* in Anglo-American law' (1929) 29 Columbia Law Review 1.

Blanke, G., 'The turning tides of Turner' (2004) 25 Business Law Review 261.

Blobel, F., Spath, P., 'The tale of multilateral trust and the European law of civil procedure' (2005) 30 European Law Review 528.

Born, G., *International Commercial Arbitration* (3rd ed., Kluwer Law International, 2009).

Bramley, M., 'Anti-suit injunctions and exclusive jurisdiction clauses' (2002) 1 Commercial Conflict of Laws 3.

Brand, R.A., 'Enforcement of foreign money-judgments in the United States: In search of uniformity and international acceptance' (1991) 67 Notre Dame Law Review 253.

Brand, R.A., 'Arbitration or litigation—choice of forum after the 2005 Hague Convention Choice of Court Agreements' (2009a) 3 Annals of the Faculty of Law in Belgrade International Edition 23.
Brand, R.A., 'European magnet and the US centrifuge' (2009b) 15 ILSA Journal of International and Comparative Law 367.
Brand, R.A., 'Recognition and enforcement of foreign judgments', Federal Judicial Center, International Litigation Guide, 2012.
Brand, R.A., Herrup, P., *The 2005 Hague Convention on Choice of Court Agreements* (CUP, 2008).
Brekoulakis, S.L., 'On arbitrability: Persisting misconceptions and new areas of concern', in Mistelis, L.A., Brekoulakis, S.L. (eds.), *Arbitrability: International and Comparative Perspectives* (Kluwer, 2009).
Briggs, A., 'Anti-European teeth for choice of court clauses' (1994) 2 Lloyd's Maritime and Commercial Law Quarterly 158.
Briggs, A., 'Anti-suit injunctions and Utopian ideals' (2004) 120 Law Quarterly Review 529.
Briggs, A., *Agreements on Jurisdiction and Choice-of-Law* (OUP, 2008).
Brittain, J.T., Jr., 'Foreign forum selection clauses in the federal courts' (2001) 23 Houston Journal of International Law 305.
Buchanan, R., 'Jurisdiction and procedure of the court of justice of the European Communities' (1974) 8 Vanderbilt Journal of Transnational Law 673.
Carbonneau, T.E., Janson, F., 'Cartesian logic and frontier politics' (1994) 2 Tulane Journal of International and Comparative Law 193.
Centre for Strategy and Evaluation Services, 'Data Collection and Impact Analysis', 17 December 2010, available at http://ec.europa.eu/justice/civil/files/study_cses_brussels_i_final_17_12_10_en.pdf, accessed on 14 January 2011.
Chatterjee, C., 'The legal effect of the exclusive jurisdiction clause in the Brussels Convention in relation to banking matters' (1995) 10 Journal of International Banking Law 334.
Chavier, T.L., 'Equitable relief—international anti-suit injunction' (1990) 14 Suffolk Transnational Law Journal 259.
Chen, H., Howes, B.T., 'The enforcement of foreign arbitration awards in China' (2009) Bloomberg Law Reports: Asia Pacific.
Clarke, A, 'Differing approach to commercial litigation in the European Court of Justice and the courts of England and Wales' (2007) 18 European Business Law Review 101.
Clarkson, C.M.V., Hill, J., *The Conflict of Laws* (4th ed., OUP, 2011).
Coakley, C, 'The growing role of customised consent in international commercial arbitration' (2000) 29 Georgia Journal of International and Comparative Law 127.
Coe, J.J., 'Book review: The principles and practice of international commercial arbitration' (2009) 113 Penn State Law Review 1369.
Cohen, M.M., 'Arbitration "agreements in writing"' (1997) 13 Arbitration International 273.
Collins, L.M., Morse, C.G.J., McClean, D., Briggs, A., Harris, J., McLachlan, C., Dickinson, A., McEleavy, P. (eds.), *Dicey, Morris and Collins: Conflict of Laws* (14th ed., Sweet & Maxwell, 2006).
Collins, L.M., Morse, C.G.J., McClean, D., Briggs, A., Harris, J., McLachlan, C., Dickinson, A., McEleavy, P. (eds.), *Dicey, Morris and Collins: Conflict of Laws* (14th ed. with 4th Cumulative Supplement, Sweet & Maxwell, 2010).

Corsico, J., '*Forum non conveniens*' (2003) 97 Northwestern University Law Review 1853.

Cremades, B.M., Madalena, I., 'Parallel proceedings in international arbitration' (2008) 24 Arbitration International 507.

Crystal, N.M., Giannoni-Crystal, F., 'Enforceability of forum selection clauses: A "Gallant Knight" still seeking Eldorado' (2012) 8 South Carolina Journal of International Law and Business 203.

Cunningham, L.A., 'Rhetoric versus reality in arbitration jurisprudence' (2012) 75 Law and Contemporary Problems 129.

De Oliveira, L.V.P., 'Brazil: Can labour disputes be submitted to arbitration?' (2012) 15 International Arbitration Law Review N25.

De Werra, J., 'Arbitrating international intellectual property disputes' (2012) 3 International Business Law Journal 299.

Dickinson, A., 'A charter for tactical litigation in Europe?' (2004) 3 Lloyd's Maritime and Commercial Law Quarterly 273.

Du, H.F., 'An empirical study on cross-border jurisdiction in Chinese courts' (2007) 2 Jurist (Fa Xue Jia) 152 (in Chinese).

Dubay, C., 'From *forum non conveniens* to open forum' (2011) 3 George Mason Journal of International Commercial Law 1.

Dundas, H.R., 'Court-compelled mediation and the European Convention on Human Rights Article 6' (2010) 76 Arbitration 343.

Dutson, S., Howarth, M., 'After West Tankers' (2009) 75 Arbitration 334.

Elcin, M., *Lex Mercatoria in International Arbitration Theory and Practice* (EUI PhD Thesis, 2012).

European Commission, *Green Paper on the Review of Council Regulation (EC) No 44/2001 on Jurisdiction and the Recognition and Enforcement of Judgments in Civil and Commercial Matters* (Brussels, 2009).

European Commission, *Report on the Review of Council Regulation (EC) No 44/2001 on Jurisdiction and the Recognition and Enforcement of Judgments in Civil and Commercial Matters* (Brussels 2009).

Fawcett, J.J., 'General report', in Fawcett, J.J. (ed.), *Declining Jurisdiction in Private International Law* (OUP, 1995).

Fawcett, J.J., Carruthers, J, *Cheshire, North and Fawcett: Private International Law* (14th ed., OUP, 2008).

Fawcett, J.J., Torremans, P., *Intellectual Property and Private International Law* (1st ed., OUP, 1998).

Fawcett, J.J., Torremans, P., *Intellectual Property and Private International Law* (2nd ed., OUP, 2011).

Fentiman, R, 'Jurisdiction agreements and forum shopping in Europe' (2006) 21 Journal of International Banking and Financial Law 304.

Fentiman, R., *International Commercial Litigation* (OUP, 2010).

Finizio, S.P., 'The partial arbitrator: US developments relating to arbitrator bias' (2004) 7 International Arbitration Law Review 88.

Force, R, 'The position in the United States on foreign forum selection and arbitration clauses, *forum non conveniens* and antisuit injunctions' (2011) 35 Tulane Maritime Law Journal 401.

Fraterman, J., 'Article 337(2) of the Ilo Constitution' (2011) 42 Georgetown Journal of International Law 879.

Garnett, R., 'The Hague Choice of Court Convention: Magnum Opus or Much Ado About Nothing' (2009) 5 Journal of Private International Law 161.

Gertz, C.M., 'The selection of choice of law provisions in international commercial arbitration' (1991) 12 Northwestern Journal of International Law and Business 163.

Graffi, L.D., 'Securing harmonized effects of arbitration agreements under the New York Convention' (2006) 28 Houston Journal of International Law 663.

Gray, A., '*Forum non conveniens* in Australia' (2009) 38 Common Law World Review 207.

Greenberg, S., Kee, C., Weeramantry, J.R., *International Commercial Arbitration* (CUP, 2011).

Gropper, A.L., 'The arbitration of cross-border insolvencies' (2012) 86 American Bankruptcy Law Journal 201.

Grossberg, J.D., 'The Magnuson-Moss Warranty Act, the Federal Arbitration Act, and the Future of Consumer Protection' (2008) 93 Cornell Law Review 659.

Gunerozbek, M.D., *The United Nations Convention on Contracts for the International Carriage of Goods Wholly or Partley by Sea* (Springer, 2011).

Haight, G.W., *Convention on the Recognition and Enforcement of Foreign Arbitral Awards* (United Nations Economic and Social Council, 1958).

Haines, A.D., 'Choice of court agreements in international litigation: Their use and legal problems to which they give rise in the context of the interim text', Prel. Doc. No 18, HCCH Choice of Court Convention 2005 Preliminary Documents, February 2002.

Haloush, H.A., Malkawi, B.H., 'Internet characteristics and online alternative dispute resolution' (2008) 13 Harvard Negotiation Law Review 327.

Hanotiau, B., 'The law applicable to the issue of arbitrability' (1998) 7 International Business Law Journal 755.

Hare, C., 'A lack of restraint in Europe' (2004) 63 Cambridge Law Journal 570.

Harris, J, 'Jurisdiction clauses and void contracts', (1998) 23 European Law Review 279.

Harris, J., 'Harris on West Tankers' (2009), available at http://conflictoflaws.net/2009/harris-on-west-tankers, accessed on 21 December 2012.

Hartley, T.C., 'The scope of the Convention' (1991) 16 European Law Review 529.

Hartley T.C., 'Brussels jurisdiction and judgments convention: Jurisdiction agreement and lis alibi pendens' (1994) 19 European Law Review 549.

Hartley, T.C., 'Interim measures under the Brussels jurisdiction and judgments convention' (1999) 24 European Law Review 674.

Hartley, T.C., 'How to abuse the law and (maybe) come out on top' (2002) 13 Kings College Law Journal 139.

Hartley, T.C., 'Preliminary draft convention on exclusive choice of court agreements, enforcement of judgments' (2003, Prel. Doc. No 25).

Hartley, T.C., 'The European Union and the systematic dismantling of the common law of conflict of laws' (2005) 54 ICLQ 813.

Hartley, T.C., 'The Hague Choice-of-Court Convention' (2006) 31 European Law Review 414.

Hartley, T.C., *International Commercial Litigation* (CUP, 2009).

Hartley, T.C, Dogauchi, M, *Explanatory Report on the 2005 Hague Choice of Court Agreements Convention* (HCCH Publications, 2007).

Haycraft, D.K., Polozola, K.P., 'Federal jurisdiction and procedure' (1998) 44 Loyola Law Review 459.

Hess, B., Pfeiffer, T., Schlosser, P., 'Report on the application of Regulation Brussels I in the Member States', Study JL S/C4/2005/03, September 2007.

Hill, J., *Cross-Border Consumer Contracts* (OUP, 2008).

Hill, R., 'The writing requirement of the New York Convention revisited' (1998) 13 Mealey's International Arbitration Report 11.

Holland, B., 'Excalibur' (2012) 78 Arbitration 81.

Holt, R.T., 'A uniform system for the enforceability of forum selection clauses in federal courts' (2009) 62 Vanderbilt Law Review 1913.

Hueske, W., 'Rule, Britannia—A proposed revival of the British anti-suit injunction in the EU legal framework' (2009) 41 George Washington International Law Review 433.

Hwang, M., Lim, K., 'Corruption in arbitration—Law and reality' (2011) available at www.arbitration-icca.org/media/0/13261720320840/corruption_in_arbitration_paper_draft_248.pd, accessed on 2 September 2012.

Illmer, M., Naumann, I., 'Yet another blow: Anti-suit injunctions in support of arbitration agreements within the European Union' (2007) 10 International Arbitration Law Review 147.

Inoue, T, 'Introduction to international commercial arbitration in China' (2006) 36 Hong Kong Law Journal 171.

James, S., Lambert, R., 'Arbitration in the finance sector' (2006) 9 International Arbitration Law Review 40.

Jenard, P., 'Report on the Convention on Jurisdiction and the Enforcement of Judgments in Civil and Commercial Matters' (1979) [1979] OJ C 59/1.

Jiang, Z., 'Federal arbitration right, choice-of-law clauses and state rules and procedure' (1992) 22 Southwestern University Law Review 159.

Joseph, D., *Jurisdiction and Arbitration Agreements and their Enforcement* (Sweet & Maxwell, 2005).

Kahn-Freund, O., 'Jurisdiction agreements: Some reflections' (1977) 26 ICLQ 825.

Kaplan, N., 'Is the need for writing as expressed in the New York Convention and the Model Law out of step with commercial practice?' (1996) 12 Arbitration International 27.

Kaye, P., 'Forensic submission as a bar to arbitration' (1993) 12 Civil Justice Quarterly 359 .

Kennett, W., '*Forum non conveniens* in Europe' (1995) 38 Cambridge Law Journal 552.

Kessedjian, C., 'Synthesis of the work of the Special Commission of June 1997 on international jurisdiction and the effects of foreign judgments in civil and commercial matters', Prel. Doc. No 8 of November 1997.

Kim, G.G., 'After the ECJ's West Tankers' (2011) 12 Cardozo Journal of Conflict Resolution 573.

Kollewijn, R.D., *American-Dutch Private International Law* (New York, 1961).

Korn, J.B., 'Changing our perspective on arbitration' (1991) 1991 University of Illinois Law Review 67.

Kovacas, R., 'A transnational approach to the arbitrability of insolvency proceedings in international arbitration' (2012), available at www.iiiglobal.org/component/jdownloads/viewdownload/391/5914.html, accessed on 1 April 2013.

Kramer, X.E., 'Abolition of exequatur under the Brussels I Regulation: Effecting

and protecting rights in the European judicial area' (2011) 4 Netherlands Internationaal Privaatrecht 633.
Kruger, T., 'Anti-suit injunction in the European judicial space: Turner v. Grovit' (2004) 53 ICLQ 1030.
Kruger, T., 'The 20th session of the Hague Conference: A new Choice of Court Convention and the issue of EC membership' (2006) 55 ICLQ 447.
Kulpers, J.J., 'Party autonomy in the Brussels I Regulation and the Rome I Regulation and the European Court of Justice' (2009) 10 German Law Journal 1505.
Landau, T., 'The requirement of a written form for an arbitration agreement', in Van Den Berg, A.J. (ed.), *International Commercial Arbitration* (Kluwer, 2002).
Landi, N., 'Arbitrability of antitrust claims' (2005) 9 Vindobona Journal of International Commercial Law and Arbitration 313.
Lando, O., 'The *lex mercatoria* in international commercial arbitration' (1985) 34 ICLQ 747.
Layton, A., 'Layton on West Tankers' (2009), available at http://conflictoflaws.net/2009/layton-on-west-tankers, accessed on 21 December 2012.
Layton, L., Mercer, H., *European Civil Practice* (2nd ed., Sweet & Maxwell, 2004).
Lazic, V., 'Arbitration and insolvency proceedings' (1999) 3 Electronic Journal of Comparative Law, available at www.ejcl.org/33/art33-2.html#N_39, accessed on 1 April 2013.
Lazic, V., 'Arbitration law reform in the Netherlands' (2007) 11 Electronic Journal of Comparative Law 1.
Lehmann, M., 'A plea for a transnational approach to arbitrability in arbitral practice' (2004) 42 Columbia Journal of Transnational Law 753.
Lenaerts, K., 'The contribution of the European Court of Justice to the area of freedom, security and justice' (2010) 59 ICLQ 255.
Lenhoff, A, 'Parties' choice of forum: Prorogation agreements' (1960) 15 Rutgers Law Review 414.
Levi-Tawil, E., 'East meets West' (2011) 12 Cardozo Journal of Conflict Resolution 609.
Levy, L., 'Arbitrability of disputes in corporate matters' (2002) 5 International Arbitration Law Review 77.
Levy, L, 'Anti-suit injunctions issued by arbitrators', in Gaillard, E. (ed.), *Anti-Suit Injunctions in International Arbitration* (Juris Publishing, 2005).
Lew, J.D.M., Mistelis, L.A., Kroll, S., *Comparative International Commercial Arbitration* (Kluwer, 2003).
Li, Z.P., Liu, L., 'Analysis of feasibility to apply *forum non conveniens* in China' (2008) 24 Tribune of Study 68.
Lipe, G.S., Tyler, T.J., 'The Hague Convention on Choice of Court Agreements' (2010) 33 Houston Journal of International Law 1.
Lord Phillips of Worth Matravers, 'Alternative dispute resolution: An English viewpoint' (2008) 74 Arbitration 406.
Lowenfeld, A.F., '*Lex mercatoria:* An arbitrator's view' (1990) 6 Arbitration International 133.
Luthin, M., 'US enforcement of foreign money judgments and the needs for reform' (2008) 14 University of California Davis Journal of International Law and Politics 111.
Magnus, U., Mankowski, P. (eds.), *Brussels I Regulation* (1st ed., Sellier European Law Publishers, 2007)

Magnus, U., Mankowski, P. (eds.), *Brussels I Regulation* (2nd ed., Sellier European Law Publishers, 2012).
Makynen, M., 'Jurisdiction and procedure' (1981) 15 Suffolk University Law Review 396.
Malloy, M.P., 'Current issues in international arbitration' (2002) 15 Transnational Lawyer 43.
Mance, J., 'Exclusive jurisdiction agreements and European ideals' (2004) 120 Law Quarterly Review 357.
Maniruzzaman, A.F.M., 'The *lex mercatoria* and international contracts: A challenge for international commercial arbitration?' (1999) 14 American University International Law Review 657.
Mante, J., 'Arbitrability in the context of Ghana's new arbitration law' (2012) 15 International Arbitration Law Review 31.
Mantilla-Serrano, F., 'International arbitration and insolvency proceedings' (1995) 11 Arbitration International 51.
Marcus, D., 'The perils of contract procedure' (2008) 82 Tulane Law Review 973.
Materna, M.G., 'Unnecessary consternation' (2011) 11 Pepperdine Dispute Resolution Law Journal 571.
McDougall, A., 'International arbitration and money laundering' (2005) 20 American University International Law Review 1021.
McLachlan, C., '*Lis pendens* in international litigation' (2008) 336 Hague Recueil des Cours 201.
McLachlan, C., Shore, L., Weiniger, M., *International Investment Arbitration* (OUP, 2010).
McLaughlin, J.T., Genevro, L., 'Enforcement of arbitral awards under the New York Convention: Practice in US courts' (1986) 3 International Tax and Business Law 249.
Merrett, L., 'The enforcement of jurisdiction agreements within the Brussels I Regulation' (2006) 55 ICLQ 315.
Merrett, L., 'Article 23 of the Brussels I Regulation' (2009) 58 ICLQ 545.
Michell, M., 'Forum selection clauses and fundamental breach' (2002) 36 Canadian Business Law Journal 453.
Mistelis, L.A., *Pervasive Problems in International Arbitration* (Kluwer, 2006).
Mistelis, L.A., 'Arbitrability—International and comparative perspectives', in Mistelis, L.A., Brekoulakis, S.L. (eds.), *Arbitrability: International and Comparative Perspectives* (Kluwer, 2009).
Moberly, M.D., 'Enforcing forum selection clauses in state court' (2009) 39 Southwestern Law Review 265.
Moberly, M.D., Lisenbeen, A., 'Enforcing forum selection clauses in Arizona' (2010) 46 Arizona Attorney 54.
Moses, M.L., *The Principles and Practice of International Commercial Arbitration* (2nd ed., CUP, 2012).
Moss, G.C., *International Commercial Arbitration* (Tano Aschehoug, 1999).
Mourre, A., Lahlou, Y., 'The construction of the European judicial space' (2004) 4 International Business Law Journal 538.
Muller, C., *International Arbitration—A guide to the complete Swiss case law (unreported and reported)* (Schulthess, 2004).
Munro, C.M., 'Marc Rich v Impianti' (1992) 3 International Company and Commercial Law Review 116.

Mustill, M. J., Boyd, S.C., Andrews, N., *Commercial Arbitration* (Butterworths, 1989).

Nanda, V.P., Pansuis, D.K., *Litigation of International Disputes in US Courts* (Thomson Reuters, 2012).

Nicholls, C., Daniel, T., Bacarese, A., Hatchard, J., *Corruption and Misuse of Public Office* (2nd ed., OUP, 2011).

Nurmela, I., 'Sanctity of dispute resolution clauses: Strategic coherence of the Brussels system' (2005) 1 Journal of Private International Law 115.

Nuyts, A., *Study on Residual Jurisdiction: General Report* (European Commission, 2007).

Nygh, P., *Autonomy in International Contracts* (OUP, 1999).

Padis, G., 'Arbitration under siege' (2013) 91 Texas Law Review 665.

Palser, E., 'The end for *forum non conveniens*' (2006) 1 Nottingham Law Journal 32.

Parish, M., 'The proper law of an arbitration agreement' (2010) 76 Arbitration 661.

Park, W.W., 'Illusion and reality in international forum selection' (1995) 30 Texas International Law Journal 135.

Park, W.W., Yanos, A.A., 'Treaty obligations and national law' (2006) 58 Hastings Law Journal 251.

Peel, E., 'Arbitration and anti-suit injunctions in the EU' (2009) 125 Law Quarterly Review 365.

Peel, E., '*Forum non conveniens* revisited' (2001) 117 Law Quarterly Review 187.

Perreau-Saussine, L., '*Forum conveniens* and anti-suit injunctions before French courts' (2010) 59 ICLQ 519.

Pien, J., 'Creditor rights and enforcement of international commercial arbitral awards in China' (2007) 45 Columbia Journal of Transnational Law 586.

Pietro, D.D., Platte, M., *Enforcement of International Arbitration Awards* (Cameron May, 2001).

Poudret, J., Besson, S., *Comparative Law of International Arbitration* (Sweet & Maxwell, 2007).

Pryles, M., 'Comparative aspects of prorogation and arbitration agreements' (1976) 25 ICLQ 543.

Purdie, J., 'Exclusive jurisdiction clauses', (2008) 158 New Law Journal 1489.

Qureshi, K., 'Staying power' (2009) 23 Lawyer 24.

Rainer, D., 'Impact of West Tankers on parties' choice of a seat of arbitration' (2009) 95 Cornell Law Review 431.

Rashid, A.A., 'The Hague Convention on Choice of Court Agreements 2005: An overview' (2005) 45 Indian Journal of International Law 558.

Redfern, A., *Law and Practice of International Commercial Arbitration* (4th ed., Sweet & Maxwell, 2004).

Reich, N., 'Transnational consumer law—Reality or fiction?' (2009) 27 Penn State International Law Review 859.

Ribstein, L.E., Kobayashi, B.H., 'State regulation of electronic commerce' (2002) 51 Emory Law Journal 1.

Ritter, M.J., 'Disputing arbitration clauses in international insurance agreements' (2012) 3 Pace International Law Review Online Companion 40.

Robert-Tissot, D., 'The battle for forum' (2005) 155 New Law Journal 1496.

Rodger, B.J., 'Interim relief in support of foreign litigation' (1999) 18 Civil Justice Quarterly 199.

Rogerson, P., 'English interference in Greek affairs' (1994) 53 Cambridge Law Journal 241.

Rosen, J.A., 'Arbitration under private international law: The doctrine of separability and competence de la competence' (1994) 17 Fordham International Law Journal 599.

Sasson, M., 'The recent "reform" of the Italian Code of Civil Procedure Chapter on Arbitration' (2007) 10 International Arbitration Law Review 1.

Schlosser, P., 'Report on the convention of October 1978 on the Accession of the Kingdom of Denmark, Ireland and the United Kingdom of Great Britain and Northern Ireland to the Convention on Jurisdiction and Enforcement of Judgments in Civil and Commercial matters and to the Protocol on its Interpretation by the Court of Justice', OJ 1979 C59/71.

Schlosser, P., 'Competence of arbitrators and of courts' (1992) 8 Arbitration International 189.

Schlosser, P., 'Jurisdiction and international judicial and administrative cooperation' (2000) 284 Recueil des Cours 13.

Schmitz, A.J., 'Refreshing contractual analysis of ADR agreements by curing bipolar avoidance of modern common law' (2004) 9 Harvard Negotiation Law Review 1.

Schulz, A., 'Report on the First Meeting of the Informal Working Group on the Judgments Project—October 22–25, 2002', HCCH, Prel. Doc. No 20 of November 2002 (2002a).

Schulz, A., 'Reflection paper to assist in the preparation of a Convention on Jurisdiction and Recognition and Enforcement of Foreign Judgments in Civil and Commercial Matters', Hague Conference, Prel. Doc. No 19, August 2002 (2002b).

Schulz, A., 'The Hague Convention on Choice of Court Agreements' [2005] Yearbook of Private International Law 1.

Shine, P., 'Establishing jurisdiction in commercial disputes: Arbitral autonomy and the principle of kompetenz-kompetenz' (2008) 3 Journal of Business Law 202.

Shipman, S., 'Court approaches to ADR in the civil justice system' (2006) 25 Civil Justice Quarterly 181.

Siegel, A.M., 'The court against the courts: hostility to litigation as an organizing theme in the Rehnquist court's jurisprudence' (2006) 84 Texas Law Review 1097.

Sifakis, N., 'Exclusive jurisdiction clauses' (2006) 12 Journal of International Maritime Law 307.

Simons, T., 'Cross-border "torpedo" actions' (2003) 5/6 European Legal Forum 287.

Simons, T., Calabresi-Scholz, S., 'Lugano Convention Article 21' (2007) 6 European Legal Forum 296.

Slater, A.G., '*Forum non conveniens*: A view from the shop floor' (1988) 104 Law Quarterly Review 554.

Snyckers, F., 'Civil and constitutional jurisdiction and procedure' (1997) Annual Survey of South African Law 657.

Soltysinski, S., 'Choice of law and choice of forum in transnational transfer of technology transactions' (1986) 196 Recueil Des Course 239.

Souza, F.D., 'The recognition and enforcement of commercial arbitral awards in the People's Republic of China' (2006) 30 Fordham International Law Journal 1318.

Stein, A. R., '*Forum non conveniens* and the redundancy of court-access doctrine' (1985) 133 University of Pennsylvania Law Review 781.

Steinbruck, B., 'The impact of EU law on anti-suit injunctions in aid of English arbitration proceedings' (2007) 26 Civil Justice Quarterly 358.

Steinle, J., Vasilliades, E., 'The enforcement of jurisdiction agreements under the Brussels I Regulation: Reconsidering the principle of party autonomy' (2010) 6 Journal of Private International Law 565.

Strong, S.I., 'Navigating the borders between international commercial arbitration and US federal courts' (2012) 2012 Journal of Dispute Resolution 119.

Symeonides, S.C., Perdue, W.C., von Mehren, A.T., *Conflict of Laws: American, Comparative, International* (1st ed., Thomson West, 1998).

Tan, D., 'Damages for breach of forum selection clauses, principled remedies, and control of international civil litigation' (2005) 40 Texas International Law Journal 623.

Tang, Z., *Electronic Consumer Contracts in the Conflict of Laws* (Hart, 2009).

Tang, Z.S., 'Conflicts of jurisdiction and party autonomy in EU' (2012a) 59 LIX Netherlands International Law Review 321.

Tang, Z.S., 'Effectiveness of exclusive jurisdiction clauses in the Chinese courts' (2012b) 61 ICLQ 459.

Tang, Z.S., 'Parallel proceedings and anti-arbitration injunction' (2012c) 7 Journal of Business Law 589.

Taylor, D.H., 'Forum selection clause: A tale of two concepts' (1993) 66 Temple Law Review 785.

Tett, R., 'Donahue v Armco: A sensible and pragmatic approach to anti-suit injunctions' (2003) 109 British Insurance Law Association Journal 7.

Thrope, J., 'A question of intent: Choice of law and the international arbitration agreement' (1999) 54 Dispute Resolution Journal 16.

Tieder, J.B., 'Factors to consider in the choice of procedural and substantive law in international arbitration' (2003) 20 Journal of International Arbitration 393.

Tu, G., 'The Hague Choice of Court Convention—A Chinese perspective' (2007) 55 American Journal of Comparative Law 347.

Tu, G., '*Forum non conveniens* in the People's Republic of China' (2012) 11 Chinese Journal of International Law 341.

Tweeddale, A., Tweeddale, K., 'Incorporation of arbitration clauses revisited' (2010) 76 Arbitration 656.

von Mehren, A., 'Theory and practice of adjudicatory authority in private international law: A comparative study of the doctrines, policies and practices of common-and-civil-law systems' (2002) 295 Recueil des Cours 9.

Wall, C.J., 'The framework for mediation in Hong Kong' (2009) 75 Arbitration 78.

Walt, S., 'Decision by division: The contractarian structure of commercial arbitration' (1999) 51 Rutgers Law Review 369.

Wan, E.X., Speech on 6 June 2008 at the 50th Anniversary Symposium of the New York Convention, 6 June 2008, available at www.rucil.com.cn/article/default.asp?id=798, accessed on 4 October 2013.

Wang, M., 'Dancing with the dragon' (2009) 29 Northwestern Journal of International Law and Business 309.

Westbrook, J.L., 'International arbitration and multinational insolvency' (2011) 29 Penn State International Law Review 635.

Wetter, G., 'Issues of corruption before international tribunals' (1994) 10 Arbitration International 277.

Whincop, M.J., 'Conflicts in the Cathedral: Towards a theory of property rights in private international law' (2000) 50 University of Toronto Law Journal 41.
Williams, H., 'Anti-suit injunctions: Damp squib or another shot in the maritime locker' (2006) 20 Australia and New Zealand Maritime Law Journal 4.
Wilson, J., 'Anti-suit injunctions' (1997) Journal of Business Law 424.
Wilson, J., 'Three if by equity' (2004) 19 St John's Journal of Legal Comment 772.
Woodward, W. Jr., 'Saving the Hague Choice of Court Convention' (2008) 29 University of Pennsylvania Journal of International Law 657.
Wright, M.J., 'Enforcing forum-selection clauses' (2011) 44 Loyola of Los Angeles Law Review 1625.
Wyss, N., 'First options of Chicago v Kaplan' (1997) 72 Tulane Law Review 351.
Yackee, J.W., 'Choice of law considerations in the validity and enforcement of international forum selection agreements' (2004a) 9 UCLA Journal of International Law and Foreign Affairs 43.
Yackee, J.W., 'A matter of good form' (2004b) 53 Duke Law Journal 1179.
Yetter, P., 'The evolution of forum-selection-clause enforcement in Texas' (2010) 73 Texas Bar Journal 274.
Youssef, K., 'The death of inarbitrability', in Mistelis, L.A., Brekoulakis, S.L. (eds.), *Arbitrability: International and Comparative Perspectives* (Kluwer, 2009).
Zadkovich, J., 'International commercial arbitration and the Bribery Act 2010' (2011) 14 International Arbitration Law Review 103.
Zadkovich, J., Roberts, N., 'West Tankers 2012: Pro-arbitration through enforcement of declaratory awards' (2012) 15 International Arbitration Law Review 51
Zhang, M., 'International civil litigation in China: A practical analysis of the Chinese judicial system' (2002) 25 Boston College International and Comparative Law Review 59.
Zhang, S.Z., Xu, X.D., Li, X., 'The difficulty and outlet of choice of foreign courts' (2010) China Law Journal, available at www.kingandwood.com/article.aspx?id=Forum-Shopping-for-Dispute-Resolution-Hurdles-and-Solutions&language=zh-cn##1, accessed 4 October 2013.
Zhang, X.C., 'The agreement between mainland China and the Hong Kong SAR on mutual enforcement of arbitral awards' (1999) 29 Hong Kong Law Journal 463.
Zhao, X.W., 'Reforming Chinese arbitration law and practices in the global economy' (2006) 31 University of Dayton Law Review 421.
Zimmerman, J., 'Restrictions on forum selection clauses in franchise agreements and the Federal Arbitration Act' (1998) 51 Vanderbilt Law Review 759.

Index